BERLIN

Bilder einer Metropole
Art and Architecture

BERLIN

Bilder einer Metropole
Art and Architecture

Mit Texten von
with texts by
Edelgard Abenstein

h.f.ullmann

Inhalt

Eine kurze (Kunst-)Geschichte Berlins

9 Stadt der Kurfürsten und preußischen Könige

18 Im Zeichen des Kaiserreiches

32 Spuren des Aufbruchs, der Diktatur und Zerstörung

34 Von der Frontstadt zum Symbol der deutschen Einheit

Öffentliche Räume

45 Preußens Militär als Taufpaten und
die repräsentativsten Plätze der Stadt

64 Boulevards für Flaneure und
Geschäftsmeilen für Einkäufer

78 Magistrale, Wasserstraßen und Brücken

Gebäude und Ensembles der Macht

88 Kanzleramt und Schloss Bellevue

92 Reichstag und das Band des Bundes

111 Rathäuser, Botschaften und Ländervertretungen

Der Kronschatz der Stadt

122 Museumsinsel – „Tempelstadt der Künste" und
Weltkulturerbe

162 Das Herzstück des preußischen Berlin

186 Kulturforum – neue Architektur für Alte Meister
und klassische Moderne

224 Zwischen Kreuzberg und Wannsee –
vom Jüdischen Museum bis zur Liebermann-Villa

264 Zeitgenössische Kunst – Kunstszene Berlin

Aufführungsstätten der Kultur

274 Theaterbühnen von Reinhardt bis zum Boulevard

279 Musiktheater und Konzerthäuser von Weltruf

285 Filmtheater, Kulturarena, Freilichtbühnen

Medien, Messen, Verkehrsareale

292 Türme des Funks und Fernsehens

297 Kongress- und Messeanlagen

299 Flughäfen von Weltbedeutung

303 Bahnhöfe im großen und im kleinen Stil

Wohnen, Arbeiten, Sport

308 Villen Wohnhäuser und Siedlungen

320 Büros, Banken und Wissenschaft

326 Antikisierender und minimalistischer Sportstättenbau

Glaubenshäuser, Friedhöfe, Denkmäler

336 Kirchen, Synagogen und Moscheen

348 Letzte Ruhestätten

358 In Erinnerung an Sieger, Retter, Opfer und Helden

Schlösser und Gärten

366 In der Stadt: Charlottenburg und Jagdschloss Grunewald

372 Am Rand gelegen: Tegel, Spandau, Friedrichsfelde, Köpenick

382 Am Wasser gebaut: Pfaueninsel, Glienicke, Babelsberg

Drüben in Potsdam

392 Das Paradies von Sanssouci

406 Neuer Garten und Pfingstberg

410 Die geschichtsträchtige Stadt

422 Werkregister

426 Namen- und Ortsregister

431 Abbildungsnachweis

Content

A Brief (Art) History of Berlin

9 City of Electors and Prussian Kings

18 Under the Sign of Empire

32 Traces of Departure, Dictatorship and Destruction

34 From Front City to the Symbol of German Unity

Public Spaces

45 Prussia's Military as Godfather and
the City's Most Representational Spaces

64 Boulevards for Flaneurs and
Outdoor Shopping Malls for Shoppers

79 Magistrals, Waterways and Bridges

Buildings and Complexes of Power

88 Chancellor's Office and Bellevue Palace

92 Reichstag and the Federal Band

111 City Halls, Embassies and Federal States' Missions

Crown Jewels of the City

122 Museum Island – "Temple of the Arts" and
World Heritage

162 The Centerpiece of Prussian Berlin

186 Culture Forum – New Architecture for Old Masters and
Classical Modernity

224 Between Kreuzberg and Wannsee –
from the Jewish Museum to Liebermann Villa

264 Contemporary Art – Art Scene Berlin

Cultural Performance Spaces

274 Stages from Reinhardt to the Boulevard

279 Musical Theaters and Concert Halls of World Renown

285 Movie Theaters, Culture Arena, Open Air Stages

Media, Trade Fairs, Traffic Areas

292 Radio and Television Towers

297 Congressional and Trade Facilities

299 Airports of World Renown

303 Train Stations in Big and Small Ways

Residence, Work, Sports

308 Villas, Apartment Houses and Settlements

320 Offices, Banks and Science

326 Faux-Antique and Minimalist Sports Facilities

Devotional Buildings, Cemeteries, Monuments

336 Churches, Synagogues and Mosques

348 Final Resting Places

358 In Memory of Victors, Saviors, Victims and Heroes

Palaces and Gardens

366 In the City: Charlottenburg and Grunewald Hunting Palace

372 Sitting on the Edge: Tegel, Spandau, Friedrichsfelde, Köpenick

382 Built on the Water's Edge: Pfaueninsel, Glienicke, Babelsberg

Over there in Potsdam

392 Sanssouci Paradise

406 New Garden an Pfingstberg Hill

410 The Historic City

422 Index of Works

426 Index of Names and Places

431 Illustration Credits

BERLIN et CÖLN.
Capitale de Prusse.

W ie", so sinnierte ein französischer Besucher Berlins 1806 voller Bewunderung, „wie konnte bloß jemand auf die Idee kommen, in all dem Sand eine Stadt zu gründen?" Der Reisende hieß Stendhal und war von zuhause anderes gewöhnt. In Paris, dem Nabel der damaligen Welt, lebten zum Ende des Ancien Régime 700 000 Einwohner, während die Hauptstadt Preußens gerade ein Viertel davon zählte. Berlin kennt keine baulichen Zeugnisse früher Zivilisationen, denn die Römer kamen nicht bis in die märkische Streusandbüchse. Erst sehr spät taucht es in einer Urkunde des Jahres 1237 auf, und zwar nicht mit dem Namen „Berlin", sondern mit der später einverleibten Zwillingsstadt „Cölln". Wenige Zeugen sind aus dem 13. Jahrhundert erhalten geblieben: die mehrfach umgebaute Nikolaikirche, die Marienkirche, neben der alten Stadtmauer die Ruine der gotischen Klosterkirche, die kleine Heiliggeist-Spitalkapelle und der Juliusturm der Spandauer Zitadelle.

P. von der Aa, *Ansicht der Städte Berlin und Cölln von Norden gesehen* (View from the North of the Cities of Berlin and Cölln), um/c. 1729, Kupferstich, spätere Kolorierung/color added later.

Vorhergehende Seite/Previous page: *Vue Perspective de la Ville de Berlin Capital du Royaume de Prusse* (Perspektivische Ansicht der Stadt Berlin, Hauptstadt des Königreichs Preußen/Perspective View of the City of Berlin, Royal Capital of Prussia), um/c.1760, altkolorierter Kupferstich/ old-colored copper engraving, 26 x 41 cm, Paris (Daumont).

H ow," thus pondered a French visitor to Berlin in 1806, full of admiration, "how could anyone come up with the idea of founding a city on all this sand?" The traveler's name was Stendhal and he was used to quite different things at home. The navel of the world at the time, Paris had 700,000 inhabitants at the end of the Ancien Régime, while Prussia's capital had but a quarter of that. Berlin is devoid of architectural remnants left over by early civilizations, since the Romans did not reach the Brandenburgian sandbox. It makes its appearance rather late in a document dating back to the year 1237 – and not under the name of "Berlin" but under the name of its sister city, "Cölln," which it later absorbed. Few monuments testifying to the 13th century have survived: repeatedly remodeled Nikolai Church, St Mary's Church, the ruin of Gothic Franciscan Monastery Church next to the old town wall, small Holy Ghost Hospital Chapel, and Julius Tower of Spandau Citadel.

Stadt der Kurfürsten und preußischen Könige

Erst nach dem Dreißigjährigen Krieg, der das ohnehin karge Brandenburg von Grund auf verwüstet hatte, begann sich Berlin zu einer Stadt von Einfluss zu entwickeln. Das verdankt sie der Einwanderungspolitik des Großen Kurfürsten. Mit qualifizierten Zuwanderern vor allem aus Frankreich und den Niederlanden ließ er die Residenz nach Plänen von Johann Gregor Memhardt neu anlegen. Ein geometrisches Grundraster aus langen Geraden, allen voran die Straße Unter den Linden, gab die künftige Stadtentwicklung vor.

Erst eine Generation später, unter dem ehrgeizigen Kurfürsten Friedrich III., der sich 1701 zum König Friedrich I. in Preußen krönen ließ, wurde in Berlin erstmals Architektur von europäischem Rang gebaut: das Zeughaus, die Dome am Gendarmenmarkt und die barocke Erweiterung des Schlosses. Neben Johann Arnold Nering und Eosander von Göthe setzten die Leistungen von Andreas Schlüter ästhetische Maßstäbe. Wichtige Impulse für die Kunst und das kulturelle Leben gingen von

Links/Left: Matthias Czwiczek (um/c. 1600–1652), *Der Große Kurfürst und seine Gemahlin Luise Henriette von Oranien* (The Great Elector and His Wife Louise Henriette of Orange), 1649, Öl auf Leinwand/oil on canvas, 260 x 212 cm.

Anton Graff (1736–1813), *Friedrich Wilhelm II. von Preußen* (Frederick William II of Prussia), 1792, Öl auf Leinwand/ oil on canvas, 76 x 61 cm.

City of Electors and Prussian Kings

Berlin began to develop into a city of consequence only after the Thirty Years' war which had absolutely devastated Brandenburg, a barren spot of land in any case. It owed this progress to the immigration policies of the Great Elector. Using qualified immigrants, foremost from France and the Netherlands, he had the royal residence city planned from scratch based on layout designs by Johann Gregor Memhardt. A geometrical basic grid composed of long straight lines, chief among them Unter den Linden Boulevard, predetermined its future urban development.

Architecture of European distinction was not built in Berlin until a generation later, under ambitious Elector Frederick III who had himself crowned King Frederick I in Prussia in 1701: the Armory, the cathedrals on Gendarmen Market and the Baroque expansion of the palace. The achievements of Andreas Schlüter, next to those of Johann Arnold Nering and Eosander von Göthe, set aesthetic benchmarks. Important

Königin Sophie Charlotte aus, die das später nach ihr benannte Schloss Charlottenburg veranlasste und den Philosophen Gottfried Wilhelm Leibniz nach Berlin holte. 1696 wurde die Akademie der Künste gegründet, 1700 folgte die Akademie der Wissenschaften, die Königliche Bibliothek wurde ausgebaut – alles im Dienste der neuen Macht- und Prachtentfaltung von Europas jüngstem Königreich. Mit dem Prunk des französischen Sonnenkönigs am Hof von Versailles konnte man freilich hierzulande nicht mithalten. Am allerwenigsten Ehrgeiz in dieser Richtung zeigte Friedrich Wilhelm I., dem man den Beinamen „Soldatenkönig" gab. Der widmete sich allerdings nicht nur dem Ausbau des Militärwesens, auch die Charité, das große Bürgerhospital, geht auf ihn zurück, ebenso wie die drei markanten Platzanlagen, die bis heute die Mitte Berlins prägen: das Rondell des Mehringplatzes, das Oktogon des Leipziger Platzes und das Karree des Pariser Platzes am Brandenburger Tor.

Unter Friedrich II., den man schon zu Lebzeiten „den Großen" nannte, avancierte das Königreich Preußen zur fünften Großmacht in Europa, nach Österreich, Frankreich, Russland und Großbritannien. Und Berlin wurde zu einer Stadt, in der Handel, Wissenschaften und Künste blühten. Zusammen mit seinem alten Jugendfreund Knobelsdorff konzipierte er eine Art architektonisches Regierungsprogramm, das nach ihm be-

Carl Friedrich Schmid
(1799 – um/c. 1860),
Karl Friedrich Schinkel, 1832,
Öl auf Leinwand/oil on canvas,
48 x 48 cm, Alte Nationalgalerie.

impulses for art and culture originated from Queen Sophie Charlotte, who initiated construction of Charlottenburg Palace, later named in her honor, and who summoned philosopher Gottfried Wilhelm Leibniz to Berlin. The Academy of Arts was founded in 1696; the Academy of Sciences followed suit in 1700; the Royal Library was expanded – all in the service of the freshly flourishing power and glory of Europe's youngest kingdom. Of course, domestic efforts fell short of the splendor of the French Sun King at the court of Versailles. Frederick William I, nicknamed the "Soldier King," showed the least inclination for such ambitions. However, he did not focus exclusively on the expansion of military power; he also initiated construction of Charité Hospital, the great civilian infirmary, as well as of three striking public squares that determine Berlin's central area to the present day: the "Rondell" of Mehringplatz, the "Oktogon" of Leipziger Platz and the "Karree" of Pariser Platz at Brandenburg Gate.

Under Frederick II, called "the Great" even during his lifetime, the Kingdom of Prussia developed into the fifth major power in Europe, following Austria, France, Russia, and Great Britain. And Berlin grew to be a city encouraging the trades, sciences and arts to flourish. Jointly with his old childhood friend Knobelsdorff, he conceived a type of architectural government program resulting in the creation of Forum Fridericianum on

nannte Forum Fridericianum an der Straße Unter den Linden mit Opernhaus, St. Hedwigs-Kathedrale, der Alten Bibliothek sowie dem Prinz-Heinrich-Palais, der heutigen Humboldt-Universität. Bis heute repräsentiert das monarchische Ensemble den Geist jener Zeit, die friderizianische Staatsauffassung, in der die Toleranz gegenüber anderen Glaubensrichtungen ebenso großgeschrieben wurde wie die Förderung von Bildung, Wissenschaft und Künsten. Die Malerei jener Epoche prägten ganz entscheidend der Franzose Antoine Pesne, den schon Friedrich I. berufen hatte, und der Danziger Daniel Chodowiecki.

Zur wahren Talentschmiede in allen kulturellen Disziplinen aber wurde die Stadt unter dem Nachfolger Friedrichs des Großen. Eine Blütezeit hob an, die bis zum Wiener Kongress anhielt und dem geistigen Zentrum Weimar durchaus ebenbürtig war. Friedrich Wilhelm II. regierte zwar nur elf Jahre, aber diese Zeit war reich an künstlerischen Taten. Während seiner Regentschaft wuchs der Bürgersinn und entsprechend wich der geschmacksbildende Einfluss zurück, durch den die Souveräne bislang ihren Regierungsepochen ein eigenes Gesicht aufgeprägt hatten. Ein erstarkendes Bürgertum machte sich weitgehend unabhängig davon. Nur Friedrich Wilhelm IV. und Kaiser Wilhelm II. haben sich später noch einmal energisch in den Gang der Kunstgeschichte eingemischt. Unter dem „Viel-

Karl Friedrich Schinkel (1781–1841), *Blick in Griechenlands Blüte* (Glimpse of Greece's Golden Age), 1825, Kopie/copy by Wilhelm Ahlborn (1796–1857), nach dem Gemälde/after the painting, 1836, Öl auf Leinwand/oil on canvas, 94 x 235 cm, Alte Nationalgalerie.

Unter den Linden Boulevard with the Opera House, St Hedwig's Cathedral, the Old Library, as well as Prince Henry's Palace, today's Humboldt University. To the present day, this royal complex represents the spirit of that time, the Friderician idea of statehood which attached as much importance to tolerance towards other faiths as to the promotion of education, science and art. The art of painting prevalent during this period was decisively influenced by French painter Antoine Pesne, appointed by Frederick I, and by Gdansk painter Daniel Chodowiecki.

But it was under his successor, Frederick the Great, that the city developed into a veritable fount of creativity in all cultural disciplines. A period of artistic flowering began that lasted until the Congress of Vienna and that could compete with the intellectual center that was Weimar. Although Frederick William II governed for only eleven years, the period of his tenure was rich in artistic achievements. Bourgeois civic sensibility matured during his reign, while the influence of aesthetic taste, hitherto used by sovereign rulers to leave their mark on their epochs, waned. Gaining in confidence, the middle classes for the most part declared their independence from such sovereignty. Only Frederick William IV and Emperor William II once again inserted themselves forcefully into the course of cultural history. Friderician Rococo said goodbye under the "Much

14

geliebten", ein Beiname, der sich seinem Hang zu erotischen Eskapaden verdankt, verabschiedete sich das friderizianische Rokoko, der Klassizismus, der für die Ideale einer freiheitlichen Bürgergesellschaft stand, behauptete sich. Als fulminanten Auftakt der neuen Architektur baute Carl Gotthard Langhans das Brandenburger Tor, Johann Gottfried Schadow setzte die Quadriga darauf. An der Bauakademie lehrten Vater und Sohn Gilly, die Schinkel den Weg zum Klassizismus wiesen. August Wilhelm Iffland brachte das deutschsprachige Schauspiel zum Erblühen und machte aus dem bis dahin provinziellen Königlichen Schauspielhaus ein weltstädtisches Theater. Durch den Goethe-Freund Carl Friedrich Zelter bekam die Singakademie nationale Reputation. Berlin wurde die Stadt der literarischen Salons und der deutschen Romantiker mit den Schlegel-Brüdern, Heinrich von Kleist und E.T.A Hoffmann.

Der überragende Architekt dieser Epoche war Karl Friedrich Schinkel. Mit ihm gewann Berlin eine ästhetische Qualität von europäischer Ausstrahlung. Seinem Genie verdankt die Stadt

Vorhergehende Seite/Previous page: Friedrich Wilhelm Klose (1804 – nach/after 1871), *Die neue Bauschule, von der Schlossbrücke aus gesehen – Die Werderschen Mühlen* (The New Academy of Architecture, as Seen from Palace Bridge – The Werder Mills), 1836, Öl auf Leinwand/oil on canvas, 42,5 x 55 cm.

Beloved," a nickname he earned because of his penchant for erotic escapades; Neoclassicism, standing for the ideals of a liberal civic society, asserted itself. As fulminant prelude to the new architecture, Carl Gotthard Langhans built Brandenburg Gate; Johann Gottfried Schadow put the Quadriga on top. Father and son Gilly, showing Schinkel the way toward Neoclassicism, taught at the Academy of Architecture. August Wilhelm Iffland made German-language drama flourish and turned the hitherto provincial Royal Schauspielhaus into a cosmopolitan theater. With Carl Friedrich Zelter, a friend of Goethe's, the Academy of Singing acquired national renown. Berlin became the city of literary salons and German Romantics under the influence of the Schlegel brothers, Heinrich von Kleist and E.T.A Hoffmann.

The preeminent architect of the period was Karl Friedrich Schinkel. Because of him, Berlin gained an aesthetic quality of European significance. It is not only excellent buildings, such as the New Guard House, the Schauspielhaus Theater and

nicht nur exzellente Gebäude wie die Neue Wache, das Schauspielhaus und das Alte Museum. Schinkels gesamte Arbeit von den Bauten über die Malerei bis zum Entwurfdesign trägt in ihren Ausdrucksmitteln die typisch maßvolle Eleganz, die spröde Harmonie, die man seither als Preußens Stil bezeichnet. Ganz besonders machte seine Fähigkeit Schule, schlichte Nutzbauten durch gelungene Proportionen und feine Profile gewissermaßen zu adeln. Über den Klassizismus hinaus fand er im kubischen Rohziegelbau der Bauakademie neue Zweckformen für kommende Bauaufgaben des 19. Jahrhunderts. Die stilistische Brillanz spiegelt sich in jedem seiner Werke, bis zu Möbel-, Geräte- und Gefäßentwürfen. Sie prägten das Berliner Kunsthandwerk weit über das Bauhaus und die Neue Sachlichkeit hinaus.

Im Umkreis von Schinkel wirkten kongenial der Bildhauer Christian Daniel Rauch und ganz besonders der Landschafts- und Gartenarchitekt Peter Joseph Lenné. Durch die Werke seiner zahlreichen Schüler wie Stüler, Strack und Persius, der so-

Carl Pescheck (1803–1847), *Panoramische Ansicht von Berlin, vom Zeughaus aus gesehen* (Panoramic View of Berlin, as Seen from the Armory), um / c. 1830, altkolorierter Kupferstich / old-colored copper engraving, nach einem Gemälde von / after a painting by Johann Carl Enslen (1759–1848), 30,7 x 71 cm.

the Old Museum, that the city owes to his genius. From buildings to paintings to design sketches, Schinkel's entire body of works is characterized in its expressive media by a restrained elegance, a stubborn harmony, since then designated as hallmarks of Prussia's style. Especially influential was his ability to, as it were, ennoble modest functional buildings by giving them felicitous proportions and fine profiles. Transcending Neoclassicism, he discovered new forms for future architectural projects of the 19th century in the cubic raw brick building of the Academy of Architecture. This stylistic brilliance was reflected in every single one of his works, all the way to his designs for furniture, tools and bowls. They left their mark on Berlin's decorative arts far beyond the influence of the Bauhaus and New Objectivity.

The sculptor Christian Daniel Rauch and especially the landscape and garden architect Peter Joseph Lenné were congenially working in Schinkel's vicinity. Through the works of his numerous students such as Stüler, Strack and Persius,

Links/Left: Carl Joseph Begas (1794–1854), *Peter Joseph Lenné*, um/c. 1850, Öl auf Leinwand/ oil on canvas.

Carl Adolph Henning (1809–1900), *Christian Daniel Rauch*, 1849, Öl auf Leinwand/oil on canvas, 65,5 x 58,5 cm.

genannten Schinkel-Schule, zu der man selbst Friedrich Wilhelm IV. zählte, blieb sein Einfluss bis zur Gründerzeit spürbar, in zahllosen Kirchen, Schulen, Kommunalbauten, Wohn- und Rathäusern. Den wichtigsten Beitrag zur Malerei der Frühromantik hat in Berlin ebenfalls Schinkel geleistet, der in den ersten beiden Jahrzehnten des 19. Jahrhunderts ideale Landschaften schuf in stetem heimlichen Wettbewerb mit Caspar David Friedrich, dessen Werke das Königshaus, aber auch private Sammler ankauften. In deren Nachfolge erwarb sich Carl Blechen mit seiner impulsiven Malweise Reputation, die weit über die Stadtgrenzen hinausging.

Wie eine Chronik der laufenden Ereignisse begleiten die sachlichen Veduten Eduard Gaertners den Aufstieg der preußischen Hauptstadt. Deren wachsende Prosperität und ihre Anziehungskraft boten der Porträtmalerei das ganze Jahrhundert hindurch eine lukrative Basis, von Carl Begas bis Franz Krüger, der in seinen Paraden durchaus mit Witz die Berliner Gesellschaft darstellte. Auf dem Feld der Historienmalerei wartet die Stadt schon um 1800 mit Darstellungen aus der vaterländischen Geschichte auf. Unübertroffen ist darin dann Adolph von Menzel, der mit seinen Gemälden über das Leben Friedrichs des Großen etwa dem Genre eine neue Richtung gab, denn er kommt ohne Pathos und Heroisierung aus. Alles andere als ein Hofmaler, verschrieb er sich nach seinen ersten,

the so-called Schinkel School which even included Frederick William IV, his influence remained recognizable in countless churches, schools, municipal constructions, residential buildings and city halls up to the Wilhelminian Gründerzeit period. Schinkel also made the most important contribution to early Romanticism's art of painting in Berlin, as he created ideal landscapes in the first two decades of the 19th century in an ongoing, secret competition with Caspar David Friedrich, whose works were bought by the royal family, but also by private collectors. As their successor, Carl Blechen acquired renown far transcending Berlin's city limits with his impulsive manner of painting.

Like a chronicle of current events, Eduard Gaertner's vedutas follow the rise of the Prussian capital. Its growing prosperity and attractiveness provided portrait painters with a lucrative source of income throughout the century, from Carl Begas to Franz Krüger, whose pictures of parades depicted the entire scope of Berlin society with quite a bit of humor. In the field of historical painting, the city serves up representations of patriotic history as early as the years around 1800. Unsurpassed in this genre is Adolph von Menzel, who gave it a new direction with paintings like those on the life of Frederick the Great, since he cannot make do without pathos and heroization. Not at all a court painter, he dedicated himself to Realism after his

den Impressionismus vorwegnehmenden Bildern dem Realismus. Malend und zeichnend hielt er fest, wie sich Berlin von einer Residenzstadt zur Industriemetropole entwickelte. Menzel ist somit der bedeutendste Chronist des modernen Lebens in Berlin.

Zum ersten Mal in der Geschichte der Malerei wird bei ihm die Maschine sowie deren Herrschaft über den Menschen zum Thema. Von England aus hatte die industrielle Revolution auch Preußen erreicht, und Berlin entwickelte sich dank Eisenbahn und Dampfmaschinen zum wirtschaftlichen Schrittmacher in Deutschland. Freilich wuchsen auch die sozialen Gegensätze. Arbeitsuchende strömten in Massen in die Stadt und waren mit Wohnraum und einer funktionstüchtigen Infrastruktur zu versorgen. Die schuf von 1862 an der Stadtbaurat James Hobrecht mit einem Masterplan, der die Weichen stellte für die hoch verdichtete Bebauung ganzer Viertel und Straßen-

Eduard Gaertner (1801–1877), *Hof der königlichen Porzellan-manufaktur Berlin, Leipziger Straße 4* (Courtyard of the Royal Porcelain Manufactory Berlin, 4 Leipziger Straße), 1818, Feder und Wasserfarben/pen and watercolor, 31,8 x 47,4 cm, Märkisches Museum.

first paintings, which prefigure Impressionism. Painting and drawing, he recorded how Berlin developed from a royal residence city to an industrial metropolis. Menzel is therefore the most significant chronicler of modern life in Berlin.

For the first time in the history of painting, the machine and its mastery over mankind was raised as an issue. Coming from England, the Industrial Revolution had finally arrived in Prussia; and Berlin developed into Germany's economic pace-setter, thanks to the railroad and steam engines. Of course, social discrepancies increased as well. People looking for employment flocked to the city in droves and had to be supplied with housing and a functional infrastructure. The latter was created starting in 1862 by Municipal Planning Advisor James Hobrecht whose master plan set the course for the dense development of entire quarters and city blocks by

18

blöcke mit hintereinander gestaffelten vier- bis fünfgeschossigen Mietshäusern. Die Anfänge der für Berlin bis heute so charakteristischen Straßenzüge liegen in dieser Zeit. So umstritten die neue Stadtplanung damals auch war, ihre großzügigen Straßenanlagen haben sich bewährt. Sie sind in der Lage, selbst die Verkehrsströme des 21. Jahrhunderts aufzunehmen.

Im Zeichen des Kaiserreiches

Mit der Reichsgründung von 1871 war Berlin Hauptstadt des Kaiserreiches geworden, und die Dynamik der neuen Rolle veränderte auch dank der Reparationszahlungen Frankreichs das Erscheinungsbild der Stadt vollkommen. Ein furioser wirtschaftlicher Aufschwung setzte ein. Aus der übersichtlichen Residenz der ersten Monarchen wird eine Stadt der Massen auf dem Weg in die Moderne. Mit 2,7 Millionen Einwohnern ist

Adolph von Menzel (1815–1905), *Krönung Wilhelms I. zum König von Preußen am 18. Oktober 1861 in der Schlosskirche zu Königsberg* (Coronation of William I as King of Prussia on October 18, 1861, in the Palace Church at Königsberg), Ölskizze/oil sketch, November 1861, Öl auf Leinwand/ oil on canvas, 74,5 x 100 cm, Alte Nationalgalerie.

building four- to five-story tenements stacked one behind the other. The origins of the street layout so typical of Berlin date back to this period. As controversial as this new urban planning was at the time, its composition of spacious streets has stood the test of time. They are even able to accommodate 21st century traffic flows.

Under the Sign of Empire

When the Empire was founded in 1871, Berlin was made its capital, and the dynamics of its new role changed its physiognomy entirely, aided in part by the reparations paid by France. A period of furious economic boom ensued. Out of the clearly arranged residential seat of the first monarchs, there emerged a city of the masses on its way to Modernity. Counting 2.7 million inhabitants at the end of the century, Berlin had become

Unten/Below: Adolph von Menzel (1815–1905), *Hinterhaus und Hof* (Rear of House and Backyard), 1844 (Hinterhof des Hauses Berlin, Zimmerstraße 4, wo Menzel bis 1845 wohnte/backyard of the house on 4 Zimmerstraße, Berlin, where Menzel lived up to 1845), Öl auf Leinwand/oil on canvas, 45 x 62 cm, Alte Nationalgalerie.

Rechts/Right: Adolph von Menzel (1815–1905), *Palaisgarten des Prinzen Albrecht* (The Palace Garden of Prince Albert), 1846 (Blick aus Menzels Wohnung/view from Menzel's apartment, Berlin, Schöneberger Straße 18), überarbeitet/revised 1876, Öl auf Leinwand/oil on canvas, 68 x 86 cm, Alte Nationalgalerie.

Berlin am Ende des Jahrhunderts die am dichtesten besiedelte Stadt der Welt. Rund um die historische Innenstadt wuchs innerhalb von wenigen Jahrzehnten ein gewaltiger Ring von dicht bebauten Mietshausvierteln mit Kirchen, Schulen, Krankenhäusern, Badeanstalten und öffentlichen Parkanlagen. Was noch an Architektur aus dem Mittelalter oder aus der Renaissance vorhanden war, musste oft den neu geschaffenen Wohnquartieren weichen – oder den Visionen eines auf Pomp und Repräsentation ausgerichteten kaiserlichen Stilwillens. Grandiose Bauten für staatliche Einrichtungen wie Ministerien und Gerichte bestimmten den Wilhelminismus auf baulicher Seite, allen voran das Reichstagsgebäude und der Berliner Dom. Auch das Bode-Museum, die Kaiser-Wilhelm-Gedächtniskirche oder das backsteinerne Postfuhramt in der Oranienburger Straße zeigen den Gestus imperialer Prachtentfaltung. Mit herrschaftlichen Fassaden schmückten sich auch die Mietshäuser, mit kolossalen Formen, Kuppeln, Turmaufsätzen und Erkern. Bis heute bestimmt der Eklektizismus der Gründerjahre, der sich wie in einem Musterkatalog aus Stilmitteln früherer Epochen bediente, das Bild der Stadt. Das Bürgertum zog es vor allem in Richtung Westen, an den neu angelegten

Das denkmalgeschützte Tor des ehemaligen Borsigwerks im Bezirk Tegel, eingeweiht 1898.

Landmark-protected gate of the former Borsig factory in the district of Tegel, dedicated in 1898.

Vorhergehende Seite / Previous page: Karl Eduard Biermann (1803–1892), *Die Borsig'sche Werkstatt am Oranienburger Tor in Berlin* (Borsig Factory at Oranienburg Gate in Berlin), 1847, Aquarell / watercolor, Borsig'sche Vermögensverwaltung / Borsig Estate.

the most densely populated city in the world. Around its historical city center, there emerged within the span of a few centuries an enormous ring of densely built-up tenement districts with churches, schools, hospitals, public baths, and public parks. What little architecture had survived from the Middle Ages or the Renaissance now frequently had to make way for these newly created residential quarters – or for the visions of an imperial will to style focused on pomp and representation. Grandiose buildings for state-run institutions such as ministries and courts determined the architectural aspect of Wilhelminianism, foremost among them the Reichstag building and Berlin Cathedral. The Bode Museum, Kaiser Wilhelm Memorial Church or the brick-built, horse-powered Postal Office on Oranienburger Straße likewise reveal this drive to imperial magnificence. Apartment buildings as well were decorated with stately façades featuring colossal forms, domes, turrets, and oriels. Having helped itself to stylistic devices from earlier epochs as if from a sample catalog, Wilhelminian Gründerzeit eclecticism still determines Berlin's cityscape to the present day. The well-to-do middle classes were mostly attracted to the West, to newly constructed Kur-

Unten: Anhalter Bahnhof, nach Plänen von Franz Schwechten, 1874–80, Eingangsfront, Foto von Lucien Levy, um 1885; 1959 wurde das Gebäude gesprengt.

Below: Anhalt Train Station, designed by Franz Schwechten, built in 1874–80, entrance façade, photo by Lucien Levy, c. 1885; the building was demolished in 1959.

Rechts: Denkmalgeschützte AEG-Turbinenfabrik, Entwurf Peter Behrens, Berechnung Karl Bernhard, 1909, ursprüngliche Länge 124 m, Höhe 25 m.

Right: Landmark-protected AEG Turbine Factory, design: Peter Behrens, structural engineering: Karl Bernhard, 1909, original length: 124 m, height: 25 m.

Anton von Werner (1843–1915),
Der Kongress zu Berlin (Berliner
Kongress 13. Juni bis 13. Juli 1878,
Zusammenkunft der europäischen
Großmächte und der Türkei unter
Vorsitz Bismarcks zur Neuordnung
der Verhältnisse auf dem Balkan),
1881, Öl auf Leinwand,
360 x 615 cm, Rotes Rathaus.

Anton von Werner (1843–1915),
Congress of Berlin (Berlin Congress
of June 13 to July 13, 1878,
conference of Europe's major
powers and Turkey under the
presidency of Bismarck to
reorganize the countries of the
Balkans), 1881, oil on canvas,
360 x 615 cm, Red City Hall.

Anton von Werner (1843–1915),
*Die Eröffnung des Deutschen
Reichstages im Weißen Saal
des Berliner Schlosses durch
Wilhelm II. am 25. Juni 1888*, 1888,
erste Version zum Monumental-
gemälde von 1893, Öl auf Leinwand, 102,5 x 152,5 cm.

Anton von Werner (1843–1915),
*The Opening of the German
Reichstag in the White Hall of the
Berlin Palace by William II on
June 25, 1888*, 1888, colored
sketch for the monumental
painting of 1893, oil on canvas,
102.5 x 152.5 cm.

Max Slevogt (1868–1932),
Der verlorene Sohn
(The Prodigal Son), 1898/99,
Triptychon/triptych, Öl auf
Leinwand/oil on canvas,
Mittelbild/central panel,
111 x 98 cm, Flügel je/each
wing 111 x 50 cm.

Kurfürstendamm mit seinen prunkvollen Wohnpalästen oder in die noblen Villenkolonien, die im Grunewald und am Wannsee wie Pilze aus dem Boden schossen.

Die Architektenstars der Zeit waren hier beschäftigt, u. a. Hermann Muthesius, Bernhard Sehring, Paul Baumgarten. Allerorten ließ die Lust am Ornament städtische Schmuckplätze entstehen, jede Grünfläche wurde mit Skulpturen des „Berliner Realismus" dekoriert. In den stilistischen Wirrwarr des Historismus „Inseln des Geschmacks" zu platzieren, die neue Stadtlandschaft mit „demokratischen" Wegmarken zu versehen, war der pädagogische Impuls des Stadtbaurats Ludwig Hoffmann, als er das Virchow-Krankenhaus wie ein hochfunktionales Barockschloss, das Märkische Museum als öffentlich begehbare Stadtgeschichte anlegte. Die ersten Linien der Hoch- und Untergrundbahn wurden gebaut. Vor den Toren der ehemaligen Stadtmauer entstanden ringförmig um das Zentrum große Bahnhöfe und riesige Fabrikareale: neue Gebäudetypen, in denen sich eine eigene technische Ästhetik abzeichnete. Peter Behrens baute die berühmte Turbinenhalle für die AEG, Alfred Messel entwarf seine weltbekannten großen Kaufhäuser: Wie schon einmal zur Schinkel-Zeit kündigte sich eine neue Architektur an, die auf Europa Einfluss gewinnen sollte.

Auch in der bildenden Kunst holte Berlin auf. Während die Kaiserproklamation in Versailles ein letztes Mal die Hofkunst mit aller Macht zurückgerufen hatte – davon zeugt die

fürstendamm with its ostentatious residential palaces or to the elegant villa colonies that sprang up like mushrooms in Grunewald and on Lake Wannsee.

Star architects of the period were commissioned for these jobs, e.g., Hermann Muthesius, Bernhard Sehring, Paul Baumgarten. Delight in ornamentation resulted in the creation of ubiquitous open spaces that were urban gems; every green space was decorated with sculptures in the style of "Berlin Realism." To insert "islands of good taste" into the stylistic hodgepodge of Historism, to furnish this new cityscape with "democratic" markers, such was the pedagogical impulse of Municipal Planning Advisor Ludwig Hoffmann when he designed Virchow Hospital as a Baroque palace furnished with state-of-the-art equipment or the Brandenburg Museum as publicly accessible city history. The first lines of the elevated and underground railway were constructed. Laid out in ring form around the center outside the gates of the former city wall, large train stations and gigantic factory areas emerged: new types of buildings featuring a distinctive kind of technological aesthetics. Peter Behrens built the famous Turbine Hall for AEG; Alfred Messel designed his world-renowned, large department stores: As once before during Schinkel's time, a period of new architecture influencing Europe was heralded.

In the fine arts, Berlin caught up as well. While the Emperor's Proclamation in Versailles had summoned back courtly arts with all its might for one last time – the Victory Column is proof

Siegessäule ebenso wie das Werk Anton von Werners und die Denkmalflut des ausgehenden 19. Jahrhunderts – erhob sich gegen die offiziell geförderte Kultur subversiv ein neuer Zeitgeist.

Max Liebermann gründete 1892 zusammen mit Walter Leistikow und Max Slevogt die erste Berliner Sezession, die zum Zentrum des deutschen Impressionismus wurde. In seinen Bildern erhob er nicht nur den arbeitenden Menschen in unpathetischer Schlichtheit zur Kunst, er porträtierte auch die geistige Elite seiner Zeit. Und er malte die Berliner Natur, Gärten am Wannsee, stille Alleen, als heitere Seelenlandschaften. Damit beginnt, vom Kaiser als „Rinnsteinkunst" geschmäht, die moderne Malerei in Berlin – mit Käthe Kollwitz, Lovis Corinth, Heinrich Zille, dem Porträtisten des „Miljöhs", der auch die Fotografie als neues künstlerisches Medium nutzte, und den 1910 aus Dresden übergesiedelten Brücke-Künstlern.

Max Slevogt (1868–1932), *Badehaus an der Havel* (Bathhouse on the Havel), 1912, Öl auf Leinwand/oil on canvas, 65,5 x 80,5 cm.

of this as much as Anton von Werner's body of works and the late 19th century flood of monuments – a new *Zeitgeist* rose up subversively against such officially sponsored culture.

In 1892 Max Liebermann, with Walter Leistikow and Max Slevogt, founded the First Berlin Secession, which became central to German Impressionism. His paintings not only raised the worker to the level of art in a style of unsentimental simplicity; he also portrayed the intellectual elite of his time. And he painted Berlin nature, gardens on Lake Wannsee, quiet tree-lined avenues, as carefree landscapes of the soul. Vilified as "gutter art" by the emperor, modern painting in Berlin thus began – with Käthe Kollwitz, Lovis Corinth, Heinrich Zille (portraitist of the "Miljöhs," or milieus, who also used photography as a new artistic medium), and the Brücke artists who moved to the city from Dresden in 1910.

Oben: Heinrich Zille (1858–1929), *Berliner Strandleben* (Berlin Beach Life), 1912, schwarze Kreide, Aquarell und Deckfarbe/black chalk, watercolor and opaque watercolor, 31,9 x 49,3 cm, Stiftung Stadtmuseum/City Museum Foundation.

Heinrich Zille als Fotograf des Elends und des Alltags der einfachen und der armen Leute: Holzsammlerinnen am Exerzierplatz in Charlottenburg (oben) und Marktszene auf dem Friedrich-Karl-Platz, heute Klausener Platz, um 1900.

Heinrich Zille as photographer of the misery and everyday life of the poor and humble: Women wood gatherers on Exerzierplatz in Charlottenburg (above) and market scene on Friedrich-Karl Square, now Klausener Platz, c. 1900.

Links: Heinrich Zille (1858–1929), *Gesellschaft in Altberliner Destille* (Get-Together in Old Berlin Pub), 1905, schwarze Kreide, Feder und Aquarell/black chalk, pen and watercolor, 26,3 x 25,2 cm.

Zille-Fotos um 1900: Werkstatt eines Schumachers, Kinder und Straßenszene in Charlottenburg, Eckkneipe in der Hirtenstraße.

Zille photos c. 1900: Cobbler's workshop, children and street scene in Charlottenburg, corner pub on Hirtenstraße.

Spuren des Aufbruchs, der Diktatur und Zerstörung

Der Erste Weltkrieg fegte die Monarchie hinweg. Doch die junge Republik hatte keinen leichten Start. Politisch und wirtschaftlich instabil, war ihr nur eine kurze Phase der Prosperität vergönnt. Die wirkte auf Kunst und Architektur geradezu beflügelnd. Wieder einmal wurde ein neues, ein anderes Berlin geboren. Es avancierte zum Experimentierfeld kühner Entwürfe mit sich ständig wandelnden Stilrichtungen: Expressionismus, Neue Sachlichkeit, Gartenstadtmodelle und die klassische Moderne des Bauhauses. Ab Mitte der Zwanzigerjahre setzte ein regelrechter Bauboom ein. Die neuen Aufgaben hießen Wohnsiedlungen, Sportanlagen, Filmpaläste, Ausbau des Nahverkehrsnetzes, Bauten der Elektrizitäts- und Wasserversorgung und Flughäfen. Der technische Fortschritt brachte in der 3,8 Millionen-Stadt, der größten Industriemetropole des Kontinents, vollkommen neue Bautypen in einer Vielfalt hervor, von der die Stadt bis in unsere Tage zehrt.

Auch in der Unterhaltungsindustrie – im Film, Theater, Sport – und auch im Journalismus fand die fruchtbarste Periode des 20. Jahrhunderts in Berlin statt. Hier fanden die radikalen Innovationen in den bildenden Künsten, in Literatur und auf der Bühne statt. Sie alle lebten und arbeiteten in Berlin: Maler wie Otto Dix, George Grosz, John Heartfield, Max Beckmann und Hannah Höch. Schriftsteller wie Gottfried Benn, Bertolt Brecht, Kurt Tucholsky und Alfred Döblin. Kurt Weill und Paul Hindemith komponierten, Max Reinhardt und Gustaf Gründgens schrieben Theatergeschichte, Fritz Lang schuf die großen Filmklassiker. Die deutsche Hauptstadt wurde zum internationalen Umschlagplatz künstlerischer Ideen – bis 1933. Dann machte die NS-Diktatur mobil gegen alles, was sie als „Groß-

„Neugestaltung der Reichshauptstadt", Modell der von den Nationalsozialisten geplanten Nord-Süd-Achse durch Albert Speer, 1938/39; im Vordergrund das Triumphtor nach Entwurf Hitlers, im Hintergrund links der Südbahnhof, Foto um 1939.

"Redesigning the Capital of the Reich," model of the North-South Axis designed by Albert Speer for the National Socialists, 1938/39; in the foreground: the Arch of Triumph designed by Hitler, in the background, left: Southern Train Station, photo c. 1939.

Traces of Departure, Dictatorship and Destruction

World War I blew away the monarchy. However, the young republic did not have an easy start. Politically and economically unstable, it was granted only a short period of prosperity. Its influence on art and architecture, though, was veritably inspirational. Once again, a new, a different Berlin was born. It developed into an experimental testing ground for bold designs featuring constantly changing styles: Expressionism, New Objectivity, models of garden cities, and classical Bauhaus Modernism. In the mid-1920s, a veritable building boom broke out. The new assignments were called: residential settlements, sports facilities, movie theater picture palaces, expansion of the local transit network, public utility buildings for electricity and water supplies, and airports. Such technological progress in a city of 3.8 million inhabitants, the largest industrial metropolis in Europe, produced entirely new building types in so much variety that the city is still saturated with them to the present day.

The entertainment industry – film, theater, sports – and journalism also enjoyed their most productive periods of the 20th century in Berlin. This was the place for radical innovation in the visual arts, in literature and on the stage. They all lived and worked in Berlin: painters like Otto Dix, George Grosz, John Heartfield, Max Beckmann, and Hannah Höch; writers like Gottfried Benn, Bertolt Brecht, Kurt Tucholsky, and Alfred Döblin. Kurt Weill and Paul Hindemith composed music; Max Reinhardt and Gustaf Gründgens made theater history; Fritz Lang created great motion picture classics. The German capital developed into an international hub for the exchange of ideas on art – up to 1933. Then the National Socialist dictatorship mobilized against everything it conceived of as "metropolitan

stadtdekadenz" ansah. Im besonderen Maße traf die Juden-verfolgung die Kreativen aus der Kultur.

Der Nationalsozialismus betrachtete die Architektur als „steingewordene Weltanschauung". Einige der monumenta-len Großbauten haben den Krieg überlebt, die Verwaltungsge-bäude am Fehrbelliner Platz, das Reichsluftfahrtministerium von Ernst Sagebiel, der Flughafen Tempelhof und das Olym-pia-Gelände. Ab 1937 plante Albert Speer „nach den Ideen des Führers" den Umbau Berlins zur „Welthauptstadt Germania", eine gigantische, 300 Meter breite und sieben Kilometer lan-ge, von Monumentalbauten flankierte Via triumphalis sollte als Nord-Süd-Achse durch Berlin geschlagen werden. Der Aus-bruch des Krieges beendete die bereits begonnenen Abriss-arbeiten. Am Ende des Krieges – Berlin hatte die schlimmsten Bombenangriffe erlebt, kein anderer Ort wurde so häufig Ziel alliierter Flugzeuge – war die ehemalige Reichshauptstadt das größte zusammenhängende Ruinengebiet Europas.

Modell der 1938/39 geplanten monumentalen Kongresshalle für 100 000 Menschen, Entwurf von Albert Speer; daneben als Größenvergleich Modelle des Brandenburger Tors und des Reichstags, Foto um 1939.

Model of the monumental Congress Hall planned in 1938/39 for 100,000 people, design by Albert Speer; next to it: models of Brandenburg Gate and the Reichstag for size comparison, photo c. 1939.

decadence." Their persecution of the Jews hit especially hard those creative in cultural life.

For National Socialism, architecture was "ideology become stone." Some of its monumentalist buildings have survived the war, such as the administrative building on Fehrbelliner Platz, the Reich Aviation Ministry by Ernst Sagebiel, Tempelhof Air-port, and the Olympic grounds. Starting in 1937, Albert Speer planned, "after ideas by the Führer," the rebuilding of Berlin into the "World Capital of Germania"; a gigantic 300-meter-wide and 7-kilometer-long *via triumphalis*, flanked by monu-mental buildings, was to be cut through Berlin in the form of a North-South Axis. The outbreak of the war put an end to the labors of demolition that had just begun. By the close of the war – Berlin had suffered the worst bombing raids, no other site had been as frequent a target of Allied warplanes as was this city – the former capital of the Reich had become the largest, contiguous field of ruins anywhere in Europe.

Von der Frontstadt zum Symbol der deutschen Einheit

Nach der Teilung Deutschlands wurde Berlin zum Spielball des Kalten Krieges. Entlang der politisch-ideologischen Fronten in zwei verschiedene Städte getrennt, vollzog sich hier der Wettstreit der Systeme hart im Raum. Während im Westen die Moderne der Weimarer Republik wieder als architektonisches Leitbild belebt wurde, herrschte im Osten eine monumental-traditionalistische Sprache vor. Markante Prestigeobjekte waren das Hansaviertel im Tiergarten einerseits, die Stalin-später Karl-Marx-Allee, die erste „sozialistische Straße" andererseits. Mit dem Mauerbau 1961, der West-Berlin komplett isolierte, verlief die Stadtentwicklung endgültig getrennt voneinander. Der für den Westen verlorenen Museumsinsel wurde mit dem Scharounschen Konzept das Kulturforum entgegengestellt. Das Zentrum der „Hauptstadt der DDR" lag zwischen neuen Straßenschneisen am Alexanderplatz, mit dem Fern-

Alfred Stiller (1879–1954), *Liebknecht-Luxemburg-Gedenk-demonstration im Januar 1948 auf dem Friedhof von Friedrichsfelde* (Liebknecht-Luxemburg Memorial Demonstration Held in January 1948 on the Friedrichsfelde Cemetery), 1948, Öl auf Pappe/oil on cardboard, 84 x 90 cm, Deutsches Historisches Museum/German Historical Museum.

From Front City to Symbol of German Unity

After Germany's division, Berlin became a pawn in the Cold War. Separated into two different cities along political and ideological frontlines, it provided the space for harsh competition between the two systems. While Weimar Republic Modernism was revived as architectural model in the West, a monumental-traditionalist language predominated in the East. Striking objects of prestige were the Hansa Quarter in Tiergarten on one side and Stalin Avenue, later called Karl Marx Avenue, the first "socialist street," on the other. When the Wall was built in 1961, completely isolating West Berlin, development of the two cities proceeded henceforth in a segregated manner. Museum Island, lost to the West, was countered with Scharoun's concept of the Culture Forum. The center of the "Capital of the GDR" was located between new boulevards cut out at Alexanderplatz, with the Television Tower as central point of reference.

Prachtstraße der DDR, erbaut 1952–60, einst Stalinallee, seit 1961 Karl-Marx-Allee; Fassaden mit historischer Straßenlaterne, „Zuckerbäcker-Stil"-Details und Kupppelturm am Frankfurter Tor.

Flagship boulevard of the GDR, built in 1952–60, formerly Stalin-allee, since 1961: Karl-Marx-Allee; façades with historical street lamp, "gingerbread style" details and domed tower at Frankfurt Gate.

sehturm als zentralem Bezugspunkt. Obwohl eigentlich wiederaufbaufähig, wurde das Stadtschloss gesprengt; die „Platte" bildete das Leitmedium der Wohnungsbauprogramme der DDR. An den Peripherien wuchsen riesige Trabantenstädte in die Höhe, in beiden Teilen der Stadt. Erst in den Siebzigerjahren vollzog sich in West-Berlin mit dem Einzug der Postmoderne sowie dem IBA-Programm der „behutsamen Stadterneuerung" und der „kritischen Rekonstruktion" alter Stadtstrukturen eine Wende. Ost-Berlin setzte mit dem historisierenden Wiederaufbau des zerstörten Nikolai-Viertels Akzente. Durch ihr anregendes, nicht zuletzt durch die politische Lage bestimmtes Klima zog die Stadt selbst zu Zeiten des Eisernen Vorhangs Künstler an. Die Gruppe der „jungen Wilden", die einen neuen expressiven Stil kreierten, oder die „Schule der Neuen Prächtigkeit", die sich der figurativen Malerei sowie einem satirischen Realismus verschrieben.

Mit dem Fall der Mauer 1989 begann für Berlin eine neue Zeitrechnung. Die Stadt ist zu einem Mekka der modernen Architektur geworden. Am Brandenburger Tor und am Potsdamer Platz, wo das Mauer-Niemandsland die Stadthälften durchtrennte, in der Friedrichstraße und um den Reichstag herum entstand eine neue Mitte. Das Regierungsviertel wurde aus dem Boden gestampft, Industriebrachen zu urbanem Leben erweckt, Großprojekte in Angriff genommen wie das des Zentralbahnhofs, mit dem sich Berlin zum ersten Mal in seiner Geschichte eine gigantische Drehscheibe ins Zentrum der Stadt gestellt hat. Nach dem Bauboom der Neunzigerjahre zeigt sich eine Metropole, die moderner ist und vitaler als viele andere. Sie knüpft an lange vergessene Traditionen an und hat dabei eine überraschende Vielfalt an Formen hervorgebracht – in der Architektur wie in der Kunstszene. Ihre historische Mitte schließlich gewinnt sie mit dem Nachbau des Schlosses zurück. Das schon vor hundert Jahren von Karl Scheffler geprägte Wort, welches Berlin eine geradezu ewige Wandlungsfähigkeit attestiert, scheint sich wieder einmal zu bewahrheiten.

Rechts/Right:
Matthias Koeppel (geb./b. 1937), *Die Öffnung der Berliner Mauer* (The Opening of the Berlin Wall), 1996/97, Triptychon-Mittelteil/ central panel of the triptych, Öl auf Leinwand/oil on canvas, 400 x 440 cm, Abgeordnetenhaus von Berlin/Berlin House of Representatives.

Unten: East Side Gallery, nach der Maueröffnung 1989 von 118 Künstlern aus über 20 Ländern bemaltes Stück der Berliner Mauer zwischen Ostbahnhof und Oberbaumbrücke, seit 1991 unter Denkmalschutz; hier zwei besonders populäre Werke.

Below: East Side Gallery, after the 1989 Wall opening, 118 artists from over 20 countries covered this section of the Berlin Wall between Ostbahnhof and Oberbaum Bridge with paintings; landmark-protected since 1991; here: two especially popular works.

Although its reconstruction was possible, City Palace was blown up and demolished. "Plattenbau" panels constituted the leading building material for GDR housing development programs. Giant satellite cities soared upwards along the peripheries of both city sections. It was not until the 1970s that a change of direction occurred in West Berlin, aided by the introduction of Post-Modernism into the city, as well as the IBA program of "Careful Urban Renewal" and "Critical Reconstruction" of old urban structures. East Berlin made an impression with its historicizing reconstruction of destroyed Nikolai Quarter. The city's stimulating ambience, last not least the result of political conditions, has always attracted artists, even during the era of the Iron Curtain: the group "Young Fauves" who created a new, expressive style, or the "School of New Magnificence" that dedicated itself to figurative painting as well as a type of satirical Realism.

When the Wall fell in 1989, Berlin started a new calendar. The city has become a Mecca of modern architecture. At Brandenburg Gate and on Potsdamer Platz where the no-man's-land of the Wall once cut the city in two, on Friedrichstraße and around the Reichstag, a new city center has come into being. The government district was constructed from scratch; industrial wastelands were sparked into urban life; large-scale projects were broached, such as the Central Railway Station, making it the first time in its history that Berlin has placed a giant transit hub into its very center. Following the building boom of the 1990s, a metropolis has emerged that is more modern and vital than many others. It has picked up the thread of traditions long forgotten and has thus produced a surprising variety of forms – in architecture as much as in the arts scene. And finally, it will regain its historical center with the reconstruction of City Palace. Coined some one hundred years ago, Karl Scheffler's phrase that ascribes a downright perennial power of transformation to Berlin seems to be speaking the truth yet another time.

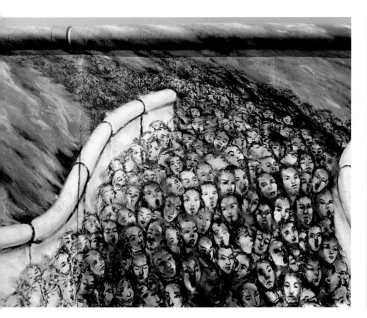

Spektakuläre Dachkonstruktion
des Sony Centers mit sieben
angrenzenden Gebäuden aus
Stahl und Glas, Helmut Jahn,
1996–2000, Dachhöhe 67 m,
freie Spannweite 102 m.

Spectacular roof construction
at the Sony Center with seven
adjoining buildings made of
steel and glass, Helmut Jahn,
1996–2000, roof height: 67 m,
clear span: 102 m.

Ansichten des geplanten Schloss-Wiederaufbaus nach Entwürfen von Franco Stella: Rekonstruiert werden die barocken Stadtfassaden sowie die des Schlüterhofs und die Kuppel des Schlosses (links). Ostfassade sowie Westwand des Schlüterhofes (unten) werden in Form einer offenen Loggia mit Belvedere neu entworfen.

Views of the planned reconstruction of City Palace after designs by Franco Stella: The Baroque city façades and those of the Schlüterhof as well as the palace dome will be rebuilt (left). The eastern façade and western wall of the Schlüterhof (below) will be newly designed in the form of an open loggia with belvedere.

Öffentliche Räume

Public Spaces

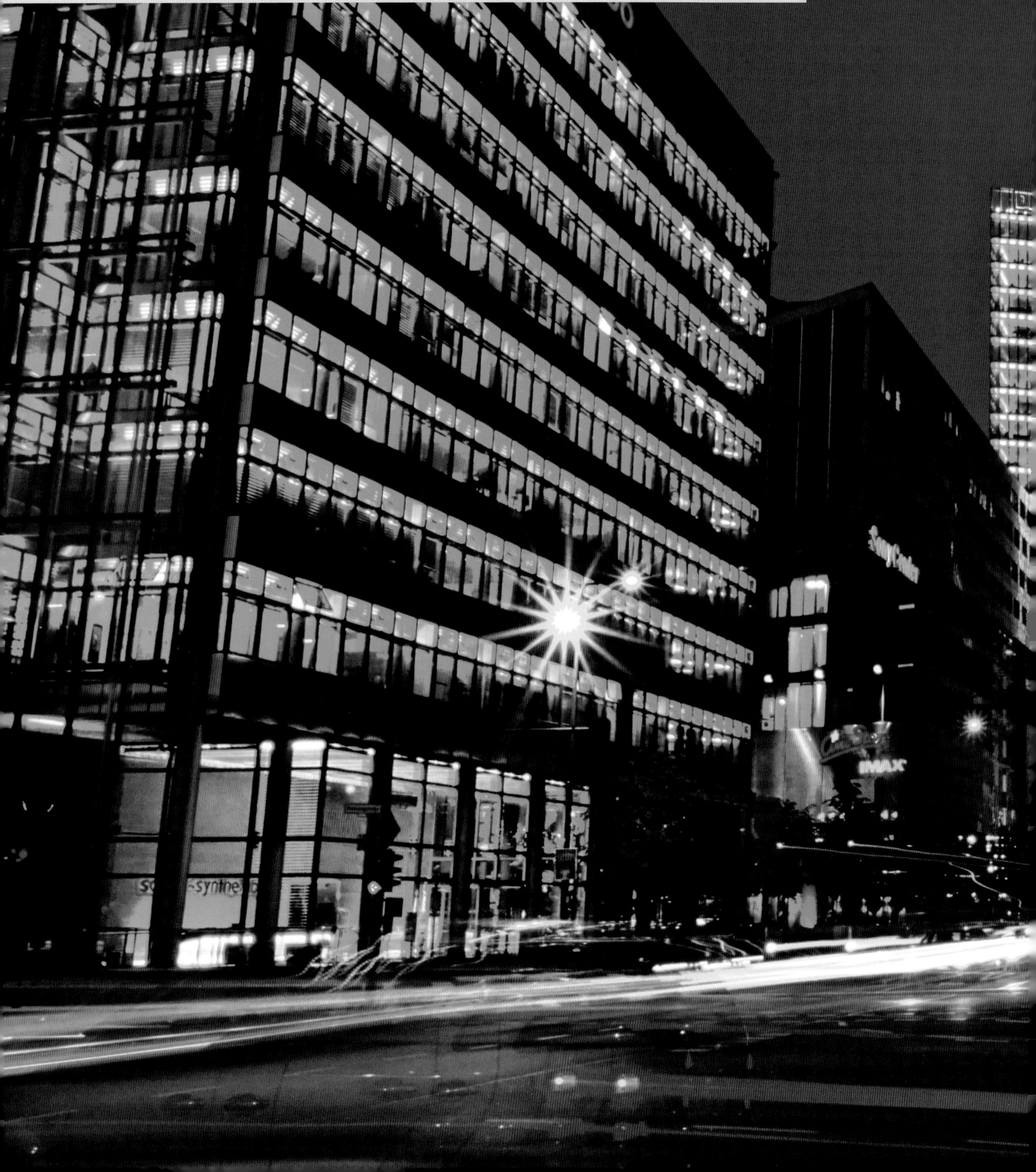

Aufmarsch- und Exerzierplätze, Markt- und Kirchplätze – im Laufe seiner über 750-jährigen Geschichte ent standen in Berlin fast alle bekannten Platztypen. Freilich, nicht jedem sieht man seine Herkunft an. Der heutige „Salon" der Stadt, der Gendarmenmarkt, oder „die gute Stube", der Pariser Platz, zeugen kaum mehr von ihrer – militärischen – Vergangenheit. Ganz anders die Verkehrsknotenpunkte, die ab der Jahrhundertwende mit den S-Bahnhöfen neue Stadträume entstehen ließen, so der Mexikoplatz rund um das Jugendstiljuwel des Zehlendorfer Bahnhofs. Eine Berliner Besonderheit sind die am Zeichentisch entworfenen Anlagen, die schönen „möblierten" Schmuckplätze. Zu ihnen zählen der Rüdesheimer Platz in Wilmersdorf mit Brunnen und Figuren, der Schöneberger Viktoria-Luise-Platz mit Kolonnade und Bassin mit Fontäne, der Kollwitz-Platz am Prenzlauer Berg mit seiner parkartigen Anlage in der Mitte oder auch der Savignyplatz im Herzen Charlottenburgs, der trotz des Verkehrs auf der Kantstraße noch etwas vom alten Berlin bewahrt hat. Als öffentliche Räume bilden diese Plätze die Mitte eines Viertels. Sie sind Treffpunkt für alle, zugleich Erholungsstätten, an denen sich gelebte Urbanität entdecken lässt. Jüngstes und gelungenstes Beispiel für einen ganz neuen Platztypus ist der elegante, 1998 von Hans Kollhoff und Helga Timmermann entworfene Walter-Benjamin-Platz an der Leibnizstraße, beweist er doch, wie ein offener Raum zu der ihn umschließenden Bebauung nicht nur gehört, sondern durch sie erst entsteht.

Seit 1814, als die preußischen Truppen Frankreichs Hauptstadt eroberten, trägt das Areal seinen Namen: der Pariser Platz mit dem Brandenburger Tor. Und obenauf die Quadriga.
Vorhergehende Seite:
Die Potsdamer Straße durchschneidet den Potsdamer Platz.

Since 1814, when Prussian troops captured the capital of France, the site has borne its current name: Paris Square with Brandenburg Gate. On top, the Quadriga.
Previous page:
Potsdam Street cuts through Potsdam Square.

Parade and drill grounds, market places and church yards – in the course of its more than 750 years of history, about every well-known type of open space has emerged in Berlin. Admittedly, not all of them give evidence of their every original use today. The present-day "salon" of the city, the Gendarmenmarkt, or its "best room," Pariser Platz, display more of its – military – past. Quite different are the traffic hubs that created new urban spaces with the arrival of the S-Bahn railway stations around the turn of the century, such as Mexiko-platz which emerged around the Art Deco jewel that is Zehlen-dorf Train Station. A Berlin specialty are those areas explicitly designed by architects, the beautifully "furnished," decorative squares. Among them are Rüdesheimer Platz in Wilmersdorf with fountains and statues, Schöneberger Viktoria Luise Platz featuring colonnades and a pond with water-jet, Kollwitz Platz on Prenzlauer Berg with a park-like layout at its center, or also Savignyplatz in the heart of Charlottenburg, which preserves something of Old Berlin in spite of heavy traffic on Kantstraße. As public spaces, these areas constitute the center of a city quarter. This is where everyone meets, where people can rest and really discover the urban experience. The most recent and successful example of an entirely new type of public space is elegant Walter Benjamin Platz on Leibnizstraße, designed in 1998 by Hans Kollhoff and Helga Timmermann; it proves how an open space not only belongs to the buildings that surround it but is actually created by them.

Oben: Mit der neuen US-Botschaft nach Plänen des Büros Moore Ruble Yudell wurde 2008 die letzte Lücke im Gesamtensemble Pariser Platz geschlossen.

Unten: Blick zur Nordseite mit Haus Liebermann (Kleihues), Palais am Pariser Platz (Winking/ Froh) und Dresdner Bank (Gerkan, Marg und Partner).

Above: The new United States Embassy Building designed by Moore Ruble Yudell in 2008 has closed the last gap in the Paris Square complex.

Below: View to the north with Liebermann House (Kleihues), Palace at Paris Square (Winking/ Froh) and Dresdner Bank (Gerkan, Marg and Partner).

Preußens Militär als Taufpaten und die repräsentativsten Plätze der Stadt

Zunächst hieß er Quarree, als Friedrich Wilhelm I. ihn neben dem Oktogon am Leipziger Platz und dem Rondell am Mehringplatz als dritten großen Platz der Stadt anlegen ließ. Nach der Eroberung von Paris durch die preußischen Truppen erhielt der Platz 1814 seinen jetzigen Namen. Damals war der *Pariser Platz* mit barocken Palais und klassizistischen Stadtvillen dicht umbaut und gehörte zu den nobelsten Adressen Berlins. Einträchtig neben preußischen Staatsministern und Militärs wohnten hier auch Künstler wie der Komponist Giacomo Meyerbeer. Achim von Arnim wuchs hier auf, und Max Liebermann residierte bis zu seinem Tod 1935 neben dem Brandenburger Tor. Im Zweiten Weltkrieg wurde der Pariser Platz stark zerstört. Lediglich Reste der Akademie der Künste blieben bestehen. Erst nach dem Fall der Mauer konnte ab 1993 mit dem Wiederaufbau des Platzes als Gesamtensemble begonnen werden. Hier-

Nach Plänen von Carl Gotthard Langhans 1791 fertiggestellt: das Brandenburger Tor. 1793 kam Johann Gottfried Schadows Quadriga mit der Siegesgöttin Eirene hinzu.

Completed in 1791, designed by Carl Gotthard Langhans: Brandenburg Gate. Johann Gottfried Schadow's Quadriga with Irene, Goddess of Victory, was added in 1793.

Prussia's Military as Godfather and the City's Most Representational Spaces

Originally, it was called "Quarree," when Frederick William I had installed it as the city's third largest public space, next to the "Oktogon" of Leipziger Platz and the "Rondell" of Mehringplatz. After Paris was conquered by Prussian troops, the space acquired its current name in 1814. In those days, *Pariser Platz* was densely surrounded by Baroque mansions and Neoclassicist urban villas; and it was one of the city's finest residential areas. Prussian Ministers of State and military families lived here in peaceful harmony with artists such as Giacomo Meyerbeer, the composer. Achim von Arnim grew up here, and Max Liebermann lived next to Brandenburg Gate until his death in 1935. During World War II, Pariser Platz was heavily damaged. Nothing but remnants of the Academy of Arts remained standing. Reconstruction of the area as a comprehensive design could be launched only after the fall of the Wall, in 1993.

H. A. Forst nach/after
F. A. Schmidt, *Brandenburger Tor
und Pariser Platz* (Brandenburg
Gate and Paris Square), um/
c. 1820, kolorierte Lithographie/
hand-colored lithograph.

zu erließ der Berliner Senat Gestaltungssatzungen, die Ge-
bäudehöhe, Material und Fassadenaufriss vorschrieben. Als
Ausnahme wurde nur der umstrittene Entwurf von Günter Behnisch für die Glasfassade der Akademie der Künste geneh-
migt. Wie historische Elemente und moderne Bauweise sich
in „kritischer Rekonstruktion" vereinigen, zeigen die beider-
seits des Tores entstandenen Gebäude, das Haus Sommer mit
der Commerzbank und das Haus Liebermann (Josef Paul
Kleihues), an der Nordseite das Palais am Pariser Platz (Bernhard Winking/Martin Froh), die Dresdner Bank (Gerkan, Marg
und Partner), die neue Französische Botschaft (Christian de
Portzamparc) sowie als großer Schlussstein der benachbarte
Bau, u. a. für die Fotosammlung The Kennedys. An der Süd-
westecke erhebt sich die US-Botschaft (Moore, Rubel, Yudell),
deren Sicherheitsbedürfnis einen ganzen Straßenzug verlegen
ließ. Daneben schließt sich die DZ-Bank von Frank O. Gehry an.
Die Bauordnung zwang auch ihn zu gestalterischer Disziplin,
so dass sich das für ihn typische architektonische Wunder-
werk nun im Inneren entfaltet. Weit in die Wilhelmstraße hin-

To do so, the Berlin Senate enacted design statutes that prescribed building height, materials and front elevation. Only
Günter Behnisch's controversial design for the glass façade of
the Academy of Arts was granted an exception. How historical
elements and modern building methods merge to from "critical reconstruction" is exemplified by the buildings flanking
the gate: House Sommer with Commerzbank and House
Liebermann (Josef Paul Kleihues); the Palais at Pariser Platz
(Bernhard Winking/Martin Froh) on the north side; the
Dresdner Bank building (Gerkan, Marg und Partner), the French
Embassy (Christian de Portzamparc), as well as – conceived as
a grand keystone – the neighboring building, which also houses
the photograph collection, The Kennedys. The southwestern
corner is the site of the US Embassy (Moore, Rubel, Yudell); for
security reasons, an entire street had to be relocated to accommodate it. Next door we find the DZ Bank by Frank O. Gehry.
Building regulations also forced him to exercise discipline in
design, so that the architectural marvels so typical of this
architect now unfold in its interior. The new building of the

ein reicht der Neubau des Luxushotels Adlon (Patzschke, Klotz & Partner).

Das bekannteste Bauwerk Berlins war jahrzehntelang ein Symbol der geteilten Stadt. Von Wachtürmen flankiert, stand das *Brandenburger Tor* verloren im Niemandsland an der Staatsgrenze der DDR. Mauer und Todesstreifen versperrten den Zugang. Dabei hatte das schöne frühklassizistische Tor einst die Ideale einer freiheitlichen Bürgergesellschaft um 1800 repräsentiert. Das einzige erhalten gebliebene Stadttor Berlins wurde unter Friedrich Wilhelm II. zwischen 1789 und 1791 nach Plänen von Carl Gotthard Langhans errichtet. Vorbild waren die Propyläen der Akropolis. Langhans' auch im europäischen Vergleich fulminante Neuschöpfung ist ein Sandsteinbau mit fünf Durchfahrten, die auf beiden Seiten durch jeweils sechs fünfzehn Meter hohe dorische Säulen markiert sind. Die beiden flankierenden Torhäuser wurden 1868 von dem Schinkel-Schüler Johann Heinrich Strack angefügt. Die das Tor krönende Quadriga (1793) mit der geflügelten Friedensgöttin Eirene sowie die Entwürfe zu den Reliefs an den

Charles Meynier (1768–1832), *Napoleons Einzug in Berlin am 27. Oktober 1806* (Entry of Napoleon into Berlin on October 27, 1806), 1810, Öl auf Leinwand/ oil on canvas, 330 x 493 cm, Musée National du Château de Versailles.

luxury Hotel Adlon (Patzschke, Klotz & Partner) extends far into Wilhelmstraße.

Berlin's most famous structure was a symbol of the divided city for decades. Flanked by watchtowers, *Brandenburg Gate* stood lost in no-man's-land at the GDR border. Wall and death strip barred any access. And yet, the beautiful early Neoclassicist gate once represented the ideals of liberal civil society around 1800. The only one left of Berlin's city gates was constructed in 1789–1791 under Frederick William II based on designs by Carl Gotthard Langhans. It was modeled on the Propylaea of the Acropolis. Even as compared to other structures in Europe, Langhans' creation is a brilliant novelty; the sandstone building has five gateways that are distinguished on both sides by six 15-meter-tall Dorian columns. The two flanking gatehouses were added in 1868 by Schinkel student Johann Heinrich Strack. The Quadriga (1793) with Irene, the winged goddess of peace, crowning the gate, as well as the designs for the bas-reliefs on its interiors were fashioned by Johann Gottfried Schadow. It was Napoleon who first bestowed

Innenseiten fertigte Johann Gottfried Schadow. Es war Napoleon, der dem Brandenburger Tor erstmals eine politische Bedeutung verlieh, als er nach dem Sieg bei Jena 1806 an der Spitze seiner Garden in Berlin einmarschierte. Die Quadriga ließ er nach Paris schaffen, bis Feldmarschall von Blücher sie acht Jahre später im Triumph zurückbrachte. Nun wurde das Tor zum Denkmal für die Befreiungskriege, die einstige Friedensgöttin mit dem von Schinkel hinzugefügten Eisernen Kreuz und Adler zur Viktoria. Fortan diente es als Kulisse für staatliche Feiern. Hier fand 1871, nach dem Sieg über Frankreich, der prunkvolle Einmarsch deutsch-preußischer Truppen statt. Die Nationalsozialisten feierten am 30. Januar 1933 die Machtergreifung mit einem Fackelzug. Bei Kriegsende wehte auf dem Tor symbolträchtig die rote Fahne der Roten Armee. Als am 9. November 1989 die Mauer fiel, ging ein Bild um die Welt: das Brandenburger Tor, bestürmt von jubelnden Menschenmassen. Seither steht es für die Erfahrung, dass „die deutsche Geschichte nicht nur Irr- und Sonderwege, sondern auch glückliche Wendungen kennt". (Günter de Bruyn)

Der schönste Platz Berlins aber ist der *Gendarmenmarkt* – ein Ensemble gelungener Symmetrie und architektonischen Ebenmaßes. Seinen Namen verdankt er dem Kürassierregiment „Gens d'armes", das Mitte des 18. Jahrhunderts hier seine Wachen und Stallungen hatte. Im Krieg stark beschädigt,

Gendarmenmarkt als Ensemble architektonischen Ebenmaßes. Unten: Deutscher Dom mit dem Schiller-Denkmal von Reinhold Begas; rechts unten: das von Schinkel entworfene Schauspielhaus und der Französische Dom.

Gendarmen Market as a composition of architectural harmony. Below: German Cathedral with Schiller Monument by Reinhold Begas; below right: Schauspielhaus, designed by Schinkel, and French Cathedral.

political significance to Brandenburg Gate when, after his 1806 victory at Jena, he marched into Berlin at the head of his guards. He had the Quadriga removed to Paris until Field Marshall von Blücher triumphantly returned her eight years later. Thus the gate became a monument to the Liberation Wars; the erstwhile goddess of peace, newly equipped with an Iron Cross and an eagle by Schinkel, was made Victoria, goddess of victory. Since then, it has served as backdrop for ceremonies of state. It was here that in 1871, after their victory over France, magnificently decked out German-Prussian troops marched back into the city. The National Socialists celebrated their seizure of power on January 30, 1933, with a torchlight procession. By the end of the war, the Red Army's red flag was flying atop the gate, heavy with symbolism. When the Wall fell on November 9, 1989, an image was broadcast around the world: Brandenburg Gate, stormed by jubilant crowds. Since then, it stands for the experience that "German history is informed not only by aberrations and special paths but also by fortunate turns" (Günter de Bruyn).

The most beautiful square in Berlin, however, is the *Gendarmenmarkt* – a merger of successful symmetry and architectural harmony. It owes its name to the Regiment of Cuirassiers called "Gens d'armes" that had its guardhouses and stables here in the mid-18th century. Heavily damaged in the war, it was given

erhielt er 1950, anlässlich der 250-Jahrfeier der dort angesiedelten Deutschen Akademie der Wissenschaften, seine alte Gestalt zurück. Mittelpunkt des Platzes ist das klassizistische Schauspielhaus von Karl Friedrich Schinkel, das heutige Konzerthaus. Es wurde 1818 bis 1821 auf den Grundmauern des 1817 abgebrannten Nationaltheaters errichtet.

Der Französische Dom an der Nordseite des Platzes entstand 1701 bis 1705 nach den Plänen von Jean Louis Cayart für die seit 1685 nach Berlin eingewanderten Hugenotten. Sein Pendant, der Deutsche Dom auf der gegenüberliegenden Seite des Platzes, wurde zur gleichen Zeit nach Plänen von Martin Grünberg für die preußische lutherische Bevölkerung gebaut. Auf seinen Stufen bahrte man 1848 die bei den Barrikadenkämpfen getöteten Demokraten, die Märzgefallenen, auf. Ihre charakteristischen Kuppeltürme ebenso wie die klassizistischen Vorbauten erhielten die Dome unter Friedrich II. Carl von Gon-

Der Potsdamer Platz in Zeugnissen der Schwarzweißfotografie. Oben ein Blick auf das Grandhotel Bellevue mit Werbung für das Varieté Wintergarten, Foto 1925. Rechts oben: eine Luftaufnahme von 1923, Fotopostkarte.

Potsdam Square as documented by black-and-white photography. Above, a view of Grand Hotel Bellevue with an ad for Varieté Wintergarten, photo 1925. Above right: an aerial photograph of 1923, photographic postcard.

back its original aspect in 1950 on the occasion of the 250th anniversary of the German Academy of Sciences located there. The square's central feature is the Neoclassicist Schauspielhaus by Karl Friedrich Schinkel, today's Concert Hall. It was built in 1818–1821 on the foundations of the National Theater that had been gutted by fire in 1817.

Based on designs by Jean Louis Cayart, the French Cathedral on the north side of the square was constructed in 1701–1705 for the Huguenots who had immigrated to Berlin since 1685. Its counterpart, the German Cathedral on the other side of the square, was built during the same period for the Prussian Lutheran population based on designs by Martin Grünberg. Democrats killed in 1848 during street battles, the March Dead, were laid out on its steps. The cathedrals acquired their distinctive domed towers as well as Neoclassicist front buildings under Frederick II. Carl von Gontard modeled them after

tard orientierte sich dafür an römischen Vorbildern. Pate standen die Zwillingskirchen auf der Piazza del Popolo. In der Mitte: Reinhold Begas' Schiller-Denkmal (1859).

Das Vorzeigeobjekt der Stadtplaner ist eigentlich gar kein Platz, wie der Name nahelegt: Hier am *Potsdamer Platz* ist eine Stadt in der Stadt entstanden. Das war nicht immer so. Einst das verkehrsreichste Areal Europas, das Luxushotels säumten und legendäre Etablissements wie das Café Josty oder das Haus Vaterland, schlug am Potsdamer Platz das heimliche Herz der Stadt. Und hier gab sich das neue „homogene Weltstadtpublikum" (Siegfried Kracauer) ein Stelldichein. Nach der nahezu kompletten Zerstörung im Zweiten Weltkrieg lag das gesamte Terrain brach und gehörte – eine Wüste inmitten der Stadt – jahrzehntelang zum Todesstreifen der Mauer. Heute steht der neue Potsdamer Platz mit seiner Mischung aus Entertainment, Kunst am Bau, Musicaltheater, Traditions-

Roman prototypes. Further inspiration were the twin churches of the Piazza del Popolo. In the center: Reinhold Begas' Schiller Monument (1859).

The city planners' flagship object is actually no square at all, although the name says so: Here at *Potsdamer Platz*, a city within a city has come to be. That was not always the case. Once the busiest traffic area in Europe, surrounded by luxury hotels and legendary establishments such as Café Josty or House Vaterland, Potsdamer Platz once harbored the secret heart of the city. It was here that the new "homogeneous metropolitan audience" (Siegfried Kracauer) congregated. After being almost completely destroyed in World War II, the entire terrain lay fallow and, for decades, belonged to the death strip along the Wall – a desert at the heart of the city. Today, the new Potsdamer Platz is again synonymous with the pulsating life of Berlin featuring a mixture of entertainment, art in architecture,

restaurants wie dem historischen Weinhaus Huth, Bars, Kinos, Grand Hotels, Einkaufsmall und Büros wieder als Synonym für das pulsierende Leben Berlins. Mit seinen beiden unterschiedlichen Zentren, dem Sony-Komplex und dem DaimlerChrysler-Areal, knüpft er wieder an den alten Vorkriegsmythos an. Dabei wurde auf der Grundlage eines Masterplans von Heinz Hilmer und Christoph Sattler nach traditionellem Berliner Blockschema an den rekonstruierten Straßenzügen entlang gebaut.

Renzo Piano, den bei den vielfältigen 19 Gebäuden des DaimlerChrysler-Quartiers weitere Architekten wie Richard Rogers, Arata Isozaki und Jos Rafael Moneo unterstützten, entwarf Musicaltheater, Spielbank und Imax-Kino am Marlene-Dietrich-Platz sowie das in ockerfarbenes Terrakotta gekleidete und mit einem grünen Würfel gekrönte debis-Haus. Helmut Jahns Sony Center hingegen stammt aus einer Hand und präsentiert eine geschlossene Glas-Stahl-Architektur, die in der Mitte eine von einem Zeltdach überspannte Plaza entstehen lässt. Dort hat ein von den Bomben verschonter Überrest des Grand Hotels Esplanade nobles Asyl gefunden. 1995 wurde er mitsamt dem berühmten Kaisersaal von seinem 75 Meter entfernten originalen Standort hierher verlegt. Sony-Turm, Pianos spitzwinkliges Bürohaus und Hans Kollhoffs treppenförmiges Backsteingebäude bilden das neue Wahrzeichen des Platzes, ein markantes Ensemble, das zum Leipziger Platz hin – der sich in neuer Gestalt zum alten Achteck formt – ein Tor andeutet und diesen geradewegs mit dem Kulturforum verbindet.

Die Gegenwart des Potsdamer Platzes: Seit den Neunzigerjahren ist hier eine hochmoderne Stadt in der Stadt entstanden, unter Mitwirkung vieler Architekten von Weltruf.

Potsdam Square today: Since the 1990s, an ultra-modern city within the city has emerged here with the collaboration of many architects of world renown.

musical theater, traditional restaurants such as the historical Weinhaus Huth, bars, movie theaters, grand hotels, a shopping mall, and offices. Its two different centers, the Sony Complex and the DaimlerChrysler Area, allow it to tie in again with the old prewar myth. The basis for its construction was a master plan by Heinz Hilmer and Christoph Sattler that observed traditional Berlin perimeter block development so as to build along reconstructed streets.

Supported by additional architects such as Richard Rogers, Arata Isozaki and Jos Rafael Moneo when designing the various 19 buildings of the DaimlerChrysler Quartier, Renzo Piano designed the Musical Theater, gambling casino and Imax cinema on Marlene Dietrich Platz as well as the debis house, clad with ocher-colored terracotta panels and crowned with a green cube. Helmut Jahn's Sony Center, on the other hand, was designed by a single architect and presents a closed glass-and-steel structure that forms a plaza covered by a tent roof at its very center. Spared by the bombs, a remnant of the Grand Hotel Esplanade has found classy asylum there. It was transferred here in 1995 from its original site 75 meters away, together with the famous Kaisersaal (emperor's hall). The Sony Tower, Piano's sharp-angled office building and Hans Kollhoff's staircase-like brick building constitute the new landmarks of the square, a remarkable ensemble that suggests a gateway in the direction of Leipziger Platz – which has reclaimed its old octagon shape albeit in a new guise – and that links the latter in a straight line with the Kulturforum.

Nüchtern und glanzlos, laut und geschichtsträchtig: Mit seinen Ausmaßen von drei Hektar ist der *Alexanderplatz* der weiträumigste Platz Berlins – und der Ort, an dem am 4. November 1989 eine halbe Million Menschen machtvoll das Ende der DDR ausriefen. Aus der Trümmerwüste des alten „Alex", der seinen Namen einem Staatsbesuch des Zaren Alexander I. im Jahre 1805 verdankt, war nach dem Krieg ein um ein Vierfaches vergrößertes Areal entstanden, das bis heute durch planwirtschaftlich nüchternes Baugefüge beherrscht wird. Die DDR-Vergangenheit Berlins spiegelt kein Platz der Stadt so sehr wider wie der Alexanderplatz. Aus der Vorkriegszeit haben sich lediglich die beiden Bürohäuser von Peter Behrens, das Alexander- und das Berolinahaus (1932), erhalten. Bis 1969 funktionierten die Ostberliner Planer den Platz komplett um: Die verkehrsberuhigte Zone in der Mitte flankieren einander kreuzende Verkehrstangenten und einzelne Baublöcke; darunter das Centrum-Warenhaus, an dessen Stelle einst das legendäre Kaufhaus Tietz stand, heute Kaufhof, das Haus der Presse (Berliner Verlag), das Haus der Elektrotechnik (Umwelt- und Familienministerium) sowie das Haus des Reisens (Weekend-Club); dazu das Haus des Lehrers, das in einem umlaufenden Wandbild (1964) von Walter Womacka das gesellschaftliche Leben im Sozialismus zeigt, und das höchste Hotel der Stadt, heute Park Inn. Den Mittelpunkt der Anlage bilden die Urania-Weltzeituhr und der Brunnen der Völkerfreundschaft

1929 veröffentlichte Alfred Döblin *Berlin – Alexanderplatz*, dem Roman folgte bereits zwei Jahre später der Film mit Heinrich George als Franz Biberkopf.
Rechts: Weltzeituhr und Fernsehturm, die heutigen Wahrzeichen des Alexanderplatzes.

In 1929, Alfred Döblin published his novel *Berlin – Alexanderplatz*; all but two years later, it was turned into a movie with Heinrich George as Franz Biberkopf.
Right: World Time Clock and Television Tower, present-day emblems of Alexander Square.

Sober and lusterless, noisy and pregnant with history: Extending across three hectares, *Alexanderplatz* is the most spacious square in Berlin – and the site where, on November 4, 1989, half a million people powerfully proclaimed the end of the GDR. Out of the rubble of the old "Alex," which owes its name to an 1805 state visit by Czar Alexander I, an area four times as large as the original emerged after the war; up to the present day, it has been dominated by a sober, socialist-planned, economy-style architectural complex. Berlin's GDR past is reflected by no other public space as much as by Alexanderplatz. The only prewar buildings to survive are the two office buildings by Peter Behrens, the Alexander and Berolina Houses (1932). By 1969, East Berlin city planners had completely reconfigured the square: The traffic-exempt zone in the center is flanked by criss-crossing transit thoroughfares and solitary building blocks; among these are Centrum Department Store, built on the former site of legendary Kaufhaus Tietz and occupied today by Kaufhof, the House of the Press (Berliner Verlag), the House of Electro-Technology (Department of the Environment and Family Affairs) as well as the House of Travel (Weekend Club), also the House of the Teacher that features a mural (1964) by Walter Womacka showing social life under Socialism and wrapping all around the building, and the tallest hotel of the city, today's Park Inn. Central features of the area are the Urania World Time Clock and the Fountain of International

Oben: Blick auf die 1929 bis 1932 nach Plänen von Peter Behrens errichteten Bürohäuser am Alexanderplatz. Unten: Die preisgekrönten Entwürfe von Hans Kollhoff für die Neubebauung des Areals sehen dreizehn 138- bis 142-geschossige Türme vor.

Above: View of office buildings on Alexander Square, built in 1929–1932 based on designs by Peter Behrens. Below: Hans Kollhoff's prize-winning designs for the reconstruction of the square envisioned thirteen towers, 138–142 stories tall.

aus den 1960er-Jahren. Noch immer lässt das Klein-Manhattan, das hier mit Kollhoffs Hochhauspark bereits 1993 geplant wurde, auf sich warten, auch wenn seit Jahren schon die Pressluft-hämmer und wie eh und je der Verkehr hier regieren, ganz so wie in Alfred Döblins berühmtem Roman „Berlin Alexanderplatz".

Heute oft verwandelt, zweckentfremdet oder ganz verschwunden sind die ältesten Plätze Berlins, die als Märkte an Verkehrskreuzungen entstanden waren wie der Molkenmarkt, der Cöllnische Fischmarkt oder der Neue Markt vor der Marien-kirche. Nichts erinnert hier mehr an das spätmittelalterliche Viertel, wo einst Lessing und Fontane flanierten, wo Moses Mendelssohn wirkte und Minna von Barnhelm logierte. Zwischen Kirche, Rotem Rathaus und Marx-Engels-Denkmal ist ein Drittel von Alt-Berlin unter Rasen, Rabatten und Pflaster begraben. Heute zeigt sich hier stattdessen in Gestalt einer namenlosen, leeren Fläche ein real existierendes Stück Hauptstadt der DDR. Dagegen hat für *Spittel- und Molkenmarkt* die Zukunft schon begonnen. Der historische Stadtgrundriss wird

Eduard Gaertner (1801–1877), *Der Spittelmarkt* (Hospital Market), 1833, Öl auf Leinwand/oil on canvas, 48,5 x 78,5 cm.

Linke Seite/left page: Johann Heinrich Hintze (1800–1862), *Der Neue Markt mit der Marienkirche* (New Market with St Mary's Church), Öl auf Leinwand/oil on canvas, 64 x 47 cm.

Friendship from the 1960s. Little Manhattan, originally planned in 1993 when Kollhoff proposed his Highrise Park, is still waiting to be built, even though jackhammers and good old traffic have dominated the area for years now, just like in Alfred Döblin's famous novel, "Berlin Alexanderplatz".

Berlin's oldest public spaces that once emerged as market places at transit intersections, such as Molken Market, Cölln Fish Market or New Market in front of St Mary's Church, have often been transformed, redesigned for different uses or have entirely disappeared today. Nothing here commemorates the late medieval quarter where once Lessing and Fontane went out for a stroll, where Moses Mendelssohn was at work and Minna von Barnhelm had lodgings. Flanked by a church, Red City Hall and the Marx Engels Monument, a third of Old Berlin has been buried under lawns, flower beds and pavements. Instead, a real, existing piece of the GDR capital presents itself here today in the shape of a nameless, empty expanse. The *Spittel and Molken Market*, on the other hand, have already

wieder belebt. Beide, heute kaum mehr als Plätze erkennbar, an der Hauptverbindung zwischen Ost und West, an der Leipziger- bzw. Gertraudenstraße gelegen, warten darauf, in ihrer ursprünglichen Geometrie rekonstruiert und bebaut zu werden.

Am Zentrum der City-West führen die großen Geschäftsmeilen entlang: Kurfürstendamm, Tauentzien-, Kant- und Budapester Straße – und mittendrin der *Breitscheidplatz*. Schon in den 1920er-Jahren pulsierte um die Kaiser-Wilhelm-Gedächtniskirche das kulturelle Leben mit Cafés und Kabaretts, Theatern und großen Uraufführungskinos neben noblen Wohnquartieren und ersten Einkaufsadressen. Nach den schweren Verwüstungen des Zweiten Weltkriegs nahm die Gegend mit Hochhäusern und Zeilenbauten eine ganz neue Gestalt an, während der S- und U-Bahnhof Zoo nach der Teilung der Stadt die Funktion des West-Berliner Hauptbahnhofs übernahm. Nach den Plänen von Paul Schwebes und Hans Schoszberger entstanden in den Jahren 1955 bis 1957 der Zoobogen, das Bauensemble mit Bikinihaus, in dem in den 1970er-Jahren die Kunsthalle untergebracht war, und der Zoo-Palast, bis 1999 Ort der Berliner Filmfestspiele. Das unter Denkmalschutz stehende Kino ist als Einziges aus der Ära der großen Lichtspielhäuser um den Kurfürstendamm erhalten geblieben und wird bald umgebaut, ohne den Stil der 1950er-Jahre zu gefährden. Weithin sichtbar: die Ikone des Wirtschaftswunders, das Europa-Center.

Breitscheidplatz mit Kaiser-Wilhelm-Gedächtniskirche (oben) und dem *Weltkugelbrunnen* des Bildhauers Joachim Schmettau von 1983 (rechts).

Breitscheid Square with Emperor William Memorial Church (above) and *World Globe Fountain* by sculptor Joachim Schmettau, 1983 (right).

Rechte Seite, oben: Der Lustgarten, aus der Perspektive des Berliner Doms; unten: mit Schinkels Altem Museum und dem Reiterstandbild Friedrich Wilhelms III., Photochrom, um 1890/1900.

Right page, above: Pleasure Garden, as seen from Berlin Cathedral; below: with Schinkel's Old Museum and the equestrian statue of Frederick William III, photochrome, c. 1890/1900.

ventured into the future. Their historical city groundplan will be revived. Almost unrecognizable as public spaces today, both of them are located on the main axis linking East and West, on Leipziger and Gertraudenstraße, respectively, and both await their restoration to original specifications on the level of layout and architecture.

Grand shopping streets line the center of City West: Kurfürstendamm, Tauentzienstraße, Kantstraße, and Budapester Straße – and in their midst, *Breitscheidplatz*. Cultural life with cafés and cabarets was vibrant around Kaiser Wilhelm Memorial Church already back in the 1920s; theaters and grand world premiere movie palaces stood next to elegant residential quarters and premier retail venues. When World War II had wreaked havoc on the area, it acquired an entirely new aspect dominated by highrises and *Zeilenbau* housing slabs while, after the city's division, the urban rail and subway station Zoo took on the function of West Berlin's central railway station. The Zoobogen was constructed in 1955–1957 based on designs by Paul Schwebes and Hans Schoszberger – the architectural ensemble with Bikinihaus that, in the 1970s, housed the Kunsthalle, and the movie theater Zoo Palast, until 1999 the venue for the Berlin International Film Festival. Protected by landmark status, this movie theater is the only one to survive from the era of the grand "Lichtspielhäuser" on Kurfürstendamm; it will soon be remodeled without detracting from its 1950's design. Visible from afar: the economic miracle icon, the Europa Center.

Prospect oder Weg, gegen dem Thier-Garden vor Berlin

1. Oberst von Weilers Gartl. 3 Königl. Stall
2. Alt Marinus Garten

Linden Allee
1691.

Bibl. Reg.
Berol.

Johann Stridbeck ad vif del.
1691.

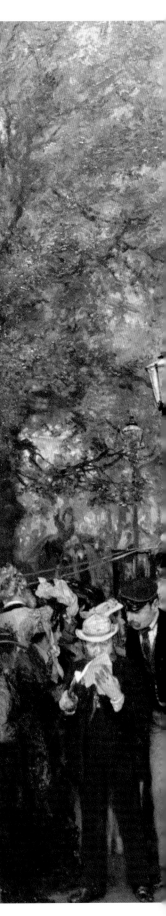

Oben/Above: Lovis Corinth
(1858–1925), *Berlin, Unter den
Linden*, 1922, Öl auf Leinwand/
oil on canvas, 70 x 90 cm, Von der
Heydt-Museum Wuppertal.

Rechts/Right: Adolph von Menzel
(1805–1905), *Abreise König
Wilhelms I. zur Armee am 31. Juli
1870* (Departure of King William I
for the Army on July 31, 1870),
1871, Öl auf Leinwand/oil on
canvas, 63 x 78 cm,
Alte Nationalgalerie Berlin.

Boulevards für Flaneure und Geschäftsmeilen für Einkäufer

Prachtboulevard, preußische Via triumphalis, Flaniermeile – die Linden, wie die Berliner sagen, führen vom alten Zentrum Berlins, von der Spreeinsel, wo einst das königliche Schloss stand, bis zum Brandenburger Tor. In glanzvoller Abfolge markieren die Bauten *Unter den Linden* die Geschichte der preußischen Architektur vom Barock bis zum Klassizismus. Was zunächst nur ein holperiger Reitweg war, wurde nach dem

Unter den Linden: Blick von der Schloss-Brücke auf Kronprinzen-palais (links) und Staatsoper, im Vordergrund zwei historische Kandelaber.

Unter den Linden: View of Crown Prince's Palace (left) and State Opera from Palace Bridge, in the foreground: two historical candelabra.

Boulevards for Flaneurs and Outdoor Shopping Malls for Shoppers

Flagship boulevard, Prussian *via triumphalis*, strollers' promenade – the Linden, as Berliners call it, leads from the old center of Berlin, Spree Island where the royal palace once stood, to Brandenburg Gate. In glorious sequence, the buildings *Unter den Linden* earmark the history of Prussian architecture from the Baroque to Neoclassicism. Originally nothing but a bumpy bridle path, it was planted with linden trees after the

Dreißigjährigen Krieg auf Wunsch des Großen Kurfürsten mit Linden bepflanzt. Ein erstes Wohnhaus, die spätere Stadtkommandantur, entstand 1653/54. Das erste repräsentative Gebäude, einen richtungsweisenden Barockbau, ließ König Friedrich I. an der Allee errichten: das Zeughaus. Als nächster entfaltete Friedrich der Große eine rege Bautätigkeit. Neben dem Kronprinzenpalais, dem einzigen Zeugnis aus der Ära seines Vaters, des Soldatenkönigs, hielten nun preußisches Rokoko und Frühklassizismus Einzug: das Forum Fridericianum mit Opernhaus, die St.-Hedwigs-Kathedrale und das Palais für

Christian Daniel Rauch (1777–1857), *Reiterstandbild Friedrich des Großen* (Equestrian Statue of Frederick the Great), 1851, Bronze, Höhe/height 13,5 m.

Unten: Schinkels Neue Wache (rechts) und Humboldt-Universität.
Below: Schinkel's New Guard House (right) and Humboldt University.

Thirty Years' War at the behest of the Great Elector. Its first residential building, the city garrison or Stadtkommandantur, was built in 1653/54. King Frederick I had the first representational building built on the avenue, a trendsetting Baroque structure: the Armory. Frederick the Great was next in line to engage in intense building activity. Prussian Rococo and early Neoclassicism now made their appearance next to the Crown Prince's Palace, the only building dating back to the era of his father, the Soldier King: the Forum Fridericianum with Opera House, St Hedwig's Cathedral and the Palace for Prince Hein-

den Prinzen Heinrich, die jetzige Humboldt-Universität; später kam die Königliche Bibliothek hinzu. Dem Pariser Vorbild gemäß wurde die Straße auf beiden Seiten mit vierstöckigen Palais für ihre adligen Bewohner bebaut. Unter Friedrich Wilhelm II. erhielt sie mit dem Brandenburger Tor ihren krönenden Abschluss. Schinkels Neue Wache schließlich, die Schlossbrücke sowie das Museum am Lustgarten, ein erstes bürgerliches Haus für die Künste, verleihen der Straße bis heute ihren architektonischen Glanz. Nach 1945 lag die Straße in Trümmern. Wertvolle Bauten wie das Kronprinzenpalais und die Oper wurden durch Richard Paulick aufwendig rekonstruiert.

Über 3,3 Kilometer zieht sich die *Friedrichstraße* schnurgerade durch die Stadtmitte: Sie war einmal die längste Straße Berlins. Mit ihrer Mischung aus Tingel-Tangel und Varietés bildete sie traditionell den Gegenpol zum Neuen Westen am Kurfürstendamm, wo „geistige Intimität und Witz" (Walther Kiaulehn) herrschten, während hier weltstädtisches Amüsement für den Massengeschmack angeboten wurde. Damals hieß die Friedrichstraße „Saufstraße", die Leipziger Straße mit den Warenhäusern war die „Kaufstraße", die noblen Linden feierte man als „Laufstraße".

Durch die fast vollständige Zerstörung im Zweiten Weltkrieg sind in der Friedrichstraße heute kaum noch ein Dutzend historischer Häuser zu finden. Während der DDR-Zeit führte sie eine Existenz am Rande. Nach dem Fall der Mauer wurde hier

Die Friedrichstraße um 1930, mit dem Eingang zur U-Bahnstation Stadtmitte.

Friedrichstraße c. 1930, with entrance to underground railway station Stadtmitte.

Linke Seite, oben:
Vor dem berühmten Café Bauer an der Ecke Unter den Linden, als noch die Pferdedroschken fuhren, Photochrom, um 1890.
Unten: Bahnhof Friedrichstraße mit Eisenbahnbrücke, kolorierte Postkarte, um 1905.

Left page, above:
In front of famous Café Bauer at the corner of Unter den Linden Blvd. with horse-drawn carriages still in service, photochrome, c. 1890.
Below: Friedrichstraße train station with railway bridge, hand-colored postcard, c. 1905.

rich, today's Humboldt University; the Royal Library was added at a later date. True to its Paris model, the street was built up on both sides with four-story mansions for its aristocratic residents. It acquired its crowning glory under Frederick William II with the construction of Brandenburg Gate. Schinkel's New Guardhouse finally, the Palace Bridge as well as the Museum at Pleasure Garden, the first house of the arts for the middleclass citizen, have been imparting their architectural brilliance to the avenue up to the present day. After 1945, the street lay in ruin. Valuable buildings such as the Crown Prince's Palace and the Opera were elaborately reconstructed by Richard Paulick.

For 3.3 kilometers, *Friedrichstraße* runs straight as an arrow through the center of the city: It was once the longest street in Berlin. With its mixture of honkytonk clubs and varietés, it posed a traditional counterpoint to the New West at Kurfürstendamm, where "intellectual intimacy and wit" (Walther Kiaulehn) were king, while here cosmopolitan amusement for mainstream tastes was offered. In those days Friedrichstraße was called "Saufstraße" or "drinking street"; Leipziger Straße with its department stores was a "Kaufstraße" or "shopping street," while classy Linden was feted as a "Laufstraße" or "strolling street."

Because of its almost complete destruction in World War II, barely a dozen historical buildings have survived on Friedrichstraße. During the GDR period, it led a marginal existence.

Lichtkegel des 1996 eröffneten
französischen Kaufhauses
Galeries Lafayette im Quartier 207
in der Friedrichstraße.

Light cone of the French
department store Galeries
Lafayette in Quarter 207 on
Friedrichstraße, opened in 1996.

Rechte Seite, oben:
Moderne Glas- und Stahlprismen,
Fassaden-Lichtbänder mit
Elementen aus Klassizismus und
Art déco zeichnen das Quartier
206 aus. Ein Werk der Architekten
Pei Cobb Freed & Partners.
Unten: Glasfassade des exklusiven
Kaufhauses Galeries Lafayette,
nach Entwürfen von Jean Nouvel.

Right page, above: Modern glass
and steel prisms, clerestory
strip-lights with Neoclassicist
and Art Déco elements across the
façade distinguish Quarter 206.
A work by architects Pei Cobb
Freed & Partners.
Below: Glass façade of the high-
end department store Galeries
Lafayette, based on designs by
Jean Nouvel.

Prunkfassade eines Wohnhauses am Kurfürstendamm, Olivaerplatz. Rechts: Neues Kranzler-Eck mit dem alle Dimensionen sprengenden Glasbau von Helmut Jahn, 1998–2000.

Magnificent façade of a residence on Kurfürstendamm, Oliva Square. Right: New Kranzler Corner with the humungous glass building by architect Helmut Jahn, 1998–2000.

im großen Stil gebaut, und die Friedrichstraße bekam eine vollständig neue Funktion.

Zunächst gab es nur einen Reitweg, der die Residenzstadt mit den Jagdgründen im Grunewald und dem gleichnamigen Jagdschloss (1542) verband. Als Berlin mit der Reichsgründung zur kaiserlichen Kapitale aufstieg, entwickelten sich *Kurfürstendamm* und *Tauentzienstraße* rasch zur teuersten Wohnlage Berlins. Es entstanden herrschaftliche Mietshäuser in allen Stilen und Stilgemischen mit teilweise riesigen Wohnungen – zum Beispiel 575 Quadratmeter in Hausnummer 60. Empfangshalle, Salons, Kabinette und Schlafzimmer waren in diesen Häusern in genau festgelegter Abfolge angeordnet. Vom Dienstpersonal wurden sie durch den Hof über eigene Treppenhäuser betreten. Heute sind in den häufig bereits nach dem Krieg aufgeteilten Wohnungen Arztpraxen und Büros untergebracht.

After the fall of the Wall, Friedrichstraße was built up again in grand style and assigned an entirely new function.

Originally only a bridal path linked the royal residence city with the hunting grounds in Grunewald and the homonymous Hunting Palace (1542). When Berlin rose to the status of imperial capital after the founding of the Reich, *Kurfürstendamm* and *Tauentzienstraße* quickly developed into the most expensive residential areas of Berlin. Palatial apartment buildings in all kinds of styles and stylistic mixtures came into being containing apartments of sometimes gigantic proportions – for example, 575 square meters in No. 60. The layout sequence of lobby, parlors, closets, and bedrooms was strictly prescribed in these buildings. The servants accessed them from the courtyard via separate stairwells. Already subdivided after the war, these apartments frequently house doctors' and administrative offices today.

Europa-Center, fotografiert durch die Skulptur *Berlin* der Künstler Brigitte und Martin Matschinsky-Denninghoff sowie eine Innenansicht der Geschäftsetagen (rechts).

Europa Center, photographed by way of *Berlin*, a piece of sculpture by artists Brigitte and Martin Matschinsky-Denninghoff, as well as an interior view of the business floors (right).

Ab 1910 war der Neue Westen mit dem Kurfürstendamm und der Tauentzienstraße als pulsierenden Lebensadern auch das „Industriegebiet der Intelligenz" (Erich Mühsam). Hier versammelte sich fast die gesamte Avantgarde, hier hatte sie mit dem Café des Westens (heute Café Kranzler) und dem Romanischen Café (dort, wo heute das Europa-Center steht) ihr Zentrum und ihre Bühne. Hier standen die großen Filmpaläste, Revuetheater und Kabarettbühnen. Im Eckhaus zur Fasanenstraße befand sich das von Rudolf Nelson gegründete Nelson-Theater, in dem 1926 Josephine Baker im knappen Bananenkostüm Berlin eroberte. Nur unweit davon bespielte Max Reinhardt, Regiestar des Deutschen Theaters, zwei weitere Bühnen, die 1924 von ihm gegründete Komödie und das Theater am Kurfürstendamm, in dem 1931 die Brecht-Weill-Oper „Aufstieg und Fall der Stadt Mahagonny" uraufgeführt wurde. Die beiden Theatersäle, Zeugnisse eines eleganten Art déco, sind heute in eine Bausünde der 1970er-Jahre, das Kudamm-Karree, einbezogen – mit ungewisser Zukunft. Der größte Teil dieser Welt aber ging im Dritten Reich und im Bombenhagel unter. Fast die Hälfte der Bebauung war am Ende des Zweiten Weltkriegs zerstört, der Rest stark beschädigt. Zwischen den Ruinen öffnete das Hotel Kempinski 1952 seine Tore, 1958 das Café Kranzler mit der berühmt gewordenen, markisenbewehrten Rotunde, die heute von Helmut Jahns gläsernem Riegelbau des Victoria-Areals überragt wird. Auch wenn der Kurfürs-

Über drei Etagen erstreckt sich die 13 m hohe Uhr der fließenden Zeit von Bernhard Gitton, ein Kunstwerk und ein wissenschaftliches Objekt zugleich.

Taking up three floors, the 13-meter-tall Clock of Flowing Time by Bernhard Gitton is both, a work of art and a scientific object.

From 1910 onward, the New West with Kurfürstendamm and Tauentzienstraße as its vibrant arteries also functioned as the "industrial area of the intellect" (Erich Mühsam). Almost all of the avant-garde set did its socializing here; it was here, at the Café des Westens (today's Café Kranzler) and the Romanisches Café (once located at the site of today's Europa Center), that they found their center and their stage. The grand movie palaces stood here, the revue theaters and cabaret stages. The corner building at Fasanenstraße housed the Nelson Theater, founded by Rudolf Nelson, where in 1926 Josephine Baker conquered Berlin in her scanty banana outfit. Not far from there, Max Reinhardt, star director of the Deutsches Theater, put on plays at two additional theaters, the Komödie, founded by him in 1924, and the Theater am Kurfürstendamm, where in 1931 Brecht's and Weill's opera, "Rise and Fall of the City of Mahagonny," had its world premiere. These two theater halls, heritage structures in the style of an elegant Art Déco, have nowadays been integrated into an architectural sin of the 1970s, the Kudamm-Karree – though their future is uncertain. The better part of that world, however, was lost in the Third Reich and a hail of bombs. Almost half of the buildings were destroyed at the end of World War II. Amidst the ruins, Hotel Kempinski opened its door in 1952; in 1958, Café Kranzler followed suit with its famous, marquee-fitted rotunda, much overshadowed today by Helmut Jahn's glass and steel-frame building of the

tendamm nach dem Fall der Mauer Funktionsverluste hinzu-
nehmen hatte, beginnt er sich mit neuer Architektur wieder einmal zu behaupten.

Es gehört zu Berlin wie der Reichstag und das Brandenburger Tor: Mit 60.000 Quadratmetern Verkaufsfläche ist das *Kaufhaus des Westens* (*KaDeWe*) das größte Warenhaus des Kontinents – und eine touristische Attraktion. Seit jeher gilt der
wuchtige Sandsteinbau mit der gläsernen Tonne als erste
Adresse für den gehobenen Geschmack.

Dabei war die Konkurrenz groß in der Hauptstadt der Waren-
häuser, die schon vor dem Ersten Weltkrieg zu den leistungs-
fähigsten und besten der Welt zählten: Tietz am Alexanderplatz
etwa oder Alfred Messels „Berliner Louvre", wie Fedor von

Links: Einkaufsstraße Tauentzien
mit Gedächtniskirche und der
Skulptur *Berlin* von Brigitte und
Martin Matschinsky-Denninghoff.
Unten: Nobelkaufhaus KaDeWe.

Left: Shopping street Tauentzien
with Memorial Church and *Berlin*,
a piece of sculpture by Brigitte
and Martin Matschinsky-
Denninghoff. Below: Classy
department store KaDeWe.

Victoria Areal. Even if Kurfürstendamm had to suffer loss of
function after the fall of the Wall, it has once again begun to
reassert itself by means of new architectural components.

It belongs to Berlin like the Reichstag and Brandenburg Gate:
With 60,000 square meters of shopping area, the *Kaufhaus des
Westens* (*KaDeWe*) is the largest department store on the
continent – and a tourist attraction. The massive sandstone
building with the "glass barrel" has always been considered a
premier venue for shoppers with upscale taste.

This is so even though there was much competition in this
capital of department stores which, even before World War I,
were among the most productive and best in the world: Tietz on
Alexanderplatz, for example, or Alfred Messel's "Berlin Louvre,"

Berliner Warenhausgeschichte:
Großer Lichthof im Kaufhaus
Wertheim in der Leipziger Straße,
erbaut bis 1906 nach Plänen von
Alfred Messel; Fotografie
(Autotypie), um 1927.

Berlin department store history:
Large atrium in Wertheim
Department Store on Leipziger
Straße, completed in 1906,
designed by Alfred Messel;
photograph (autotype), c. 1927.

„Brunnen-Lichthof" im Kaufhaus
Wertheim mit der Strumpfwaren-
Abteilung nach Erweiterungs-
baumaßnahmen 1927;
Farbdruck nach kolorierter
Fotografie, um 1927.

"Fountain Atrium" in Wertheim
Department Store with hosiery
department after expansion/
remodeling, 1927; color print of
a hand-colored photograph,
c. 1927.

Zobeltitz das Kaufhaus Wertheim in der Leipziger Straße nannte. Mit fünf Etagen war das von Johann Emil Schaudt entworfene Haus an der Tauentzienstraße bei der Eröffnung 1907 das größte Deutschlands, und die Gegend um die Gedächtniskirche stieg zum florierenden „Neuen Westen" auf. Während mit Karstadt am Hermannplatz ein weiteres Kaufhaus der Superlative entstand, wurde das KaDeWe 1927 von der Tietz-Gruppe übernommen, die wenige Jahre später von den Nationalsozialisten enteignet und „arisiert" wurde. 1943 stürzte ein Bomber in das Dachgeschoss des Kaufhauses, das fast vollständig ausbrannte. 1950 wurde es neu eröffnet – als einziges Zeugnis aus der großen Warenhausära Berlins.

Kaufhaus Karstadt am Neuköllner Hermannplatz, erbaut 1927–29 nach Entwürfen des Architekten Philipp Schäfer; Fotopostkarte, um 1935.

Karstadt Department Store on Hermannplatz in Neukölln, built in 1927–29, designed by architect Philipp Schäfer; photographic postcard, c. 1935.

as Fedor von Zobeltitz called Wertheim department store on Leipziger Straße. At five stories tall, the building designed by Johann Emil Schaudt on Tauentzienstraße was the largest in Germany at its opening in 1907; and the area around Gedächtniskirche grew to be the flourishing district of "Neuer Westen." While Karstadt on Hermannplatz was opened as yet another department store of superlatives, the KaDeWe was taken over in 1927 by the Tietz Group which, a few years later, was dispossessed by the National Socialists and "Arianized." In 1943, a bomber plunged into the top floor of the store which was almost completely gutted. In 1950, it was reopened – as the only surviving building of Berlin's great era of department stores.

Magistrale, Wasserstraßen und Brücken

Von Ost nach West wird Berlin von zwei großen Achsen durchschnitten, von zwei Magistralen. Wie zufällig spiegeln sie die unheilvolle Geschichte der Stadt: Die *Straße des 17. Juni* führt vom östlichen Rand des alten Zentrums über das Brandenburger Tor bis an die westliche Stadtgrenze; die *Karl-Marx-Allee*, das längste Baudenkmal Deutschlands, bildet unter verschiedenen Namen die Ausfallstraße vom Alexanderplatz bis an die östliche Peripherie. Auf 1,7 Kilometern stellt die ehemalige Große Frankfurter Straße, die zwischen 1952 und 1960 von den Kollektiven Hartmann/Henselmann/Hopp/Leucht/Paulick/Souradny als Paradestraße der DDR gebaut wurde und bis kurz nach dem Mauerbau Stalinallee hieß, die Architektur des Sozialistischen Realismus zur Schau. Ausgerechnet hier entzündete sich am 1. Juni 1953 der durch russische Panzer am 17. Juni blutig niedergeschlagene Arbeiteraufstand.

Es war diese Straße, die ursprünglich das Sommerschloss der ersten Preußenkönigin Sophie Charlotte (heute Schloss Charlottenburg) mit der Berliner Residenz verband und die der Königin zu Ehren 330 Jahre lang Charlottenburger Chaussee hieß. Erst während des Nationalsozialismus wurde sie im Zuge des geplanten Umbaus von Berlin zur „Welthauptstadt Germania" auf die heutige Breite gebracht. Die so entstandene Repräsentationsstraße erhielt 1935 den offiziellen Namen Ost-West-Achse. Außerdem wurde die einst den Königsplatz (heute Platz der Republik) schmückende Siegessäule 1938 auf den Großen Stern umgesetzt. Seitdem stellt sie das weithin sichtbare Erkennungszeichen der Straße des 17. Juni dar, die ihren Namen seit dem Senatsbeschluss vom 22. Juni 1953 in Erinnerung an den Volksaufstand in der DDR trägt. Die inzwischen denkmalgeschützten typischen Straßenlaternen hat Albert Speer gestaltet. Während die alliierten Westmächte hier bis 1989 alljährlich ihre Truppenparaden abhielten, ist die Straße heute das städtische Terrain für Großveranstaltungen jeder Art.

Unglaublich, aber wahr: Mit über tausend *Brücken* besitzt Berlin mehr als doppelt so viele wie die Brückenstadt Venedig. Spree, Havel und die vielen Kanäle, das waren über Jahrhunderte die Lebensadern der Stadt. Diesem zweihundert Kilometer umspannenden Wasserstraßennetz verdankt Berlin einen Gutteil seines wirtschaftlichen Aufschwungs.

Einst Repräsentationsstraße
zwischen zwei königlichen
Schlössern: die Ost-West-Achse
mit dem Großen Stern (unten),
seit 1938 geschmückt von der
umgesetzten Siegessäule.

Former representational
boulevard connecting two royal
palaces: the East West Axis with
the Great Star (below), since
1938 decorated with the
relocated Victory Column.

Magistrals, Waterways and Bridges

Berlin is transected from East to West by two great axes, or two magistrals. As if by accident, they reflect the city's calamitous history: The *Straße des 17. Juni* leads from the eastern rim of the old city center via Brandenburg Gate up to the western city limit; *Karl-Marx-Allee*, the longest architectural monument in Germany, constitutes, under various names, the arterial road from Alexanderplatz up to the eastern periphery. Built in 1952–1960 by the collectives of Hartmann/Henselmann/Hopp/Leucht/Paulick/Souradny as a GDR flagship boulevard and called Stalinallee until shortly after the building of the Wall, the former Große Frankfurter Straße showcases the architecture of Socialist Realism on a 1.7-kilometer stretch. It was here of all places that the Workers' Uprising was sparked on June 1, 1953, and bloodily put down by Russian tanks on June 17.

This was the street that originally linked the summer palace (today Charlottenburg Palace) of the first Prussian queen, Sophie Charlotte, with the royal residence of Berlin and which, in honor of the queen, bore the name of Charlottenburger Chaussee for 330 years. Only during the era of National Socialism was it enlarged to its current width in the wake of the planned remodeling of Berlin into the "World Capital of Germania." The representational boulevard thereby created was given the official name of East-West Axis in 1935. Additionally, the Victory Column that had once graced Königsplatz (today's Platz der Republik) was moved to the Great Star in 1938. Since then, it constitutes the highly visible emblem of the Straße des 17. Juni, which received its name by Senate decree on June 22, 1953, to commemorate the People's Uprising in the GDR. The characteristic street lamps, by now landmark protected, were designed by Albert Speer. While the Allied Western forces conducted their annual military parades here until 1989, the avenue today serves as urban terrain for all sorts of mass events.

Incredible, but true: At more than one thousand *bridges*, Berlin has more than double the number of bridges than Venice, the city of bridges. Spree, Havel and numerous canals: those were the city's lifelines for centuries. It is to this water network extending for two hundred kilometers that Berlin owes a large part of its economic boom.

Einst Paradestraße der Hauptstadt der DDR: Deutschlands längstes Baudenkmal führt über den Strausberger Platz (oben) und passiert die Türme des Frankfurter Tors (unten).

Former flagship boulevard of the GDR capital: Germany's longest architectural monument runs by Strausberg Square (above) and past the towers of Frankfurt Gate (below).

Eduard Gaertner (1801–1877),
Ansicht der Schlossbrücke
(View of Palace Bridge), 1861,
Öl auf Leinwand/oil on canvas,
90 x 125,5 cm.

Die Schlossbrücke (1821–24),
Entwurf: Karl Friedrich Schinkel.
Umrissstich: Ferdinand Berger
nach Zeichnung Schinkels, 1819.
Die Marmorstandbilder, ebenfalls
von Schinkel entworfen, wurden
erst 1853–57 errichtet.

Palace Bridge (1821–24),
design: Karl Friedrich Schinkel.
Silhouette etching: Ferdinand
Berger after a Schinkel drawing,
1819. The marble statues, likewise
designed by Schinkel, were not
mounted until 1853–57.

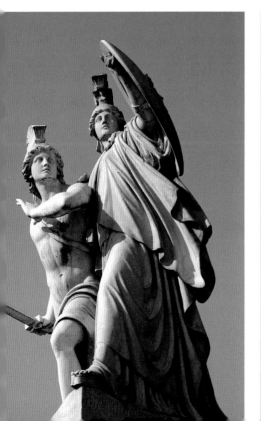

Oben/Above: Maximilian Roch
(1793–?), *Lange Brücke und Schloss*
(Long Bridge and Palace), 1842,
Öl auf Leinwand/oil on canvas,
99 x 152 cm, Märkisches Museum.

Unten/Below: Eduard Gaertner
(1801–1877), *Die Königsbrücke*
(King's Bridge), 1832, Öl auf
Leinwand/oil on canvas,
53,5 x 87 cm, Märkisches Museum.

Die Oberbaumbrücke über die Spree. Das neugotische Bauwerk mit seinen beiden 34 m hohen Türmen wurde 1894–96 nach Plänen von Otto Stahn erbaut.

Oberbaum Bridge across the Spree. The Neo-Gothic structure with its two 34-meter-tall towers was built in 1894–96 based on designs by Otto Stahn.

Linke Seite: Die Moltkebrücke aus rotem Sandstein und mit Bild- und Skulpturenschmuck aus der Wilhelminischen Zeit führt über die Spree nahe dem Bundeskanzleramt. Sie wurde erbaut nach Plänen von Otto Stahn 1886–91.

Left page: Moltke Bridge made of red sandstone and decorated with images and sculptures from the Wilhelminian Era leads across the Spree near the Office of the Federal Chancellor. It was built in 1886–91 based on designs by Otto Stahn.

Rechts: Der Preußische Adler auf der Weidendammer Brücke, eine der ersten gusseisernen Brücken in Mitteleuropa. Baumeister war ebenfalls Otto Stahn.
Unten: Über die Havel verbindet die Glienicker Brücke Berlin und die Stadt Potsdam.

Right: Prussian Eagle on Weidendamm Bridge, one of the first cast iron bridges in Central Europe, likewise designed by master builder Otto Stahn.
Below: Spanning the Havel, Glienicke Bridge links Berlin and Potsdam.

Gebäude und Ensembles der Macht
Buildings and Complexes of Power

Von den einstigen Schaltzentralen der politischen Macht ist wenig geblieben in Berlin. Das alte Schloss überdauerte nur in Gestalt des Balkons, von dem aus Karl Liebknecht 1918 die „freie sozialistische Republik" proklamiert hatte. Die Wilhelmstraße, Regierungsmeile des Kaiserreichs, der Weimarer Republik und des Nationalsozialismus, wurde im Zweiten Weltkrieg nahezu ausgelöscht und danach zu einem Wohnquartier.

Kanzleramt und Schloss Bellevue

Heute verteilen sich die Ämter der Bundesregierung auf neue und alte Gebäude in den Bezirken Tiergarten und Mitte. Zentrum ist das Areal zwischen Reichstag und Spree, wo sich bis in die 1940er-Jahre hinein eine bürgerliche Wohngegend mit spätklassizistischen Villen und Botschaften ausdehnte, das Alsenviertel. Hitlers Architekt Albert Speer plante hier die Große Volkshalle, wofür noch vor den großen Bombenangriffen ein Großteil des Viertels abgerissen wurde. Nach Kriegsende lag das Gelände brach, bis die Mauer fiel – und Berlin 1990 zur

Reihe oben:
Bundeskanzleramt, Teilansicht der Deckenkonstruktion im südwestlichen Flügel und Blick auf die Etagen (rechte Seite).

Row above:
Chancellor's Office, partial view of the ceiling structure in the southwestern wing and view of the floors (right page).

Vorhergehende Seite/Previous page: Bundeskanzleramt/ Chancellor's Office (1997–2001), Axel Schultes, Charlotte Frank.

Little is left in Berlin of the former control centers of power. The old palace only survived in the shape of the balcony from which Karl Liebknecht proclaimed the "free socialist republic" in 1918. Wilhelmstraße, government boulevard of the Empire, the Weimar Republic and National Socialism, was all but obliterated during World War II and thereafter transformed into a residential quarter.

Chancellor's Office and Bellevue Palace

Today, the offices of the federal government are distributed across new and old buildings in the districts of Tiergarten and Mitte. The area between Reichstag and Spree is their center that, up to the 1940s, was the site of a middleclass neighborhood featuring late Neoclassicist villas and embassies – the Alsenviertel. Hitler's architect, Albert Speer, had this site earmarked for his planned Great Hall of the People; the better part of the quarter was razed for that project even before the great air raids. After the end of the war, the area lay fallow

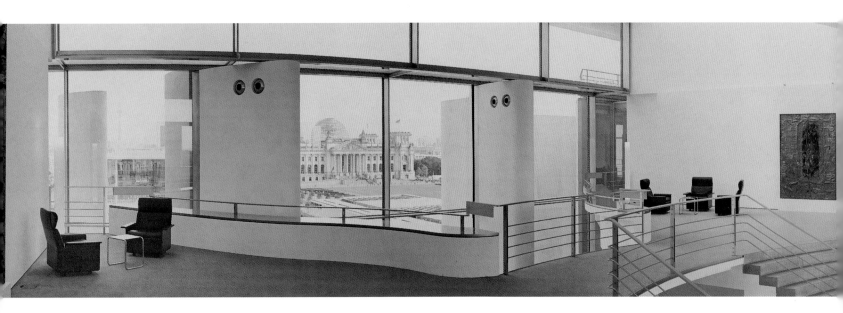

Hauptstadt wurde. Ein Jahr später wurde der Umzug von Parlament und Regierung aus Bonn beschlossen.

Den Generalplan für die neue Gestaltung entwickelten 1991 die Berliner Architekten Axel Schultes und Charlotte Frank. Programmatisch und gleichermaßen radikal wird darin das neue Regierungsviertel zum „Band des Bundes" erklärt. Über neunhundert Meter lang legt es sich wie ein weißer Riegel aus ineinander verwobenen Baukörpern über den Spreebogen und vollzieht eine Art symbolischen Brückenschlag zwischen den einstmals durch die Mauer getrennten Stadthälften, die, bis heute sichtbar, genau entlang des Marie-Elisabeth-Lüders-Hauses verlief. Vom ersten Spatenstich an bis zur Eröffnung des letzten Baus 2003 vergingen nur sechs Jahre.

Das *Bundeskanzleramt*, gleichfalls von Schultes und Frank entworfen, machte den Anfang. Es ist zwar nicht der größte, aber der wohl imposanteste Neubau des Ensembles. Die langen Beton- und Sandsteinfassaden der Bürotrakte und der Leitungsbau bilden eine dreiflügelige Anlage. Nur zum Reichstag hin öffnet sich eine augenfällige Schaufront mit ihrem

Unten: Innenansichten des Bundeskanzleramts. Skylobby mit Blick zum Reichstagsgebäude (linke Seite) sowie Foyer und Treppenaufgänge.

Below: Interior views of the Chancellor's Office. Sky lobby with view of the Reichstag building (left page) as well as foyer and stairways.

until the fall of the Wall – and Berlin became the federal capital in 1990. One year later, the move of parliament and government from Bonn to Berlin was decided.

The general layout for the new design was developed in 1991 by Berlin architects Axel Schultes and Charlotte Frank. Programmatic and simultaneously radical, their vision declared the new government district a *"Band des Bundes,"* a 'Federal band' or also 'bond.' Over nine hundred meters long and composed of intricately woven structures, it lies across Spreebogen like a white tie-bar and builds a symbolic bridge between the two halves of the city once divided by the Berlin Wall whose exact course is visible still today, running the length of Marie Elisabeth Lüders House. The Band's completion took only six years from the groundbreaking ceremony to the opening of the final building in 2003.

The *Chancellor's Office*, also designed by Schultes and Frank, was the first. It was not the largest, but arguably the most commanding new building of the complex. The long concrete and sandstone façades of the office tracts and the main building

Ehrenhof, der mit Eduardo Chillidas „Berlin"-Skulptur geschmückt ist. Im mittleren Kubus befindet sich die eigentliche Machtzentrale, der Kabinettssaal im sechsten Stock und darüber das Kanzlerbüro. Nach Westen verbindet eine Brücke den Amtssitz mit dem sich über das Wasser hinweg fortsetzenden Kanzlergarten. Dass sich die Regierungszentrale nicht in architektonische Konkurrenz zum Sitz des Parlaments, dem Reichstag gegenüber, begibt, sondern sich als primus inter pares in das Band der Bundesbauten eingliedert, wird gleichfalls als symbolträchtig angesehen. Einziger Zeuge aus der Vergangenheit ist die benachbarte Schweizer Botschaft. Das Palais von 1871 (Friedrich Hitzig), das 2001 einen festungsartigen Anbau (Diener & Diener) erhielt, behauptet sich inmitten von Neubauten als letzte Hinterlassenschaft des historischen Alsenviertels.

Noch älter ist der Amtssitz des Bundespräsidenten, der westlich, Spree abwärts liegt: *Bellevue*, ein nobles Schloss im Park, repräsentativ, aber nicht einschüchternd, vornehm, ohne aufzutrumpfen. 1786 errichtete Michael Philipp Daniel Boumann die elegante Dreiflügelanlage für den Prinzen August Ferdinand von Preußen, den jüngsten Sohn des Soldatenkönigs, dem sein Friedrichsfelder Schloss zu weit vor den Stadttoren lag. Boumann orientierte sich bei seinem Entwurf an der kurz zuvor fertig gestellten Residenz in Wörlitz und schuf damit das erste königlich-preußische Schloss in frühklassizistischem Stil. Im heute rekonstruierten ovalen Festsaal, den Carl Gotthard Langhans 1791 gestaltete, waren Friedrich Schiller und Napoleon zu Gast. Später richtete Friedrich Wilhelm IV. in der Residenz die „Vaterländische Galerie" ein, das erste Museum für zeitgenössische Kunst in Preußen. Gleichzeitig wurde der Park

Rechte Seite: Schloss Bellevue mit dem ellipsenförmigen Bau des Bundespräsidialamts nahe dem großen Stern. Darunter: Frontansicht des Amtssitzes des Bundespräsidenten.

Right page: Bellevue Palace with the elliptical building of the Federal President's Office near the Great Star. Beneath: Front view of the federal president's official residence.

Die umlaufenden, zum Lichthof hin offenen Galerien im Inneren des Bundespräsidialamts (1996–98), entworfen von Martin Gruber und Helmut Kleine-Kraneburg.

Circumambient galleries opening upon the atrium inside the Federal President's Office (1996–98), designed by Martin Gruber and Helmut Kleine-Kraneburg.

form three wings. They open up only towards the Reichstag where they display a striking front enclosing a Court of Honor decorated with Eduardo Chillida's "Berlin" sculpture. The actual center of power is located in the center cube; the Cabinet Hall is on the sixth floor while the Chancellor's Office lies above. A bridge links the office with the Chancellor's Garden extending across the water on both sides of the Spree. That this center of the federal government does not see itself in architectural competition with the seat of Parliament, the Reichstag on the other side, but defines itself as integral *primus inter pares* among all federal Band buildings, is likewise considered deeply symbolic. The only building commemorating the past is the neighboring Swiss Embassy. The Palace building dating back to 1871 (Friedrich Hitzig), enlarged by a fortress-like annex in 2001 (Diener & Diener), asserts itself in the midst of new buildings as the final vestige remnant of the historical Alsen Quarter.

Even older is the official seat of the federal president, located to the west, down the Spree: *Bellevue*, a noble palace in the park, representational, but not intimidating, lofty, but without arrogance. Michael Philipp Daniel Boumann built the elegant three-wing facility in 1786 for Prince August Ferdinand of Prussia, the youngest son of the Soldier King, who thought his Friedrichsfeld Palace lay too far outside the city gates. Taking his cues from the Royal Residence recently built in Wörlitz, Boumann thus created the first royal Prussian palace in the early Neoclassicist style. The oval banqueting hall, designed by Carl Gotthard Langhans in 1791 and now reconstructed, once hosted Friedrich Schiller and Napoleon. Later, Frederick William IV had the "Fatherland Gallery" installed in the build-

für die Öffentlichkeit zugänglich gemacht. Das stark kriegszerstörte Bellevue wurde mehrfach grundlegend restauriert und modernisiert. Nebenan ist von 1996 bis 1998 das Bundespräsidialamt – entworfen von Martin Gruber und Helmut Kleine-Kraneburg – hinzugekommen, eine vierstöckige, in hochglänzende, schwarze Granitplatten gekleidete Ellipse mit einem Innenhof.

Reichstag und das Band des Bundes

Kaum ein anderes Gebäude repräsentiert so viele Wendepunkte in der deutschen Geschichte wie der *Reichstag* – seit 1999 Sitz des Deutschen Bundestages. Philipp Scheidemann rief hier am 9. November 1918 die Republik aus. Kuppel und Plenarsaal brannten in der Nacht zum 28. Februar 1933 vollständig aus, was die Nationalsozialisten zum Anlass nahmen, zunächst die Reichtagsbrandverordnung zu erlassen und später das berüchtigte Ermächtigungsgesetz durchzusetzen, das ihre Alleinherrschaft besiegelte. 1945 hissten Soldaten der Roten Armee die rote Fahne auf dem Dach. Mit dem Bau des Parlaments war nach der Reichsgründung, die 1871 aus der preußischen Kapitale Berlin die Reichshauptstadt machte, der Frankfurter Architekt und Palladio-Liebhaber Paul Wallot be-

Oben: Albrecht Kurz (1858–1928), *Das Reichstagsgebäude*, um 1900, Farblithographie, 32 x 41,5 cm.
Rechts oben: Eduard Obermayer (1831–1916), *Reichstags-Gebäude zu Berlin. Westfront*, Kupferstich.
Unten: Seit 1999 befindet sich im umgebauten Reichstag der Plenarsaal des Deutschen Bundestags.

Above: Albrecht Kurz (1858–1928), *Reichstag Building*, c. 1900, color lithography, 32 x 41.5 cm.
Right above: Eduard Obermayer (1831–1916), *Reichstag Building. Western façade*, copper engraving.
Below: Since 1999, the plenary hall of the German Parliament has been located in the remodeled Reichstag.

ing – the first museum for contemporary art in Prussia. The park was opened to the public at the same time. Heavily damaged by the war, Bellevue was thoroughly renovated and modernized several times. Next door, the Office of the Federal President – designed by Martin Gruber and Helmut Kleine-Kraneburg – was added in 1996–1998, a four-story ellipse clad with high gloss, black granite slabs and an interior courtyard.

Reichstag and the Federal Band

Almost no other building has represented as many turning points in German history as the *Reichstag* – since 1999, the seat of the German Bundestag. Here, Philipp Scheidemann proclaimed the Weimar Republic on November 9, 1918. Dome and plenary hall were completely gutted by fire during the night of February 28, 1933, an event used by the National Socialists to enact the Reichstag Fire Decree and, later, to push through the infamous Enabling Act that sealed their dictatorship. In 1945, soldiers of the Red Army hoisted the Red Flag on its roof. After the founding of the Empire, which changed Berlin's status from Prussian to imperial capital in 1871, Frankfurt architect and Palladio fan Paul Wallot was assigned to construct the Parliament building. The massive cuboid, chiefly designed in the

Sir Norman Fosters Glaskuppel auf dem Reichstag: 800 t Stahl und Glas, 40 m Durchmesser, 23,5 m in der Höhe, 360 einzelne Spiegel. Und ein Blick für die Besucher in den Plenarsaal.

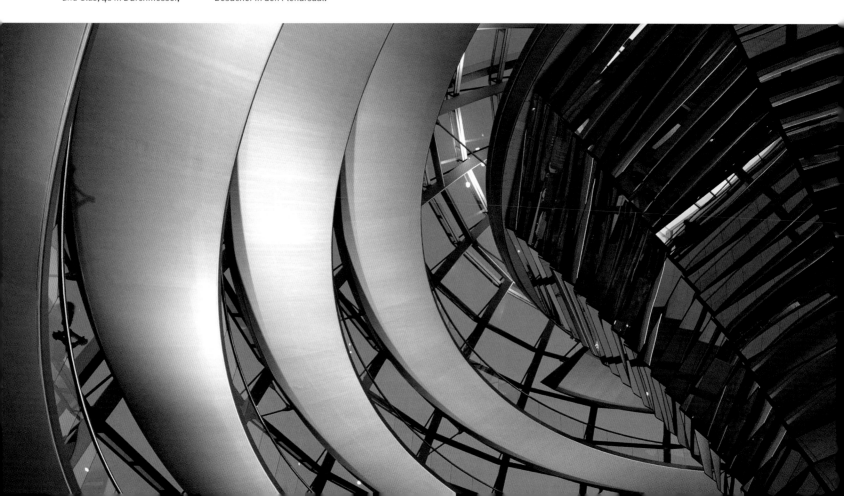

Sir Norman Foster's glass dome on the Reichstag building: 800 tons of steel and glass, 40 m in diameter, 23.5 m high, 360 single mirrors. And a view of the plenary hall for visitors.

Gerhard Richter, *Schwarz Rot Gold* (Black Red Gold), 1998, farbemailliertes Glas (colored enamel on glass), 2072 x 317 cm, Reichstag, Westvorhalle/western lobby, Kunstsammlung des Deutschen Bundestages/ German Bundestag Art Collection.

Rupprecht Geiger, *Rot 2000, 875 /99* (Red 2000, 875 / 99), Kleiner Protokollraum des Reichstags/Small Protocol Room of the Reichstag, 1999, fluoreszierende Farben/ fluorescent colors, Kunstsammlung des Deutschen Bundestages/German Bundestag Art Collection.

auftragt worden. Der hauptsächlich im Stil der italienischen Hochrenaissance gehaltene, durch vier Ecktürme bewehrte, wuchtige Quader wurde von 1884 bis 1894 errichtet. Während er dem Schloss und dem damaligen Regierungsviertel seine Rückseite zuwandte, öffnete sich seine Hauptfassade zum Königsplatz hin. Schon allein die Kuppel aus Stahl und Glas – ein vielfach bewundertes technisches Meisterwerk – rief die Missbilligung Kaiser Wilhelms II. hervor, konkurrierte sie doch provokativ mit der des Schlosses. Für ihn stellte der Bau „den Gipfel der Geschmacklosigkeit" dar; den Reichstag nannte er „Reichsaffenhaus". So dauerte es bis 1916, ehe er sein Einverständnis erklärte, die von Peter Behrens gestaltete Inschrift „Dem Deutschen Volke" über dem Westportal anbringen zu lassen. Der im Zweiten Weltkrieg schwer beschädigte Reichstag wurde in den Sechzigerjahren durch den Architekten und Professor Paul Baumgarten (1900–1984) wiederaufgebaut, wobei ein Großteil des plastischen Fassadenschmucks abgetragen und Überreste des historischen Inneren zerstört wurden.

Nach der deutschen Wiedervereinigung waren die Meinungen über die neuerliche Nutzung des geschichtsbeladenen Bauwerks geteilt. Erst durch Christos und Jeanne-Claudes Verhüllung im Sommer 1995 änderte sich die Stimmung.

Norman Foster gelang es schließlich, die historische Bausubstanz so in den Umbau zu integrieren, dass ein würdevolles, hochfunktionales und modernes Parlament entstand. Dabei dominiert die Geschichte weder die Gegenwart noch umgekehrt. Fosters Meisterleistung ist die neue, mittels einer doppelten Rampenspirale begehbare, gläserne Kuppel, die Einblick in den riesigen Plenarsaal erlaubt.

Unterirdisch ist der Reichstag durch einen Fußgängertunnel mit den Büros der Bundestagsabgeordneten verbunden, die sich in dem gegenüberliegenden, langgestreckten Neubauriegel auf beiden Ufern der Spree befinden. Im *Paul-Löbe-Haus* (2001), das von Stephan Braunfels konzipiert und nach dem Sozialdemokraten und Präsidenten des Reichstags Paul Löbe (1875–1967) benannt wurde, ist allein die zentrale Halle mit ihren ausladenden Galerien über 150 Meter lang. Acht Rotunden beherbergen hier die Sitzungssäle für die Ausschüsse sowie Büros für die Parlamentarier. Im Sinne einer „gläsernen Demokratie" wurde bei der Gestaltung viel Wert auf Offenheit und Transparenz gelegt. Besonders reizvoll sind die Treppe an der Spree und die Promenade mit Blick auf die verschiedenen Regierungsbauten.

Das am anderen Ufer als *Marie-Elisabeth-Lüders-Haus* (2003) fortgesetzte Gebäude ist durch eine zweistöckige Fußgängerbrücke angebunden. Unter dem Dach des ebenfalls von Braunfels entworfenen Gebäudes ist Platz für eine der größten Parlamentsbibliotheken der Welt. Elegante Treppen durchziehen den Bau und führen zum Wasser hinab. Der Name erinnert an die liberale Politikerin Marie-Elisabeth Lüders (1878–1966).

Nördlich des Paul-Löbe-Hauses ist nach Plänen des Wiener Architekten Gustav Peichl eine futuristisch wirkende Kindertagesstätte für Bundestagsmitarbeiter entstanden. An seiner Seite führt die elegante Kronprinzenbrücke des Spaniers Santiago Calatrava hinüber zum Haus der Bundespressekonferenz.

style of the Italian High Renaissance and furnished with four corner towers, was built in 1884–1894. Turning its back on the Palace and former government district, its main façade opened up towards Königsplatz. The steel and glass dome alone – a technological masterpiece much admired in various quarters – occasioned the disapproval of Emperor William II, since it provocatively competed with that of the Palace. For him, this building represented the "pinnacle of poor taste"; William II called the Reichstag the "Imperial Monkey House." So it was not until 1916 (during World War I) that he gave his approval to have architect and designer Peter Behrens' inscription "To the German People" affixed above the west portal. Heavily damaged during World War II, the Reichstag was reconstructed in the 1960s by architect and Professor Paul Baumgarten (1900–1984); most of the sculptural décor on the façade was removed and remnants of the historical interior were destroyed in the process.

After German reunification, opinions about putting this historically burdened building to new use were divided. Only when Christo and Jeanne-Claude wrapped it in the summer of 1995 did the mood change.

Norman Foster, finally, was able to so integrate its historical architectural substance with the remodeling as to create a dignified, highly functional and modern Parliament. As a result, neither does history dominate the present nor vice versa. Foster's masterpiece is the new glass dome, accessible via a double spiral ramp that grants visitors a view down into the gigantic plenary hall.

The Reichstag is connected via an underground pedestrian tunnel with the delegates' offices of the Bundestag; they are housed in the elongated new building spread out across from it on both sides of the Spree. The *Paul Löbe House* (2001), conceived by Stephan Braunfels and named after Social Democrat and President of the Reichstag Paul Löbe (1875–1967), contains a central hall with projecting galleries that is more than 150 meters long. Eight rotundas house the conference halls for caucuses as well as offices for parliamentarians. To symbolize "crystalline democracy," much attention was paid to openness and transparency. Especially appealing are the staircase by the Spree and the promenade with a view of various government buildings.

The building continues on the other side of the river as *Marie Elisabeth Lüders House* (2003) which is accessed via a two-story pedestrian bridge. Under the roof of this building, likewise designed by Stephan Braunfels, there is space for one of the largest parliamentary libraries in the world. Elegant staircases run throughout the building and lead down to the water. Its name commemorates liberal German politician Marie-Elisabeth Lüders (1878–1966).

To the north of Paul Löbe House, a futuristic daycare center for the children of Bundestag staff members was built based on designs by Viennese architect Gustav Peichl. Next to it, the elegant Crown Prince Bridge, designed by Spanish architect Santiago Calatrava, leads across the river to the House of the Federal Press Conference.

Georg Baselitz, *Friedrichs Melancholie*, 1998, Öl auf Leinwand/oil on canvas, ca. 500 x 400 cm, des Reichstag, Südportal/southern entrance, Kunstsammlung des Deutschen Bundestages/German Bundestag Art Collection.

Joseph Beuys (1921–1986), *Tisch mit Aggregat* (Desk with Power Unit), 1958/1985, Bronze, im Reichstag, Abgeordneten-Restaurant/Delegates' Restaurant, Kunstsammlung des Deutschen Bundestages/German Bundestag Art Collection.

98

Christian Boltanski, *Archiv
der Deutschen Abgeordneten*
(Archive of the German
Delegates), Reichstag,
Untergeschoss des
Osteingangs/basement of
the eastern entrance.

Rechts/Right:
Hans Haacke, *DER BEVÖLKERUNG*
(To the Population), 2000/08,
Reichstag, nördlicher Lichthof/
northern light-well, 21 x 7 m,
Kunstsammlung des Deutschen
Bundestages/German Bundestag
Art Collection, Stefan Müller.

Der größte der Bundestagsneubauten, das *Jakob-Kaiser-Haus* (2002), trägt den Namen des Mitbegründers der CDU (1888–1961). In durchlichteter Architektur lebt hier das alte Dorotheenviertel mit seinen zahlreichen historischen Grundrissen, seiner kleinteiligen Struktur wieder auf. Restaurierte Altbauten sind als Zeitzeugen integriert, so das Reichspräsidentenpalais von Paul Wallot und die Kammer der Technik.

Zur Spree hin zeigen sich offene Höfe. Wie ein vielteiliges Puzzle wirkt dieses Gesamtensemble mit seinen insgesamt 1745 Abgeordneten- und Fraktionsbüros, das von draußen vielerlei Ein- und Durchblicke gewährt. Mit dieser Nachbarschaft erhielt der Reichstag nun endlich seine einst städtische Umgebung zurück.

Reihe oben, von links: Blick auf das Regierungsviertel am Spreebogen („Band des Bundes"), Jakob-Kaiser-Haus, Paul-Löbe-Haus und der Innenhof der Bundespressekonferenz.

Row above, from left: View of the Government District at Spreebogen, Jakob Kaiser House, Paul Löbe House and the interior courtyard of the Federal Press Conference building.

The largest of the new buildings of the Bundestag, the *Jakob Kaiser House* (2002), bears the name of the co-founder of the CDU (1888–1961). The old Dorotheen Quarter with its numerous historical ground plans and low density construction is revived here in an architecture permeated by light. Restored old buildings are integrated as historical witnesses, such as the Imperial Presidential Palace by Paul Wallot and the Chamber of Technology.

Courtyards open up towards the Spree. With its 1,745 offices for delegates and parliamentary parties, the complex seems like an intricate puzzle that grants all sorts of insights and perspectives to passers-by. This neighborhood finally brings back the Reichtag's former urban environment.

Neuartig ist auch das *Kunst-am-Bau-Projekt*, das die vier Häuser des Bundestags mit ganz besonderem Glanz versieht, neben dem Reichstag das Paul-Löbe-, Elisabeth-Lüders- und Jakob-Kaiser-Haus. Allen voran sind es die Werke von zeitgenössischen Künstlern, die großenteils eigens für diesen Auftritt im Bundestag geschaffen wurden. 111 Maler und Bildhauer, Video- und Installationskünstler waren eingeladen, mit ihren Werken die neuen Parlamentsbauten auszugestalten, von Gerhard Altenbourg bis Neo Rauch, von Anselm Kiefer bis Gerhard Richter. Doch nicht nur deutsche Künstler kommen zu Wort. Wie schon mit dem englischen Architekten Norman Foster wurden auch „Vertreter" der anderen Alliierten des Zweiten Weltkriegs zur Mitarbeit aufgefordert. Aus Frankreich

Linke Seite, unten: Kanzleramt, von der Spreeseite aus gesehen.
Unten: Eine zweistöckige Fußgängerbrücke verbindet das Paul-Löbe-Haus (links) mit dem Marie-Elisabeth-Lüders-Haus.

Left page, below: Chancellery, as seen from the Spree.
Below: A two-story pedestrian bridge connects Paul Löbe House (left) with Marie Elisabeth Lüders House.

Another novelty is the *Art-in-Architecture Project* that lends a very special brilliance to the four Bundestag Houses – the Reichstag as well as the Paul Löbe, Elisabeth Lüders and Jakob Kaiser Houses. This is due, above all, to the works by contemporary artists chiefly created for their Bundestag performance. From Gerhard Altenbourg to Neo Rauch, Anselm Kiefer to Gerhard Richter – 111 painters and sculptors, video and installation artists, were invited to furnish the new Parliament buildings with their works. But not only German artists had their say. As is the case with English architect Norman Foster, "representatives" of the other Allied Forces of World War II were also summoned. From France this includes Christian Boltanski who reveals the democratic "foundations" support-

ist das u. a. Christian Boltanski, der mit seinem „Archiv der Deutschen Abgeordneten" die demokratischen „Grundmauern" aufzeigt, die das politische Geschehen tragen. Der russische Künstler Grisha Bruskin macht in 115 Einzelbildern durchaus ironisch auf Missverständnisse in der symbolischen Wahrnehmung des Reichstags aufmerksam.

Auch Jenny Holzer (USA) schuf etwas Spezifisches: eine Stahlstele, auf der im Parlament gehaltene Reden samt Zwischenrufen in Leuchtschrift vom Boden zur Decke laufen. Günther Ueckers Andachtsraum hebt die gemeinsamen Ursprünge von jüdischer, christlicher und muslimischer Religion hervor, Georg Baselitz interpretiert die deutschen Sehnsuchtsworte „Melancholie" und „Abgrund", wie sie auch von Politikern gern zitiert werden, in einer großformatigen Caspar-David-Friedrich-Paraphrase. Entstanden sind beeindruckende Rauminstallationen, die auch besichtigt werden können.

Während in anderen Parlamentsgebäuden dieser Welt Bilder des Nationalgeschehens hängen, hat man sich in Berlin für ein Bekenntnis zur zeitgenössischen Kunst entschieden, laut Experten einzigartig auf der Welt. Außerdem werden Werke aus der 1969 begründeten, durch jährliche Ankäufe erweiterten Kunstsammlung in einer besonderen, öffentlich zugänglichen Halle im Marie-Elisabeth-Lüders-Haus präsentiert, neben zahlreichen Wechselausstellungen zeitgenössischer Kunst.

Die hauseigene Kollektion besteht mittlerweile aus über 4000 Gemälden, Grafiken und Drucken, die auch zwischen den Büros, Konferenzräumen und Fluren rotieren.

Links: Blick aus dem Paul-Löbe-Haus (2001, Stephan Braunfels) auf das benachbarte Kanzleramt. Unten: der Innenhof des Hauses.

Left: View of the Chancellery from adjacent Paul Löbe House (2001, Stephan Braunfels). Below: the interior courtyard of the house.

ing political events with his "Archive of the German Delegates." Russian artist Grisha Bruskin calls somewhat ironic attention to the misunderstandings informing people's symbolic perception of the Reichstag in 115 single pictures.

American artist Jenny Holzer also created something specific: a steel stele showing Parliament speeches including heckles in the form of neon inscriptions running from floor to ceiling. Günther Uecker's Chamber of Devotion highlights the common origin of the Jewish, Christian and Muslim religions; Georg Baselitz interprets two German words connoting longing – "Melancholie" and "Abgrund" (abyss) – that are often cited by politicians in the form of a large format paraphrase of Caspar David Friedrich. Thus were created impressive spatial installations that can also be visited.

While other Parliament buildings in the world exhibit images of national history, Berlin has opted for a commitment to contemporary art. According to experts, this is unique in the world. In addition, works from the art collection founded in 1969 and annually enlarged through further purchases are shown in a publicly accessible hall in Marie Elisabeth Lüders House – next to numerous traveling exhibitions of contemporary art.

The in-house collection by now consists of over 4,000 paintings, graphic art works and prints that also rotate among offices, conference rooms and corridors.

But art is also visible on the outside. Next to the pedestrian bridge that accompanies the "Leap over the Spree" (Stephan

Rechts: Christiane Möbius, *Rennachter*, im Jakob-Kaiser-Haus (fünf Architektenteams, 2002). Unten: Die Rotunde im Marie-Elisabeth-Lüders-Haus nach Plänen von Stephan Braunfels. Das Innere des Betonzylinders beherbergt den Lesesaal der Bibliothek des Deutschen Bundestages.

Right: Christiane Möbius, *Eight-Seater Racing Canoes*, in the Jakob Kaiser House (five architecture teams, 2002). Below: Rotunda in Marie Elisabeth Lüders House designed by Stephan Braunfels. The interior of the concrete cylinder houses the reading room of the German Bundestag Library.

Doch auch von außen lässt sich Kunst besichtigen. Neben der Fußgängerbrücke, die den „Spree-Sprung" (Stephan Braunfels) der Bundestagsgebäude begleitet, ragen an der Ostwand des Paul-Löbe-Hauses zwei grüne Skulpturen zehn Meter in die Höhe: Neo Rauchs Werk „Mann auf der Leiter". Nachts leuchten sie weithin übers Wasser der Spree. Daneben das kunterbunte Innere eines Restaurants: „Untitled Restaurant" heißt Jorge Pardos' Installation aus zahlreichen Kugellampen und mit Intarsien gestalteten Tischen und Stühlen, die aus einem gewöhnlichen Speisesaal einen Kunstraum machen.

Gegenüber strahlt Imi Knoebels „Rot, Gelb, Weiß, Blau 1-4" durch die gläserne Fassade des Elisabeth-Lüders-Hauses nach draußen. Die Mauer, die das Jakob-Kaiser-Haus einfriedet, ist durchsichtig und trägt das „Grundgesetz 49", die Grundrechte, auf denen die junge deutsche Demokratie 1949 aufbaute – ein Werk des israelischen Künstlers Dani Karavan.

Während die Regierung den Beginn einer neuen Ära für Berlin mit neuer Architektur betonte, brachte man die *Ministerien* mehrheitlich kostensparend in modernisierten Altbauten in Mitte oder am Rande des Tiergartens unter. Das war, architektonisch gesehen, nicht unbedingt ein Nachteil. Dabei nahm man – neben einstigen Regierungsgebäuden der DDR – auch wieder in Betrieb, was durch den Nationalsozialismus historisch „kontaminiert" war; das ehemalige Reichsluftfahrtminis-

Linke Seite: Das Ministerium des Inneren, von der Spreeseite gesehen und ein Blick auf den Innenhof.
Unten: Erweiterungsbau des Auswärtigen Amts, 1996–99, nach Plänen der Architekten Thomas Müller und Ivan Reimann.

Left page: Ministry of the Interior, view from the Spree, and view of the interior courtyard.
Below: Extension of the Foreign Office, 1996–99, based on designs by architects Thomas Müller and Ivan Reimann.

Braunfels) performed by the Bundestag buildings, two green sculptures rise up ten meters high on the eastern wall of the Paul Löbe House: Neo Rauch's "Man on the ladder." Illuminated by night, their glow travels far across the water of the Spree. Next to it, the motley colored interior of a restaurant: "Untitled Restaurant" is the name of Jorge Pardos' installation composed of numerous spherical lamps as well as tables and chairs with colored inlays that transform an ordinary cafeteria into a space of art.

Across from it, Imi Knoebel's "Red, Yellow, White, Blue 1-4" blazes through the glass façade of the Elisabeth Lüders House. The wall, enclosing the Jakob Kaiser House, is transparent and bears the inscription of "Grundgesetz 49," the basic rights on which the young German democracy was founded in 1949 – a work by Israeli artist Dani Karavan.

While the government signaled the beginning of a new era with new architecture, the *Federal Ministries* for the most part were housed in modernized old buildings in Mitte or at the edge of Tiergarten to save costs. From an architectural perspective, that was not always a drawback. In addition to former GDR government buildings, structures historically "contaminated" by National Socialism were also put to use once more – Hermann Göring's former Reich Air Ministry, for example, which had survived the air war that had been planned here un-

Das Bundesratsgebäude, einst erste Kammer des Preußischen Landtags. In der Wandelhalle: die Installation *Die drei Grazien*, geschaffen von der Künstlerin Rebecca Horn.

Federal Council building, former first Chamber of the Prussian Diet. In the foyer: the installation *The Three Graces*, created by artist Rebecca Horn.

Im Rücken des Bundesrats-
gebäudes: die ehemalige
Zweite Kammer des Preußischen
Landtags, Friedrich Schulze,
1892–98, heute Berliner
Landesparlament; unten:
die Eingangshalle.

At the rear of the Bundesrat
building: the former Second
Chamber of the Prussian
Parliament, Friedrich Schulze,
1892–98, now: Berlin State
Parliament; below:
the entrance hall.

terium Hermann Görings etwa, das den Luftkrieg, der hier geplant wurde, unbeschadet überstanden hatte. Mit seiner glatten Marmorkalkfassade und den Fensterbändern, die Schießscharten ähneln, ist das Gebäude das einzige Relikt aus der Zeit, als die Wilhelmstraße synonym für eine zerstörerische Weltpolitik stand. 1935/36 nach Plänen von Ernst Sagebiel in Rekordzeit errichtet, wurde es in der DDR als Haus der Ministerien genutzt und beherbergte in den 1990er-Jahren die Zentrale der Treuhandanstalt. Seit 1992 heißt es Detlev-Rohwedder-Haus und ist Sitz des Bundesfinanzministeriums.

Eine Gedenktafel an der Leipziger Straße erinnert an die Protestveranstaltung von Bauarbeitern am 16. Juni 1953, die zum

Haus der Bundespressekonferenz am Spreebogen (ganz rechts) nach Entwürfen von Johanne und Gernot Nalbach, 1998–2000; daneben Bürokomplexe und Fernsehturm.

Federal Press Conference building at Spreebogen (far right) based on designs by Johanne and Gernot Nalbach, 1998–2000; next to it: office tracts and TV Tower.

scathed. With its smooth marble-lime façade and ribbon windows that resemble crenels, the building is the only relic of the period when Wilhelmstraße was synonymous with a destructive world politics. Based on designs by Ernst Sagebiel and built in record time in 1935/36, it was used by the GDR as House of Ministries and, in the 1990s, housed the headquarters of the Treuhand privatization agency. In 1992, it was renamed Detlev Rohwedder House and has since served as the seat of the Federal Ministry of Finance.

A memorial plaque on Leipziger Straße commemorates the protest by construction workers on June 16, 1953, that led to the People's Uprising the next day. That architecture can serve

Volksaufstand am nächsten Tag führte. Dass Architektur als Mahnung an die Geschichte dienen kann, zeigen auch andere Amtsbauten, die in der Neugestaltung ihre vormalige Nutzung nicht verschweigen: das Bundesministerium für Arbeit und Soziales etwa, das Sitz der Propagandazentrale von Joseph Goebbels war, oder das Auswärtige Amt in der ehemaligen Reichsbank (1934–1940).

Das Verteidigungsministerium nutzt den sogenannten Bendlerblock an der Stauffenbergstraße, von dem aus deutsche Generäle im 20. Jahrhundert zwei Angriffskriege befehligten und das zugleich die Zentrale der Widerstandskämpfer gegen Hitler war – heute „Gedenkstätte Deutscher Widerstand".

Willy-Brandt-Haus, Parteizentrale der SPD, Helge Bofinger, 1993–96, und das Konrad-Adenauer-Haus, Parteizentrale der CDU, Petzinka, Pink und Partner, 1998–2000.

Willy Brandt House, SPD party headquarters, Helge Bofinger, 1993–96, and Konrad Adenauer House, CDU party headquarters, Petzinka, Pink and Partner, 1998–2000.

as a warning to history is also demonstrated by other official buildings that do not silence their prior uses in their remodeled forms: the Federal Ministry of Labor and Social Affairs, for example, that was the seat of Joseph Goebbels' Headquarters of Propaganda, or the Foreign Office in the former Reichsbank (1934–1940).

The Federal Ministry of Defense occupies the so-called Bendlerblock at Stauffenbergstraße from where German generals commanded two wars of aggression in the 20th century, and which was, at the same time, the headquarters of the resistance fighters against Hitler – today's "German Resistance Memorial Center."

Rathäuser, Botschaften und Ländervertretungen

Nicht nach politischen Farbwerten ist das Rote Rathaus benannt, sondern nach dem leuchtenden Backstein, aus dem es von 1861 bis 1869 nach den Plänen des Stüler-Schülers Hermann Friedrich Waesemann errichtet wurde. Während der Rundbogenstil der Fassade an die märkische Baukunst anknüpft, verweisen das Blockhafte des Gebäudes und der stumpfe, 94 Meter hohe Turm, der stolz die Kuppel des Königsschlosses überragte, auf die Rathaustypen Italiens und Flanderns. Ein erstarkendes Berliner Bürgertum setzte so ein weithin sichtbares Zeichen. Der auf der Höhe des ersten Stocks umlaufende Terrakottafries erzählt in 36 Tafeln die lokale Geschichte bis zur Reichsgründung. Das im Zweiten Weltkrieg stark beschädigte Gebäude wurde nach der Teilung der Stadt zum Sitz des Ost-Berliner Magistrats, die westliche Regierung zog ins Schöneberger Rathaus. Dessen schlichter Bau von 1914 (Peter Jürgensen und Jürgen Bachmann) geriet mit Regierenden Bürgermeistern wie Ernst Reuter und Willy Brandt immer wieder ins Blickfeld der Weltöffentlichkeit. Hier bekannte sich John F. Kennedy 1963 in seiner berühmten Rede („Ich bin ein Berliner") zu der Frontstadt als Bollwerk der westlichen Hemisphäre. Im Turm läutet bis heute jeden Mittag die 1950 von den USA gestiftete, der Liberty Bell in Philadelphia nachgebildete Freiheitsglocke. Senat und Regierender Bürgermeister kehr-

Der Pfeiler-Wimperg-Giebel des Köpenicker Rathauses, Hans Schütte, 1901–04, Klinkerbau in Formen der märkischen Backsteingotik.
Linke Seite: Das Rote Rathaus (Hermann Friedrich Waesemann, 1861–1869) mit Neptunbrunnen.
Unten: Der Säulensaal mit seinen Skulpturen, ist ausgemalt nach dem Vorbild des Palazzo Pubblico im toskanischen Siena.

The ornamental Gothic gable of Köpenick City Hall, Hans Schütte, 1901–04, clinker-brick building in Brandenburg Gothic brick style.
Left page: Red City Hall (Hermann Friedrich Waesemann, 1861–1869) with Neptune Fountain.
Below: The Hall of Columns with its sculptures is painted after its model, the Palazzo Pubblico in Tuscan Siena.

City Halls, Embassies and Federal States' Missions

Berlin's Rotes Rathaus, or Red City Hall, is not named for its symbolic color but for the brightly colored bricks out of which it was built in 1861–1869, based on designs by Stüler student Hermann Friedrich Waesemann. While the round-arch style of its façade ties in with Brandenburgian architecture, the blocky quality of the building and its blunt-topped, 94-meter-tall tower that proudly rose up above the dome of the Royal Palace, refers back to Italian and Flemish city hall types. Gaining in confidence, the Berlin bourgeoisie thereby sent a signal visible from afar. On 36 panels, the terracotta frieze encircling the building on the first floor narrates local history up to the founding of the Empire. Heavily damaged during World War II, the building served as seat for the East Berlin Magistrate after the city's division; the Western city government moved into Schöneberg City Hall. Its modest building of 1914 (Peter Jürgensen and Jürgen Bachmann) repeatedly attracted international attention with such mayors as Ernst Reuter and Willy Brandt. It was here that, in 1963, John F. Kennedy, in his famous speech ("Ich bin ein Berliner"), announced his commitment to the frontline city as a bulwark of the Western hemisphere. Every day at noon, up to the present day, the Freedom Bell, donated by the United States and modeled on Liberty Bell in Philadelphia, chimes from its tower. On October 1, 1991, the Senate and governing

In den Ministergärten.
Die Vertretung des Bundeslandes
Hessen, Michael Christl und
Joachim Bruchhäuser, 1998–2001.
Links: Die Vertretung des Bundes-
landes Baden-Württemberg,
Dietrich Bangert, 1998–2000.

In the Ministerial Gardens.
The Mission of the Federal State
of Hesse, Michael Christl and
Joachim Bruchhäuser, 1998–2001.
Left: The Mission of the Federal
State of Baden-Württemberg,
Dietrich Bangert, 1998–2000.

ten am 1. Oktober 1991 wieder ins Rote Rathaus zurück, das seitdem offiziell Berliner Rathaus heißt.

Seit jeher residierten die Großen der Weltpolitik rund um den Pariser Platz, die USA, Frankreich, England und Russland – und sie tun dies heute wieder. Wer dort nicht unterkam, verteilte sich über die Stadt. Während viele der derzeit 182 in Deutschland akkreditierten Staaten ihren diplomatischen Sitz im früheren Ost-Berlin oder im südwestlich gelegenen Dahlem behalten haben, hat der Tiergarten seinen einstigen Status als Botschaftsbezirk wiedergewonnen. Die dort unter den Nationalsozialisten propagierte Großform zeigen die ehemalige Japanische, Italienische und Spanische Botschaft, nach Kriegszerstörung und Wiederaufbau, heute jedoch in abgewandelter Weise. Daneben machen viele Neubauten mit gelungenen Entwürfen auf sich aufmerksam: der des österreichisch-finnischen Architektenduos Alfred Berger und Tiina Parkkinen für die Nordischen Botschaften etwa, deren Gemeinschaftshaus hinter kupfergrüner Lamellenfassade Transparenz und Verbundenheit demonstriert; oder die daneben liegende Botschaft Mexikos mit ihrer monumentalen Front aus schräggestellten, weißen Betonstützen von Teodoro González de León

Die Vertretungen der Bundesländer Saarland (links),
Alt + Britz, 1998–2000,
und Rheinland-Pfalz, Heinle,
Wischer und Partner, 1999-2000.

The Missions of the Federal
States of Saarland (left),
Alt + Britz, 1998–2000, and of
Rhineland-Palatinate, Heinle,
Wischer and Partner, 1999–2000.

mayor returned to the Rotes Rathaus – since then officially renamed Berlin City Hall.

The great names of world politics have always resided around Pariser Platz: the United States, France, England, and Russia – and they do so again today. Those who did not find a space there spread out all across the city. While many of the 182 states currently thus accredited in Germany retained their diplomatic seat in former East Berlin or in southwestern Dahlem, others moved to Tiergarten that has reclaimed its former status as an embassy district. Today, however, after wartime destruction and reconstruction, the large format once propagated by the National Socialists is being exhibited differently by the former Japanese, Italian and Spanish Embassies. Next to them, many new buildings call attention to themselves because of their successful designs: the Nordic Embassies, for example, by the Austrian-Finnish architect duo Alfred Berger and Tiina Parkkinen, whose Community House behind a copper-green lamella façade demonstrates transparency and connection; or the Mexican Embassy next door, by Teodoro González de León and Francisco Serrano, with its monumental front made of obliquely positioned, white con-

Eingangsbereich der Britischen
Botschaft (1998–2000) in der
Wilhelmstraße, innen und außen.
Motto des Architekten Michael
Wilford: „Ein Gebäude des
21. Jahrhunderts, eine Collage
aus Alt und Neu."

Entrance area of the British
Embassy (1998–2000) on
Wilhelmstraße, interior and
exterior. Architect Michael
Wilford's motto: "A building of
the 21st century, a collage of
old and new."

BRITISH EMBASSY

Rechts: Botschaft Chinas, einst DDR-Gewerkschaftszentrale – mit neuer Aluminium-Fassade. Unten: Die Indische Botschaft, mit roh gebrochenem Sandstein verkleidet, Léon Wohlhage Wernik Architekten, 1999–2001.

Right: Chinese Embassy, former headquarters of the GDR Trade Union – with new aluminum façade. Below: Embassy of India, clad with roughcast sandstone, Léon Wohlhage Wernik Architects, 1999–2001.

und Francisco Serrano. Für die österreichische Gesandtschaft, die vom Potsdamer Platz aus das Entree zum Diplomatenviertel bildet, entwarf Architekt Hans Hollein einen dreiteiligen Komplex in farbenfrohen und bewegten, teils kubischen, teils elliptischen Formen.

Auch die Bundesländer sind in der Hauptstadt mit neuer Architektur präsent. Mitten im Botschaftsviertel residieren die Vertretungen von Bremen und Baden-Württemberg; in den Ministergärten, mit Blick auf Reichstag und Brandenburger Tor, die Länder Niedersachsen, Schleswig-Holstein, Rheinland-Pfalz, Saarland, Mecklenburg-Vorpommern und Hessen. Von hier aus sind die Wege kurz zum Preußischen Herrenhaus an der Leipzigerstraße, in dem das politische Organ der Länder, der Bundesrat, seit dem Jahr 2000 seinen Sitz hat.

Und selbstverständlich dokumentieren auch die beiden größten Volksparteien der Republik, dass sie architektonisch auf der Höhe der Gegenwart angekommen sind: die SPD im Willy-Brandt-Haus (1993–1996) bediente sich eines schon durch die IBA preisgekrönten Entwurfs von Helge Bofinger: Der schiffsähnliche Bau aus Glas, hellem Kalkstein und bläulichem Metall versieht das Viertel der südlichen Friedrichstraße mit einem auffälligen städtebaulichen Akzent. Einem ähnlichen Modell folgt das Konrad-Adenauer-Haus, das wenige Kilometer westlich von der Konkurrenz gleichfalls auf den Landwehrkanal blickt. Auch die Zentrale der CDU (1998–2000), nach Plänen von Petzinka, Pink und Partner, nimmt Anleihen bei maritimen Vorbildern.

Die Italienische Botschaft im Stil eines Renaissance-Palazzos.
Vittorio de Feo und Stefan Dietrich, 1999–2003.
Rechte Seite: Die Nordischen Botschaften mit einem Gemeinschaftshaus (oben) und separaten Eingangsbereichen.
Alfred Berger und Tiina Parkkinen, 1997–99.

The Italian Embassy in the style of a Renaissance palace.
Vittorio de Feo and Stefan Dietrich, 1999–2003.
Right page: The Nordic Embassies with a communal building (above) and separate entrance areas.
Alfred Berger and Tiina Parkkinen, 1997–99.

crete supports. For the Austrian Embassy, which forms the entrance to the Diplomats' Quarter as seen from the direction of Potsdamer Platz, Hans Hollein designed a three-part complex featuring colorful and dynamic, partly cubic, partly elliptical forms.

The federal states are likewise present in the capital with new architecture. The diplomatic missions of Bremen and Baden-Württemberg reside in the middle of the Embassy Quarter; those of Lower Saxony, Schleswig-Holstein, Mecklenburg-Western Pomerania, Saarland, Rhineland-Palatinate, and Hesse sit in the Ministers' Gardens, with a view of the Reichstag and Brandenburg Gate. It is a short walk from here to the Prussian House of Lords on Leipzigerstraße where, since 2000, the political organ of the states, the Bundesrat, has its seat.

And of course, the two largest political parties of the Republic demonstrate as well that they have arrived, architecturally speaking, in the present tense: the SPD in the Willy Brandt House (1993–1996) used an IBA prize-winning design by Helge Bofinger: The ship-like building made of glass, bright limestone and blue-tinted metal lends a striking architectural accent to the quarter of southern Friedrichstraße. Also looking onto the Landwehrkanal a few kilometers west of the competition, the Konrad Adenauer House has emulated a similar model. The CDU headquarters (1998–2000), based on designs by Petzinka, Pink and Partner, likewise borrows from maritime examples.

Oben: Die Botschaft der
Niederlande, aus Stahlbeton,
Naturstein und Alu-Fassade,
Rem Koolhaas, 2002–04;
links: im Empfangsbereich
begrüßt Andy Warhol
(1928–1987), *Reigning Queens –
Queen Beatrix of the
Netherlands*, 1984, Siebdrucke,
39 x 31 cm, courtesy of the
Netherlands Embassy.

Above: The Netherlands Embassy
made of reinforced concrete,
natural stone, aluminum façade,
Rem Koolhaas, 2002–04;
left: Andy Warhol (1928–1987)
welcomes visitors in the
reception area, *Reigning Queens
– Queen Beatrix of the Netherlands*, 1984, screen prints,
39 x 31 cm, courtesy of the
Netherlands Embassy.

Links: Südafrikas Botschaft,
Büro mma architects (Luyanda
Mpahlwa, Alun Samuels),
1999–2001, davor die Skulptur
von Speelman Mahlangu (1958–
2004), *Prayer for Peace*, Bronze.

Left: South African Embassy,
mma architects (Luyanda
Mpahlwa, Alun Samuels),
1999–2001, in front: a sculpture
by Speelman Mahlangu (1958–
2004), *Prayer for Peace*, bronze.

Rechts: Die Botschaft von
Mexiko mit ihrer
charakteristischen
Betonrippenfassade, Teodoro
González de León und Francisco
Serrano, 1999–2000.

Right: The Embassy of Mexico
with its characteristic
ribbed concrete façade,
Teodoro González de León
and Francisco Serrano,
1999–2000.

Der Kronschatz der Stadt

Crown Jewels of the City

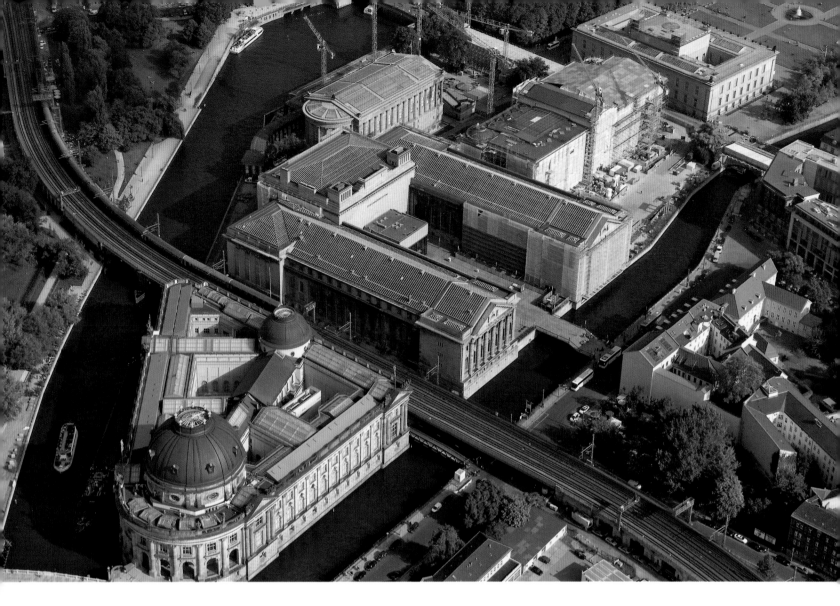

Der Kronschatz Berlins sind seine Museen. Die Kapitale besitzt etwa 170 davon, und sie verteilen sich über die ganze Stadt: von den großen Ensembles auf der Museumsinsel, am Kulturforum beim Potsdamer Platz und im Zentrum Dahlem, über das Jüdische Museum und die Berlinische Galerie in Kreuzberg bis zur Liebermann-Villa am Wannsee, vom Naturkundemuseum in Mitte bis nach Schloss Friedrichsfelde. Eine Menge National- und Weltkultur, Natur- und Technikgeschichte also.

Museumsinsel – „Tempelstadt der Künste" und Weltkulturerbe

Einer der größten Museumskomplexe der Welt liegt auf einer Insel in der Spree und ist ganz der europäischen Kunst und der Archäologie gewidmet. Als erster Bau entstand hier Karl Friedrich Schinkels (Altes) Museum, das die Kunst im Sinne des Humboldtschen Bildungsideals allen Berliner Bürgern zugänglich machte. Doch schon bei der Eröffnung 1830 zeigte sich, dass die auf Zuwachs angelegten Sammlungen mehr Raum benötigten. Also ordnete Friedrich Wilhelm IV. (noch als Kronprinz) 1841 an, das gesamte Areal zu einer „Freistätte für Kunst und Wissenschaft umzuschaffen". So wuchs im Laufe von hundert Jahren das Ensemble von fünf imposanten Museumsbau-

Langgestreckt zieht sich die Museumsinsel mit (von links) dem Bode-Museum, dem Pergamonmuseum, der Alten Nationalgalerie sowie dem Neuen und dem Alten Museum.

Museum Island is a long stretch of land on which are located (from left) the Bode Museum, Pergamon Museum, Old National Gallery, as well as the New and the Old Museum.

Vorhergehende Seite: Die Büste der Königin Nofretete, 1340 v. Chr.

Previous page: Queen Nefertiti's bust, 1340 BC.

Berlin's crown jewels are its museums. The capital has about 170 of these; and they are scattered all over the city: from the great complexes on Museum Island, the Culture Forum at Potsdamer Platz and in the center of Dahlem, the Jewish Museum and Berlin Gallery in Kreuzberg to Villa Liebermann on Lake Wannsee; from the Museum of Natural History to Friedrichsfelde Palace. This means a lot of national and world culture, natural and technological history.

Museum Island – "Temple of the Arts" and World Heritage

One of the largest museum complexes in the world is situated on an island in the Spree and is wholly dedicated to European art and to archaeology. Its first building was Karl Friedrich Schinkel's (Old) Museum that made art accessible to all Berlin citizens, in keeping with Humboldt's educational ideals. But when it was opened in 1830, it was already apparent that the collections, intended for growth, would require more space. So in 1841, Frederick William IV (still a Crown Prince) gave the order to have the entire area "transformed into a sanctuary for art and science." Thus the complex of five imposing museums developed over the period of a century: In 1859, the New

ten: 1859 kam das Neue Museum hinzu, 1876 die Alte Nationalgalerie, 1904 das Bode-Museum und 1930 das Pergamonmuseum. Im Zweiten Weltkrieg wurden die Museen zu etwa siebzig Prozent zerstört. „Ein geistiges Weltgebäude", wie Ludwig Justi, ehemals Direktor der Nationalgalerie, die Museumsinsel genannt hat, war in sich zusammengestürzt und wurde ab 1950 nur notdürftig als Heimstatt für die Kunst wieder tauglich gemacht. Dann kam 1989/90 die politische Wende und mit ihr der Enthusiasmus der Erneuerung. 1999 wurde der Masterplan zur Wiederherstellung der Museen und zur Neuordnung der nach dem Krieg in Ost und West geteilten Sammlungen beschlossen. Im selben Jahr ernannte die UNESCO die „Tempelstadt der Künste" zum Weltkulturerbe. Was einst als „preußische Akropolis" begann, führt jetzt wieder auf nur einem Quadratkilometer durch sechstausend Jahre Geschichte und durch die Hochkulturen in Orient und Okzident, von den Ursprüngen der europäischen Kunst im Zweistromland und in Ägypten über die klassische Antike, Mittelalter, Renaissance und Barock bis zur Malerei des Impressionismus.

Wie eine Arche liegt das *Bode-Museum* im Wasser: An der Nordspitze der Insel, wo sich die Spreearme vereinigen, entstand um 1900 ein neues Museum, das die enorm gewachsenen Bestände der Gemälde- und Skulpturengalerie aufnehmen

Im Bode-Museum auf der Museumsinsel werden die Skulpturensammlung und das Museum für Byzantinische Kunst, das Münzkabinett und Werke der Gemäldegalerie präsentiert.

The Bode Museum on Museum Island presents the Sculptures Collection and the Museum for Byzantine Art, the Coin Cabinet and works from the Picture Gallery.

Museum was added; in 1876, the Old National Gallery; in 1904, the Bode Museum; and in 1930, the Pergamon Museum. During World War II, up to seventy percent of the museums were destroyed. "An intellectual edifice of the world," as Museum Island was called by Ludwig Justi, former director of the National Gallery, had collapsed; its makeshift restoration as a functioning home for the arts was begun in 1950. Then the political turning point came in 1989/90 that fueled an enthusiastic desire for renewal. In 1999, the master plan was finalized to restore the museums and to reorganize the collections that had been divided after the war into East and West holdings. That same year, UNESCO assigned the status of World Heritage Site to this "temple of the arts." What once began as a "Prussian Acropolis," now again guides visitors, across the space of one square kilometer, through six thousand years of history and information on advanced cultures of the Orient and Occident, from the origins of European art in Mesopotamia and Egypt, across Classical Antiquity, the Middle Ages, Renaissance and Baroque, up to the art of Impressionism.

Bode Museum emerges from the water like an ark: At the northern tip of the island, where the two arms of the Spree merge, a new museum was built around 1900 that was to house the enormously expanded collections of the Picture and

Links: Das Treppenhaus im Bode-Museum.

Rechts: Das Museum besitzt ein weltweit einzigartiges Ensemble an Reliefs des fränkischen Bildhauers Tilman Riemenschneider (um 1460/65–1531). Den 13 Werken ist ein eigener Saal gewidmet, darunter befindet sich auch die Reliefgruppe *Die heilige Anna mit ihren drei Ehemännern*, um 1510, Lindenholz, Höhe 115 cm. Die Skulpturengruppe stand vermutlich in der Anfang des 19. Jh. abgerissenen Marienkapelle am Milchmarkt in Rothenburg ob der Tauber.

Left: Staircase inside the Bode Museum.

Right: The museum owns a set of reliefs unique in the world by Frankish sculptor Tilman Riemenschneider (c. 1460/65–1531). These 13 works are housed in a hall by themselves; among them is the relief composition *Saint Anne and Her Three Husbands*, c. 1510, linden wood, height: 115 cm. This group of statues was probably set up in a church torn down in the early 19th century: St Mary's Chapel on Milk Market in Rothenburg on the Tauber.

Max Liebermann (1847–1935),
Wilhelm von Bode, 1904,
Oil on canvas/Öl auf Leinwand,
114 x 92 cm, Alte Nationalgalerie.

Links/Left: Tilman Riemenschneider
(um/c. 1460/65–1531),
*Die Erscheinung Christi vor Maria
Magdalena* vom Magdalenen-
Rentabel zu Münnerstadt (Christ
Appearing to Mary Magdalena,
from the Magdalene Altarpiece
at Münnerstadt), 1490–92,
Lindenholz/linden wood,
143,5 x 102 cm, Bode-Museum.

Oben: Giovanni Pisano
(um 1250 – um 1328), *Leib Christi
mit Engeln*, Kanzellesepult,
um 1300, Relief aus Marmor,
Herstellungsort Toskana/Italien,
Bode-Museum.

Above: Giovanni Pisano
(c. 1250 – c. 1328),
Body of Christ with Angels,
pulpit c. 1300, marble relief,
production site: Tuscany/Italy,
Bode Museum.

sollte. Der von Wilhelm II. favorisierte Architekt Ernst von Ihne errichtete es 1897 bis 1904 in neobarockem Stil, mit einer florentinischen Basilika in der Mittelachse und einer mächtigen Kuppel über der Eingangshalle. Zunächst nach dem 1888 verstorbenen Kaiser Friedrich III. benannt, erhielt es 1956 seinen heutigen Namen nach dem Gründungsdirektor Wilhelm von Bode (1854–1929). Dem einstigen Leiter der Gemäldegalerie und Direktor der Königlichen Museen gelangen dank seiner ausgezeichneten Beziehungen zu Künstlern und Sammlern viele spektakuläre Ankäufe – Werke, die auch heute noch den Schwerpunkt der Sammlung bestimmen.

Die Ende der 1990er-Jahre begonnene Generalinstandsetzung wurde 2006 abgeschlossen. Seitdem präsentiert sich

Sculpture Gallery. An architect favored by William II, Ernst von Ihne, built it in 1897–1904 in the Neo-Baroque style, with a Florentine basilica on its center axis and a mighty dome above the entrance hall. First named after Emperor Frederick III who had died in 1888, it received its current name in 1956 when it was renamed after its founding director, Wilhelm von Bode (1854–1929). The former head of the Picture Gallery and director of the Royal Museums was able to purchase many spectacular works due to his excellent contacts with international artists and collectors – works that still constitute the center of the collection.

The museum's comprehensive restoration, begun in the late 1990s, was completed in 2006. Since then, the Bode Museum

das Bode-Museum als erste Adresse für europäische Bild-hauerei vom frühen Mittelalter bis zum 18. Jahrhundert mit einem Schwerpunkt auf Werken der deutschen Spätgotik von Hans Multscher, Hans Brüggemann, Nicolaus Gerhaert von Leyden, Hans Leinberger und vor allem Tilman Riemenschneider aus Würzburg. Reizvoll an der Präsentation ist der Zusammenklang zwischen Gemälden und Skulpturen, wie ihn Wilhelm von Bode schon vor hundert Jahren erprobt hat. Gemäß seiner ursprünglichen Bestimmung zeigt das Museum nun auch wieder die Byzantinische Sammlung, zu der es in Deutschland nichts Vergleichbares gibt, und das kostbare Münzkabinett, das mit gut einer halben Million Objekten zu den weltgrößten Sammlungen zählt.

Maria mit dem Jesuskind, Majolika-Relief, baugebundenes Exponat, Bode-Museum.

Mary with Baby Jesus, maiolica relief, exhibit integral to the building, Bode Museum.

has emerged as a leading institution specializing in European sculpture from the early Middle Ages through the 18th century, with an emphasis on German late Gothic works by Hans Multscher, Hans Brüggemann, Nicolaus Gerhaert von Leyden, Hans Leinberger and, above all, Tilman Riemenschneider from Würzburg. Most appealing about their presentation is the harmonious interaction between paintings and sculptures, an approach pioneered by Wilhelm von Bode one hundred years ago. True to its original calling, the museum today again exhibits its collection of Byzantine art, unrivalled anywhere else in Germany, and its valuable Coin Cabinet Collection, featuring a good half a million objects, which makes it one of the largest in the world.

Linke Seite/Left page:
Links/Left: Joseph Anton Feuchtmayer (1696–1770), *Maria*, um/c. 1717–19, Lindenholz/linden wood, Höhe/hight 163 cm, Bode-Museum.

Rechts/Right: Niclaus Gerhaert von Leyden (um/c. 1430–1473), *Die Muttergottes aus Dangolsheim* (The Dangolsheim Madonna), um/c. 1460/65).

Eine erhabene Pharao-Skulptur ziert den Eingangsbereich des Museums mit seinen weltweit einmaligen antiken Schätzen.

An exalted Pharao sculpture adorns the entrance area of the museum with its antique treasures unique in the world.

Eine Fußgängerbrücke über den Spreearm führt zum Vorplatz des Pergamonmuseums auf der Museumsinsel.

A pedestrian bridge across the arm of the Spree leads to the forecourt of the Pergamon Museum on Museum Island.

Details des Pergamonaltars:
Athena im Kampf mit Alkyoneus
(links) und *Zeus kämpft gegen
den Gigantenführer Porphyrion
und zwei jugendliche Giganten*
(rechts), Marmor, Höhe des
Frieses 2,30 m.

Details of Pergamon Altar:
Athena Fighting Alcyoneus (left)
and *Zeus Fighting Porphyrion,
Leader of the Giants, and Two
Adolescent Giants* (right),
marble, height of frieze: 2.30 m.

Pergamonaltar, um 170 v. Chr.,
Marmor, Gesamtlänge des Frieses
113 m, Breite der Freitreppe 20 m,
Pergamonmuseum.

Pergamon Altar, c. 170 B.C.,
marble, total length of frieze 113 m,
width of temple staircase 20 m,
Pergamon Museum.

ZEUS

Genau hundert Jahre nach der Eröffnung von Schinkels Museum wurde auf der Museumsinsel der Schlussstein des heutigen *Pergamonmuseums* gesetzt, als Alfred Messel und Ludwig Hoffmann für die damals schon legendäre Sammlung antiker Baukunst das weltweit erste „Architektur"-Museum (1909–1930) entwarfen. Es wurde um die Rekonstruktionen des Pergamonaltars, des Ischtar-Tors und der Prozessionsstraße von Babylon gewissermaßen herumgebaut. Später zog dann auch noch die frühislamische Mschatta-Fassade aus der jordanischen Wüstenresidenz ein. Auf dem Sumpfgelände der Museumsinsel gestalteten sich die Bauarbeiten äußerst schwierig. Ein Vorgängerbau war 1901 fertig gestellt worden, musste aber schon acht Jahre später aus statischen Gründen wieder abgerissen werden. Finanzielle Engpässe, der Erste Weltkrieg und die Novemberrevolution unterbrachen den Bauprozess, sodass das Museum erst 1930 eröffnet werden konnte.

Nur knapp ein Jahrzehnt lang waren die Schätze auf der Museumsinsel zugänglich, dann wurden ein Jahr nach Beginn des Zweiten Weltkriegs alle Berliner Museen geschlossen. Erst

Das Ischtar-Tor aus Babylon, erbaut um 580 v. Chr. unter Nebukadnezar II. (604–562 v. Chr.), mit seinen prachtvollen, farbig glasierten und gebrannten Tonziegeln, 14,73 x 15,70 m, Pergamonmuseum.

Babylonian Ishtar Gate, built around 580 BC under King Nebukadnezar II (604–562 B.C.), with its magnificent, color-glazed and burnt terracotta tiles, 14.73 x 15.70 m, Pergamon Museum.

Exactly one hundred years after the opening of Schinkel's museum, the capstone was set in place at today's *Pergamon Museum* on Museum Island, when Alfred Messel and Ludwig Hoffmann designed the world's first "Architecture" museum (1909–1930) to house the collection of ancient architecture, legendary even in those days. It was virtually built around the reconstruction of the Pergamon Altar, Ishtar Gate and the Processional Boulevard of Babylon. Later, the early Islamic Mschatta-façade of a Jordanian desert residence moved in as well. Construction was very difficult on the swampy territory of Museum Island. A precursor building was completed in 1901 but had to be demolished only eight years later for structural reasons. Financial straits, World War I and the November Revolution interrupted the building process, so that the museum's opening was postponed until 1930.

The treasures of Museum Island were accessible to the public for only a decade; then all Berlin museums closed down one year after World War II had begun. It was not until 1956 that the Pergamon Museum opened its doors once more. Since

1956 öffnete das Pergamonmuseum wieder seine Tore. Seither trägt es, nach seiner Hauptattraktion und einem der berühmtesten Bauwerke der Antike, dem Pergamonaltar, seinen Namen. 170 v. Chr. während der Herrschaftszeit des Eumenides II. zum Dank an die Götter für erwiesene „Wohltaten" errichtet, pries man den Tempel einst als eines der sieben Weltwunder. Der 113 Meter lange, heute den gesamten Saal umlaufende Fries, der einst die Außenseite des Altars schmückte, stellt den mythischen Kampf der Giganten gegen die griechischen Götter dar und war somit ein Gleichnis für den Kampf des Guten, der gerechten Ordnung und der Zivilisation gegen das Böse, die Willkür und das Chaos. Der Altar, der in byzantinischer Zeit abgerissen worden war, lag lange Zeit verschüttet, ehe er ab 1878 von einem deutschen Grabungsteam

Teil der Prozessionsstraße aus dem 6. Jh. v. Chr., der Zeit des neubabylonischen Königs Nebukadnezar II., Pergamonmuseum.

Segment of the Processional Boulevard from the 6th century B.C., the era of neo-Babylonian King Nebukadnezar II, Pergamon Museum.

then it has borne the name of its main attraction and one of the most famous ancient buildings, the Pergamon Altar. Built in 170 B.C., during the reign of Eumenides II, as an acknowledgment of "good deeds" done by the gods, the temple was once hailed as one of the Seven Wonders of the World. The 113-meter-long frieze, nowadays lining the entire hall but once decorating the external wall of the altar, represents the mythical combat of the Giants against the Greek gods; it thus furnished an analogy for the fight of the good, just order and civilization against evil, arbitrariness and chaos. The altar, demolished in Byzantine times, had long lain buried before it was uncovered, starting in 1878, by the German archaeological team headed by Carl Humann and taken to Berlin from 1880 onward. The Market Gate of Miletus (c. 120 A.D.), magnificent

unter der Leitung von Carl Humann freigelegt und ab 1880 nach Berlin gebracht wurde. Auch das Markttor von Milet (um 120 n. Chr.), prunkvolles Monument der römischen Kaiserzeit, wurde erst 1903 bis 1905 bei Ausgrabungen wieder entdeckt und mit Genehmigung der türkischen Behörden dann nach Berlin überführt. Die mit Skulpturen geschmückte Fassade des zweigeschossigen Portals blieb während des Zweiten Weltkriegs, von einer Ummauerung geschützt, im Museum. Durch einen Bombentreffer stark beschädigt, wurde das Tor 1954 notdürftig wiederhergestellt und erst jüngst fachgerecht restauriert.

Neben der Antikensammlung mit griechisch-römischer Baukunst, Skulpturen, Inschriften, Mosaiken, Bronzen und Kleinkunst beherbergt das Pergamonmuseum eine der weltweit bedeutendsten Sammlungen orientalischer Altertümer, das

Der schreitende Löwe galt als Symbol der Liebes- und Kriegsgöttin Ischtar, Detail aus der Prozessionsstraße, glasiertes Ziegelrelief, 105 x 227 cm.

The striding lion was considered a symbol of Ishtar, goddess of love and war, Detail of the Processional Boulevard, glazed brick relief, 105 x 227 cm.

monument of the Roman Empire, was also rediscovered only during excavations in 1903–1905 and taken to Berlin after clearance from the Turkish authorities was obtained. Decorated with sculptures, the façade of the two-story portal remained in the museum during World War II, protected by a strong wall built around it. Badly damaged by a bomb, the gate was provisionally repaired in 1954 and only most recently professionally restored.

Besides the Collection of Classical Antiquities featuring Greek-Roman architecture, sculptures, inscriptions, mosaics, bronzes, and small artifacts, the Pergamon Museum also houses one the world's most significant collections of Oriental antiquities – the Museum of Near Eastern History. Next to Hittite, Assyrian and Babylonian stelae, monuments

Vorderasiatische Museum. Hauptattraktion sind neben hethitischen, assyrischen und babylonischen Stelen, Denkmälern und Reliefs die Prachtbauten Babylons, die Prozessionsstraße, das Ischtar-Tor (um 580 v. Chr.) und die Thronsaalfassade des Königs Nebukadnezar II. (604–562 v. Chr.).

Die wilden Tiere auf den Wandflächen symbolisieren Babylons Hauptgottheiten: Die Löwen stellen die Göttin Ischtar dar, die Herrin des Himmels, die für die Liebe ebenso zuständig war wie für den Schutz der Armee. Die schlangenähnlichen Drachen stehen für den Stadtgott Marduk, der Fruchtbarkeit und ewiges Leben schenkte. Die Stiere verweisen auf den Wettergott Adad, zu dessen Heiligtum, den „Turm von Babel", vermutlich die Prozessionsstraße führte. Sie war ursprünglich 250 Meter lang und über zwanzig Meter breit. Das Tor bewachte einst den Zugang zu einer neunzig Meter hohen Zikkurat, einem

Assyrischer König Asarhaddon führt Besiegte am Nasenring, 7. Jh. v. Chr., babylonische Granitstele.
Rechts: Relief mit Darstellung des Wettergottes aus Tell Halaf, 9. Jh. v. Chr., Basalt, 83 x 57 cm.

Assyrian King Esarhaddon leads the vanquished by nose rings, 7th century B.C., Babylonian granite stela.
Right: Relief representing the weather god of Tell Halaf, 9th century B.C., basalt, 83 x 57 cm.

and reliefs, its main attractions are Babylon's flagship buildings: the Processional Boulevard, Ishtar Gate (c. 580 B.C.) as well as the throne room façade of King Nebukadnezar II (604–562 B.C.).

The wild animals on the walls symbolize Babylon's main gods: The lions represent the goddess Ishtar, Queen of Heaven, who specialized in love as much as in the protection of the army. The snake-like dragons stand for the city god Marduk, giver of fertility and eternal life. The bulls refer to the weather god Adad; the Processional Boulevard probably once led to his sanctuary, the "Tower of Babel." Originally, the boulevard was 250 meters long and over twenty meters wide. Ishtar Gate once guarded the entrance to a 90-meter-high *zikkurat*, a stepped temple; its original location was at the head of a stately thoroughfare traversing the ancient global metropolis.

Links/Left: Frauenstatue mit Granatapfel (Female Figure with Pomegranate), 580–60 v. Chr./ B.C., Mamor/marble, Höhe/hight 194 cm, „Berliner Göttin"/ "Berlin Goddess", Pergamonmuseum.

Rechts/Right: Kore „Ornithe", um/c. 560 v. Chr./B.C., Marmor/marble, Samos, Griechenland/Greece, Pergamonmuseum.

140

Markttor von Milet, römischer Torbau, um 120 n. Chr., durch Erdbeben zerstört, 1903 bei deutschen Grabungen gefunden, 1925–29 im Pergamonmuseum wieder aufgebaut, Marmor, Höhe 28,92 m, Foto um 1929.

Market Gate of Miletus, Roman gate building, c. 120 A.D., destroyed by earthquake, discovered during German excavations in 1903, set up in 1925–29 in the Pergamon Museum, marble, height: 28.92 m, photo c. 1929.

Stufentempel, und es stand am Beginn einer Prachtmeile durch die antike Weltmetropole. Lange kannte Europa nur das Bild, das die Bibel von der großen „Hure Babel" überliefert hatte. Dabei war das am Euphrat zwischen Kornfeldern, Palmenhainen und den legendären hängenden Gärten gelegene Babylon eine internationale Handelsstadt und die politische Machtzentrale eines Reiches, das durchaus dem späteren Imperium Romanum vergleichbar ist. Unter Verwendung der glasierten, aus zahllosen Bruchstücken zusammengefügten Originalziegel wurden Teile der Bauten in nahezu originaler Größe rekonstruiert.

Weitere Höhepunkte des Pergamonmuseums sind die Fassade des Kalifenschlosses Mschatta aus dem 8. Jahrhundert, das Aleppo-Zimmer (um 1600), die Gebetsnischen von Konya (1360) und Kaschan (1226) im Museum für Islamische Kunst, mit Werken islamischer Völker vom 8. bis ins 19. Jahrhundert, von Spanien bis Indien. Schwerpunkte sind Keramik, Buchkunst, Teppiche und Schnitzereien aus dem Vorderen Orient einschließlich Ägypten und Iran. Wie im benachbarten Neuen Museum, Friedrich August Stülers Meisterwerk des Spätklassizismus, wird auch im Pergamonmuseum weiter kräftig saniert. Die dreiflügelige Anlage soll nach Plänen von Oswald Mathias Ungers demnächst mit einem Querriegel geschlossen werden.

For a long time, Europe had known nothing but the traditional Biblical image of the great "Whore of Babylon." Instead, Babylon on the Euphrates – set among corn fields, palm groves and the legendary Hanging Gardens – was a hub of international trade and the political center of an empire quite comparable to that of the later Imperium Romanum. Covered with the original glazed tiles consisting of countless fragments, segments of the buildings were reconstructed to almost original scale.

Further highlights of the Pergamon Museum are the façade of the Mschatta Caliph's Palace from the 8th century, the Aleppo Chamber (c. 1600), and the prayer niches of Konya (1360) and Kashan (1226), exhibited in the Museum of Islamic Art that showcases works by Islamic peoples from the 8th to the 19th centuries and hailing from Spain to India. Central features are the ceramics, carpets and woodcarvings from the Near East, including Egypt and Iran. Like its neighbor, the New Museum, Friedrich August Stüler's late Neoclassicist masterpiece, the Pergamon Museum is still caught up in the process of renovation. The three-wing structure is soon to be locked by a crossbar-style transverse building designed by Oswald Mathias Ungers.

Aleppo-Zimmer/Aleppo Chamber, 1600–03, bemaltes Zedernholz/ painted cedar wood, 2,5 x 35 m, Pergamonmuseum.

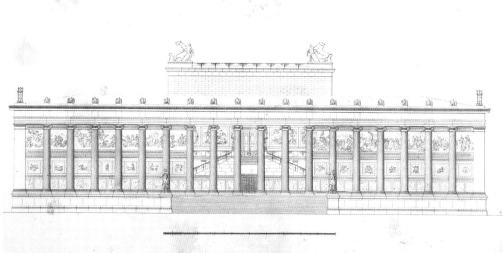

Links: Altes Museum, von
18 Säulen geschmückte Vorhalle
mit Blick zum Dom, nach Plänen
von Karl Friedrich Schinkel
(1781–1841), erbaut 1823–29.

Left: Old Museum, entrance hall
with view of cathedral, decorated
with 18 columns, built in 1823–29
based on designs by Karl Friedrich
Schinkel (1781–1841).

Zeichnungen nach K. F. Schinkel.
Oben: Carl Friedrich Thiele (um
1780–1836), *Façade der Hauptfronte des neuen Museums*,
Umrissstich.

Unten: Hans Fincke (1800–1849),
*Perspectivische Ansicht von der
Galerie der Haupt-Treppe*,
Umrissstich.

Drawings after K. F. Schinkel.
Above: Carl Friedrich Thiele
(c. 1780–1836), *Façade of the
Main Front of the new Museum*,
contour engraving.

Below: Hans Fincke (1800–1849),
*Perspectival View of the Gallery
of the Main Stairs*, contour
engraving.

Karl Friedrich Schinkel selbst hielt es für seine beste Arbeit: das *Alte Museum*, das aussah wie ein griechischer Tempel und neben Schloss, Dom und Zeughaus eine vierte Macht im Staate durchsetzte: Kunst und Kultur. Als erstes Haus in Deutschland machte das Museum (1825–1830) königliche Sammlungen öffentlich zugänglich. Das besagt schon die lateinische Inschrift an der Hauptfront: Das Haus ist „dem Studium jeder Art von Altertümern und der freien Künste" gewidmet. Zwei Skulpturen – Albert Wolffs „Löwenkämpfer" und die „Kämpfende Amazone" von August Kiss – flankieren die Freitreppe zur Vorhalle, die von 18 ionischen Säulen getragen wird. Diese wiederum sind bewacht von 18 preußischen Adlern auf dem Dach. Die große Granitschale im Lustgarten entstand 1827 nach einem Schinkel-Entwurf mit sieben Metern Durchmesser. Herzstück des Museums ist die dem römischen Pantheon nachempfundene, vollendet proportionierte, 23 Meter hohe Rotunde. In einem Ring aus zwanzig korinthischen Säulen und in den Nischen im oberen Galerieumgang fand die Sammlung antiker Statuen ihren Platz. Seit 1998 ist im Hauptgeschoss die Antikensammlung zu sehen, die sich neben dem Pergamonmuseum hier an einem zweiten Standort präsentiert. Höhepunkte der Sammlung, die nach Themen wie „Sport", „Fest", „Gelage" und „Götter" geordnet ist, sind der skythische Goldfund aus Vettersfelde, der Betende Knabe, die Thronende Göt-

Albert Wolff (1814–1892),
Löwenkämpfer (Lion Fighter),
1854–61, Bronze, Höhe/hight
445 cm, Altes Museum.

Karl Friedrich Schinkel himself thought it his best work: the *Old Museum* that looked like a Greek temple and asserted a fourth power on a par with Palace, Cathedral and Armory: that of art and culture. As the first such institution in Germany, the Museum (1825–1830) opened its royal collections to the public. The Latin inscription on the main façade already says as much: The building is dedicated "to the study of any type of antiquity and of free art." Two sculptures – Albert Wolff's "Lion Slayer" and August Kiss' "Fighting Amazon" – flank the wide outdoor steps to the vestibule that is supported by 18 Ionic columns. These in turn are guarded by 18 Prussian eagles on the roof. With a diameter of seven meters, the great granite bowl in Pleasure Garden was created in 1827 based on a design by Schinkel. The museum's centerpiece is the perfectly proportioned, 23-meter-high rotunda, modeled on the Roman Pantheon. Its collection of antique statues is housed in a circle composed of twenty Corinthian columns and in the alcoves along the upper gallery walkway. Since 1998, the Collection of Classical Antiquities can be viewed on the main floor; it is presented here in a second location, in addition to that of the Pergamon Museum. Highlights of the collection, which is organized according to themes such as "Sports," "Festivities," "Revelries," and "Gods," are the Scythian Golden Treasure of Vettersfelde, the Praying Boy, the Enthroned

tin von Tarent sowie Zeugnisse der minoischen und etruskischen Kultur. Nachdem das Ägyptische Museum seinen Standort in Charlottenburg verlassen hatte, machte es für eine Interimszeit im ersten Stock Station, bevor es mit seinen weltberühmten Glanzstücken, allen voran die 3300 Jahre alte Nofretete, in sein angestammtes Domizil zurückkehrt: in das von David Chipperfield wiederhergestellte *Neue Museum*, das seit dem Krieg Ruine war. Was an größeren Bauteilen und Raumfolgen verloren ist, zum Teil ganze Gebäudeflügel, wird nun in der Formensprache des 21. Jahrhunderts ergänzt. Leitmaterial sind Beton und unverputzter Backstein. Daneben plant der englische Architekt eine schnörkellose Kolonnadenarchitektur als zentrale Eingangshalle zu allen Museen. Sie wird den Namen des Berliner Mäzens James Simon tragen und das Neue Museum mit dem Pergamonmuseum verbinden.

Goddess of Tarent, as well as artifacts of Minoan and Etruscan culture. After leaving its old home in Charlottenburg, the Egyptian Museum stopped over for a while on the first floor, before it returned – with its world famous showpieces, above all 3,300-year-old Nefertiti – to its ancestral domicile, the *New Museum*: once a war ruin, now reconstructed by David Chipperfield. What was lost in terms of larger structural components and original suites of rooms – and entire wings were lost – is now being replaced with structures informed by an iconography of the 21th century. Their leading building materials are concrete and raw brick. Additionally, the English architect has plans for a colonnade-style structure without frills to serve as a central lobby to all museums. To be named after Berlin's patron of the arts, James Simon, it will connect the New Museum to the Pergamon Museum.

Die dem römischen Pantheon nachempfundene Rotunde im Alten Museum, 23 m hoch, 23 m Durchmesser, mit zwanzig korinthischen Säulen.

Rotunda modeled on the Roman Pantheon in the Old Museum, 23 m high, 23 m in diameter, with twenty Corinthian columns.

„Die Schöne ist gekommen", so lautet ihr Name übersetzt. Bevor die Büste der Nofretete im wiederhergestellten Neuen Museum auf der Museumsinsel als Teil der Ägyptischen Sammlung zu sehen ist, zeigt sich Berlins „schönster Schatz" in Schinkels Altem Museum. Die Büste stammt aus der 18. Dynastie, der Amarna-Zeit, um 1340 v. Chr., Kalkstein und Gips, Höhe 50 cm.

"The beautiful one has arrived," this is her name in translation. Before Nefertiti's bust can be seen in the reconstructed New Museum on Museum Island as part of the Egyptian Collection, Berlin's "most beautiful treasure" is being shown in Schinkel's Old Museum. The bust dates back to the 18th Dynasty, the Amarna Period, c. 1340 B.C., limestone and plaster, height: 50 cm.

Echnaton und seine Gemahlin
Nofretete vor der Sonnenscheibe
Atons, Reliefplatte eines Haus-
altars, Neues Reich, 18. Dynastie,
um 1350 v. Chr., Kalkstein,
Höhe 32,5 x 39 cm, Altes Museum.

Akhenaten and his spouse
Nefertiti in front of Aten's sun
disk, relief panel of a domestic
altar, New Kingdom, 18th Dynasty,
c. 1350 BC, limestone, height:
32.5 x 39 cm, Old Museum.

Porträtbüste des athenischen
Staatsmannes und Heerführers
Perikles (um 500–429 v. Chr.),
römische Kopie nach Original des
Kresilas, um 440 v. Chr.,
Höhe 54 cm, Altes Museum.

Portrait bust of Athenian
statesman and military leader
Pericles (c. 500–429 BC), Roman
copy after the original by Cresilas,
c. 440 BC, height: 54 cm,
Old Museum.

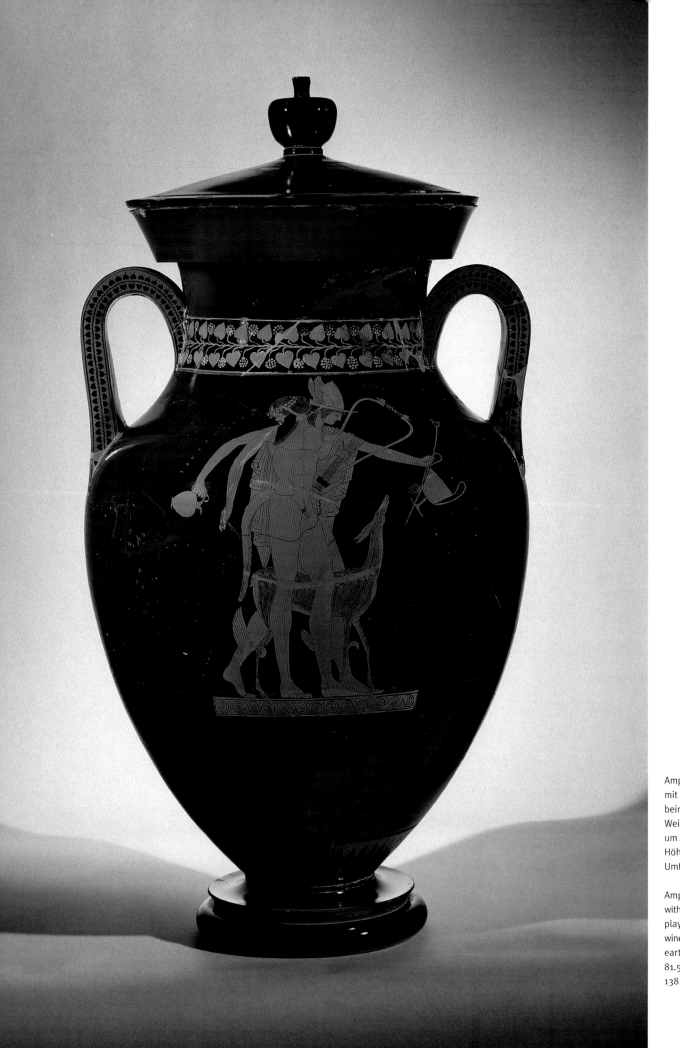

Amphora des „Berliner Malers"
mit Motiv des Silens Oreimachos
beim Leierspiel und Hermes mit
Weinkanne und Kantharos,
um 490 v. Chr., Ton, rotfigurig,
Höhe 81,5 cm (mit Deckel),
Umfang 138 cm, Altes Museum.

Amphora by the "Berlin Painter"
with motif of the Silene Oreimachos
playing the lyre and Hermes with
wine jug and kantharos, c. 490 B.C.,
earthenware, red-figure, height:
81.5 cm (with lid), circumference:
138 cm, Old Museum.

„Der betende Knabe", griechische
Bronze-Skulptur aus Rhodos,
um 300 v. Chr., bereits 1747 durch
den Ankauf für die Sammlung
Friedrich II. nach Sanssouci und
Berlin gekommen, seit 1830 im
Alten Museum ausgestellt.

"Praying Boy," Greek bronze
statue from Rhodes, c. 300 B.C.,
bought for the collection of
Frederick II and brought to
Sanssouci and Berlin as early as
1747, on exhibit in the Old
Museum since 1830.

DER DEUTSCHEN KUNST MDCCCLXXI

Alte Nationalgalerie
geöffnet

Alte Nationalgalerie auf der Museumsinsel, erbaut nach Plänen von Friedrich August Stüler und Johann Heinrich Strack, 1866–76.

Old National Gallery on Museum Island, construction based on designs by Friedrich August Stüler and Johann Heinrich Strack, 1866–76.

Allegorische Figur, den Kunstunterricht symbolisierend, von Moritz Schulz (1825–1904) an der Freitreppe der Alten Nationalgalerie.

Allegorical figure symbolizing art instruction, by Moritz Schulz (1825–1904), at the external staircase of the Old National Gallery.

Caspar David Friedrich
(1774–1840), *Frau am Fenster*
(Woman at the Window), 1822,
Öl auf Leinwand/oil on canvas,
44 x 37 cm, Alte Nationalgalerie.

Rechts/Right: Caspar David
Friedrich (1774–1840),
Greifswalder Hafen (Greifswald
Harbour), um/c. 1818–20,
Öl auf Leinwand/oil on canvas,
90 x 70 cm, Alte Nationalgalerie.

Caspar David Friedrich
(1774–1840), *Mann und Frau in
Betrachtung des Mondes*
(Man and Woman Contemplating
the Moon), 1830–35, Öl auf Lein-
wand/ oil on canvas, 34 x 44 cm,
Alte Nationalgalerie.

Was einst als Museum für zeitgenössische Malerei gedacht war, thront wie ein korinthischer Tempel aus rotem Sandstein an der Spree. Die *Alte Nationalgalerie* wurde 1866 bis 1876 nach den Plänen von Friedrich August Stüler und Johann Heinrich Strack erbaut. Über dem Eingangsportal erhebt sich seit 1886 ein von Alexander Calandrelli geschaffenes bronze-nes Reiterstandbild von König Friedrich Wilhelm IV., dem „Ro-mantiker auf dem Thron". Seine Ideen und Skizzen bestimm-ten maßgeblich den Bau.

Im Tympanon sieht man Germania als Schutzpatronin der Kunst, ein Symbol, das die um die Jahrhundertwende ent-brannten heftigen Auseinandersetzungen über die Samm-lungsankäufe begleiten sollte. Direktor Hugo von Tschudi wur-

Once intended as a Museum of Contemporary Art, it is enthroned above the Spree like a Corinthian temple made of red sandstone. The *Old National Gallery* was built in 1866–1876, based on designs by Friedrich August Stüler and Johann Heinrich Strack. A bronze equestrian statue created by Alexander Calandrelli has been towering above the entrance portal since 1886; it features King Frederick William IV, the "Romanticist on the throne." His ideas and sketches left their decisive mark on the building's construction.

The tympanum shows Germania as patroness of the arts, a symbol that was to accompany the lively conflicts sparked around the turn of the century about how to handle acquisi-tions for the collections. Director Hugo von Tschudi was even

Caspar David Friedrich
(1774–1840), *Einsamer Baum*
(Lonesome Tree), 1822, Öl auf
Leinwand/oil on canvas, 55 x 71 cm,
Alte Nationalgalerie.

de, weil er beim französischen „Erbfeind" zu viele Bilder erwarb, sogar entlassen. Heute zählen die Werke von Edouard
Manet und Claude Monet, von Edgar Degas, Auguste Renoir
und Gustave Courbet zu den Hauptattraktionen. Auch Paul
Cézannes „Mühle an der Couleuvre bei Pontoise" (1881) hängt
hier, das erste Werk des Franzosen, das je in einem Museum
ausgestellt wurde. Im Krieg zerstört, wurde die Nationalgalerie als erstes Gebäude auf der Museumsinsel wieder aufgebaut
und 1997 bis 2001 aufwendig saniert; sie zeigt heute die Kunst
des 19. Jahrhunderts. Herausragend ist die Sammlung der Malerei der Romantik. Allen voran Caspar David Friedrich, von
dem aus allen Schaffensperioden Werke zu sehen sind, so sein
„Mönch am Meer" (1808–1819) , „Der Watzmann" (1824/25)

fired because he had purchased too many paintings from the
French "arch enemy." Today, these works by Edouard Manet
and Claude Monet; Edgar Degas, Auguste Renoir and Gustave
Courbet, feature among its main attractions. Paul Cézanne's
"Mill on the Couleuvre near Pontoise" (1881) hangs here as well
– the first work of this Frenchman ever to be exhibited in any
museum. Destroyed during the war, the National Gallery was
the first building to be rebuilt on Museum Island and elaborately renovated in 1997–2001; today, it exhibits the art of the
19th century. Outstanding is its collection of Romantic paintings. Foremost among these are works by Caspar David Friedrich from all periods of his creative life, such as his "Monk by
the Sea" (1808–1819), "Watzmann Mountain" (1824/25) and

und „Das Riesengebirge" (1830–1835). Zu den Höhepunkten zählen auch Arnold Böcklins „Die Toteninsel" (1883), Anselm Feuerbachs „Gastmahl des Plato" (1873) und das reiche Werk Max Liebermanns und Adolph von Menzels, der mit dem „Balkonzimmer" (1845) den Impressionismus in Deutschland vorbereitete und u. a. mit dem „Flötenkonzert Friedrich des Großen in Sanssouci" (1850–1852) zu Berlins berühmtestem Maler avancierte.

Auch die Sammlung der Skulpturen ist bemerkenswert, vor allem Johann Gottfried Schadows Prinzessinnengruppe, sein Grabmal des Alexander Graf von der Mark, aber auch Werke von Antonio Canova, Christian Daniel Rauch, Reinhold Begas und Auguste Rodin.

Caspar David Friedrich (1774–1840), *Mondaufgang am Meer* (Moonrise by the Sea), 1822, Öl auf Leinwand/oil on canvas, 55 x 71 cm, Alte Nationalgalerie.

"Riesengebirge Mountains" (1830–1835). Other highlights are Arnold Böcklin's "The Island of Death" (1883), Anselm Feuerbach's "Plato's Symposium" (1873) and the abundant works by Max Liebermann and Adolph von Menzel, who blazed a trail for Impressionism in Germany with his "Balcony Room" (1845) and who acquired the status as Berlin's most famous painter with, e.g., his "Flute Concert by Frederick the Great in Sanssouci" (1850–1852).

The Sculpture Collection is likewise remarkable, especially Johann Gottfried Schadow's Princess Group and his Tomb of Alexander Graf von der Mark, but also works by Antonio Canova, Christian Daniel Rauch, Reinhold Begas und Auguste Rodin.

Max Liebermann (1847–1935),
Flachsscheuer in Laren
(Flax Spinning in Laren), 1887,
Öl auf Leinwand/oil on canvas,
135 x 232 cm, Alte Nationalgalerie.

Unten/Below: Adolph von Menzel
(1815–1905), *Eisenwalzwerk*
(Iron Rolling Mill), 1872–75,
Öl auf Leinwand/oil on canvas,
153 x 253 cm, Alte Nationalgalerie.

Wilhelm von Schadow (1788–1862), *Die Brüder Schadow mit Thorvaldsen* (The Schadow Brothers with Thorvaldsen), (von links/from left: Ridolfo Schadow, Bertel Thorvaldsen, Wilhelm Schadow), Öl auf Leinwand/oil on canvas, 92 x 118 cm, Alte Nationalgalerie.

Gustave Courbet (1819–1877), *Die Welle* (The Wave), 1869/70, Öl auf Leinwand/oil on canvas, 112 x 144 cm, Alte Nationalgalerie.

Auguste Rodin (1840–1917),
Der Denker (The Thinker), 1881–83,
Bronze, 71 x 39 x 56,5 cm,
Alte Nationalgalerie.

Das Herzstück des preußischen Berlin

Was auch Lindenforum heißt, ist Berlins größtes Freiluft-museum: das nach Friedrich II. benannte *Forum Fridericianum*. Mit den das Ensemble umrahmenden Gebäuden zählt es zu den bemerkenswertesten Sehenswürdigkeiten der Stadt. Im Zentrum steht die 1741 bis 1743 im Stil eines korinthischen Tempels errichtete Königliche Oper, die heutige Staatsoper Unter den Linden. Georg Wenzeslaus von Knobelsdorff schuf damit das erste freistehende Opernhaus Deutschlands.

Ebenfalls nach seinen Plänen führte Johann Boumann d. Ä. zwischen 1747 und 1773 den Bau der katholischen St.-Hed-wigs-Kathedrale aus, die nach den Schlesischen Kriegen ein Zeichen friderizianischer Toleranz setzen sollte. Vorbild für den

Vorhergehende Seite/Previous page: Eduard Gaertner (1801–1877), *Blick vom Dach der Friedrich-Werderschen Kirche auf das Friedrichsforum* (View of Frederick's Forum from the Roof of Friedrich-Werder Church), 1835, Öl auf Leinwand/oil on canvas, 94 x 147 cm, Märkisches Museum.

The Centerpiece of Prussian Berlin

Also called Lindenforum, it is Berlin's largest open-air museum: the *Forum Fridericianum*, named after Frederick II. Including the buildings framing the ensemble, it is one of the city's most remarkable places of interest. Its central feature is the Royal Opera, built in 1741–1743 in the style of a Corinthian temple, today called State Opera Unter den Linden. Georg Wenzeslaus von Knobelsdorff created it as the first detached opera house in Germany.

Also basing himself on his designs, Johann Boumann the Elder expanded Catholic St Hedwig's Cathedral in 1747–1773, which was to signal Frederickian tolerance after the Silesian Wars. Its domed structure with columned portico was

Kuppelbau mit dem Säulenportikus als Eingangshalle war das Pantheon in Rom. In die Westseite des Platzes schwingt sich die effektvolle Fassade der „Kommode" genannten ehemaligen Königlichen Bibliothek, die 1775 bis 1780 nach einem für die Wiener Hofburg vorgesehenen Entwurf von Johann Bernhard Fischer von Erlach entstand; heute beherbergt sie die Juristische Fakultät der Humboldt-Universität. Im Alten Palais daneben lebte Wilhelm I. fünfzig Jahre lang zunächst als Kronprinz, dann als König und Kaiser. Die Humboldt-Universität gegenüber war ursprünglich als Palais für Prinz Heinrich, den Bruder Friedrichs des Großen, gedacht und wurde 1748 bis 1766 von Johann Boumann d. Ä. nach Entwürfen von Knobelsdorff erbaut. Das im Krieg weitgehend zerstörte Platzensemble ist ab den 1950er-Jahren sorgfältig rekonstruiert worden.

Oben, links: Das Zeughaus, Barockbau von 1706, beherbergt heute das Deutsche Historische Museum.
Rechts: Der rückseitige Anbau des Museums mit gläsernem Treppenhaus, I.M. Pei, 1998–2004.

Above, left: Armory, Baroque building of 1706, today it houses the German Historical Museum.
Right: The rear extension of the Museum with glass-fronted stairway, I.M. Pei, 1998–2004.

modeled on the Roman Pantheon. The western side of the plaza features the dramatic façade of the former Royal Library, nicknamed "Kommode," or "Chest of Drawers," and built in 1775–1780, based on a design by Johann Bernhard Fischer von Erlach originally intended for the Vienna Hofburg; today it is the home of Humboldt University's School of Law. For about fifty years, William I lived in the Old Palace next door, first as crown prince, then as king and emperor. Just opposite, Humboldt University was originally conceived as a palace for Prince Henry, brother to Frederick the Great; it was designed by Knobelsdorff and built in 1748–1766 by Johann Boumann the Elder. Most of the square was destroyed by the war, but the ensemble has been carefully reconstructed since the 1950s.

Innenansicht des gläsernen
Anbaus am Deutschen
Historischen Museum/Interior
view of the glass addition to the
German Historical Museum,
I.M. Pei, 1998–2004.

Peter Paul Rubens (1577–1640), *Karl V., Portrait mit dem Kommandostab* (Charles V, Portrait with Baton), 1603, Kopie nach verlorenem Gemälde von Tizian (copy after a lost painting by Titian), 1548, Öl auf Leinwand/oil on canvas, 111,5 x 89,5 cm, Deutsches Historisches Museum/German Historical Museum.

Links: Eine von insgesamt 22 Masken sterbender Krieger des Bildhauers und Architekten Andreas Schlüter im Innenhof des Zeughauses.

Left: One of 22 masks of dying warriors by sculptor and architect Andreas Schlüter in the inner courtyard of the Armory.

Der Innenhof des Deutschen Historischen Museums im Zeughaus ist seit 1999 mit einem transparenten Dach überspannt.

The interior courtyard of the German Historical Museum in the Armory has been covered by a transparent roof since 1999.

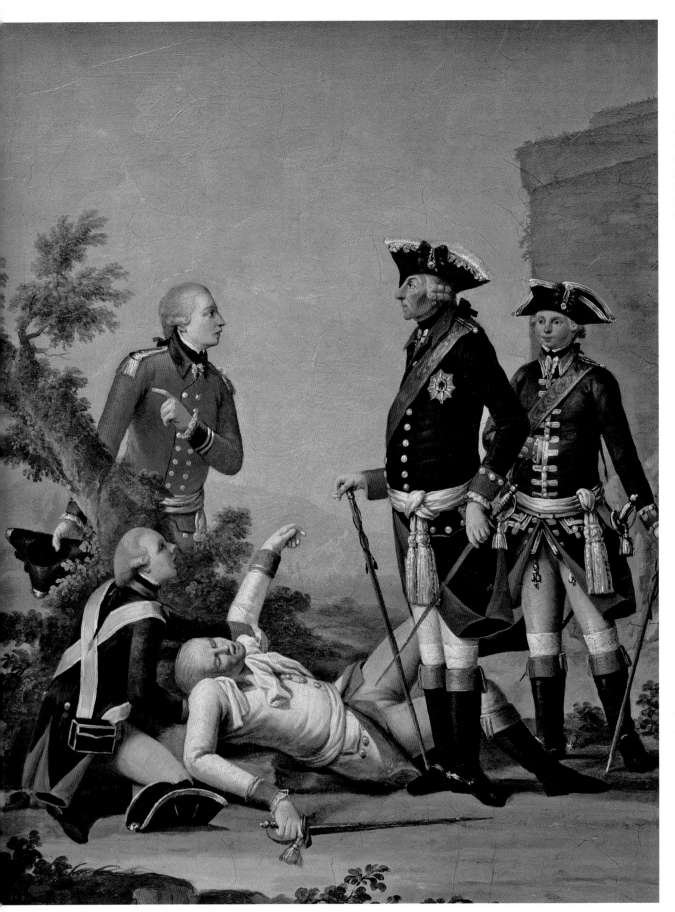

Unbekannter Künstler/unknown artist, *Friedrich der Große ehrt einen gefallenen Offizier* (Frederick the Great Honors a Fallen Officer), 1790, Öl auf Leinwand/oil on canvas, Deutsches Historisches Museum/ German Historical Museum.

Daniel Bretschneider d. J./ the Younger (1623–1658), *Stammbaum einer sächsischen Familie* (Genealogical Tree of a Saxon Family), Öl auf Leinwand/ oil on canvas, 39 x 29 cm, Deutsches Historisches Museum/ German Historical Museum.

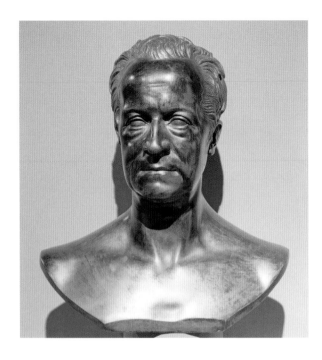

Christian Daniel Rauch
(1777–1857), *Karl August von
Hardenberg*, Porträtbüste/
portrait bust, 1816, Eisenguss/
cast iron, Höhe/hight 46,5 cm,
Deutsches Historisches Museum/
German Historical Museum.

Franziska Kobes (um/c. 1803–?),
Berliner Marktszene
(Berlin Market Scene), um/c. 1830,
Öl auf Leinwand/oil on canvas,
79 x 63,5 cm,
Deutsches Historisches Museum/
German Historical Museum.

Der bedeutendste noch existierende Barockbau Berlins hat in nur elf Jahren vier Architekten beansprucht: Johann Arnold Nering, Martin Grünberg, Andreas Schlüter und Jean de Bodt. 1706 wurde das Gebäude, in dem heute das *Deutsche Historische Museum* residiert, seiner Bestimmung übergeben: Während Preußens Aufstieg zur europäischen Großmacht diente das *Zeughaus* als Waffenarsenal, was den Berliner Märzrevolutionären Anlass bot, es 1848 zunächst erfolgreich zu stürmen. Nach der Reichsgründung war es bis zum Zweiten Weltkrieg Waffen- und Kriegsmuseum. Von 1952 bis 1990 zeigte hier das Museum für Deutsche Geschichte der DDR seine Sicht auf die „revolutionären Traditionen des Deutschen Volkes". Es ist im Deutschen Historischen Museum aufgegangen, das sich nach Jahren des Provisoriums seit 2006 neu präsentiert. Die Geschichte Deutschlands wird hier kontrovers ausgestellt, im europäischen Zusammenhang und in ihrer regionalen Vielfalt. Aus mehr als dreihundert Jahren sind Kostüme, Bilder, Spielzeug, Alltagsgegenstände, Urkunden, Möbel und vieles mehr zusammengetragen. Neben den Militaria ist die Plakatsammlung von internationaler Bedeutung. Im Schlüterhof, der von

Berlin's most important, still existing Baroque building took eleven years to build and used four architects in the process: Johann Arnold Nering, Martin Grünberg, Andreas Schlüter, and Jean de Bodt. Now housing the *German Historical Museum*, the building was first dedicated in 1706: During Prussia's ascent to the status of a major European power, the *Armory* was first used as a weapons' depot, which was incentive enough for Berlin March revolutionaries to raid it – successfully, at first – in 1848. After the founding of the Empire, it served as a museum of weapons and war until World War II. From 1952 to 1990, the Museum for German History of the GDR used it to exhibit its own view of the "revolutionary traditions of the German people." It was absorbed by the German Historical Museum that, after years of makeshift arrangements, emerged with a new look in 2006. Germany's history is now on display in a manner inviting debate – in its European context and its regional multiplicity. Three hundred years of collecting produced costumes, pictures, toys, everyday objects, certificates, furniture, and much more. Besides artifacts of military history, it also features a poster collection of international

William Pape (1859–1920),
Die kaiserliche Familie im Park zu Sanssouci (The Imperial Family in Sanssouci Park), 1891,
Öl auf Leinwand/oil on canvas,
270 x 185 cm,
Deutsches Historisches Museum/
German Historical Museum.

Fritz Paulsen (1838–1898),
Bei der Stellenvermittlung – Gesinde-Vermietungsbureau
(At the Employment Agency;
Menial Staff Rental Office), 1881,
Öl auf Leinwand/oil on canvas,
89,5 x 135 cm,
Deutsches Historisches Museum/
German Historical Museum.

170

Otto Antoine (1865–1951),
Leipziger Platz, um/c. 1910,
Öl auf Leinwand/oil on canvas,
51,7 x 86 cm,
Deutsches Historisches Museum/
German Historical Museum.

Otto Griebel (1895–1972),
Die Internationale,
(The International), 1928/30,
Öl auf Leinwand/oil on canvas,
124 x 185 cm,
Deutsches Historisches Museum/
German Historical Museum.

Ieoh Ming Pei, einem Walter-Gropius-Schüler, mit einer Glas-Stahl-Konstruktion überdacht wurde, befinden sich als Hauptattraktion die „Masken der Sterbenden Krieger", um 1695 von Andreas Schlüter geschaffen. Vergangenheit und Gegenwart zeigen sich nicht nur in den Exponaten des Museums, sondern auch im Nebeneinander von Altbau und dem neu gestalteten Stadtraum: Pei entwarf die neue Ausstellungshalle als einen luftigen Baukörper aus Glas und Stein, der einen optischen Angelpunkt schafft zwischen Museumsinsel und den Linden, deren ältestes Gebäude das Zeughaus ist.

Daneben erhebt sich Schinkels *Neue Wache* (1816–1818), von einem Kastanienwäldchen beschirmt, das schon Friedrich Wilhelm III. anlegen ließ. Im Inneren der heutigen „Zentralen Gedenkstätte der Bundesrepublik Deutschland für die Opfer von Krieg und Gewaltherrschaft" befindet sich Käthe Kollwitz' Skulptur „Mutter mit totem Sohn".

Wo heute der mächtige Bau der *Humboldt-Universität* Unter den Linden mit seinem dreigeschossigen Haupttrakt steht, hatte Friedrich der Große zunächst einen Königspalast geplant. Der sollte gegenüber von Oper, Kathedrale und Bibliothek auf dem Forum Fridericianum die enge Allianz zwischen Monarchie, Kunst und Wissenschaft repräsentieren. Von diesem Plan blieb, in verkleinerter Form, die Stadtresidenz für den Bruder des Königs. Friedrich Wilhelm III. stiftete sie dann der Berliner Universität, die bis 1946 seinen Namen trug. Ihre Grün-

W. Loeillot, *Die Universität*, (The University), um/c. 1840, kolorierte Kreidelithographie/ colored chalk lithography, 21 x 29 cm.

relevance. The Schlüterhof, covered by Ieoh Ming Pei, a Walter Gropius student, with a glass and steel construction, features as its main attraction the "Masks of the Dying Warriors," created by Andreas Schlüter around 1695. Past and present are not only modalities of the exhibits but also emerge in the way in which this traditional building and Berlin's newly configured city space coexist: Pei designed the new exhibition hall as an airy structure made of glass and stone that creates an optical pivot between Museum Island and Linden Boulevard, the oldest building of which is the Armory.

Schinkel's *New Guard House* (1816–1818) is located next door, protected by a small chestnut grove first planted under Frederick William III. Inside the current "Central Memorial of the Federal Republic of Germany for the Victims of War and Tyranny," there is Käthe Kollwitz' sculpture "Mother with Dead Son."

At the site of the current massive structure of *Humboldt University* on Unter-den-Linden Boulevard with its three-story main tract, Frederick the Great had originally planned a royal palace. It was to represent the close alliance of monarchy, art and science once it was built just across from the Opera, Cathedral and Library on Forum Fridericianum. All that remains of this project is a reduced version of the urban residence for the king's brother. Frederick William III donated it to Berlin's university, which then bore his name until 1946. Its founding

dung ist vor allem auf Betreiben Wilhelm von Humboldts im Zuge der Reformbewegungen zustande gekommen. Humboldt entwarf eine „Universitas litterarum", in der die Einheit von Lehre und Forschung ebenso herrschen sollte wie der Anspruch, die Studenten allseitig humanistisch zu bilden. Dieser Gedanke erwies sich als erfolgreich, verbreitete sich weltweit und ließ in den folgenden anderthalb Jahrhunderten viele Lehranstalten gleichen Typs entstehen. 1810 nahm die Berliner Universität ihren Betrieb auf. Ihr erster gewählter Rektor war der Philosoph Johann Gottlieb Fichte.

Neben Georg Wilhelm Friedrich Hegel waren es Friedrich Schleiermacher, Ludwig Feuerbach, Jacob und Wilhelm Grimm, die rasch den Ruhm der Universität als Talentschmiede für die Geisteswissenschaft verbreiteten. Von Beginn an bestimmten mit Christoph Wilhelm Hufeland und Albrecht Daniel Thaer aber auch die Naturwissenschaftler das Profil der Fakultäten.

„Kommode" am Bebelplatz, 1775–80 entstanden als Königliche Bibliothek im Rahmen des von Knobelsdorff konzipierten Forum Fridericianum, ist heute Sitz der Juristischen Fakultät der Humboldt-Universität.

"Commode" on Bebelplatz, created in 1775–80 as Royal Library in the context of Knobelsdorff's design for the Forum Fridericianum, today the seat of Humboldt University's Law School.

was achieved primarily through the initiative of Wilhelm von Humboldt in the wake of reform movements. Humboldt designed a "Universitas litterarum," for which the oneness of teaching and research was to be as central as the demand to teach students in a comprehensively humanistic manner. This idea proved to be successful; it was disseminated all over the world and spawned several similar institutions of learning in the ensuing one and a half centuries. Berlin University began operating in 1810. Its first elected president was the philosopher Johann Gottlieb Fichte.

Besides Georg Wilhelm Friedrich Hegel, those who were most instrumental in quickly spreading the university's reputation as a hotbed for the humanities were Friedrich Schleiermacher, Ludwig Feuerbach, Jacob and Wilhelm Grimm. From the start, though, the natural sciences – led by scientists such as Christoph Wilhelm Hufeland and Albrecht Daniel Thaer – also

Links: Erst Stadtresidenz des Bruders von Friedrich II., Friedrich Wilhelm III., dann gestiftet der humanistischen Bildungsidee: die Humboldt-Universität.

Left: Initially, the city residence of Frederick II's brother, Frederick William III, then donated to serve the humanistic idea of education: Humboldt University.

Oben: Innenansicht der Bibliothek des Jacob-und-Wilhelm-Grimm-Zentrums der Humboldt-Universität, Architekt: Max Dudler, fertiggestellt 2009.

Above: Interior view of the library of the Jacob and Wilhelm Grimm Center of Humboldt University, architect: Max Dudler, completed in 2009.

Rechts unten: Georg Friedrich Weitsch (1758–1828), *Alexander von Humboldt*, 1806, Öl auf Leinwand/oil on canvas, 126 x 93 cm, Alte Nationalgalerie. J. L. Raab nach/after Franz Krüger, *Wilhelm v. Humboldt*, Stahlstich (steel engraving), um/c. 1840.

Oben: Theobald Reinhold
Freiherr von Ör (1807–1885),
*Weimars goldene Tage /
Der Weimarer Musenhof*, 1860,
Holzstich nach Zeichnung.
Friedrich Schiller liest u. a. vor
Herzoginmutter Amalie, dem
Herzogpaar Karl August und
Luise, Goethe, Wieland, Herder
und den Humboldt-Brüdern.

Above: Theobald Reinhold
Freiherr von Ör (1807–1885),
*Weimar's Golden Days / Weimar
Court of the Muses*, 1860,
woodcut after drawing.
Friedrich Schiller reads to
Dowager Duchess Amalia, the
ducal couple Karl August and
Louise, Goethe, Wieland, Herder,
the Humboldt brothers, et al.

Friedrich Georg Weitsch
(1758–1828), *Alexander von
Humboldt und Aimé Bonpland im
Tal von Tapia am Fuß des Vulkans
Chimborazo*,
(Alexander von Humboldt and
Aimé Bonpland in the Valley of
Tapia at the Foot of Chimborazo
Volcano), 1810, Öl auf Leinwand/
oil on canvas, 162 x 226 cm.

Marchais & Bouquet nach einer
Skizze von/after a sketch by
Louis de Riens, *Volcans d'air de
Turbaco*, um/c. 1800, Aquatinta,
aus/from
Alexander von Humboldt,
Vue des cordillieres, Paris 1810–15.

Nicht zuletzt dank der Förderung Alexander von Humboldts, dem zweiten Namenspatron, wurde die Universität schnell Wegbereiter vieler neuer Disziplinen. Insgesamt 29 Nobelpreise zeugen von der überragenden wissenschaftlichen Leistung ihrer Gelehrten wie Robert Koch, Albert Einstein oder Theodor Mommsen. 1829 wurde die Charité eingegliedert, von 1913 bis 1920 das U-förmige Haupthaus durch Ludwig Hoffmann spiegelbildlich erweitert. Nach der Zerstörung durch Bombenangriffe im Zweiten Weltkrieg 1944/45 baute man die gesamte Anlage nach dem historischen Vorbild wieder auf. Seit 1949 trägt sie den Namen ihres Erfinders, Wilhelm von Humboldt.

Eduard Ender (1822–1883), *Humboldt und Bonpland am Orinoco*, um/c. 1800, Öl auf Leinwand/oil on canvas, 80 x 150 cm, Akademie der Wissenschaften/ Academy of Sciences.

Nächste Seiten/Next pages: Eduard Gaertner (1801–1877), *Der Schlüterhof des Stadtschlosses* (Schlüter Courtyard of City Palace), um/c. 1830, Öl auf Leinwand/ oil on canvas, 97 x 155 cm.

determined the character of the departments. Due, last not least, to the support of Alexander von Humboldt, after whom the university was then named, it quickly became a trailblazer of many new disciplines. Twenty-nine Nobel Prizes prove the outstanding scientific achievements of such scholars as Robert Koch, Albert Einstein or Theodor Mommsen. Charité Medical School was absorbed in 1829; its horseshoe-style main building was enlarged by Ludwig Hoffmann who added a mirroring structure in 1913–1920. After its destruction by bombs in 1944/45, the entire complex was reconstructed, patterned on its historical model. Since 1949, it has borne the name of its founder Wilhelm von Humboldt.

Einst war es die prunkvolle Mitte Berlins: Das barocke *Hohen-zollernschloss*, das 1945 fast vollständig ausbrannte und 1950 gesprengt wurde, soll wiedererstehen. Die jahrelang heftig geführte Debatte ist 2008 mit dem preisgekrönten Entwurf des Italieners Franco Stella zu einem Ende gekommen. Die Pläne sehen die Rekonstruktion dreier barocker Fassaden, des legendären Schlüterhofs sowie der Schinkelschen Kuppel vor. Bis 2015 wird in der Kubatur der alten Residenz ein modernes Kulturzentrum heranwachsen, das Humboldt-Forum. Hier werden die bislang in Dahlem ansässigen außereuropäischen Museen einziehen, die Landesbibliothek sowie die wissenschaftlichen, teilweise auf das berühmte Brüderpaar zurückgehenden Sammlungen der Humboldt-Universität. Berlin gewinnt mit diesem Schauhaus der Weltkunst seine historische Mitte zurück und – ein neues Wahrzeichen.

W. Loeillot, *Das Königliche Schloss* (The Royal Palace), um/c. 1850, Kreidelithographie/chalk lithography, 21,5 x 29 cm.

Rechts oben/Right above: F. Mesmer, *Angriff der Kavallerie auf das vor dem Schloss versammelte Volk am 18. März* (Cavalry Attack on the People Assembled in Front of the Palace on March 18), 1848, Aquarell/watercolor.

Unten/Below: Das Schloss und der Lustgarten (Palace and Pleasure Garden), koloriertes Foto/hand-colored photo, 1898.

Once it was the glorious center of Berlin: Baroque *Hohen-zollern Palace*, almost completely gutted by fire in 1945 and then blown up in 1950, is to be resurrected. The vehement debates of the past few years came to an end in 2008 when the prize-winning design by Italian architect Franco Stella was selected. His plans project the reconstruction of three Baroque façades, the legendary Schlüterhof as well as Schinkel's cupola. By 2015, a modern cultural center will have been developed within the cubage of the old Royal Residence: the Humboldt Forum. Museums specializing in non-European cultures, currently housed in Dahlem, will move there, as will Berlin's Regional Library and the scientific collections of Humboldt University, which, in part, derive from those seeded by the famous brothers. With this new venue for international art, Berlin will regain its historical center – and acquire a new emblem.

Franz Krüger (1797–1857),
*Die Huldigung der preußischen
Stände vor Friedrich Wilhelm IV.
in Berlin am 15. Oktober 1840*
(The Prussian Estates Render
Obeisance to Frederick William IV
in Berlin on October 15, 1840),
Öl auf Leinwand/oil on canvas,
301 x 436 cm.

Letzte Spuren des barocken
Stadtschlosses: Die Skulptur
Winter von Balthasar Permoser,
1706–08, stützt den Balkon
des erhaltenen ehemaligen
Schlossportals IV.
Unten: Die von Genien flankierte
Wappenkartusche.

Final traces of Baroque City
Palace: The sculpture *Winter*
by Balthasar Permoser, 1706–08,
supports the balcony of surviving
former palace portal IV.
Below: Heraldic cartouche
flanked by putti.

Eine verschwundene Welt in Schwarzweiß – Bilddokumente aus dem Berliner Stadtschloss 1905 bis 1918, von oben links gegen den Uhrzeigersinn: Teesalon der Königin Elisabeth mit Skulpturen von Christian Friedrich Tieck, Wendeltreppe und großes Treppenhaus, Schweizer-Saal, die Erasmus-Kapelle (unter Friedrich Wilhelm IV. Arbeitszimmer), Schreibzimmer Friedrich des Großen (später der Königin Elisabeth), die Brandenburgische (auch Rote-Adler-)Kammer.

A vanished world in black and white – pictorial documents from Berlin City Palace 1905 to 1918, counter-clockwise from upper left: Tea salon of Queen Elisabeth with sculptures by Christian Friedrich Tieck, spiral staircase and great stairwell, Swiss Hall, Erasmus Chapel (used as study under Frederick William IV), Frederick The Great's writing room (later Queen Elisabeth's), Brandenburgian (also Red Eagle) Chamber.

Kulturforum – neue Architektur für Alte Meister und klassische Moderne

Zwischen Tiergarten, Potsdamer Platz und Landwehrkanal erstreckt sich das Kulturforum mit seinen architektonischen Solitären rund um die 1846 von Friedrich August Stüler errichtete St. Matthäuskirche, einen Ziegelbau im italo-romanischen Stil. In diesem Ensemble ist die europäische Kunst versammelt. Der Gedanke eines neuen Kulturzentrums im Westteil der Stadt geht auf Hans Scharoun zurück, der schon in seinem „Kollektivplan" von 1946 ein „Kulturband" entlang der Spree entwarf und auch in den 1950er-Jahren allen politischen Widrigkeiten zum Trotz immer eine Kulturlandschaft für Gesamtberlin im Sinn behielt. Darin war zwischen den Linden im Osten und dem Schloss Charlottenburg im Westen ein weiterer kultureller Knotenpunkt genau in der Mitte vorgesehen. So entstanden auf dem durch Hitlers Baupläne für eine gigantische neue Hauptstadt schon vor und vollends während des Krieges durch Bomben verwüsteten Areal als Eckpfeiler zuerst die Philharmonie, die Staatsbibliothek und die Neue Nationalgalerie. Nachdem die Mauer die Teilung längst zementiert hatte, folgten Musikinstrumenten-Museum, Kunstgewerbemuseum und der Kammermusiksaal, später das Kupferstichkabinett und

Das weltweit einzigartige Ensemble an der Potsdamer Straße: das Kulturforum u. a. mit Philharmonie, Kammermusiksaal, Staatsbibliothek, der Neuen Nationalgalerie, Gemäldegalerie. Der Vater des Gesamtplans war Hans Scharoun (1893–1972).

The complex on Potsdamer Straße is unique in the world: Culture Forum with Philharmonic Hall, Hall for Chamber Music, State Library, New National Gallery, Picture Gallery, et al. Its comprehensive design was fathered by Hans Scharoun (1893–1972).

Culture Forum – New Architecture for Old Masters and Classical Modernity

The Culture Forum with its architectural singularities ranges across an area bordered by Tiergarten, Potsdamer Platz and Landwehrkanal and gathered around St Matthew's Church, a brick structure built by Friedrich August Stüler in 1846 in the Italian-Romanesque style. European art has its collective home inside this complex. The idea of a new cultural center in the western part of the city goes back to Hans Scharoun whose "collective plan" of 1946 projected a "Culture Band" running along the Spree, and who, even in the 1950s and in spite of all political adversities, always kept in mind a unified cultural landscape for all of Berlin. It stipulated an additional cultural hub exactly midway between the Linden in the East and Charlottenburg Palace in the West. Thus were created, on the site first devastated by Hitler's architectural designs for a gigantic new capital and then utterly destroyed during the war, the initial cornerstone buildings consisting of the Philharmonic Hall, the State Library and the New National Gallery. After the Wall had long consolidated the city's division, the Museum of Musical Instruments, the Museum of Decorative Arts and the Chamber Music Hall followed suit and, sometime later, the

die Kunstbibliothek. Den Schlussstein in einer mehr als dreißigjährigen Planungs- und Baugeschichte setzte die 1998 eröffnete Gemäldegalerie. Die Architekten Hilmer & Sattler entwarfen den sachlichen Neubau an der Südwest-Ecke des Kulturforums.

Die Sammlung europäischer Malerei vom 13. bis zum 18. Jahrhundert, heute in der *Gemäldegalerie*, zählt mit Recht zu den größten und weltweit bedeutendsten und blickt auf eine wechselvolle Geschichte zurück. Eröffnet wurde sie 1830 in dem von Schinkel entworfenen Königlichen Museum am Lustgarten, dem heutigen Alten Museum. Den Grundstock bildeten die Kunstsammlungen des Großen Kurfürsten und Friedrichs des Großen. Unter Wilhelm von Bode, dem Direktor von 1890 bis 1929, gelangten sie bald zu internationalem Ruhm. Von 1904 an wurden sie im damaligen Kaiser-Friedrich-Museum, dem heutigen Bode-Museum, präsentiert. Der Zweite Weltkrieg richtete großen Schaden an. Mehr als vierhundert großformatige Werke gingen verloren oder wurden zerstört. Die anschließende Spaltung Berlins riss auch die Sammlung auseinander. Nachdem die Bilder auf Ost und West verteilt waren, im Bode-Museum und im Museum Dahlem, sind sie auf dem Kulturfo-

Die von Säulen durchzogene Wandelhalle der 1998 eröffneten Gemäldegalerie (Architekten: Heinz Hilmer, Christoph Sattler, Thomas Albrecht) ziert die Brunneninstallation *5-7-9 Serie* von Walter de Maria.

Opened in 1998, the Picture Gallery has a foyer articulated by columns (architects: Heinz Hilmer, Christoph Sattler, Thomas Albrecht) and adorned with the fountain installation *5-7-9 Series* by Walter de Maria.

Museum of Prints and Drawings and the Art Library. The capstone to this planning and construction phase of more than thirty years was set in place in 1998 with the opening of the Picture Gallery. The architects Hilmer & Sattler designed the sober and functional new building on the southwestern corner of the Kulturforum.

The collection of European paintings from the 13th through the 18th centuries, now housed in the *Picture Gallery*, rightly counts among the greatest and most important collections worldwide and looks back on a colorful history. It was opened in 1830 in the Royal Museum at Pleasure Garden, today's Old Museum. Its original holdings were seeded by the art collections of the Great Elector and Frederick the Great. Under Wilhelm von Bode, museum director in 1890–1929, they soon acquired international fame. As of 1904, they were exhibited in the former Kaiser Friedrich Museum, called Bode Museum today. World War II did a lot of damage. More than four hundred large-scale works were lost or destroyed. Berlin's subsequent division further disintegrated the collection. While the paintings were divided between East and West, the Bode and Dahlem Museums, they have now been reunited at the

rum wieder vereint. Kern des Gebäudes ist eine dreischiffige Wandelhalle, die bis auf ein in der Mitte platziertes Wasserbecken von Walter de Maria leer ist. Um die Halle herum liegen 72 Säle und Kabinette, die rund tausend Hauptwerke präsentieren, in der Studiengalerie des Untergeschosses sind weitere vierhundert Gemälde ausgestellt. Sammlungsschwerpunkte der Gemäldegalerie bilden die deutsche und italienische Malerei des 13. bis 16. Jahrhunderts und die niederländische Malerei des 15. und 16. Jahrhunderts. Glanzstücke sind Werke von Albrecht Dürer, Lucas Cranach d. Ä., Hans Memling und Pieter Bruegel d. Ä. Den Höhepunkt der Sammlung stellen die Holländer und Flamen des 17. Jahrhunderts dar, besonders die Werke Rembrandts und immer noch „Der Mann mit dem Goldhelm" (um 1650/55), obwohl als gesichert gilt, dass

Blick in die modernen Ausstellungsräume der Gemäldegalerie.

View of the modern exhibition rooms of the Picture Gallery.

Culture Forum. The building's core is a triple-nave foyer, which is empty except for a central water basin by Walter de Maria. Surrounding the foyer are 72 halls und cabinets which showcase around one thousand major works; four hundred additional paintings are on display in the Studies Gallery on the lower floor. Central features of the Picture Gallery collection are 13th–16th century paintings by German and Italian masters and 15th–16th century paintings by Dutch masters. Highlights are works by Albrecht Dürer, Lucas Cranach the Elder, Hans Memling, and Pieter Bruegel the Elder. The collection's top attractions are Dutch and Flemish masters of the 17th century, especially Rembrandt's works – and, still, "Man with a Golden Helmet" (around 1650/55), even though it is now considered certain, that it was not painted by the master's hand and merely

Antonio del Pollaiuolo
(um/c. 1432–1498), (auch
zugeschrieben/also attributed
to Domenico Veneziano,
um/c. 1400/10–1461),
Profilbildnis einer jungen Frau
(Profile Portrait of a Young
Woman), um/c. 1465/70,
auf Pappelholz/on cottonwood,
52,5 x 36,5 cm, Gemäldegalerie.

190

Bartolome Bermejo (Bartolomé
de Cardenás) (um/c. 1440–1500),
Marientod
(Death of the Virgin Mary),
um/c. 1460/65, Öl auf Holz/oil on
wood, 63 x 41 cm, Gemäldegalerie.

Rechts/Right: Martin Schongauer
(um/c. 1450–1491),
Die Geburt Christi
(Birth of Christ), um/c. 1480,
Eichenholz/oak, 37,5 x 28 cm,
Gemäldegalerie.

Albrecht Dürer (1471–1528),
Jakob Fugger II. (der Reiche/the
Rich), um/c. 1518, Öl auf
Lindenholz/oil on linden wood,
64 x 49,5 cm, Gemäldegalerie.

Links/Left: Caravaggio
(eigentl./orig. Michelangelo
Merisi) (1571–1610), *Amor als
Sieger* (Amor Victorious), 1601/02,
Öl auf Leinwand/oil on canvas,
156 x 113 cm, Gemäldegalerie.

er nicht von des Meisters Hand, sondern nur aus seiner Werkstatt stammt. Dazu kommen Bildnis-, Genre- und Landschaftsgemälde u. a. von Frans Hals, Jacob van Ruisdael und Peter Paul Rubens. Französische Malerei ist u. a. mit Antoine Watteau und Nicolas Poussin vertreten, unter den Spaniern ragen El Greco und Diego Velázquez, unter den Engländern Joshua Reynolds und Thomas Gainsborough hervor.

Schon 1994 eröffnete das *Kupferstichkabinett* mit einer Überblicksschau, die den reichen Bestand an Holzschnitten, Bleistiftzeichnungen und Lithografien vom 14. bis 20. Jahrhundert exemplarisch aufblätterte. Bereits 1652 begann die Sammlungsgeschichte: Der Große Kurfürst kaufte damals 2500 Zeichnungen für die Hofbibliothek. König Friedrich Wilhelm III. gründete dann 1831 das Kupferstichkabinett, das mittlerweile 110 000 Handzeichnungen, Aquarelle, Gouachen

Links/Left: Jacob Cornelisz van Amsterdam (um/c. 1470–1533), *Die Heilige Elisabeth von Thüringen* (Saint Elisabeth of Thuringia) und/and *Die Heilige Anna Selbdritt* (Saint Anne with Virgin and Child), um 1515/20. Rückseiten der Seitenflügel eines Flügelaltars/reverse of wings of a winged altar, auf Eichenholz/on oak, je/each 50 x 17 cm, Gemäldegalerie.

Rechts/Right: Lucas Cranach d. Ä./the Elder (1472–1553), *Der Sündenfall* (Fall of Man), 1533, auf Rotbuche/on copper beech, 50,4 x 35,5 cm, Gemäldegalerie.

fashioned by his workshop. Other works include portrait, genre and landscape paintings by, e.g., Frans Hals, Jacob van Ruisdael and Peter Paul Rubens. French masters are represented by, e.g., Antoine Watteau and Nicolas Poussin; El Greco and Diego Velázquez are preeminent among the Spanish, and Joshua Reynolds and Thomas Gainsborough have pride of place among the English.

Back in 1994, the *Museum of Prints and Drawings*, opened its doors with a survey exhibit providing a sample showing of its rich holdings in woodcuts, pencil drawings and lithographs from the 14th through the 20th centuries. Its history of collection began as early as 1652: That is when the Great Elector bought 2,500 drawings for the Library of the Court. King Frederick William III then founded the Museum of Prints and Drawings in 1831, which by now owns 110,000 hand

und Pastelle sowie 520 000 Drucke, mit Originalgrafik illustrierte Bücher und einige hundert Inkunabeln besitzt. Von mittelalterlichen Manuskripten über Zeichnungen des Renaissancemalers Tizian und Radierungen des Berliners Daniel Chodowiecki bis ins 20. Jahrhundert und zur Fotografie reicht die Palette. Besonders reich sind die Bestände an früher italienischer, altdeutscher und niederländischer Grafik und Zeichnungen, u. a. von Botticelli und Dürer, sowie an Arbeiten von Schinkel und Menzel. Einen der Schwerpunkte bilden Rembrandts Radierungen. Sein Werk liegt im Kupferstichkabinett fast vollständig vor. Von den ihm einst zugeschriebenen 150 Zeichnungen hat zwar nur etwa die Hälfte der strengen Kritik moderner Forschung standgehalten, aber auch diese Zahl wird von keinem anderen Museum erreicht.

Links/Left: Battista Dossi (um/c. 1495–1548), *Venus und Amoretten in einer Landschaft* (Venus with Cupids in Landscape), um/c. 1546/48, Öl auf Pappelholz/oil on cottonwood, 65 x 47 cm, Gemäldegalerie.

Rechts/Right: Jan Gossaert, genannt/known as Jan Mabuse (um/c. 1478/88–1532), *Neptun und Amphitrite*, 1516, Öl auf Holz/oil on wood, 188 x 124 cm, Gemäldegalerie.

drawings, watercolors, gouaches, and pastels, as well as 520,000 prints, books with original illustrations and some one hundred incunabula. Its gamut runs from medieval manuscripts to drawings by Renaissance painter Titian and etchings by Berlin artist Daniel Chodowiecki, into the 20th century and up to photography. Especially rich are its holdings in early Italian, old German and Dutch graphic arts and drawings, e.g., by Botticelli and Dürer, as well as in works by Karl Friedrich Schinkel and Adolph von Menzel. Rembrandt's etchings constitute one of the core collections. Almost his entire body of works is on hand at the Museum of Prints and Drawings. Of the 150 drawings once attributed to him, only about half have stood the strict test of modern research, but even this number has not been reached by any other museum.

Die Entwicklung des europäischen Kunsthandwerks wird im benachbarten Gebäude gezeigt, von Rolf Gutbrod im Stil des Brutalismus entworfen, der schon bei seiner Eröffnung 1985 auf wenig Sympathie traf. Dabei verfügt das 1867 gegründete *Kunstgewerbemuseum* als älteste Einrichtung seiner Art in Deutschland über einen erlesenen Bestand europäischen Kunsthandwerks vom frühen Mittelalter bis in die Gegenwart, vom berühmten Welfenschatz aus dem 11. bis 15. Jahrhundert über das Lüneburger Ratssilber aus dem 15. bis 17. Jahrhundert bis zu einem Verwandlungstisch von Abraham Roentgen aus dem Frühklassizismus und zu den Gläsern von Émile Gallé aus dem 19. Jahrhundert. Die Neue Sammlung zeigt Kunsthand-

Pieter Bruegel d. Ä./the Elder (um/c. 1525/30–1569), *Die niederländischen Sprichwörter* (Dutch Proverbs), 1559, Öl auf Eichenholz/oil on oak, 117 x 163 cm, Gemäldegalerie.

The development of European arts and crafts is on display in the building next door, designed by Rolf Gutbrod in the style of Brutalism, which did not engender a lot of sympathy even in 1985 when it was first opened. Nevertheless, the *Museum of Decorative Arts*, founded in 1867 and the oldest institution of its kind in Germany, owns select holdings of arts and crafts objects dating back to the early Middle Ages through the present day, from the famous Guelph Treasure from the 11th–15th centuries to the Lüneburg Council Silverware from the 15th–17th centuries, to a convertible table by Abraham Roentgen dating back to early Neoclassicism and glassware by Émile Gallé from the 19th century. The New Collection

Tizian, eigentl./orig. Tiziano
Vecelli(o) (1477 oder um/
or c. 1488/90–1576),
Selbstbildnis (Self-Portrait), 1562,
Öl auf Leinwand/oil on canvas,
96 x 75 cm, Gemäldegalerie.

Tizian, eigentl./orig. Tiziano
Vecelli(o) (1477 oder um/
or c. 1488/90–1576),
Venus mit dem Orgelspieler
(Venus and the Organist),
um 1550/52, Öl auf Leinwand/
oil on canvas, 115 x 210 cm,
Gemäldegalerie.

Rechts/Right: Georges de La Tour
(1593–1652), *Die Erbsenesser*
(The Pea Eaters), um 1618,
Öl auf Leinwand/oil on canvas,
74 x 87 cm, Gemäldegalerie.

Links/Left: Pieter de Hooch (1629–1684), *Die Mutter* (The Mother), um/c. 1661/63, Öl auf Leinwand/oil on canvas, 92 x 100 cm, Gemäldegalerie.

Oben/Above: Pieter Bol (1622–1674), *Stilleben mit totem Hasen* (Still Life with Dead Hare), 1645/55, Öl auf Leinwand/oil on canvas, 64 x 80,5 cm, Gemäldegalerie.

Rembrandt, Harmensz van Rijn
(1606–1669), *Moses zerschmettert die Gesetzestafeln* (Moses
Smashing the Tables of Law), 1659,
Öl auf Leinwand/oil on canvas,
169 x 137 cm, Gemäldegalerie.

Links/Left:
Rembrandt, Harmensz van Rijn
(1606–1669), *Jakobs Kampf mit
dem Engel* (Jacob Wrestling with
the Angel), um 1660,
Öl auf Leinwand/oil on canvas,
137 x 116 cm, Gemäldegalerie.

Jan Vermeer van Delft
(1632–1675), *Das Glas Wein*
(The Glass of Wine),
um/c. 1661, Öl auf Leinwand/
oil on canvas, 66,3 x 76,5 cm,
Gemäldegalerie.

Rechts/Right: Jan Vermeer van
Delft (1632–1675), *Junge Dame
mit Perlenhalsband* (Young Lady
with Pearl Necklace), um/c. 1664,
Öl auf Leinwand/oil on canvas,
51,2 x 45,1 cm, Gemäldegalerie.

werk, Mode und Industriedesign der Gegenwart. Das Museum befand sich bis 1921 im Martin-Gropius-Bau und danach bis 1939 im Berliner Stadtschloss.

Ein Teil der Sammlungen wurde nach dem Krieg im Schloss Köpenick neu zusammengestellt, der andere Teil war im Charlottenburger Schloss untergebracht, bevor er in den Neubau am Kulturforum umzog. Schloss Köpenick bleibt mit zwanzig Epochenräumen eine Dependance des Museums.

Als Teil des Deutschen Gewerbemuseums, des heutigen Kunstgewerbemuseums, wurde 1867 die *Kunstbibliothek* gegründet. Sie ist mit ihren rund 400.000 Bänden eine der bedeutendsten kunstwissenschaftlichen Spezialbibliotheken in Deutschland. Seit 1994 befindet sie sich ebenfalls am Kulturforum Potsdamer Platz. Mit ihren bedeutenden Beständen – Sammlung der Handzeichnungen (ca. 30 000 Architekturzeichnungen), Ornamentstichsammlung, Lipperheidesche Kostümbibliothek, Sammlung der Plakat- und Reklamekunst, Gebrauchsgraphische Sammlung, Sammlung Buchkunst, Sammlung Fotografie – bietet die Kunstbibliothek ein breites Forschungsangebot.

Links/Left: Thomas Gainsborough (1727–1788), *Die Marsham-Kinder* (The Marsham Children), 1787, Öl auf Leinwand/oil on canvas, 243 x 182 cm, Gemäldegalerie.

Rechts/Right: Giovanni Battista Tiepolo (1696–1770), *Das Martyrium der Hl. Agathe* (The Martyrdom of St Agatha), um/c. 1756, Öl auf Leinwand/ oil on canvas, 184 x 131 cm, Gemäldegalerie.

showcases contemporary arts and crafts, fashion and industrial design. Up to 1921, the museum was housed in the Martin Gropius building and thereafter through 1939, in Berlin's City Palace.

A part of its collections was newly assembled at Köpenick Palace after the war, the other part was housed in Charlottenburg Palace, before it moved to the new building on the Culture Forum. Köpenick Palace with its twenty period rooms remains a Dependance, or branch, of the museum.

The *Art Library* was founded in 1867 as part of the German Crafts Museum, today's Museum of Decorative Arts. It has approximately 400,000 volumes and ranks among Germany's leading institutions specializing in literature concerning the history of art. It also moved to the Culture Forum on Potsdamer Platz in 1994. The library offers a broad range of impressive collections including: an important collection of about 30,000 architectural drawings, ornamental prints and drawings, the Lipperheide costume library, posters and advertisements, the collection of graphic design, the collection book design, and the collection of photographs.

Antoine Watteau (1684–1721),
Der Tanz (The Dance), um/c. 1719,
Öl auf Leinwand/oil on canvas,
97 × 116 cm, Gemäldegalerie.

Pieter Bruegel d. Ä./the Elder
(um/c. 1525/30–1569),
Der Alchimist (The Alchemist),
1558, Ausschnitt/detail,
Federzeichnung/pen-and-ink
drawing, bräunliche Tinte/
brownish ink, 30,8 x 45,3 cm,
Kupferstichkabinett/Museum of
Prints and Drawings.

Hans Baldung Grien
(1484/85–1545),
Der Hexensabbat (Witches'
Sabbath), 1510,
Holzschnitt/woodcut,
ohne Tonplatte/without color
woodblock, 37,9 x 26 cm,
Kupferstichkabinett/Museum of
Prints and Drawings.

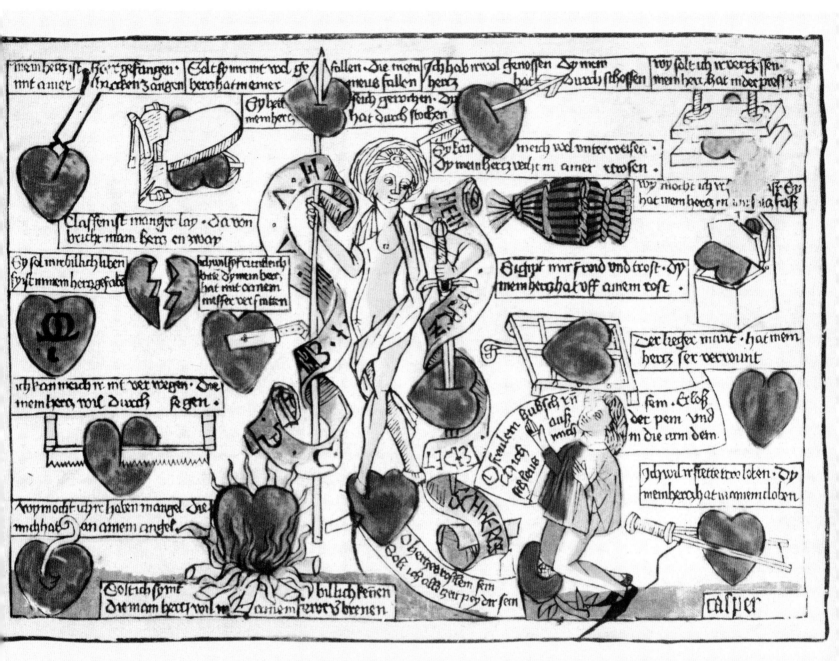

Meister Caspar von Regensberg,
Die Macht der Frau Minne
(The Power of Lady Love),
kolorierter Einblattholzschnitt/
hand-colored single-leaf wood cut,
15. Jh./15th century,
Kupferstichkabinett/Museum of
Prints and Drawings.

Albrecht Dürer (1471–1528),
Dürers Mutter (Dürer's Mother),
1514, Kohlezeichnung auf Papier/
charcoal on paper, eigenhändig
beschriftet/inscribed by the
artist, 42 x 30 cm,
Kupferstichkabinett/Museum of
Prints and Drawings.

Links/Left: Rembrandt,
Harmensz van Rijn (1606–1669),
Selbstbildnis mit Pelzmütze
(Self-Portrait in Fur Hat), 1631,
Radierung/etching, 6,4 x 6 cm,
Kupferstichkabinett/Museum of
Prints and Drawings.

Daniel Nikolaus Chodowiecki
(1726–1801),
Türkische Reitergruppe
(Group of Turkish Riders), 1763,
Aquarell/watercolor,
11,2 x 17,2 cm,
Kupferstichkabinett/Museum of
Prints and Drawings.

Mathis Gothart Grünewald
(um/c. 1470/75–1528),
*Figurenstudie zu dem Heiligen
Antonius des Isenheimer Altars*
(figure study of St. Anthony of the
Isenheim Altar), um 1512/16,
Kreidezeichnung auf Papier/
chalk drawing on paper, 29 x 20 cm,
Kupferstichkabinett/Museum of
Prints and Drawings.

Adolph von Menzel (1815–1905),
*Arbeiter an der Deichsel des
Transportwagens* (Workers at the
Drawbar of the Trolley), 1872/74,
Teilstudie für das Gemälde
Eisenwalzwerk, (detail study for
his painting *Steel Rolling Mill*),
Bleistift auf Papier/pencil on
paper, 40 x 26,2 cm,
Kupferstichkabinett/Museum of
Prints and Drawings.

Arnold Boecklin (1827–1901),
Kentaur und Nymphe (1855),
Aquarell auf bräunlichem Karton
(watercolor on brownish carton),
19,4 x 21,1 cm,
Kupferstichkabinett/Museum of
Prints and Drawings.

Paul Gauguin (1848–1903),
Die Entführung der Europa
(The Abduction of Europe),
um/c. 1896/98, Holzschnitt,
seitenverkehrter Abzug vom
originalen Holzstock/woodcut,
reverse copy of original woodblock, 24 x 23 cm,
Kupferstichkabinett/Museum of
Prints and Drawings.

Heinrich Zille (1858–1929),
Krach in der Destille
(Ruckus at the Pub), undat.,
Kreidezeichnung/chalk drawing,
29,7 x 37,1 cm,
Kupferstichkabinett/Museum of
Prints and Drawings.

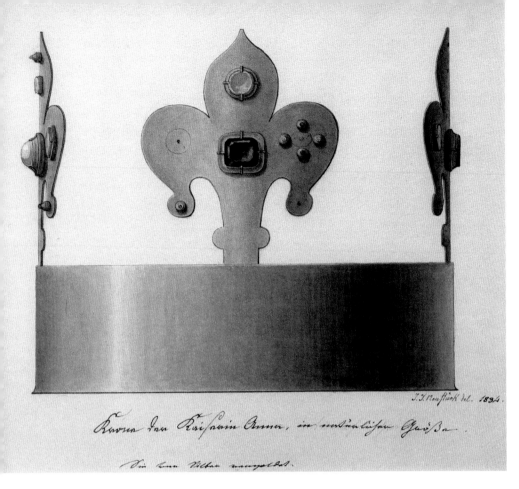

Karan der Kaiserin Anna, in natürlicher Größe.

Die ... Silber ...

Schätze aus dem Berliner Kunstgewerbemuseum I:
Oben links: Grabkrone der Königin Anna, Gemahlin König Rudolf I., 1281, vergoldetes Silberblech, Höhe 14 cm, Durchmesser 17,6 cm.

Unten links: Heinrichskreuz, Deutschland, um 1025, vordere Seite mit Goldblech, Goldfiligran, Silberperlen, Edelsteine, Glasflüsse, Rückseite Silberblech, vergoldet, Höhe 51,2 cm.

Unten rechts: Armreliquiar des Heiligen Georg, Braunschweig, um 1350, Silberblech, getrieben, gestanzt, graviert und vergoldet, Edelsteine und Glasflüsse, Höhe 55,3 cm.

Treasures of the Berlin Museum of Decorative Arts I:
Above left: Burial crown of Queen Anna, consort of King Rudolf I, 1281, gilded sheet silver, height: 14 cm, diameter: 17.6 cm.

Below left: Henry's Cross, Germany, c. 1025, front faced with sheet gold, gold filigree, silver pearls, gems, glass paste; back with sheet silver, gilded, height: 51.2 cm.

Below right: Arm reliquary of St. George, Braunschweig, c. 1350, sheet silver, hammered, embossed, engraved, and gilded; gems and glass paste; height: 55.3 cm.

Schätze aus dem Berliner Kunstgewerbemuseum II:
Oben rechts: Frühstück-Service der Königlich Preußischen Porzellanmanufaktur (KPM), um 1780, Porträtmedaillons nach antiken Münzen.

Unten links: Kette des Schwanen-ritterordens, Kopie, 1887 oder früher, nach verschollenem Original aus dem 15. Jh., Kupfer, vergoldet, Länge 50 cm.

Unten rechts: KPM-Porzellan, um 1780, Deckeltasse mit Silhouette Katharinas der Großen, Initiale 'E(katerina)' in originaler Leder-schatulle, Apothekerbüchse mit Porträt Friedrichs II. von Preußen.

Treasures of the Berlin Museum of Decorative Arts II:
Above right: Breakfast table set made by the Royal Prussian Porcelain Manufactory (KPM), c. 1780, portrait medallions modeled on antique coins.

Below left: Necklace of the Order of the Swan Knights, copy, 1887 or earlier, after the lost original from the 15th century, copper, gilded, length: 50 cm.

Below right: KPM porcelain, c. 1780, lidded cup with silhouette of Catherine the Great, initialed 'E(katerina)' in original leather casket; medicine box with portrait of Frederick II of Prussia.

214

Die nach einem Entwurf von
Ludwig Mies van der Rohe
(1886–1969) im Jahr 1968
eröffnete Neue Nationalgalerie
mit der Plastik von Henry Moore,
Der Bogenschütze, 1964.

The New National Gallery,
designed by Ludwig Mies van der
Rohe (1886–1969), opened in
1968, with Henry Moore's
sculpture, *The Archer*, 1964.

Wahrzeichen von Anfang an:
Installation von Alexander Calder
(1898–1976), *Köpfe und Schwanz*,
1965, im Hintergrund die
St.-Matthäus-Kirche von Friedrich
August Stülers .

Emblematic right from the start:
Alexander Calder (1898–1976),
Heads and Tail, 1965, in the
background: Friedrich August
Stüler's St. Matthew's Church.

Seit ihrer Eröffnung im Jahr 1968 ist Ludwig Mies van der Rohes *Neue Nationalgalerie* ein architektonisches Monument, das in seiner Anziehungskraft mit den darin ausgestellten Sammlungen konkurriert. Die Stahlkonstruktion einer Glashalle mit freitragendem, quadratischem Dach knüpft an eine Reihe ähnlicher Hallenprojekte in Mies van der Rohes Werk an. Die erste Fassung dieses Bautyps entwarf er für ein Verwaltungsgebäude von Bacardi-Rum auf Kuba, das aber nie ausgeführt wurde. Auffällig ist die Beziehung zwischen dem gläsernen Tempel und den klassizistischen Bauten von Karl Friedrich Schinkel und seinen Nachfolgern, mit denen die Geschichte der Berliner Museen so untrennbar verbunden ist.

Der neue Bau in West-Berlin beherbergte bis zum Fall der Mauer die Werke aus der (Alten) Nationalgalerie, die nach dem Krieg im Westen geblieben waren, und die 1945 gegründete Sammlung der Galerie des 20. Jahrhunderts, die den Verlust von über vierhundert Werken der Moderne durch die Naziherrschaft wieder gutmachen sollte. Seit der Umstrukturierung der Museen im wiedervereinten Berlin sind in der Neuen

Zu den herausragenden Künstlern der Sammlung der Neuen Nationalgalerie gehören, von oben links dieser Seite nach unten rechts der nächsten Seite, Max Beckmann (Foto 1938), Rudolf Belling (im Berliner Atelier 1926), George Grosz (an der Staffelei, undat.), Hannah Höch (in ihrem Atelier in Berlin-Heiligensee, 1970), Paul Klee (1921), Salvador Dalí (um 1960), Otto Dix (1947), Lyonel Feininger (1931), Oskar Kokoschka (um 1925), Edvard Munch (1943) und Pablo Picasso (mit bemalter Keramikschale, 1948).

Since its opening in 1968, Ludwig Mies van der Rohe's *New National Gallery* has functioned as an architectural monument whose attractiveness makes it compete with its own exhibitions. Its steel-framed glass hall topped by a cantilever, square roof ties it to a series of similar hall projects by Mies van der Rohe. He designed the first version of this building type for an administrative structure commissioned by Bacardi Rum in Cuba but never realized. The relationship between this glass temple and Neoclassicist buildings by Karl Friedrich Schinkel and his successors is quite striking, given that the history of Berlin's museums is so intrinsically bound up with the latter.

Until the fall of the Berlin Wall, the new building in West Berlin served as a home for the works of the (Old) National Gallery, which had remained in the West after the war, and for the collection of the "Gallery of the 20th Century," founded in 1945 and intended to compensate for the loss, due to the Nazi regime, of over four hundred modern works. Since the restructuring of the museums in reunified Berlin, sculpture and

Nationalgalerie Skulpturen und Gemälde vom Beginn des 20. Jahrhunderts bis in die 1960er-Jahre beheimatet, vom Expressionismus, Kubismus, Bauhaus, Surrealismus und Verismus bis zur Neuen Sachlichkeit. Hinzu kommt eine feine Sammlung amerikanischer Malerei der 1960er- und 1970er-Jahre.

Zu den Kernstücken gehören elf Gemälde von Max Beckmann, die einen Querschnitt durch sein Schaffen ab 1906 bieten, Werke von Edvard Munch, Ernst Ludwig Kirchner, Lyonel Feininger, Oskar Kokoschka, Otto Dix, George Grosz, Hannah Höch, Paul Klee, Wassily Kandinsky, Pablo Picasso, Joan Miró, Salvador Dalí, Yves Klein, Lucio Fontana, Morris Louis und Johannes Grützke sowie das letzte Gemälde des New Yorkers Barnett Newman „Who's Afraid of Red, Yellow and Blue IV" (1969/70), dessen „Broken Obelisk" (1963) auch die Eingangsfront ziert.

Obwohl die permanente Schau schon spektakulär ist, wird sie oft von den Sonderausstellungen übertroffen. Dann aber kann die Sammlung des Hauses meist nicht gezeigt werden.

Among the outstanding artists of the New National Gallery collection are, from the upper left of the previous page to the lower right of this page, Max Beckmann (photo 1938), Rudolf Belling (in his Berlin studio, 1926), George Grosz (at the easel, undated), Hannah Höch (in her studio in Berlin-Heiligensee, 1970), Paul Klee (1921), Salvador Dali (c. 1960), Otto Dix (1947), Lyonel Feininger (1931), Oskar Kokoschka (c. 1925), Edvard Munch (1943), and Pablo Picasso (with painted ceramic bowl, 1948).

paintings from the early 20th century through the 1960s are shown in the New National Gallery; these works range from Expressionism, Cubism, Bauhaus, Surrealism, and Verism, up to New Objectivity. There is also a fine collection of American paintings of the 1960s and 1970s.

Among the gallery's core exhibits are eleven paintings by Max Beckmann, which present a cross-section of his work starting in 1906, works by Edvard Munch, Ernst Ludwig Kirchner, Lyonel Feininger, Oskar Kokoschka, Otto Dix, George Grosz, Hannah Höch, Paul Klee, Wassily Kandinsky, Pablo Picasso, Joan Miró, Salvador Dalí, Yves Klein, Lucio Fontana, Morris Louis, and Johannes Grützke as well as the final painting by New York artist Barnett Newman, "Who's Afraid of Red, Yellow and Blue IV" (1969/70), and whose "Broken Obelisk" (1963) also graces the entrance patio.

Even though the permanent exhibits of the New National Gallery are quite spectacular, they are frequently surpassed by the special exhibits. During those times, the regular collection is usually not on display.

Lesser Ury (1861–1931),
Nollendorfplatz bei Nacht
(Nollendorfplatz at Night), 1925,
Öl auf Leinwand/oil on canvas,
72,5 x 54,5 cm, Neue National-
galerie.

Links/Left: Ernst Ludwig Kirchner
(1880–1938), *Potsdamer Platz*,
1914, Öl auf Leinwand/oil on
canvas, 200 x 150 cm,
Neue Nationalgalerie.

August Macke (1887–1914),
Bildnis Franz Marc
(Portrait Franz Marc), 1910,
Öl auf Pappe/oil on cardboard,
50 x 39 cm, Neue Nationalgalerie.

Paula Modersohn-Becker
(1876–1907), *Selbstbildnis, Akt*
(Self-Portrait, Nude), 1906,
Öl auf Leinwand/oil on canvas,
170 x 70 cm, Neue Nationalgalerie.

Wilhelm Lehmbruck (1881–1919),
Große Kniende (Large Kneeling
Woman), 1911, Bronzeguss nach
Steinguss/bronze casting after
stone casting, Höhe/hight 178 cm,
Neue Nationalgalerie.

Wilhelm Lehmbruck (1881–1919),
Torso der Großen Stehenden
(Torso of Large Standing Woman),
1910, Steinguss/stone casting,
Höhe/hight 120 cm,
Neue Nationalgalerie.

László Moholy-Nagy (1895–1946),
Komposition Z VIII, 1924,
Leimfarbe auf Leinwand/
distemper on canvas, 114 x 132 cm,
Neue Nationalgalerie.

Rechts/Right:
Max Ernst (1891–1976),
Capricorne, 1948/1964, farbig
gefasster Gips/slightly colored
plaster of Paris, 246 x 210 x 155 cm,
Neue Nationalgalerie.

Zwischen Kreuzberg und Wannsee – vom Jüdischen Museum bis zur Liebermann-Villa

Spätestens mit dem Bau der Mauer behauptete sich West-Berlin auch als neue Museumsstadt. Neben den „Zwillingen", Sammlungen also, die ein Pendant im Ostteil der Stadt hatten, zeugen davon noch immer die damals neu gegründeten Häuser wie das Bauhaus-Archiv am Tiergarten, das Bröhan-Museum, das neben dem Charlottenburger Schloss mit dem Museum Berggruen und der Sammlung Scharf-Gerstenberg einen neuen Schwerpunkt der Moderne setzt, oder das Georg-Kolbe-Museum nahe dem Olympiastadion. Im Süden West-Berlins formierte sich ein weiteres Zentrum der Kultur mit den Dahlemer außereuropäischen Sammlungen und dem Brücke-Museum. Hier befindet sich mit dem Jagdschloss Grunewald das älteste Renaissancezeugnis auf Berliner Boden.

Johann Erdmann Hummel (1769–1852), *Die Granitschale im Berliner Lustgarten* (Granite Bowl in Pleasure Garden), 1831, Öl auf Leinwand/oil on canvas, 66 x 88 cm, Märkisches Museum.

Between Kreuzberg and Wannsee – from the Jewish Museum to Liebermann Villa

No later than the building of the Wall did West Berlin also begin asserting itself as a new city of museums. Apart from the "twins," those collections having their counterpart in the Eastern part of the city, it is the newly founded museums of that time which prove this still today: such as the Bauhaus Archive at Tiergarten; the Bröhan Museum that, along with the Berggruen Museum next to Charlottenburg Palace and the Collection Scharf-Gerstenberg, provides a new focus on modernism; or the Georg Kolbe Museum close to the Olympic Stadium. Another cultural center emerged in southern West Berlin featuring the non-European collections in Dahlem and the Brücke Museum. Grunewald Hunting Palace is located here, the oldest Renaissance building on Berlin soil. Construction began

Carl Hasenpflug (1802–1858),
Die Domkirche in Berlin
(Berlin Cathedral), 1825,
Öl auf Leinwand/oil on canvas,
58,6 x 76,2 cm,
Märkisches Museum.

Ab 1542 nach einem Entwurf von Caspar Theyss für den Kurfürsten Joachim II. „im grünen Walde" errichtet, präsentiert es neben einem Jagdzeugmagazin auch eine Sammlung hochwertiger Gemälde von deutschen und niederländischen Künstlern aus dem 16. bis 19. Jahrhundert. Das Haus am Waldsee zeigt in einer stattlichen Villa wechselnde Ausstellungen mit zeitgenössischer Kunst. Aus dem einstigen Landgut, der Domäne Dahlem, ist im alten Dorfkern ein Freilichtmuseum geworden. Das Alliierten Museum auf dem Gelände des ehemaligen Outpost-Kinos der US-Streitkräfte zeigt neben einem originalen „Rosinenbomber" aus der Blockadezeit Berlins ein Kontrollhäuschen vom Checkpoint Charlie und alles, was an den Viermächtestatus der geteilten Stadt erinnert.

Seit über 130 Jahren blättert das *Märkische Museum* die geschichtliche und städtebauliche Entwicklung Berlins durch die

in 1542; designed by Caspar Theyss, the palace was built "in the green forest" for Elector Joachim II; in addition to a depot of hunting implements, it also showcases a collection of valuable paintings by German and Dutch artists of the 16th–19th centuries. The Haus am Waldsee presents varying exhibits of contemporary art in a grand villa setting. The old village center of the former country estate Dahlem Domain has since been transformed into an open-air museum. Apart from an original "Raisin Bomber" airplane from the times of the Berlin blockade, the Allied Museum on the site of the former Outpost Cinema of the American Army also exhibits a Checkpoint Charlie cabin and just about anything that commemorates the status of the divided city under the Four Power Agreement.

For over 130 years, the *Museum of the Mark Brandenburg* has been examining Berlin's historical and architectural develop-

Carl Graeb (1816–1884),
Das alte Berliner Rathaus
(Old City Hall in Berlin), 1867,
Öl auf Leinwand/oil on canvas,
76 × 94,5 cm,
Märkisches Museum.

Jahrhunderte auf, von den dörflichen Anfängen bis zur größten deutschen Stadt heute. Das Gebäude entstand von 1901 bis 1907 nach Plänen des Berliner Stadtbaurats Ludwig Hoffmann. Davor war das 1874 gegründete Museum provisorisch im Palais Podewils untergebracht. Hoffmann konstruierte es nach Vorbildern der Backsteingotik und Renaissance. Die märkische Region, die im Museum dokumentiert wird, kommt bereits in der Architektur zur Anschauung: Der walmdachbekrönte Turm ist dem Bergfried der Bischofsburg in Wittstock nachempfunden, die Schaugiebel und die Ornamentik der gotischen Fassade kopieren die St. Katharinenkirche in Brandenburg/Havel. Auch der Roland, der als Reproduktion vor dem Haupteingang des Museums steht, stammt in seinem Entwurf von dort. Die Innenräume inszenieren bestimmte Stimmungen,

ment throughout the centuries, from its rural beginnings to its status as Germany's greatest city today. The museum was built in 1901–1907 based on designs by Berlin city surveyor Ludwig Hoffmann. In earlier times, the museum, established in 1874, was provisionally housed at Podewils Palace. Hoffmann modeled his structure on Gothic brick buildings and Renaissance predecessors. Also documented by the museum, Brandenburg region already reveals itself in the building's architecture: The tower with its hipped roof imitates the castle tower of Bishop Castle in Wittstock; the gable tops and other ornaments of the gothic façade copy St Catharine's Church in Brandenburg/Havel. The "Roland" reproduction in front of the museum's main entrance is from the same region. The interior rooms project certain moods to bring the past back

um vergangene Zeiten erlebbar zu machen: Schwerter und Ritterrüstungen werden in der mittelalterlichen Waffenhalle mit Sterngewölbe gezeigt, sakrale Kunstwerke in der gotischen Kapelle.

Herausragende Stücke in dieser eigenwilligen Architektur-assemblage sind etwa das einzige erhaltene Originalteil der Quadriga vom Brandenburger Tor, ein Pferdekopf, Gemälde von Anton von Werner und Edvard Munch, die Abteilung Theater- und Literaturgeschichte von 1750 bis 1933, eine einzigartige Sammlung von Musikautomaten und das Kaiserpanorama.

Der bedeutende historische Museumsbau ist das Stammhaus der Stiftung Stadtmuseum, die 1995 im Zuge der Neuordnung der Berliner stadthistorischen Sammlungen entstand. Dazu gehören dreizehn über die Stadt verteilte Museen wie das

Links/Left: Karl Wilhelm Wach (1787–1845) nach/after P.E. Stroehling, *Königin Luise als Hebe vor dem Brandenburger Tor* (Queen Louise as Hebe in front of Brandenburg Gate), 1812, Öl auf Kupfer/oil on copper, 62 x 46 cm, Märkisches Museum.

Emil Koller (tätig/fl. 1828–47), *Kurrendesänger* (Carol Singers), 1847, 63 x 71 cm, Märkisches Museum.

to life: Swords and knights' armor are shown in the medieval armory with stellar vault, religious art in the Gothic chapel.

There are some extraordinary pieces amidst this idiosyncratic architectural assemblage, for example, the sole surviving original fragment of the Quadriga on Brandenburg Gate: a horse's head; paintings by Anton von Werner and Edvard Munch; the section for theater and literary history from 1750 to 1933; a unique collection of some jukeboxes, and the Emperor Panorama.

This important historicist museum building serves as headquarters of the Berlin City Museum Foundation, established in 1995 following the reorganization of Berlin's city-historical collections. The foundation is composed of thirteen museums located all across the city, including Ephraim Palace,

Rechts oben/Right above:
Leopold Zielke (um/c. 1790–1861),
Vor den Toren Berlins
(Outside the Gates of Berlin),
1845, Aquarell/watercolor,
30 x 41 cm, Märkisches Museum.

Johann Heinr. Hintze (1800–1861),
*Blick auf die Kurfürstenbrücke
vom Mühlendamm aus*
(View of the Bridge of the Elector
from Mühlendamm), um/c. 1830,
Öl auf Holz/oil on wood, 60 x 76 cm,
Märkisches Museum.

August von Rentzell (1810–1891),
*Gegend von Treptow mit Aussicht
auf Stralau* (Area of Treptow with
view of Stralau), um/c. 1840,
Öl auf Leinwand/oil on canvas,
34 x 58 cm, Märkisches Museum.

Unten links: Gewerkschaftsfahne
der Berliner Zigarrenarbeiter, 1858;
rechts: „Wappen der Königlichen
Haupt- und Residenz-Stadt
Berlin", Farblithographie, um 1840,
von Hildebrandt nach Asmus,
Märkisches Museum.

Below left: Labor Union Flag of
Berlin's Cigar Workers, 1858;
right: "Coat of Arms of the Royal
Capital and Residence of Berlin",
color lithography, c. 1840,
by Hildebrandt after Asmus,
Märkisches Museum.

Ephraim-Palais, die Nikolaikirche, das Sportmuseum in Marzahn und Schloss Friedrichsfelde.

1975 von einer um den Kunsthistoriker Eberhard Roters versammelten Gruppe kunstsinniger Bürger gegründet, wurde die *Berlinische Galerie* schnell zu einer weit über die Grenzen der Stadt hinaus wirksamen, äußerst experimentierfreudigen Institution. Nach wechselnden Stationen ist das Museum für Moderne Kunst, Fotografie und Architektur 2004 gleich hinter

Anton von Werner (1843–1915), *Kriegsgefangen* (Prisoner of War), 1886 (Szene aus dem Deutsch-Französischen Krieg 1870–71/Scene from the Franco-Prussian War), Öl auf Leinwand/oil on canvas, 106 x 157 cm, Berlinische Galerie.

Nikolai Church, the Sports Museum in Marzahn, and Friedrichsfelde Palace.

Founded in 1975 by a group of art-minded citizens gathered around art historian Eberhard Roters, *Berlin Gallery* rapidly developed into an institution extremely eager to try out new things and active far beyond Berlin city limits. After moving from site to site, the Museum of Modern Art, Photography and Architecture found a home in 2004 in a former glass ware-

dem Jüdischen Museum in einem ehemaligen Glaslager von 1965 untergekommen. Die Industriehalle, die in einem von der Internationalen Bauausstellung hervorgebrachten Wohngebiet liegt, wurde nach Entwürfen des Architekten Jörg Fricke zu einem funktionalen großzügigen Haus für moderne Kunst umgebaut. Mehr als siebenhundert Werke von 1870 bis heute sind in der Dauerausstellung zu sehen: die Sezessionisten und die Jungen Wilden, Dada und Fluxus, Neue Sachlichkeit

Max Beckmann (1884–1950), *Die Straße* (The Street), 1914, Öl auf Leinwand/oil on canvas, 171 x 72 cm, Berlinische Galerie.

Rechts/Right: Lesser Ury (1861–1931), *Berliner Straßenszene* (Street Scene), 1889, Öl auf Leinwand/oil on canvas, 107 x 68 cm.

house built in 1965, just behind the Jewish Museum. This factory building, located in an area made prominent by the International Architecture Exhibition, was transformed into a functional, generous house of modern art based on designs by architect Jörg Fricke. More than seven hundred works from 1870 to the present day are on permanent exhibit: so the the works of Secessionists and the New Fauves, Dada and Fluxus, New Objectivity and Expressionism, Russians in Berlin,

Ernst Ludwig Kirchner (1880–1938),
Kauerndes Mädchen (Crouching
Girl), um/c. 1910,
Aquarell, Kreide auf bräunlichem
Papier/watercolor, chalk on
brownish paper, 43,8 x 33,8 cm,
Berlinische Galerie.

Links/Left:
Georg Baselitz (geb./b. 1938),
Ein moderner Maler
(A Modern Painter), 1966,
Öl auf Leinwand/oil on canvas,
162 x 130 cm, Berlinische Galerie.

und Expressionismus, Russen in Berlin, die Avantgarde in Architektur und Fotografie, Berlin unterm Hakenkreuz, die Stadt in Trümmern, Ost-Berlin und West-Berlin, die vereinte Metropole und die kreative zeitgenössische Szene. Das Spektrum reicht von Malerei, Grafik und Skulpturen über Video bis hin zur Fotografie. Im Spagat zwischen der international orientierten Nationalgalerie und dem kulturhistorischen Stadtmuseum sammelt, erforscht und präsentiert das Museum in Berlin entstandene Kunst – von Otto Dix über Heinrich Zille bis Hannah Höch, Georg Baselitz und Via Lewandowsky.

Das expressive Gebäude des *Jüdischen Museums* auf dem Grundriss einer blitzähnlichen Zickzacklinie ist ein Meisterwerk zeitgenössischer Architektur. Noch vor seiner Eröffnung 2001 war es ein Besuchermagnet. Denn Daniel Libeskinds Entwurf ist ein Kunststück der besonderen Klasse. Durch seine Zinkblechfassade, in die unregelmäßig Fensteröffnungen wie Schlitze eingeschnitten sind, gewinnt der Bau einen abstrak-

Links/Left:
Hans Baluschek (1870–1925),
Weißbieridyll (Wheat Beer Idyll),
um/c. 1902, Pastell, 98 x 66 cm,
Berlinische Galerie.

Rechts/Right:
Adelchi-Riccardo Mantovani
(geb./b. 1942), *Der Tod der Medusa*
(Death of Medusa), 1982,
Mischtechnik auf Tafel/mixed
media on board, 50 x 40 cm,
Berlinische Galerie.

the avant-garde in architecture and photography, Berlin under the swastika, the city in ruins, East Berlin and West Berlin, the unified metropolis, and the creative contemporary scene. Its gamut runs from painting, graphic arts and sculpture to video arts and photography. Straddling the divide between the internationally oriented National Gallery and the culture-and-history-focused City Museum, this museum collects, studies and presents art made in Berlin – from Otto Dix to Heinrich Zille, from Hannah Höch and Georg Baselitz to Via Lewandowsky.

Its ground plan resembling a zigzag lightning bolt, the famous expressive building of the *Jewish Museum* is a masterpiece of contemporary architecture. Even before its opening in 2001, it already functioned as a magnet for visitors – because Daniel Libeskind's design is a very special work of art. Its façade of zinc plate, into which are cut irregular window openings looking like gashes, makes the building

Franz Skarbina (1849–1910),
Auf der Digue, Ostende
(On the Boardwalk, Ostend), 1883,
Öl auf Leinwand/oil on canvas,
136 x 85,5 cm, Berlinische Galerie.

ten, zeichenhaften Charakter. Drei Achsen erschließen die asymmetrischen, spitzwinkligen Räume: Die „Achse des Exils" weist in den E. T. A. Hoffmann-Garten, die „Achse des Holocaust" endet vor einer Stahltür, hinter der sich der leere, dunkle Holocaust-Turm verbirgt, und die „Achse der historischen Kontinuität" führt in die Ausstellung, die in fünfzehn Abteilungen anhand von persönlichen Dokumenten, Zeremonialobjekten, Gemälden, Büchern, Fotografien, Münzen, Zeitungen usw. zwei Jahrtausende deutsch-jüdischer Kulturgeschichte vorstellt. Das größte jüdische Museum Europas zeigt auch, wie Deutschland durch die Vielfalt jüdischen Lebens geprägt und gestaltet wurde. Als das Museum eröffnete, erhielt Berlin nach über sechzig Jahren wieder ein Jüdisches Museum – ein erstes war im Januar 1933 eingeweiht und 1938 von der Geheimen Staatspolizei der Nationalsozialisten geschlossen worden. Nach dem Krieg wurde eine Jüdische Sammlung im damaligen Berlin-Museum gezeigt, in Philipp Gerlachs 1735 erbautem barocken Kollegienhaus, das heute gleichfalls zum Jüdischen Museum gehört.

appear abstract, symbolic. Three axes unlock the asymmetrical, sharp-angled rooms: The "Axis of Exile" points towards E. T. A. Hoffmann Garden; the "Axis of the Holocaust" dead-ends in front of a steel door behind which lies hidden the empty, dark Holocaust Tower, and the "Axis of Historical Continuity" guides visitors to the exhibition encompassing fifteen sections that showcase two millennia of German-Jewish cultural history by means of personal documents, ceremonial objects, paintings, books, photographs, coins, newspapers, etc. The largest Jewish Museum in Europe also shows how Germany was marked and shaped by the multiplicity of its Jewish life. When the museum first opened its doors in 2001, Berlin regained its first Jewish Museum in over sixty years – the first had opened in January 1933 and was closed in 1938 by the National Socialist secret police. After the war, a Jewish collection was on exhibit in the former Berlin Museum, in Philipp Gerlach's Baroque College House, built in 1735 and also belonging to the Jewish Museum today.

Wie ein Blitz schlägt der Gebäudekomplex des Jüdischen Museums mit seiner Zinkblechfassade in den Raum, Daniel Libeskind, 1992-99, eröffnet 2001.

The new building complex of the Jewish Museum with its zinc plate façade strikes into space like a bolt of lightning, Daniel Libeskind, 1992-99, opened in 2001.

Außen- und Innenansichten des Jüdischen Museums.
Oben: „Garten des Exils",
unten: Fensteröffnungen, unregelmäßig ins Zinkblech eingeschnitten wie Schlitze.

Exterior and interior views of the Jewish Museum.
Above: "Garden of Exile,"
below: window openings resembling slashes cut irregularly into the zinc plate covering.

Rechte Seite, links:
Sackler Treppe an der „Achse der Kontinuität";
rechts oben: Glashofausbau „Sukkah" nach einem Entwurf von Daniel Libeskind (2007);
unten: drei divergente Achsen: die „Achse der Kontinuität", die „Achse des Exils" und die „Achse des Holocaust".

Right page, left:
Sackler Staircase on the "Axis of Continuity";
right above: glass high-rise "Sukkah" designed by Daniel Libeskind (2007);
below: three divergent axes: the "Axis of Continuity," the "Axis of Exile" and the "Axis of the Holocaust."

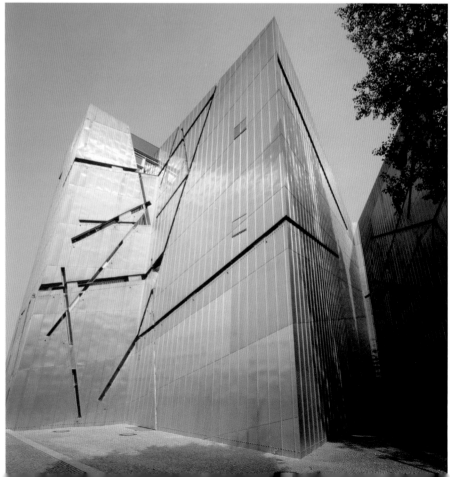

Der Berliner Neubau des *Bauhaus-Archivs*, der neben dem Museum eine Dokumentensammlung und eine Bibliothek beherbergt, wurde 1976 bis 1979 nach einem Entwurf von Walter Gropius errichtet. Der durch seine Tätigkeit als Direktor am Bauhaus zuerst in Weimar, dann in Dessau bekannte Architekt hatte nach seiner Rückkehr aus dem Exil an der Gründung des Bauhaus-Archivs seit 1961 mitgearbeitet. Sein unverwechselbares Aussehen erhält der zweigeschossige weiße Bau durch die Lichtsheds, deren Fenster nach Norden ausgerichtet sind. Diese sorgen für eine kontrollierte Lichtführung und erlauben eine optimale Präsentation der Exponate.

Der klar gegliederte, puristische Baukörper umfasst in seinem Innern das Archiv und Schauräume, in denen Sonderausstellungen und aus den Beständen Architekturmodelle, Entwürfe, Gemälde, Fotografien, Alltagsgegenstände und Möbel aus der Bauhaus-Zeit von 1919 bis 1932 präsentiert werden. Vertreten sind die Architekten Walter Gropius, Marcel Breuer und Ludwig Mies van der Rohe sowie die Künstler Oskar Schlemmer, László Moholy-Nagy, Paul Klee, Wassily Kandinsky, Johannes Itten und Marianne Brandt. Das Bauhaus-Archiv besitzt die umfangreichste Sammlung dieser weltberühmten Schule für Architektur, Design und Kunst im 20. Jahrhundert. Neben historischen Themen aus dem Umkreis des Bauhauses widmet sich das Bauhaus-Archiv auch Fragen der zeitgenössischen Architektur und dem Design.

In den nächsten Jahren wird das Museum mit dem Star-Architekten-Duo SANAA aus Tokio, Kazuyo Sejima und Ryue Nishizawa, einen dringend nötigten Erweiterungsbau entwickeln.

Das Bauhaus-Archiv nach einem Entwurf von Walter Gropius (1883–1969), erbaut 1976–79.

The Bauhaus Archive, designed by Walter Gropius (1883–1969), built in 1976–79.

Housing a museum, a collection of documents and a library, the modern Berlin building of the *Bauhaus Archive* was constructed in 1976–1979 based on a design by Walter Gropius. The architect, who became famous as Bauhaus director, first in Weimar, then in Dessau, had collaborated on founding the Bauhaus since 1961, after his return from exile. The distinctive look of the white, two-story structure is due to shed roofs whose windows face northward. They supply a controlled influx of light and so facilitate an optimal presentation of the exhibits.

The clearly articulated, purist body of the structure contains in its interior the archive and exhibition halls, where special exhibitions as well as exhibits from the permanent collections showcase architectural models, blueprints, paintings, photographs, everyday objects, and furniture from the Bauhaus period of 1919–1932. Architects Walter Gropius, Marcel Breuer and Ludwig Mies van der Rohe are as much on display as artists Oskar Schlemmer, László Moholy-Nagy, Paul Klee, Wassily Kandinsky, Johannes Itten, and Marianne Brandt. The Bauhaus Archive owns the most comprehensive collection of items by this world-famous 20th century school of architecture, design and art. Besides historical themes centering on the Bauhaus, the Bauhaus Archive also examines issues of contemporary architecture and design.

In the next few years, the museum will collaborate with SANAA, Tokyo's duo of star architects Kazuyo Sejima and Ryue Nishizawa, on developing a much needed expansion of the building.

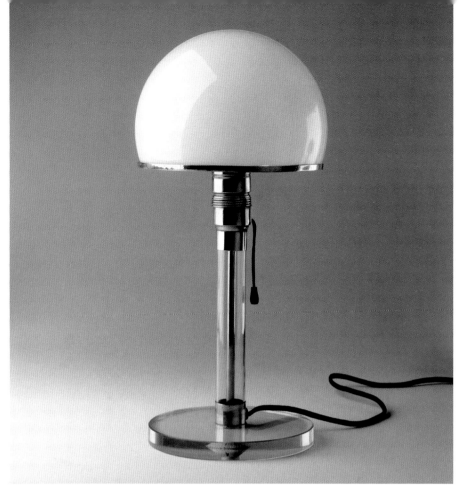

Wilhelm Wagenfeld (1900–1990), Tischleuchte (1924) mit Glasfuß oder Metallfuß, Schirm in Opalglas, Durchmesser 18 cm, Höhe 36 cm. C. J. Jucker hatte bereits 1923, ebenfalls im Auftrag des damaligen Leiters der Metallwerkstatt László Moholy-Nagy, Vorgängermodelle der Glasversion entwickelt.

Wilhelm Wagenfeld (1900–1990), Table lamp (1924) with glass base or metal base, shade made of opal glass, diameter: 18 cm, height: 36 cm. C. J. Jucker had already designed previous models of the glass version in 1923 by order of the former head of the Metal Workshop, László Moholy-Nagy.

Unten:
Marcel Breuer (1902–1981), Sessel „Wassily", 1925, Stahlrohr, verchromt und poliert, schwarzer Eisengarnstoff, 76 x 78 x 69 cm; rechts: höhenverstellbarer Drehstuhl B 7, 1926/27, Stahlrohr, verchromt, schwarz lackiertes Holz, Eisengarn, Höhe 93,5 cm.

Below:
Marcel Breuer (1902–1981), „Wassily" chair, 1925, steel tubing, chrome-plated and polished, black iron yarn fabric, 76 x 78 x 69 cm; right: height adjustable, swivel chair B 7, 1926/27, steel tubing, chrome-plated, wood with black varnish, iron yarn, height: 93.5 cm.

Die Helmut Newton Stiftung in einem ehemaligen Offizierscasino, umgebaut vom Architekturbüro Kahlfeldt 2003–04.
Oben: Foyer mit Newtons provokativer Serie *Big Nudes*, Ikonen der Fotogeschichte.
Unten: June Newton bei der Eröffnung des Hauses in Berlin vor Porträts von Helmut Newton und ihrer selbst.
Rechte Seite: Installationsansicht *Us and Them* (oben) und ein Blick in die Präsentation *A Gun For Hire*, wie Helmut Newton (1920–2004) sich selbst und seine Kunst gelegentlich bezeichnete.

The Helmut Newton Foundation housed in a former military casino, remodeled by the architectural firm of Kahlfeldt 2003–04.
Above: Foyer with Newton's provocative series "Big Nudes," icons of photo history.
Below: June Newton during the opening in Berlin in front of portraits of Helmut Newton and herself.
Right page: View of the installation *Us and Them* (above) and a glimpse of the presentation, *A Gun For Hire*, as Helmut Newton (1920–2004) occasionally called himself and his art.

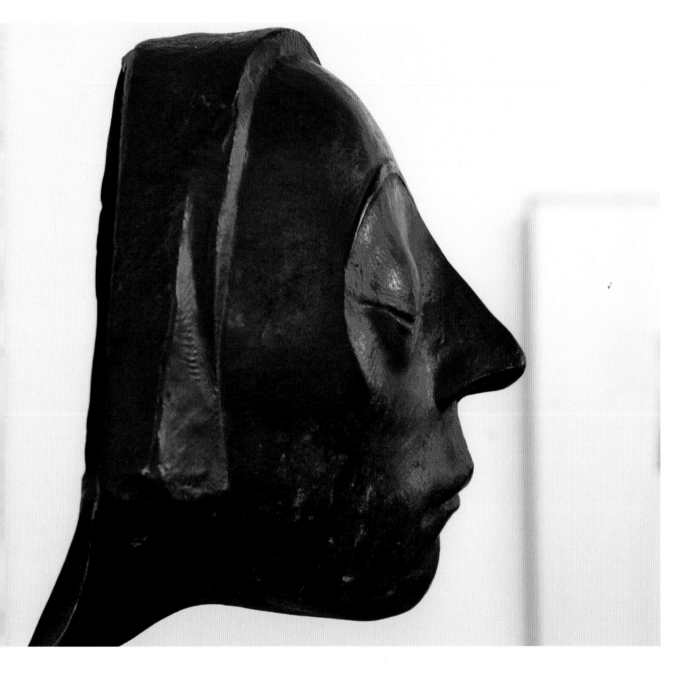

Das *Käthe-Kollwitz-Museum* im ältesten Wohnhaus in der Fasanenstraße aus dem Jahr 1871, einem spätklassizistischen Palais, ist ganz dem Schaffen der Wahlberlinerin gewidmet. Rund zweihundert Zeichnungen, Druckgrafiken und Plakate sowie das gesamte plastische Werk repräsentieren das vielfältige Œuvre einer der bekanntesten Künstlerinnen des 20. Jahrhunderts. Schwerpunkte der Kollektion bilden die Radierungen zum „Weberaufstand" (1898), der Holzschnittzyklus „Krieg" (1922/23) sowie Arbeiten zur Thematik Mutter, Kind und Krieg. Wie wichtig Käthe Kollwitz zeit ihres Lebens die genaue Selbstbeobachtung gewesen ist, zeigen ihre Selbstporträts von 1888 bis 1938. Von den mehr als hundert Zeichnungen und druckgrafischen Arbeiten aus dieser Reihe zeigt das Museum einen bedeutenden Querschnitt.

Ernst Barlach (1870–1938),
Kopf des Güstrower Ehrenmals
(Head of the Güstrow Memorial),
1927, Bronze, Höhe 35,6 cm,
Breite 33,3 cm, Tiefe 27,8 cm,
Käthe-Kollwitz-Museum.

Located in the oldest residential building on Fasanenstraße, a late Neoclassicist mansion dating back to 1871, the *Käthe-Kollwitz-Museum* is entirely dedicated to the creative activity of elective Berliner Käthe Kollwitz. About two hundred drawings, graphic prints and posters as well her entire sculptural output represent the manifold oeuvre of one of the most recognized female artists of the 20th century. Highlights of the collection are the etchings on the "Weavers' Revolt" (1898), the woodcuts cycle "War" (1922/23), as well as works on the themes of 'mother, child and war.' Her self-portraits of 1888–1938 demonstrate how important accurate self-reflection was to Käthe Kollwitz throughout her life. The museum showcases an important cross section of her more than hundred drawings and print graphical works in this series.

Mit dem Auszug der Alten Ägypter und ihrer Galionsfigur Nofretete aus dem Stülerbau gegenüber dem Schloss Charlottenburg schien der Stadtteil ins Abseits zu geraten. Doch seit sich Heinz Berggruens Sammlung hier niederließ, ist in wundersamer Zellteilung ein neues Museumsquartier entstanden, angedockt an das Jugendstil-Juwel des Bröhan-Museums. Ein aparter Schwerpunkt für die klassische Moderne etablierte sich hier.

Die private *Sammlung Berggruen* mit 165 Werken gilt als eine der weltweit bedeutendsten der klassischen Moderne. 2000, vier Jahre nach der Eröffnung des Hauses, vermachte Heinz Berggruen diesen Schatz für einen symbolischen Preis seiner Geburtsstadt Berlin. Eine Sensation – und zugleich eine Geste der Versöhnung, wie der Stifter sagte. Der jüdische

Rechts/Right: Pablo Picasso (1881–1973), *Der gelbe Pullover* (The Yellow Sweater), 1939, Öl auf Leinwand/oil on canvas, 81 x 65 cm, Sammlung Berggruen.

Unten: Ehemalige Kaserne Garde du Corps von Friedrich August Stüler (1851–59), Umbau Hilmer & Sattler und Albrecht, 1996.
Below: Former barracks Garde du Corps by Friedrich August Stüler (1851–59), remodeled by Hilmer & Sattler and Albrecht, 1996.

When the Old Egyptians and their figurehead Nefertiti moved out of the Stülerbau across from Charlottenburg Palace, this city quarter seemed to be getting relegated to the sidelines. But when Heinz Berggruen's collection moved in, docking onto the Art Nouveau jewel of the Bröhan Museum, a new museum district emerged as from a miraculous cell division. A distinctive center of gravity for classical modernism thus established itself in the area.

Comprising 165 works, the private *Berggruen Collection* is considered one of the most significant collections of classical modern art in the world. In 2000, four years after the museum's opening, Heinz Berggruen bequeathed this treasure trove for a symbolic sum to his native city of Berlin. A sensation – and also a gesture of forgiveness, as the donor said. Born in Char-

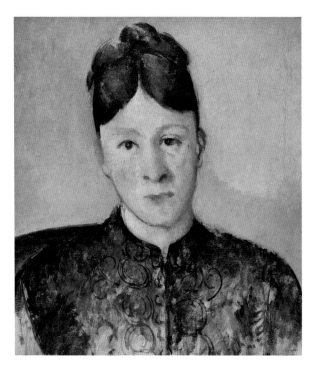

Oben/Above: Paul Cézanne
(1839–1906), *Junges Mädchen
mit Puppe* (Young Girl with Doll),
um/c. 1902/04, Öl auf Leinwand/oil
on canvas, 75 x 60 cm, Sammlung
Berggruen/Berggruen Collection.

Links/Left: Paul Cézanne
(1839–1906), *Portrait Madame
Cézanne*, um/c. 1885,
Öl auf Leinwand/oil on canvas,
46 x 38 cm, Sammlung Berggruen/
Berggruen Collection.

Oben/Above: Georges Seurat
(1859–1891), *Morgenspaziergang*
(Morning Stroll), 1884/85,
Öl auf Holz/oil on wood,
24,9 x 15,7 cm, Sammlung
Berggruen/Berggruen Collection.

Walter Leistikow (1865–1908),
Grunewaldsee oder Schlachtensee (Lake Grunewald or Lake Schlachtensee), Öl auf Leinwand/ oil on canvas, 80,5 x 121 cm, Bröhan-Museum.

Journalist Heinz Berggruen, 1914 in Charlottenburg geboren, emigrierte 1936 in die USA und gründete nach dem Zweiten Weltkrieg eine Galerie in Paris, die bald eine erste Adresse im internationalen Kunsthandel war. Berggruens vielgerühmte Freundschaften mit den Künstlern – allen voran Picasso – und seine Galeristenkontakte ermöglichten den Aufbau dieser einzigartigen Kollektion. Über siebzig höchst qualitätvolle Gemälde, Skulpturen und Papierarbeiten Picassos, von seiner Studienzeit in Madrid bis zum Spätwerk sind darin vertreten. Zu den wichtigsten Gemälden zählen der „Sitzende Harlekin" (1905) und „Der Maler und sein Modell" (1939). Daneben finden sich Hauptwerke von Paul Cézanne und Vincent van Gogh, Georges Braque und Georges Seurat, ein Raum mit Arbeiten von Alberto Giacometti und zwanzig kleinformatige Aquarelle, poetische Skripturen und fragile Malereien von Paul Klee. Das Innere des einstigen, von Friedrich August Stüler 1851 bis 1859 entworfenen Garde-du-Corps-Baus wurde für die Sammlung maßgeschneidert. Seit dem Tod Heinz Berggruens 2007 führt sein Sohn Nicolas das Erbe des Vaters fort. Fünfzig weitere Gemälde will er ins Museum nach Charlottenburg bringen, wofür das benachbarte Kommandantenhaus vorgesehen ist.

lottenburg in 1914, Jewish journalist Heinz Berggruen immigrated to the United States in 1936 and founded a gallery in Paris after World War II, which soon developed into a first port of call for the international arts' trade. Berggruen's highly praised friendships with the artists – above all with Picasso – and his gallery contacts made this unique collection possible. It showcases over seventy high-quality paintings, sculptures and works on paper by Picasso, from his student years in Madrid to his late works. His most important paintings include the "Seated Harlequin" (1905) and "The Painter and His Model" (1939). Also featured are major works by Paul Cézanne and Vincent van Gogh, Georges Braque and Georges Seurat, a room full of works by Alberto Giacometti, and twenty small-format watercolors, poetic scriptures and fragile paintings by Paul Klee. The interior of the former Garde-du-Corps building, designed by Friedrich August Stüler in 1851–1859, was custom-made for the collection. Since Heinz Berggruen's death in 2007, his son Nicolas has furthered the legacy of his father. He wants to add fifty additional paintings to the Charlottenburg museum, which will be housed in the neighboring Commander's House.

Thematisch eng an „Picasso und seine Zeit" schließt die *Sammlung Scharf-Gerstenberg* an, die 2008 in den östlichen Stülerbau einzog, wo einst das Ägyptische Museum residierte. Ihr Spektrum von herausragenden Werken des Surrealismus und seiner Vorläufer reicht von Piranesi, Goya und Redon bis zu Dalí, Magritte, Max Ernst und Dubuffet.

Jugendstil, Art Déco und Funktionalismus – Objekte der bildenden und angewandten Kunst aus drei Epochen zeigt das *Bröhan-Museum*. Es trägt den Namen des Sammlers Karl H. Bröhan, der im Jahr 1981 seine Privatsammlung, die er bis dahin in einer Dahlemer Villa gezeigt hatte, der Stadt Berlin zum Geschenk machte. Seither ist die feine Kollektion in einem ehamals zum Charlottenburger Schloss gehörenden Kasernengebäude aus der Zeit des Spätklassizismus untergebracht.

Sammlung Scharf-Gerstenberg, Gebäudeteil Marstall im Stülerbau, Gesamtumbau Gregor Sunder-Plassmann, 2008, mit der Bronzeskulptur *Figur in großer Höhe II* von Rolf Szymanski.

Scharf-Gerstenberg Collection, Marstall wing in the Stüler building, comprehensively remodeled by Gregor Sunder-Plassmann, 2008, with bronze sculpture "Figure Up High II" by Rolf Szymanski.

Thematically closely related to "Picasso and His Time" is the *Scharf-Gerstenberg Collection*, which moved into the eastern Stüler Building in 2008, the former home of the Egyptian Museum. Its gamut of extraordinary works of Surrealism and its precursors runs from Piranesi, Goya and Redon to Dalí, Magritte, Max Ernst, and Dubuffet.

Art Nouveau, Art Déco and Functionalism – objects of fine and applied arts from three periods are exhibited at the *Bröhan Museum*. It is named after collector Karl H. Bröhan who, in 1981, donated his private collection, previously exhibited only at his Dahlem villa, to the city of Berlin. Since then, the fine museum is housed in a barracks building dating back to late Neoclassicist times that once belonged to Charlottenburg Palace.

Ungewöhnlich ist die Präsentation der Stücke in Raumkunstensembles. Kunstobjekte und Gebrauchsgegenstände aus Porzellan, Keramik, Metall und Glas kombiniert mit Möbeln, Teppichen, Lampen und Gemälden werden in eleganter Wohnatmosphäre gezeigt – ein Zusammenspiel, das auch die Gleichwertigkeit verschiedener Kunstäußerungen klar veranschaulicht.

Schwerpunkte sind Arbeiten des französischen und des belgischen Art Nouveau, des deutschen und des skandinavischen Jugendstils sowie des französischen Art Déco. Die Gemäldesammlung umfasst Werke der Berliner Secession, etwa von Karl Hagemeister und Walter Leistikow. Zwei kleinere Kabinette sind dem belgischen Jugendstilkünstler Henry van de Velde und dem Wiener Secessionskünstler Josef Hoffmann gewidmet.

Rotunde mit Glasdach des Gebäudes von Friedrich August Stüler gegenüber dem Schloss Charlottenburg , Residenz der Sammlung Scharf-Gerstenberg für mindestens zehn Jahre.

Rotunda with glass roof of the building by Friedrich August Stüler vis-à-vis Charlottenburg Palace, seat of the Scharf-Gerstenberg Collection for at least ten years.

What is unusual is the presentation of items in the form of spatial art ensembles. In an elegant residential atmosphere, the artistic and utilitarian objects made of china, pottery clay, metal, and glass are exhibited in combination with furniture, carpets, lamps, and paintings – an interaction that likewise illustrates the equivalence of various artistic expressions.

Central features are works of French and Belgian Art Nouveau, of German and Scandinavian Art Nouveau (Jugendstil), and French Art Déco. Its collection of paintings features works of the Berlin Secession, e.g., by Karl Hagemeister and Walter Leistikow. Two smaller rooms are reserved for Belgian Art Nouveau artist Henry van de Velde and Viennese Secessionist Josef Hoffmann.

252

Georg Kolbe (1877–1947),
Der Morgen (Morning), Bronze,
Volkspark/People's Park
Schöneberg (Aufnahme/photo:
Barcelona, 1986)

Brunnen im Garten des
Georg-Kolbe-Museums
(Fountain in the garden of the
Georg Kolbe Museum).

Ernst Ludwig Kirchner (1880–1938),
Mit Schilf werfende Badende
(Bathers Throwing Reeds), 1910,
Farbholzschnitt/color woodcut,
19,5 x 28,5 cm, Brücke Museum.

Seine Entstehung verdankt das am Grunewald gelegene *Brücke-Museum* dem 1884 in der Nähe von Chemnitz geborenen Maler Karl Schmidt-Rottluff. Anlässlich seines achtzigsten Geburtstags übergab er Berlin im Dezember 1964 eine Schenkung von 74 eigenen Arbeiten. Sie bildet den Kern einer der bedeutendsten Sammlungen expressionistischer Kunst in Deutschland und der weltweit umfangreichsten von Werken der Künstlergruppe Die Brücke. Das Museum wurde 1966/67 nach Plänen von Werner Düttmann erbaut und steht architektonisch in der Tradition des Bauhauses. Es ist ausschließlich Arbeiten dieser avantgardistischen deutschen Künstlergruppe gewidmet. 1905 in Dresden gegründet, siedelte sie 1911 nach Berlin über, wo sie sich 1913 auflöste. Neben Werken der Gründungsmitglieder Karl Schmidt-Rottluff, Ernst Ludwig Kirchner, Fritz Bleyl und Erich Heckel, die in Dresden gemeinsam Architektur studierten, finden sich hier insgesamt mehr als vierhundert Gemälde von Max Pechstein, Otto Mueller und Emil Nolde. Ein Schwerpunkt sind zahlreiche Hauptwerke Kirchners, die einen Bogen von den Jahren in Dresden über die Berliner Großstadtbilder bis zu seiner Zeit in Davos spannen, wo er bis zu seinem Tod zurückgezogen in den Schweizer Alpen lebte und arbeitete.

Die märkische Waldlandschaft, die das Museum umgibt, spiegelt den Brücke-Grundsatz der Naturverbundenheit wider: Reizvoll wirkt sie in die Ausstellungsräume hinein.

Located close to Grunewald, the *Brücke Museum* owes its existence to painter Karl Schmidt-Rottluff, born near Chemnitz in 1884. On the occasion of his eightieth birthday, he donated 74 of his own works to Berlin in December 1964. They constitute the core of one the most significant collections of Expressionist art in Germany and the world's largest containing works by the artists' association Die Brücke (The Bridge). The museum was designed by architect Werner Düttmann and built in the Bauhaus architectural tradition in 1966/67. It is dedicated exclusively to the works of this avant-garde German artists' association. Founded in 1905 in Dresden, the group transferred to Berlin in 1911 and disbanded there in 1913. In addition to works by its founding members Karl Schmidt-Rottluff, Ernst Ludwig Kirchner, Fritz Bleyl, and Erich Heckel, all of whom went to the same architecture school in Dresden, more than four hundred works by Max Pechstein, Otto Mueller and Emil Nolde are likewise on display. Of central interest are several major works by Kirchner running the gamut from his years in Dresden, to his Berlin metropolitan paintings, to his time in Davos, where he lived a quiet life in the Swiss Alps until his death.

The Brandenburgian sylvan landscape surrounding the museum reflects the Brücke principle of closeness to nature: It enters appealingly into the areas of exhibition.

Linke Seite: Ernst Ludwig Kirchner
(1880–1938), *Artistin – Marcella*
(Female Artist – Marcella), 1910,
Öl auf Leinwand/oil on canvas,
100 x 76 cm, Brücke-Museum.

Oben links/Above right:
Erich Heckel (1883–1970),
Stehendes Kind (Standing Child),
1910, Holzschnitt/woodcut,
37,5 x 27,8 cm, Brücke-Museum.

Ernst Ludwig Kirchner (1880–1938),
Max Liebermann in seinem Atelier
(M.L. in his Studio), 1926,
Öl auf Leinwand/oil on canvas,
80 x 70 cm, Brücke-Museum.

Im Süden der Stadt, nahe dem Grunewald und dem Campus der Freien Universität gelegen, setzt das *Museumszentrum Dahlem* mit den außereuropäischen Kulturen einen besonderen Akzent. Die Pläne, dort einen solchen Museumskomplex zu errichten, stammen von Wilhelm von Bode. 1914 hatte Bruno Paul mit einem ersten Bau begonnen, der erst nach dem Zweiten Weltkrieg bezogen wurde und mit den zwischen 1966 und 1973 dazugekommenen Neubauten dem Völkerkundemuseum sowie der Gemäldegalerie im geteilten Berlin als westliche Heimstatt diente.

Heute ist hier das (umbenannte) *Ethnologische Museum* untergebracht, das mit fünfhunderttausend Objekten aus

Nordamerika-Abteilung des Ethnologischen Museums, im Vordergrund die Figur eines Kwakiutl-Häuptlings aus dem Norden von Vancouver Island, British Columbia, Kanada.

North America Division of the Ethnological Museum, in the foreground the figure of a Kwakiutl chieftain from northern Vancouver Island, British Columbia, Canada.

In the southern part of the city, close to Grunewald and the campus of Free University, *Dahlem Museum Center* has a special message to convey with its focus on non-European cultures. Plans to build such a museum complex in the area were first conceived by Wilhelm von Bode. In 1914, Bruno Paul started construction on the first building, though it was moved into only after World War II; new structures were added from 1966 to 1973. The complex served as the western home of the Museum of Ethnology (Völkerkundemuseum) and the Picture Gallery in divided Berlin.

Today the (renamed) *Ethnological Museum* is housed at this site, one of the most significant in the world with over five

allen Erdteilen, u. a. Alt-Amerika, Südsee und Afrika, eines der weltweit bedeutendsten ist. Auch das Museum für Ostasiatische Kunst und das Museum für Indische Kunst, die 2006 unter dem neuen gemeinsamen Namen *Museum für Asiatische Kunst* vereinigt wurden, sind hier beheimatet. Zu sehen sind Werke aus dem indo-asiatischen Kulturraum vom vierten Jahrtausend v. Chr. bis in die Gegenwart, japanische Malerei, ostasiatische Lackkunst und chinesische Keramik. In einen Dialog mit fernen Regionen tritt seit 2005 auch das *Museum Europäischer Kulturen* (ehemals Museum für Volkskunde), das unter dem Dach des Bruno-Paul-Baus Objekte aus dem Alltagsleben vom 18. Jahrhundert bis in die Gegenwart zeigt.

Gedenkkopf eines Königs Oba, Königreich Benin, 18. Jh., Messing, Höhe 28 cm; rechts: Bronzerelief vom Palast des Oba, ebd., 17. Jh., Höhe 52 cm, Ethnologisches Museum, Afrika Sammlung.

Memorial head of an Oba (King), Kingdom of Benin, 18th century, brass, height: 28 cm; right: bronze relief from the Palace of the Oba, ibid., 17th century, height: 52 cm, Ethnological Museum, Africa Coll.

hundred thousand objects from all continents, e.g., ancient America, the South Seas and Africa. Also located here are the Museum of East Asian and the Museum of Indian Art, which were combined in 2006 under the new, joint name of *Museum of Asian Art*. On exhibit are works from the Indo-Asian cultural area dating from the fourth millennium B.C. to the present, Japanese painting, East-Asian lacquer art, and Chinese ceramics. Since 2005, the *Museum of European Cultures* (formerly Museum of Folklore) has also entered into a dialog with remote regions. Housed in the Bruno Paul Building, it showcases objects of daily life from the 18th century to the present day.

258

Links: Sitzende Figur mit langem Rumpf, südliches Neuirland, Melanesien, erworben 1908, Holz, Farbe, Molluskenschalen, 82 x 30 cm, Ethnologisches Museum, Südsee-Abteilung.

Mitte: Große Bootshalle, Südsee-Abteilung Ethnologisches Museum. Rechts: Tanzender Ganesha, nördliches Bengalen, 11. Jh., grau-schwarzer Schiefer, 56 x 25 cm, Museum für Asiatische Kunst.

Left: Seated figure with long torso, southern New Ireland, Melanesia, acquired in 1908, wood, colored, mollusk shells, 82 x 30 cm, Ethnological Museum, South Seas Division.

Center: Great Hall of Boats, South Seas Division, Ethnological Museum. Right: Dancing Ganesha, northern Bengal, 11th century, gray-black slate, 56 x 25 cm, Museum of Asian Art.

Max Liebermann (1847–1935), *Wannseegarten mit Villa – Die Birkenallee im Wannseegarten nach Westen* (Wannsee Garden with Villa – Birch-Lined Avenue in Wannsee Garden Facing West), 1926, Öl auf Holz/oil on wood, 32 x 41 cm, Neue Nationalgalerie.

„In Liebermann bewundere ich Berlin", bekannte Thomas Mann. Schon zu Lebzeiten nannte man *Max Liebermann* einen Klassiker. Er setzte den Impressionismus in Deutschland durch und war einer der wichtigsten Wegbereiter der Moderne. Bereits Anfang 1892 gründete er mit Walter Leistikow und Max Slevogt die Berliner Secession, von 1920 bis 1932 stand er als Präsident der Preußischen Akademie der Künste vor. Liebermann suchte zeitlebens im Naturvorbild die Harmonie, was sich in der Wahl seiner Sujets widerspiegelt: Er malte badende Knaben und promenierende Sommergäste am Strand, Biergärten, stille Alleen und zunehmend sein kleines Gartenreich im Süden der Stadt. 1909 hatte er sich ein Sommerhaus am Wannsee bauen lassen, das er stolz „mein Schloss am See" nannte. Hier fand er abseits vom Großstadtbetrieb Ruhe. Mit dem Bau der Villa betraute er Paul Otto Baumgarten, den Garten gestaltete er gemeinsam mit Albert Brodersen, wobei er

"In Liebermann, I admire Berlin," Thomas Mann confessed. *Max Liebermann* was called a classic even when he was still alive. He made Impressionism fashionable in Germany and was one of the most important trailblazers of modernism. As early as 1892, he founded the Berlin Secession with Walter Leistikow and Max Slevogt; from 1920 to 1932, he presided over the Prussian Academy of Arts as its president. All his life, Liebermann looked for harmony in nature, his model, as is reflected in his selection of subjects: He painted boys bathing and summer guests strolling on the beach, beer gardens, quiet tree-strewn avenues, and increasingly his small garden empire in the south of the city. In 1909, he had a summerhouse built on Lake Wannsee that he proudly called "my castle on the lake." Here he found calm away from the bustle of the big city. He commissioned Paul Otto Baumgarten to build his villa; he himself designed the garden along with Albert Brodersen,

Links: Max Liebermann (1847–1935), *Die Blumenterrasse im Wannseegarten nach Nordwesten* (Flower Terrace in Wannsee Garden Facing Northwest), 1921, Öl auf Leinwand/oil on canvas, 50 x 75 cm.

Max Liebermann (1847–1935), *Der Garten des Künstlers in Wannsee* (The Artist's Garden in Wannsee), 1918, Öl auf Leinwand/oil on canvas, 70 x 90 cm.

sich außerdem von Alfred Lichtwark, dem Direktor der Hamburger Kunsthalle, beraten ließ. Mit dem Arrangement aus Nutz- und Blumengarten vor dem Haus und einer Blumenterrasse, Hecken, Bäumen und einer Rasenfläche zur Seeseite schuf er sich die Motive für sein Spätwerk. Mehr als zweihundert Gemälde in einem heiteren Impressionismus entstanden am Wannsee.

Vierzig davon zeigt die Präsentation in der denkmalgerecht wiederhergestellten Villa, die somit die Möglichkeit bietet, die Werke des großen Malerfürsten am Ort ihrer Entstehung zu erleben. Außerdem informiert eine Dokumentation über das Leben des Künstlers und seiner Familie.

Max Liebermann (1847–1935), *Der Künstler und seine Familie in seinem Haus am Wannsee*, 1926 , (The Artist and his Family in His House on Lake Wannsee), Öl auf Leinwand/oil on canvas, 54 x 75 cm.

Links: Max Liebermann (1847–1935), *Selbstbildnis mit Palette an der Staffelei, Profil rechts* (Self-Portrait with Palette at the Easel, profile right), 1915, Öl auf Pappe/oil on cardboard, 80 x 65 cm.

although he also took advice from Alfred Lichtwark, director of the Hamburg Kunsthalle. By planting a mixture of vegetable and flower garden in front of the house and a flower terrace, hedges, trees, and a lawn on the side of the lake, he created motifs for his late works.

More than two hundred of his works painted in a carefree Impressionist style were created at Lake Wannsee. Forty of these are on exhibit in the historically restored villa, thus providing visitors with the opportunity to experience the works of this great master painter at their production site. Additional informational materials document the life of the artist and his family.

Zeitgenössische Kunst – Kunstszene Berlin

Die Kunst boomt. Dabei gewinnt ein alter Charakterzug Berlins wieder Oberhand: Die Stadt, die immer viele Zentren besaß, nährt die Konkurrenz ihrer Kulturquartiere, und sie profitiert davon. Zwar erlebt der Stadtteil Mitte mit den wiedergewonnenen historischen Standorten Unter den Linden und auf der Museumsinsel eine kulturelle Blüte, wie sie noch nicht einmal die Glanzzeiten der 1920er-Jahre kannten, doch auch andernorts wächst Bedeutung nach. Berlin ist – urban wie kulturell – auf Dauer ein unvollendetes Projekt, das heißt: Nichts ist hierzulande verlässlicher als der Wandel.

„Die Luft knistert vor Kreativität", schrieb die „New York Times" 2008 über Berlin. Deutschlands Kapitale ist die Hauptstadt der Kunst und Künstler. In keiner anderen europäischen Stadt gibt es so viele Museen und Sammlungen, aber auch Galerien und private Ausstellungsorte. Die Zeichen stehen auf Pioniergeist und Engagement, sie stehen für Erneuerung. Was wie Konkurrenz für die Museen aussieht, verdankt sich nicht zuletzt deren Aufbruchswillen.

Die zeitgenössische Kunst der Staatlichen Museen wird seit November 1996 im *Hamburger Bahnhof* ausgestellt. Das 1845 bis 1847 von Friedrich Neuhaus in Anklängen an Schinkel und Stüler errichtete Gebäude ist der einzige erhaltene Kopfbahnhof Berlins, der damals die deutsche Haupt- mit der Hansestadt verband. Als man sich nach dessen Stilllegung 1904 entschloss, den Nutzbau in ein Verkehrs- und Baumuseum umzugestalten, entstand die große dreischiffige Eisen-Glas-Halle, die noch heute das Zentrum des Museums bildet. Direkt an der

Hamburger Bahnhof, nach Plänen von Friedrich Neuhaus, 1845–47, Umbau Josef Paul Kleihues, seit 1996 Museum für Gegenwart und somit Ausstellungsort für zeitgenössische Kunst. Die Lichtinstallation von Dan Flavin ist zum Wahrzeichen des Hauses geworden.

Hamburg Railway Station, designed by Friedrich Neuhaus, 1845–47, remodeled by Josef Paul Kleihues; since 1996 home of the Museum of the Present and thus an exhibition venue for contemporary art. Dan Flavin's light installation has become emblematic of the museum.

Contemporary Art – Art Scene Berlin

Art is booming. An old Berlin character trait is meanwhile regaining the upper hand: Having always had many centers, the city encourages competition among its cultural quarters, and it profits from it. Even though Berlin-Mitte with its regained historical sites on Unter-den-Linden Boulevard and Museum Island is experiencing a period of cultural high tide, unprecedented even during the glorious era of the 1920s, other sites are likewise gaining in significance. Berlin is – in urban as well as cultural terms – a permanently unfinished project, which is to say: Nothing is more reliable here than transformation.

"The air is bristling with creativity," the "New York Times" wrote about Berlin in 2008. Germany's capital is a cardinal center of the arts and artists. No other European city is home not only to so many museums and collections, but also galleries and private exhibition sites. The signs of the times indicate a pioneering spirit and engagement; they represent innovation. What looks like it is competing with the museums, also owes its existence to the museum's will to embark on new beginnings.

Contemporary works of art owned by the Berlin State Museums has been exhibited at *Hamburger Bahnhof* since November 1996. Constructed by Friedrich Neuhaus with hints of Schinkel and Stüler in 1845–1847, the building is the single remaining terminal station in Berlin, which formerly connected the German capital with the Hanseatic City of Hamburg. Decommissioned in 1904, the utilitarian building was to be turned into a museum of traffic and construction and so the triple-naved hall made of iron and glass was built; it still con-

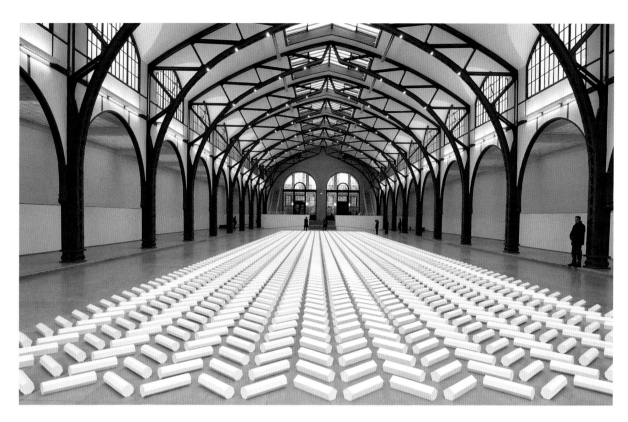

Hallen-Architektur des Museums für Gegenwart: Der schon von außen erkennbare Stil des Neoklassizismus, angelehnt an Schinkel und Stüler, wird in der dreischiffigen Eisen-Glas-Halle fortgeführt.

Hall architecture in the Museum of the Present: Already visible on the exterior, the style of Neoclassicism inspired by Schinkel and Stüler is resumed in the triple-nave iron-and-glass hall.

Links/Left: Thomas Schütte (geb./b. 1954), *The Making of Große Geister*, Flick Collection, Hamburger Bahnhof, Museum für Gegenwart.

Rechts/Right: Andreas Hofer (geb./b. 1963), *Kardinal Julian* (2006), Styropor, Gips, Lack/ styrofoam, cast, varnish, 310 x 330 x 60 cm, Friedrich Christian Flick Collection, Hamburger Bahnhof, Museum für Gegenwart.

Paul McCarthy (geb./b. 1945),
Apple Heads on Swiss Cheese,
1997–99, 2 Skulpturen/sculptures,
Fiberglas, Silikon/fibreglass,
silicone, 370 x 190 x 150 cm,
370 x 153 x 150 cm, Friedrich
Christian Flick Collection,
Hamburger Bahnhof, Museum
für Gegenwart, courtesy of the
artist and Hauser & Wirth
Zürich London.

Paul McCarthy (geb./b. 1945),
Untitled (*Michael Jackson Gold*),
1997–99, Fiberglas, Urethan-
farbe, Stahl/fibreglass, urethan-
color, steel, 268 x 242 x 140 cm,
Friedrich Christian Flick
Collection, Hamburger Bahnhof,
Museum für Gegenwart, courtesy
of the artist and Hauser & Wirth
Zürich London.

Mauer gelegen, blieb das kriegszerstörte Gebäude bis Ende der 1980er-Jahre ungenutzt. Den Umbau nahm Josef Paul Kleihues vor. Im Mittelpunkt der Präsentation befindet sich die hochrangige Privatsammlung des Berliner Kunstliebhabers Erich Marx mit Werkgruppen zeitgenössischer Künstler wie Joseph Beuys, Robert Rauschenberg und Anselm Kiefer. Aber auch neue Arbeiten von Thomas Struth, Rachel Whiteread und Andreas Gursky werden gezeigt.

Zuwachs bekam das Museum 2002 durch den Ankauf der Sammlung Marzona mit Minimal-, Konzept- und Land Art sowie 2004 durch die Leihgabe der *Friedrich Christian Flick Collection*. Die mit 150 Künstlern größte Privatsammlung zeitgenössischer Kunst präsentiert in den angrenzenden *Rieckhallen*, einem ehemaligen Speditionslager, u. a. Werke von Duane Hanson, Candida Höfer, Martin Kippenberger, Bruce Nauman, Pipilotti Rist, Thomas Ruff und Cindy Sherman. Gegenüber am Humboldthafen soll nicht nur ein neues Stadtquartier der Superklasse entstehen, hier wird auch ein neues Kunstmuseum seinen Platz haben. Bauherr: Nicolas Berggruen, der hier seine zeitgenössische Sammlung präsentieren wird. Hinter den Rieckhallen in der Heidestraße, zwischen Karosseriewerkstätten, Speditionen und Möbellagern, wächst die neue Adresse der hauptstädtischen Galerienszene heran.

Nach dem Mauerfall war es die Auguststraße, in der ein schäbiges Torhaus zum Mekka der neuen Welt wurde. Dort begann Berlins Weg zur Kunsthauptstadt Europas. In der damals baufälligen Margarinefabrik gründete Anfang der 1990er-Jahre eine Gruppe junger Leute die *Kunst-Werke*, ein heute interna-

Joseph Beuys (1921–1986), *Unschlitt/Tallow*, 1977, Sammlung/Collection Marx, Hamburger Bahnhof, Museum für Gegenwart.

stitutes the center of the museum today. Situated in the immediate vicinity of the Wall, the war-damaged building remained empty until the end of the 1980s. Josef Paul Kleihues did the remodeling. Its central exhibit is the highly ranked private collection of Berlin art lover Erich Marx that showcases groups of works by contemporary artists such as Beuys, Rauschenberg and Kiefer. But new works by Thomas Struth, Rachel Whiteread and Andreas Gursky are on also on display.

The museum's holdings were enlarged in 2002 with the purchase of the Marzona Collection, which comprises Minimal, Concept and Land Art, and with the 2004 loan of the *Friedrich Christian Flick Collection*. At 150 artists the largest private collection of contemporary art, it is housed in the adjacent *Rieck Halls*, a former freight warehouse, where it presents works by, e.g., Duane Hanson, Candida Höfer, Martin Kippenberger, Bruce Nauman, Pipilotti Rist, Thomas Ruff, and Cindy Sherman. Across from it, at Humboldthafen, a very upscale new city quarter is to be developed, but not only that: a new art museum will also find a home there. Builder-owner: Nicolas Berggruen, who will showcase his contemporary collection there. Behind the Rieck Halls on Heidestraße, among auto body shops, trucking companies and furniture warehouses, the new district for the capital's gallery scene is emerging.

After the fall of the Wall, it was on Auguststraße, where a dingy gate house turned into a Mecca of the new world. It was from there that Berlin set out to become the art capital of Europe. In the early 1990s, in a dilapidated margarine factory, a group of young people founded the *Kunst-Werke*/Art-Works,

tional bekanntes Institut für zeitgenössische Kunst, das auf fünf Etagen in dem sanierten und denkmalgeschützten Gebäude die jüngsten Entwicklungen der Gegenwartskunst präsentiert. Die ganze Gegend, ein traditioneller Arme-Leute-Bezirk mit kleinteiliger Architektur, der den Fall der Mauer in abbruchreifem Zustand erlebte, ist mittlerweile auf Hochglanz saniert. Heute findet sich in jedem zweiten Haus eine Galerie; auch Designer, Goldschmiede und Clubs haben sich niedergelassen. Das Art Forum, die Berlin Biennale, die Berliner Liste zogen nach.

Heute ist Berlin nach New York der zweitwichtigste Kunstumschlagplatz der Welt. Doch es ist auch ein Magnet für *Privatsammler*. Immer mehr von ihnen zeigen öffentlich, welche Werke ihnen wichtig sind, und zwar nicht mehr in Museen, sondern sie inszenieren ihre gekauften Werke selbst – in bizarren Räumen, an ungewöhnlichen Orten, die sie zu kleinen oder großen Kunsthallen umbauen. *Christian Boros* etwa stellt auf fünf Etagen des einzigen in der Innenstadt erhaltenen Bunkers nahe dem Deutschen Theater seine rund vierhundert Kunstwerke aus. Damien Hirst ist hier ebenso zu sehen wie Franz Ackermann, Elizabeth Peyton, Tracey Emin oder Santiago Sierra. *Erika Hoffmann* empfängt mit Werken von Andy Warhol, Bruce Nauman oder Gerhard Richter in ihrer Privatwohnung unter dem Dach einer alten Fabrik in den Sophie-Gips-Höfen. Die *Sammlung Haubrock* präsentiert sich im „Haus des Kindes" am Strausberger Platz u. a. mit Arbeiten von Günther Förg, Wolfgang Tillmanns, Gregor Schneider. Bei *Ivo*

Der Bunker von Christian Boros, ein besonders bizarrer Ort zur Präsentation von Gegenwartskunst.

Christian Boros' Bunker, an especially bizarre venue for the presentation of contemporary art.

Oben/Above: Olafur Eliasson (geb./b. 1967), *Berlin Colour Sphere*, 2006.

Rechte Seite, oben/Right page, above: Anselm Reyle (geb./b. 1979), *Life Enigma*, 2008 (links/left), Ohne Titel (Untitled), 2008 (rechts/right),

Unten links/Below left: Santiago Sierra (geb./b. 1966), Konstruktion und Installation von teerbeschichteten Formen/ Construction and Installation of Tared Forms, 2002.

Unten rechts/Below right: Monika Sosnowska (geb./b. 1972), *Ohne Titel* (Untitled), 2005.

Alle Bilder/All pictures: courtesy of Sammlung Christian Boros/ Foto Noshe.

today an internationally recognized institute of contemporary art that showcases youngest developments in the arts on five stories of the now renovated and landmarked building. The entire area, a traditional working-class district with low-density architecture that survived the fall of the Wall in a state of dereliction, has in the meantime been restored to perfection. Today, every second house has a gallery; designers, goldsmiths and nightclubs have also settled in. The Art Forum, the Berlin Biennale, and the art fair Berliner Liste followed suit.

Today, Berlin is the world's second most important trading hub for art, next to New York. But it is also a magnet for *private collectors*. More and more of them show publicly which works are important to them, and they do so no longer in museums; rather, they stage their purchased works on their own – in bizarre rooms and in unusual locations remodeled into small or big art exhibition venues. *Christian Boros*, for example, exhibits some four hundred of his collected art works on five stories of Berlin's only still existing inner-city bunker close to the Deutsches Theater. Damien Hirst can be seen here as easily as Franz Ackermann, Elizabeth Peyton, Tracey Emin, or Santiago Sierra. *Erika Hoffmann* welcomes visitors with works by Andy Warhol, Bruce Nauman or Gerhard Richter in her private apartment under the roof of an old factory in the Sophie Gips Yards. The *Collection Haubrock* is presented in the "House of the Child" at Strausberger Platz, showing works by, e.g., Günther Förg, Wolfgang Tillmanns, and Gregor Schneider. At *Ivo Wessel's* on Chausseestraße, visitors can experience

Norbert Schwontkowski
(geb./b. 1949), *Trust*, 2006,
Öl auf Leinwand/oil on canvas,
200,3 x 180,5 x 2,5 cm, courtesy
of Contemporary Fine Arts.

Wessel in der Chausseestraße sind neben Konzeptkunst Video-arbeiten von Sven Johne, Via Lewandowsky, Stefan Panhans zu erleben. *Roman Maria Koidl* hat mit seiner Sammlung ein vom Bauhaus geprägtes, mit viel Feingefühl für den neuen Nutzen hergerichtetes ehemaliges Umspannwerk hinter dem Bahnhof Charlottenburg bezogen. *Céline und Heiner Bastian* beauftragten David Chipperfield, der das Neue Museum ins 21. Jahrhundert führt, vis-à-vis mit dem Bau eines Domizils für ihre Sammlung. In das wohl spektakulärste Haus für Gegen-wartskunst in Berlin ist auch die Galerie Contemporary Fine Arts eingezogen – ein hochmodernes Schaufenster für zeitgenös-sische Kunst, direkt an der alten neuen Museumsinsel.

concept art but also video works by Sven Johne, Via Lewandowsky and Stefan Panhans. *Roman Maria Koidl* and his collection have moved into a Bauhaus-influenced former elec-tric power sub-station behind Charlottenburg Railway Station, remodeled with much sensitivity for its new usage. *Céline and Heiner Bastian* commissioned David Chipperfield, who took the New Museum into the 21st century, to build a home for their collection vis-à-vis the island. Arguably the most spectacular house for contemporary art in Berlin, the Contemporary Fine Arts gallery has also moved in – providing an ultra-modern window on contemporary art, within a stone's throw of old new Museum Island.

Von Hoch- bis Off-Kultur findet man alles in Berlin. Drei Opernhäuser, mehr als 150 Theater- und Kleinkunstbühnen, ebenso viele Kinos und acht große Sinfonieorchester von internationalem Rang. Die pulsierende Metropole hat schon immer Kulturschaffende magisch angezogen. Ihre Ausstrahlung verdankt sie nicht zuletzt dem produktiven Wechselspiel zwischen ernster Kunst und leichter Unterhaltung. So knüpfte Berlin mit dem neu eröffneten Admiralspalast 2006 direkt an seine Glanzzeit in den Goldenen Zwanzigern an. Als einer der ersten Vergnügungspaläste der Stadt bot er rund um die Uhr Amüsement aller Art. Varietés und Revuen hatten in dem Art-déco-Bau ihr Zuhause, die Comedian Harmonists feierten hier triumphale Erfolge. Im Neuen Westen baute sich auf einem Kohlenplatz der Meierei Bolle der Architekt Bernhard Sehring 1896 ein eklektizistisches Monumentaltheater, das ein bunt gemischtes Repertoire bot: das Theater des Westens. Wo einst Enrico Caruso und Maria Callas Verdi und Puccini sangen, werden heute internationale Musicals gespielt.

Oben links:
Ludwig Eduard Lütke (1801–1850), *Die Singakademie am Festungsgraben*, 1842, Farblithographie/ color lithography.

Vorhergehende Seite/Previous page: Berliner Ensemble, Zuschauerraum/auditorium, Heinrich Seeling, 1892.

Theaterbühnen von Reinhardt bis zum Boulevard

Traditionen schreibt man seit jeher groß im Kulturleben der Stadt, stößt sie aber genauso gerne wieder um. So führte Peter Stein die *Schaubühne*, die als politisch linkes Ensembletheater mit Bruno Ganz, Edith Clever und Jutta Lampe begonnen hatte, zu Weltruhm: Seine Kleist- und Tschechow-Inszenierungen, sein Antikenprojekt wurden zu international

From high to off-the-beaten-track culture – Berlin has it all. Three opera houses, more than 150 theater stages and cabarets, just as many movie theaters, and eight big symphony orchestras of international standing. The vibrant metropolis has always magically attracted creators of culture. It owes its appeal last not least to the productive interplay between serious art and light entertainment. Reopened in 2006, Berlin's Admiral's Palace thus links up with its glamorous tradition of the Golden '20s. As one of the city's first amusement centers, it provided all sorts of entertainment around the clock. Vaudeville shows and revues had their home in this Art Deco building, and the Comedian Harmonists had their greatest triumphs. In the New West, architect Bernhard Sehring built an eclecticist monumental theater for himself in 1896 on the grounds of a former coal depot belonging to the dairy-farm Bolle, which presented a colorful repertoire: the Theater of the West. Where Enrico Caruso and Maria Callas once sang Verdi and Puccini, international musicals nowadays ring from its stage.

Stages from Reinhardt to the Boulevard

Traditions have always been writ large in the cultural life of the city, but they are also just as eagerly overthrown. As such, Peter Stein made world famous the *Schaubühne*, which had started out as a politically progressive ensemble theater featuring Bruno Ganz, Edith Clever and Jutta Lampe: His Kleist and Chekhov productions and his Antiquity Project became

gefragten Exportartikeln. Gespielt wurde zunächst am Halleschen Ufer in Kreuzberg und seit 1981 im ehemaligen Universum-Kino am Lehniner Platz (Erich Mendelsohn, 1926–1928). 1999 fand ein Generationswechsel in der künstlerischen Leitung statt. Seither entwickelt sich die Schaubühne zu einem Ort für experimentelles und zeitgenössisches Repertoiretheater. Längst zum schrillen Szene-Kultobjekt und international gefeierten Aushängeschild der Berliner Bühnen avanciert ist heute die *Volksbühne* (Oskar Kaufmann, 1913/14). Daneben behaupten sich selbstbewusst die kleinen Theater, neben vielen anderen etwa die Sophiensäle, wo einst Rosa Luxemburg als Rednerin Furore machte, oder das Hebbel am Ufer, Berlins schönstes Jugendstiltheater (Oskar Kaufmann, 1907/08). Es gibt nichts, was es nicht gibt in Berlin. So erstaunt es nicht, dass den Besucher der Stadt täglich ein Angebot von bis zu 1500 Veranstaltungen erwartet.

Der Klassiker unter den Berliner Bühnen ist das *Deutsche Theater*, nicht nur was den Spielplan betrifft. Immer schon glänzte es mit großen Namen, mit Regisseuren von Heiner Müller bis Michael Thalheimer, mit seinem Ensemble erstrangiger Schauspieler wie Ulrich Mühe, Ulrich Matthes, Dagmar Manzel oder Nina Hoss. Von dem ursprünglichen Bau von Eduard Titz aus dem Jahre 1850, dem Friedrich-Wilhelmstädtischen Theater, ist nur der Zuschauerraum mit sechshundert Plätzen geblieben. 1883 erhielt das Haus seinen heutigen Namen. Otto Brahm etablierte Gerhart Hauptmann, Ibsens „Nora" feierte im Deutschen Theater ihre ersten Erfolge. 1905 übernahm Max

Max Reinhards Deutsches Theater; vom ursprünglichen Bau von Eduard Titz, 1850, ist nur der Zuschauerraum geblieben. Die neoklassizistische Fassade geht zurück auf William Müller, 1905; links daneben die Kammerspiele.

Max Reinhard's Deutsches Theater; only the auditorium from the original building by Eduard Titz, 1850, has survived. The Neoclassicist façade goes back to William Müller, 1905; next to it on the left: the Kammerspiele.

internationally popular export items. At first, the company played at Hallesches Ufer in Kreuzberg and then, since 1981, in the former Universum movie theater at Lehniner Platz (Erich Mendelsohn, 1926–1928). In 1999, its artistic leadership underwent a generational makeover. Since then, the Schaubühne has become a site for experimental and contemporary repertory theater. For a long time now, the *Volksbühne* (Oskar Kaufmann, 1913/14) has been an in-your-face cult object for the cultural scene and an internationally feted figurehead for Berlin's stages. Alongside, small theaters confidently assert themselves as well, such as the Sophiensäle, where Rosa Luxemburg once caused a furor with her speeches, or the Hebbel am Ufer, Berlin's most beautiful Art Nouveau theater (Oskar Kaufmann, 1907/08). There is nothing that Berlin doesn't have. So it is not surprising that Berlin visitors can choose daily among a selection of up to 1,500 performances.

The classic among Berlin's stages is the *Deutsches Theater* – and not only because of its repertoire. Its playbill has always been studded with big names, including directors from Heiner Müller to Michael Thalheimer, and a cast of first-class actors and actresses, such as Ulrich Mühe, Ulrich Matthes, Dagmar Manzel, or Nina Hoss. Nothing but the auditorium with six hundred seats survived of the original structure built by Eduard Titz in 1850, the Friedrich-Wilhelmstädtisches Theater. In 1883, the theater received its current name. Otto Brahm made Gerhart Hauptmann fashionable, while Ibsen's "Nora" celebrated its first successes at the Deutsches Theater. In 1905, Max Reinhardt

Reinhardt die Bühne, seine neuartigen Klassikerinszenierungen – texttreu, psychologisierend, schauspielerorientiert – schrieben Regiegeschichte. Er ließ durch William Müller die Fassade neoklassizistisch überformen und das benachbarte Casino in die *Kammerspiele* umwandeln.

Mit Autoren der Gegenwart macht das *Maxim-Gorki-Theater* auf sich aufmerksam. Das mit 440 Plätzen kleinste der Berliner Staatstheater versteckt seine noble klassizistische Fassade hinter dem Kastanienwäldchen Unter den Linden. Ursprünglich war es der älteste Konzertsaalbau der Stadt, die Sing-Akademie. Schinkel, Mendelssohn Bartholdy und Bismarck sangen in diesem renommierten Musikklub des Berliner Bürgertums. Dessen Leiter und Freund Goethes, Carl Friedrich Zelter, initiierte den Bau, der nach Schinkels Entwürfen von Carl Theodor Ottmer (1825 bis 1827) ausgeführt wurde. Aber auch schon damals nutzte man das Haus für musikferne Zwecke: Alexander von Humboldt hielt hier 1827 seine „Kosmos-Vorlesungen", nach der Märzrevolution tagte im Sommer 1848 die Konstituierende Preußische Nationalversammlung. Im Zweiten Weltkrieg schwer beschädigt, erhielt das Theater nach dem Wiederaufbau 1952 seinen jetzigen Namen.

Der Name des *Berliner Ensembles* stammt von seinem Gründer, Bertolt Brecht. So hieß die Gruppe, die sich 1949 um den Dramatiker scharte, als er nach Jahren des Exils ein Arbeitsfeld im damaligen Ost-Berlin fand. Nach einem fünfjährigen Gastspiel am Deutschen Theater machte er das Haus am Schiffbauerdamm zu seiner Spielstätte, in der er schon 1928 mit der „Dreigroschenoper" seinen ersten großen Erfolg erlebt hatte. Mit Helene Weigel, Therese Giehse und Ernst Busch führte er in Heinrich Seelings neobarockem Bau von 1892 seine Stücke und seine Theorie vom „epischen Theater", einer radikalen Abkehr vom Illusionstheater, zu internationalem Ruhm. Bahn-

„Glotzt nicht so romantisch", das Brecht-Monument des Bühnenbildners Karl-Ernst Herrmann am Berliner Ensemble.
Rechts: Das von Bertolt Brecht ab 1954 bespielte Theater am Schiffbauerdamm, erbaut 1892.

"Don't gawk so romantically," Brecht monument by stage designer Karl-Ernst Herrmann at the Berlin Ensemble Theater.
Right: Theater at Schiffbauerdamm, built in 1892, Bertolt Brecht put on plays here as of 1954.

Rechte Seite/Right page
Oben/Above: Schaubühne am Lehniner Platz, Erich Mendelsohn, 1926–28.
Unten/Below: Admiralspalast, Friedrichstraße, als Eis-Arena/as ice-skating rink, Heinrich Schweitzer, Alexander Diepenbrock, 1910, Bildpostkarte/picture postcard, um/c. 1910.

assumed command of the stage; his novel productions of the classics – faithful to the text, psychologizing, actor-oriented – went down into the annals of stage directional history. He had William Müller remodel the façade in the Neoclassicist manner and transform the casino next door into the *Kammerspiele*.

The *Maxim Gorky Theater* takes hold of its audience by featuring contemporary authors. At 440 seats the smallest of Berlin's State Theaters, it hides its elegant Neoclassicist façade behind a small grove of chestnut trees on Unter den Linden. It was originally the oldest concert hall of the city, the Sing-Akademie. Schinkel, Mendelssohn Bartholdy and Bismarck sang songs in this renowned music club of the Berlin bourgeoisie. Its director Carl Friedrich Zelter, one of the chosen few entitled to address his friend Goethe, initiated construction of the building, which was built in 1825–1827 by Carl Theodor Ottmer based on designs by Schinkel. But even in those days it was also used for purposes other than music: Alexander von Humboldt presented his "Cosmos Lectures" here in 1827; after the March Revolution, the Constitutional Prussian National Assembly held its convention there in the summer of 1848. Badly damaged in World War II, the theater acquired its current name after its reconstruction in 1952.

The name of the *Berlin Ensemble* was given by its founder, Bertolt Brecht. Such was the name of the group gathering around the dramatist in 1949 who, after returning from years of exile, had found a new field of operations in former East Berlin. After a five-year stint as guest performer at the Deutsches Theater, he made the Haus am Schiffbauerdamm his home stage; in 1928, he had already had his first great success there with his "Three Penny Opera." Accompanied by Helene Weigel, Therese Giehse and Ernst Busch, he brought international fame to his theater pieces and his theory of the

brechende Inszenierungen wurden auf die Bretter gebracht: „Der kaukasische Kreidekreis", oder „Der gute Mensch von Sezuan". Nach Brechts Tod 1956 leitete Helene Weigel das Haus allein bis ins Jahr 1971. Auch die nachfolgenden Intendanten – u. a. Ruth Berghaus, Peter Zadek und seit 1999 Claus Peymann – haben den Stil des Hauses geprägt. Nach langen Jahren der Abstinenz stehen heute neben Klassikern und Zeitgenossen erneut Brecht-Stücke auf dem Spielplan.

Musiktheater und Konzerthäuser von Weltruf

Hier erlebte die deutsche Oper schlechthin, Carl Maria von Webers „Freischütz", 1821 eine umjubelte Uraufführung, Wagner dirigierte seinen „Fliegenden Holländer" erstmalig in Berlin: Das von Schinkel 1818 bis 1821 errichtete *Schauspielhaus* am traditionsreichen Gendarmenmarkt, ein Meisterwerk klassizistischer Architektur, gehörte einst zu den ersten Theateradressen in Deutschland. 1919 in Preußisches Staatstheater umbenannt, wurde es in der Zeit der Weimarer Republik mit Leopold Jessner zur tonangebenden Bühne. In den Jahren der nationalsozialistischen Gleichschaltung versuchte Gustaf Gründgens, die „reine Kunst" mit erstklassigen Schauspielern wie Elisabeth Flickenschildt, Werner Krauß und Marianne Hoppe durch die Zeiten zu retten. Im Zweiten Weltkrieg brannte das Schauspielhaus bis auf die Außenmauern aus und wurde erst zu DDR-Zeiten (1979 bis 1984) originalgetreu rekonstruiert, wobei man das Innere jedoch völlig veränderte. An die Stelle eines Theaters mit Bühne trat ein 1850 Plätze fassender Konzertsaal mit einer an Schinkelschen Formen orientierten Ausstattung. Seit 1994 heißt das Haus *Konzerthaus Berlin*.

Schinkels Schauspielhaus, heute Konzerthaus Berlin.
Linke Seite
oben: Blick in den Konzertsaal,
unten: Umrissstiche nach Schinkel, *Ansicht aus dem Zuschauerraum auf die Scene der beim Einweihungsprolog aufgestellten Decoration* von Louis Normand (links) und *Perspektivische Darstellung des Concertsaales* von Carl F. Thiele, um 1821.

Schinkel's Schauspielhaus, now Konzerthaus Berlin.
Left page
above: Interior view of the concert hall,
below: Outline engravings after drawings by Schinkel, *View from the auditorium of the scene showing the decor set up for the inaugural prologue*, by Louis Normand (left) and *Perspectival depiction of the concert hall*, by Carl F. Thiele, c. 1821.

Konzerthaus Berlin mit Schiller-Denkmal von Reinhold Begas.

Konzerthaus Berlin with Schiller Monument by Reinhold Begas.

"epic theater," a radical turning away from illusionist theater, in Heinrich Seeling's 1892 Neo-Baroque building. Trailblazing productions were put on stage: "The Caucasian Chalk Circle" or "The Good Person of Szechwan." After Brecht's death in 1956, Helene Weigel directed the house by herself until 1971. Succeeding stage managers have likewise put their mark on the theater's style, e.g., Ruth Berghaus, Peter Zadek and, since 1999, Claus Peymann. After long years of restraint, the theater is once again producing plays by Brecht, next to classics and plays by contemporary playwrights.

Musical Theaters and Concert Halls of World Renown

Carl Maria von Weber's "Freischütz," the quintessential German opera, had its triumphant world premiere here in 1821; Wagner conducted his "Flying Dutchman" here for the first time in Berlin: Built by Karl Friedrich Schinkel in 1818–1821 and located on a square steeped in traditions, the Gendarmenmarkt, the *Schauspielhaus* is a masterpiece of Neoclassicist architecture and was once one of the best theaters in Germany. Renamed Prussian State Theater in 1919, it became the country's leading stage under Leopold Jessner in the days of the Weimar Republic. In the years of the National Socialist consolidation of power, Gustaf Gründgens tried salvaging "pure art" in dark times with first-rate actors such as Elisabeth Flickenschildt, Werner Krauß and Marianne Hoppe. During World War II, the Schauspielhaus was gutted by fire and reconstructed true to its original specifications only during GDR times (1979–1984) – though its interior was completely remodeled. Where once had been a theater with a stage, now there was a concert hall

Der größte Konzertsaal Berlins ist weltberühmt wegen seines bizarr gefalteten, zeltartigen Dachs, der golden schimmernden Außenhaut und seiner einzigartigen Akustik. Die Heimstätte der Berliner Philharmoniker, die schon immer zu den führenden Orchestern der Welt zählten, bildete den Auftakt für das neue Kulturforum am Tiergarten. Seither besitzt die *Philharmonie* auch in Architekturkreisen einen einzigartigen Klang, denn das Gebäude galt seit seiner Eröffnung 1963 als revolutionär. Der Entwurf wurde für unzählige neue Konzerthäuser kopiert. Weltweit erstmalig stellte Hans Scharoun die Musik ins Zentrum seiner zirkuszeltartigen Konstruktion, das Orchesterpodium also in die Mitte einer großen Arena. Kein Zuhörer sitzt mehr als dreißig Meter von den musizierenden Künstlern entfernt. Diese demokratische Grundidee leitete Scharoun, der schon in den 1920er Jahren Vordenker des Organischen Bauens war, bei der Gestaltung. Auf einem polygonalen Grundriss steigen die Zuschauerränge mit insgesamt 2452 Sitzplätzen wie Weinbergterrassen bis unter die Decke an. Mit ihrer einmaligen Silhouette, die auch den 1987 nach ihrem Muster entworfenen *Kammermusiksaal* charakterisiert, prägt die Philharmonie den Stadtraum am Potsdamer Platz. Das Orchester selbst besteht schon seit 1882. Hans von Bülow, Arthur Nikisch und Wilhelm Furtwängler waren stil-

Berlins größter Konzertsaal, die Philharmonie von Hans Scharoun, 1960–63.
Rechts: Philharmonie und Kammermusiksaal, die beiden aufeinander abgestimmten zeltartigen Konstruktionen auf polygonalen Grundrissen.

Berlin's largest concert hall, the Philharmonie by Hans Scharoun, 1960–63.
Right: Philharmonie and Chamber Music Hall, two complementary tent-like constructions on polygonal ground plans.

with 1,850 seats, its interior outfitted in a style reminiscent of Schinkel. Since 1994, the theater is called *Konzerthaus Berlin*.

Berlin's largest concert hall is world famous for its bizarrely folded, tent-like roof, its golden outer skin and its unique acoustics. The home of the Berlin Philharmonic Orchestra, always one of the leading orchestras in the world, was the first building to kick off construction of the new Culture Forum at Tiergarten. From that time on, the *Philharmonie* has also enjoyed special favor with architectural circles, because it has been considered revolutionary ever since its opening in 1963. Its design was copied in the building of countless new concert halls. For the first time in the world, Hans Scharoun placed music itself at the center of his circus-tent-like construction, that is, he installed the orchestra podium in the center of a large arena. No member of the audience is seated more than thirty meters away from the performing musicians. It is this democratic ideal that guides the design by Scharoun who had been a precursor of organic architecture as early as the 1920s. On a polygonal ground plan, 2,452 seats in rows are stacked up to the ceiling like terraces on a vineyard. With its unique silhouette, which also characterizes the *Kammermusiksaal* (Chamber Music Hall) that was modeled on it in 1987, the Philharmonie dominates the urban space at Potsdamer Platz. The orchestra

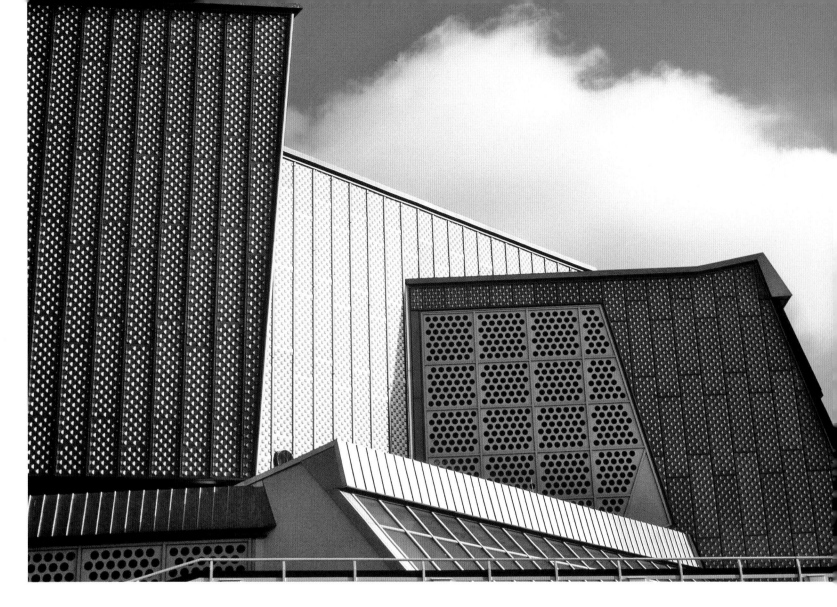

Staatsoper Unter den Linden,
G. W. von Knobelsdorff, 1741–43,
Apoll (oben) und seinen Musen
geweiht, die vom Giebel grüßen;
rechts der Zuschauerraum mit
seinen drei Rängen.

State Opera Unter den Linden,
G. W. von Knobelsdorff, 1741–43,
dedicated to Apollo (above) and
his Muses who salute from the
pediment; right: the auditorium
with its three galleries.

HANC DOMVM ARTIS COLENDAE CAVSA CONDIDIT.
ANNO MDCCCLXXXXVI BERNHARD SEHRING.

bildende Dirigenten. Ab 1954 leitete für 25 Jahre Herbert von Karajan die Philharmoniker. Ihm folgten 1989 Claudio Abbado und 2002 Sir Simon Rattle. Die ehrwürdige Institution erschließt sich derzeit mit ihrem vorbildlichen „Education-Projekt" das Publikum der Zukunft.

Berlins ältestes Opernhaus ist die *Staatsoper Unter den Linden*. 1741 hatte Friedrich II, kaum auf dem preußischen Thron, sein „Zauberschloss" mit palladianischer Front bei Georg Wenzeslaus von Knobelsdorff 1741 in Auftrag gegeben. Es war das erste freistehende Opernhaus Deutschlands sowie das damals größte in Europa – damals wie heute „Apollini et Musis", Apoll und seinen Musen geweiht. Ihren ersten künstlerischen Höhepunkt erlebte die Oper nach den Befreiungskriegen: Der berühmte Gaspare Spontini leitete das Haus, Albert Lortzing feierte Triumphe, Giacomo Meyerbeer, später Richard Strauss. Nach einem verheerenden Brand im Jahre 1843 zerstörte ein weiteres Mal der Zweite Weltkrieg das Haus. Heute zählt der Theaterbau, der von 1952 bis 1955 durch Richard Paulick nach den Knobelsdorffschen Originalplänen komplett rekonstruiert wurde, zu den schönsten Opernhäusern der Welt. Unter dem Generalmusikdirektor Daniel Barenboim pflegt man seit 1992 ein breites klassisches Repertoire, auch mit Schwerpunkten aus dem Barock und der Moderne;

Theater des Westens, Bernhard Sehring, 1895/96, Figurengruppe von Ludwig Menzel; auf dem Fries: „Dieses Haus wurde gegründet zur Pflege der Kunst."

Theater of the West, Bernhard Sehring, 1895/96, group of statues by Ludwig Menzel; on the frieze: "This House was founded to foster the arts."

itself has been in existence since 1882. Hans von Bülow, Arthur Nikisch and Wilhelm Furtwängler were its style-setting conductors. In 1954, Herbert von Karajan started conducting the Philharmonic Orchestra for the next 25 years. He was succeeded in 1989 by Claudio Abbado and in 2002 by Sir Simon Rattle. These days, the honorable institution prepares its audience of the future with its exemplary "Education Project."

Berlin's oldest opera house is the *State Opera Unter den Linden*. In 1741, just after acceding to the Prussian throne, Frederick II commissioned Georg Wenzeslaus von Knobelsdorff to build him a "Magical Palace" with a Palladian front façade. It was the first free-standing opera house in Germany and also the largest in Europe at the time – then and now "Apollini et Musis," dedicated to Apollo and his Muses. The opera house had its first artistic success after the Liberation Wars: Famous Gaspare Spontini directed the house; Albert Lortzing celebrated his triumphs, as did Giacomo Meyerbeer and then Richard Strauss. After a devastating fire in 1843, World War II destroyed the house for a second time. Reconstructed by Richard Paulick in 1952–1955 based on Knobelsdorff's original designs, the theater building today is considered one of the most beautiful opera houses in the world. Under General Music Director Daniel Barenboim, the house offers a broad classical repertoire with occasional forays

284

Babylon, Hans Poelzig, 1928/29,
als Stummfilmkino 1929
eröffnet/opened in 1929 as a
silent movie theater.

Unten/Below: Kino International,
Josef Kaiser/Heinz Aust, 1961–63,
dreigeschossiger Stahlskelettbau
mit hellem Sandstein/three-story
steel frame building with bright
sandstone.

Regie- und Gesangsstars wie Rolando Villazòn haben hier ihren Auftritt.

Traditionell profiliert sich demgegenüber die *Deutsche Oper Berlin*, mit 1885 Plätzen die größte der Stadt, durch die Uraufführung zeitgenössischer Werke, aber auch mit der „kritischen Neubefragung" des klassischen Repertoires von Mozart bis Verdi. Den Geist des Hauses, das 1956 bis 1961 von Fritz Bornemann als schlicht-eleganter Betonquader erbaut wurde, prägte einst der langjährige Generalintendant Götz Friedrich, zeitweilig mit seinem Generalmusikdirektor Christian Thielemann.

Mit der *Komischen Oper* besitzt Berlin – weltweit einmalig – drei städtische Musiktheater. Von dem ursprünglichen Gebäude in der Behrenstraße, 1892 von dem Wiener Architektenbüro Fellner & Helmer im neobarocken Stil errichtet, sind der Zuschauerraum mit seinen 1190 Plätzen sowie die prachtvolle Treppe wunderbar erhalten. Mit dem Österreicher Walter Felsenstein, der 1947 die Intendanz übernahm, erlangte die Komische Oper weltweiten Ruhm, dank der darstellerischen Maßstäbe, die er für die Opernregie setzte. Über Jahrzehnte wusste Chefregisseur Harry Kupfer dies Erbe eines „realistischen" Musiktheaters in deutscher Sprache mit Ausflügen in die leichte Operetten-Muse zu bewahren, unterstützt von namhaften Orchesterleitern wie Otto Klemperer oder Kurt Masur. Heute stehen sowohl die klassischen Werke der Opernliteratur als auch moderne Stücke auf dem Programm.

Filmtheater, Kulturarena, Freilichtbühnen

Die Geschichte des europäischen Films hat – gleichzeitig mit Paris – in Berlin angefangen: im Wintergarten-Varieté am Bahnhof Friedrichstraße, wo der Filmpionier Max Skladanowsky 1895 seine ersten Stummfilmstreifen zeigte. Und während der

Berlin und Potsdam-Babelsberg schrieben Filmgeschichte: Zu den bedeutendsten Produktionen gehörten „Metropolis" von Fritz Lang (Plakat von 1927 mit Illustration von Kurt Degen), „Der blaue Engel" von Josef von Sternberg (Uraufführungsplakat von 1929/30) und der Stummfilm „Das Cabinet des Dr. Caligari" von Robert Wiene (Plakat von 1920, Entwurf Stahl/Arpke, Farblithographie).

Berlin and Potsdam-Babelsberg made motion picture history: Among their most important productions are "Metropolis" by Fritz Lang (1927 poster with illustration by Kurt Degen), "The Blue Angel" by Josef von Sternberg (world premiere poster of 1929/30) and the silent film "The Cabinet of Dr. Caligari" by Robert Wiene (1920 poster, design by Stahl/Arpke, color lithography).

into the Baroque and the Modern; star directors and opera singers such as Rolando Villazòn perform here.

The *Deutsche Oper Berlin*, on the other hand, the city's largest opera house with a capacity of 1,885 seats, traditionally specializes in world premieres of contemporary works, but also with works that "critically re-interrogate" classical repertoires from Mozart to Verdi. The character of the opera house, built in 1956–1961 by architect Fritz Bornemann as a cuboid, concrete structure in the plain-objectivist manner, was minted some time ago by long-term General Director Götz Friedrich, at times accompanied by General Music Director Christian Thielemann.

Along with the *Komische Oper*, Berlin features three metropolitan musical theaters – this is unique in the world. The auditorium with its 1,190 seats and its magnificent staircase have wonderfully survived the passing of the original building on Behrenstraße, constructed in the Neo-Baroque style in 1892 by the Viennese architecture firm Fellner & Helmer. Becoming its director in 1947, the Austrian Walter Felsenstein brought worldwide fame to the Comic Opera because he set such high performance standards for opera direction. For decades, chief director Harry Kupfer was able to safeguard this legacy of a "realistic" musical theater in the German language with excursions into the lighter fare of operetta, supported by renowned orchestra conductors such as Otto Klemperer or Kurt Masur. Today's program features both classical works of opera literature and modern pieces.

Movie Theaters, Culture Arena, Open Air Stages

European film history was launched – alongside Paris – in Berlin: in the Wintergarten-Varieté at Friedrichstraße Railway Station, where film pioneer Max Skladanowsky showed his

Tüftler Oskar Messter die Projektionstechnik revolutionierte, kreierten Henny Porten und Asta Nielsen in einem Hinterhof ganz in der Nähe die Posen des Stummfilms vor der Kamera. Mit den Schlüsselwerken der expressionistischen Ära, „Das Cabinet des Dr. Caligari" (Robert Wiene, 1920), „Nosferatu" (Friedrich Wilhelm Murnau, 1922) oder „Dr. Mabuse, der Spieler" (Fritz Lang, 1922), setzte der deutsche Film weltweit Maßstäbe. Die hier entwickelten Kamera- und Beleuchtungstechniken nahmen Einfluss auf die gesamte internationale Filmproduktion. Berlin stieg damit zur führenden Filmmetropole Europas auf. Die UFA in Potsdam-Babelsberg entwickelte sich nach Hollywood zum zweitgrößten Filmimperium der Welt, wo internationale Klassiker wie der 1927 uraufgeführte Stummfilm „Metropolis", Fritz Langs berühmtestes Epos über eine Fabrikstadt der Zukunft, produziert wurden.

Damals traten auch die Kinos ihren rasanten Siegeszug an. 1921 gab es in der Stadt vierhundert Lichtspiele mit fast 150000 Plätzen. „Theater der kleinen Leute" nannte sie Alfred Döblin. Doch es entstanden, vor allem rund um die Gedächtniskirche, auch prächtige Filmpaläste mit Platzanweisern in Livree, Orchestern mit bis zu siebzig Musikern und einem varietéartigen Rahmenprogramm.

Musical Theater und seit 2000 zentraler Veranstaltungsort der Berliner Filmfestspiele, nach Entwürfen von Renzo Piano, 1998 fertiggestellt.

Musical Theater and the central venue for the Berlin Film Festival since 2000, completed in 1998 based on designs by Renzo Piano.

first silent film in 1895. And while Berlin tinkerer Oskar Messter revolutionized the technology of projection, Henny Porten and Asta Nielsen created the postures of silent film for the camera in a backyard close by. With the key works of the Expressionist era, "The Cabinet of Dr. Caligari" (Robert Wiene, 1920), "Nosferatu" (Friedrich Wilhelm Murnau, 1922) or "Dr. Mabuse, the Gambler" (Fritz Lang, 1922), German film production set industry benchmarks. The techniques of camera work and lighting developed in these films influenced international film production everywhere. Berlin thus became Europe's leading metropolis of movie making. UFA in Potsdam-Babelsberg grew to be the second largest film empire next to Hollywood and produced such international classics as the silent film "Metropolis", Fritz Lang's famous epic about a factory city of the future that world premiered in 1927.

Movie theaters at the time also took off on their speedy victory lap. In 1921, the city had four hundred motion picture theaters with almost 150,000 seats. Alfred Döblin called them "theaters for the common folks." But glamorous film palaces with ushers in uniform, orchestras with up to seventy musicians and vaudeville-style ancillary programs were also created, especially around Gedächtniskirche.

Als einziger Zeuge dieser Zeit ist das Kino *Babylon* in Mitte erhalten. 1929 wurde es in dem komplett von Hans Poelzig entworfenen Wohnquartier mit dem Film „Fräulein Else" eröffnet. Die Handschrift des Architekten ist unverkennbar: ein Theater mit großer Raumwirkung. Das Foyer zeigt geschmeidig gerundete Formen, die den Schwung der horizontalen Bänder an den Außenfassaden wiederholen. Im Zuschauerraum mit Empore wölbt sich über glatten Wänden eine flache Decke mit eingelassenem Oberlicht. 2001 wurde das Kino mit 450 Plätzen gemäß dem Originalzustand rekonstruiert. Ein Unikat ist die 1999 restaurierte Philips-Kino-Orgel. Als einziges Instrument ihrer Art in Deutschland begleitet sie noch heute am Originalstandort die Vorführung von Stummfilmen.

Einer der letzten Vertreter der Lichtspielära der 1950er-Jahre schließlich ist das *Kino International* nahe dem Alexanderplatz. Wie ein großes Schaufenster, das die Welt des Zelluloids auf die Straße strahlen lässt, erlaubt es einen weiten Blick auf die Karl-Marx-Allee. Mit dem gegenüberliegenden Café Moskau, den benachbarten Pavillonbauten, dem ehemaligen Hotel Berolina sowie dem Kino als Mittelpunkt entwarf Josef Kaiser einen der spannungsreichsten Komplexe des DDR-Städtebaus. 1963 eröffnet, darf sich der 551 Besucher fassende Kinosaal durchaus mit dem Platzangebot moderner Großkinos messen. Jeden Februar zu den Berliner Filmfestspielen steht das International als eine der Spielstätten des Festivals im Rampenlicht.

Der prestigereichste und größte Aufführungsort der Festspiele aber liegt am Marlene-Dietrich-Platz – ein Name, der an die Glanzzeiten des Potsdamer Platzes erinnert. Hier erleben seit dem Jahr 2000 zehn Tage lang alle Filme des Wettbewerbs ihre feierliche Premiere, auch die Eröffnungsfeier und die Ver-

Der kulturelle Veranstaltungsort Tempodrom am Anhalter Bahnhof, Meinhard von Gerkan, 2000–01, Betonkonstruktion mit zwölf Stahlstützen, Höhe 37,5 m.

The cultural venue Tempodrom at Anhalter Bahnhof, Meinhard von Gerkan, 2000–01, concrete construction with twelve steel supports, height: 37.5 m.

The single remaining architectural witness of those times is the *Babylon* movie theater in Mitte. In 1929, when it was first opened in a residential quarter designed entirely by Hans Poelzig, it showed the movie "Miss Else". The architect's handwriting is unmistakable: a theater giving guests a grand experience of architectural space. Its foyer presents lithe, rounded forms which repeat the momentum of the horizontal ties on the external façades. In the auditorium with gallery, a flat ceiling with embedded overhead light arches upward above smooth walls. In 2001, the movie theater with 450 seats was reconstructed to original specifications. Restored in 1999, its Philips Cinema Organ is a unique copy. The only instrument of its kind in Germany, it still accompanies the showing of silent movies at its original location.

One of the last representatives of the moving pictures era of the 1950s, finally, is the movie theater *Kino International* near Alexanderplatz. Letting the celluloid world shine out onto the street, its front opens up to give a wide view of Karl-Marx-Allee like a large shop window. Along with Café Moscow located across from it, the adjacent pavilion buildings, the former Hotel Berolina, as well the movie theater in the center, Josef Kaiser created one of the most intense architectural complexes of GDR urban planning. Opened in 1963, its auditorium seating 551 visitors can definitely rival the seating capacities of modern mega movie theaters. Every February during the Berlin Film Festival, the International grabs the spotlight as one of the festival's venues.

The most prestigious and largest Festival movie venue, however, is located on Marlene-Dietrich-Platz – a name reminiscent of Potsdamer Platz in its heyday. Since 2000, all films entered into the competition are given their celebrated premieres here;

gabe der offiziellen Preise finden dort statt. Das nach Plänen von Renzo Piano erbaute Haus verwandelt sich nach den Festtagen der Berlinale in ein nicht weniger festliches *Musical-Theater*, mit 1800 Sitzplätzen eines der größten Europas. Der Charlottenburger *Zoo-Palast*, in dem die Berliner Filmfestspiele 1962 aus der Taufe gehoben wurden, behält trotz des dort geplanten Umbaus seinen Glanz und bleibt ebenfalls traditioneller Spielort des Festivals.

Eine Kulturarena ganz anderen Zuschnitts ist das *Tempodrom*, in dem Konzerte, Revuen, Shows, Zirkus- und Sportveranstaltungen über die Bühne gehen. Nach Plänen Meinhard von Gerkans auf dem Areal des Anhalter Bahnhofs errichtet, zählt es mit seinem dynamischen Zeltdach zu den kühnsten Architekturentwürfen des neuen Jahrtausends in Berlin. In seiner gewagten Konstruktion erinnert es an expressionistisches Bauen in den frühen 1920er-Jahren – und an seinen kleinen Vorläufer, ein mobiles Zirkuszelt, das 1980 wie ein Ufo inmitten der Wüste des Potsdamer Platzes für alternative Kultur in West-Berlin gesorgt hatte. Später stand das Zelt lange im Tiergarten neben der Kongresshalle, wo es schließlich dem Bau des Kanzleramtes weichen musste. Unter der auf zwölf Stahlstützen ruhenden Betonkonstruktion finden 3700 Besucher Platz; in den Komplex integriert ist das Schwimmbad Liquidrom.

Besonders beliebt sind in Berlin Kulturerlebnisse unter freiem Himmel. Allen voran in der *Waldbühne*, die zweifellos zu den schönsten Freilichtbühnen Europas zählt. Nach dem Vorbild antiker Theater entworfen, platzierte sie Werner March, der 1936 gleichzeitig das nahegelegene Olympiastadion plan-

Dietrich-Eckart-Freilichtbühne, heute Waldbühne, nach Plänen von Werner March, 1934–35, ursprünglich Kult- und Feierstätte der Nationalsozialisten nach antikem Vorbild, Foto 1935.

Dietrich Eckart Open Air Stage, today's Waldbühne, based on designs by Werner March, 1934–35, originally a site for National Socialist cultic festivities modeled on ancient stages, photo 1935.

the opening ceremony and the awarding of the prizes are likewise conducted at this site. After the Berlinale is over, the house, built according to designs by Renzo Piano, transforms itself back into the *Musical Theater*, just as festive and at 1,800 seats one of the largest in Europe. Charlottenburg's *Zoo Palast*, where the Berlin Film Festival was launched in 1962, will retain its glamour in spite of its planned remodeling and will likewise remain a traditional venue for the festival.

A cultural arena of a different kind is the *Tempodrom*, which features concerts, revues, shows, circus performances and sports events. Built on the Anhalter Bahnhof area according to designs by Meinhard von Gerkan, it is one of Berlin's boldest architectural designs of the new millennium on account of its dynamic tent roof. Its daring construction is reminiscent of Expressionist buildings of the early 1920s – and of its small precursor, a mobile circus tent that produced alternative culture in West Berlin in the middle of the desert at Potsdamer Platz in 1980. Later, the tent stood for a long time in Tiergarten next to the Congress Hall before it had to yield its site to the construction of the Chancellor's Office. The concrete structure supported by twelve steel columns can accommodate 3,700 visitors; the Liquidrom, a swimming pool, is integrated into the complex.

Open-air events are especially popular in Berlin. Pride of place goes to the *Waldbühne* that is without a doubt one of Europe's most beautiful open-air stages. Modeled on ancient classical theaters, it was placed among the hills at Murellenschlucht by Werner March, who also designed nearby

te, in den Hügelzug an der Murellenschlucht. Auf den 88 Stufen des weiten Amphitheaters finden 22 000 Zuschauer Platz. Wo einst Max Schmeling boxte, ist heute ein sommerlicher Treffpunkt für Freunde der Oper, des Jazz, der Rock- und Popmusik und des Films. Traditionell intonieren hier die Berliner Philharmoniker am Ende ihrer Konzerte stets die inoffizielle Hymne der Stadt, Paul Linckes „Berliner Luft".

Was die Waldbühne für den Westen, das ist die *Wuhlheide* für den Osten der Stadt. 1950 wurde sie inmitten des Volksparks auf Trümmerschutt angelegt. 17 000 Zuschauer fasst das Oval der Open-Air-Bühne – von Pop bis Unterhaltungsmusik reicht das Spektrum der Künstler, die hier auftreten.

Seit 1982 verfügt die Waldbühne über ein Zeltdach im Bühnenbereich. Ursprünglich sollte sie 100.000 Menschen aufnehmen, heute finden hier 22.000 Zuschauer Platz.

The Waldbühne has had a tent-like stage roof since 1982. Originally intended for 100,000 spectators, today the venue has a capacity for 22,000.

Olympic Stadium in 1936. The 88 steps of the wide amphitheater can seat 22 000 spectators. Where Max Schmeling once had his boxing matches, today there is a summertime venue for friends of opera, jazz, rock, and pop music, as well as of film. At the end of their concerts, true to tradition, the Berlin Philharmonic plays the city's unofficial hymn, Paul Lincke's "Berliner Luft."

The Waldbühne is for the West, what *Wuhlheide* is for the Eastern part of the city. It was created in 1950 in the middle of the Volkspark on mounds made of wartime debris. The oval of the open-air stage can accommodate 17,000 guests – the artists performing here play music running the gamut from pop to entertainment music.

Medien, Messen, Verkehrsareale

Media, Trade Fairs, Traffic Areas

Wo die Macht ist, sind auch die Medien nicht weit. So siedelten sich, nachdem Berlin wieder zur deutschen Hauptstadt mit Regierungssitz wurde, die öffentlich-rechtlichen Anstalten nur einen Steinwurf vom neuen Regierungsviertel entfernt in neuen Domizilen an. Auch die privaten Sender suchten – in denkmalgeschützten Gebäuden – die Nähe zu Reichstag und Ministerien. Schon der erste Rundfundsender Deutschlands hatte 1923 sein Quartier im Schatten der politischen Schaltzentralen an der Wilhelmstraße aufgeschlagen. Als es im damaligen Vox-Haus am Potsdamer Platz zu eng wurde, zog der Sender in den prosperierenden Westen mit seinen neuen Quartieren um, in die heutige Masurenallee. Auch die alte Messe, die schon 1914 am Lehrter Bahnhof aus allen Nähten geplatzt war, wurde dorthin verlegt. Seither befindet sich hier eines der städtischen Medienzentren.

Türme des Funks und Fernsehens

Der von den Berlinern „Langer Lulatsch" getaufte *Funkturm* ist ein elegantes Wahrzeichen der Stadt. Er wurde 1926 zur Dritten Deutschen Funkausstellung in Betrieb genommen. Die mit Antenne 150 Meter hohe filigrane Stahlfachwerkkonstruktion, mit der Heinrich Straumer den Pariser Eiffelturm en miniature nachbaute, steht – und das ist einzigartig – auf Porzellanfüßen; sie wirken als Isolatoren, die eine Ableitung von Energie in den Erdboden verhindern. 1929 wurde von hier das erste Fernsehbild der Welt ausgestrahlt. 1945 zerstörten Granaten eine der Hauptstreben, doch der Turm blieb stehen. Von dem in 52 Metern Höhe gelegenen Restaurant und vor allem von der Aussichtsplattform unterhalb der Spitze hat man einen fantastischen Rundblick von der Havel bis nach Mitte.

Zu Füßen des Funkturms entstand damals auch das neue Messegelände für die Metropole. Der Gesamtentwurf (1928) Martin Wagners und Hans Poelzigs wurde allerdings nicht realisiert. Stattdessen führte man in den 1930er-Jahren die Pläne

Where there is power, the media are not far behind. That is why public-service broadcasting agencies settled in new homes only a stone's throw away from the new government quarter after Berlin had again become the German capital and seat of government. Private media broadcasters, too, wanted to be close to the Reichstag and Ministries – in buildings with landmark status. Even Germany's first radio broadcasting station set up camp in the shadow of the political centers of power on Wilhelmstraße in 1923. When space got tight in the former Vox House on Potsdamer Platz, the station moved to the prospering West with its new accommodations – into today's Masurenallee. The old fairgrounds, which had already been bursting at the seams at Lehrter Bahnhof in 1914, were likewise relocated there. Since that time, this area has been one of the city's media centers.

Radio and Television Towers

Nicknamed "Langer Lulatsch," (Beanpole) by Berliners, the *Radio Tower* is an elegant emblem of the city. It started operations in 1926 on the occasion of the Third German Radio Exhibition. Its delicate trussed steel construction – 150 meters high with antenna and built by Heinrich Straumer as a kind of Parisian Eiffel Tower *en miniature* – stands, and this is unique, on china feet; these act as insulators preventing the discharge of energy into the ground. In 1929, the first TV picture in the world was broadcast from here. In 1945, grenades destroyed one of its main struts, but the tower remained standing. From its restaurant, 52 meters up, and especially from the observation deck underneath its spire, visitors have a fantastic panoramic view of the area from the Havel to Mitte.

The new fairgrounds of the city at the foot of the Radio Tower also came into being in those days. The comprehensive design (1928) by Martin Wagner and Hans Poelzig, however, was not realized. Instead, Richard Ermisch's designs were implemented

von Richard Ermisch aus, die sich an dem für die Repräsenta-
tionsbauten der Nationalsozialisten üblichen Stil orientierten:
Das 1935 abgebrannte Haus der deutschen Funkindustrie von
Heinrich Straumer (1924) wurde durch die Gläserne Galerie er-
setzt. Die 35 Meter hohe Ehrenhalle bildet noch heute den Zugang zum Gelände. Daran schließen sich hundert Meter lange
Gebäude an, die Berlin seinerzeit einen pompösen Messeauf-
tritt bescherten. Das George-Marshall-Haus (1950) von Bruno
Grimmek und Werner Düttmann hingegen, eine gläserne Ausstellungshalle im südlichen Sommergarten, steht mit seiner
Leichtigkeit in größtem Gegensatz zu den nationalsozialistischen Monumentalbauten.

Ein weiterer Meilenstein deutscher Rundfunkgeschichte erhebt sich gegenüber von Funkturm und Messegelände in der
Maurenallee: Hans Poelzigs im Stil expressiver Sachlichkeit
1929 bis 1931 errichtetes erstes Funkhaus Deutschlands, das
Haus des Rundfunks. Das Gebäude hat Maßstäbe gesetzt. Die
drei viergeschossigen Bürotrakte bilden einen Innenhof, an
dem sich lärmgeschützt die akustisch empfindlichen Studios
aufreihen. Die drei Sendesäle lassen sich über die große Ein-

Seiten/Pages 290–291:
Gläserne Halle des Hauptbahn-
hofs/Central Railway Station
glass hall, Gerkan, Marg und
Partner, 2006.

Linke Seite/Left page:
Funkturm/Radio Tower,
Heinrich Straumer, 1924–26,
Messegelände/fairgrounds,
Richard Ermisch, 1935–37.

Unten: Fernsehturm/Television
Tower am/at Alexanderplatz,
Fritz Dieter, Günter Franke,
Werner Ahrend, Idee/idea
Hermann Henselmann, 1965–69.

in the 1930s, which favored the style typical of National
Socialist representative buildings: Heinrich Straumer's House
of the German Radio Industry (1924) that had been gutted by
fire in 1935 was replaced by the Glass Gallery. Its 35-meter-tall
Hall of Honor still today functions as gateway to the area.
One-hundred-meter-long buildings adjoin to it, thus granting
Berlin a pompous entrance to the trade fair in those days. The
George Marshall House (built in 1950) by Bruno Grimmek and
Werner Düttmann, on the other hand, an exhibition hall made
of glass in the southern summer garden, contrasts most
starkly in its lightness with the National Socialist monumental
edifices.

Another milestone of German radio history rises up across
from Funkturm and fairgrounds at Maurenallee. It is Hans
Poelzig's first radio building in Germany, designed in the style
of expressive Objectivity in 1929–1931: the *House of Radio
Broadcasting*. The building set standards. Its three four-story
office tracts form an interior courtyard containing a series of
acoustically sensitive studios. Its three broadcasting halls are
accessible via the large entrance hall – an atrium encircled by

gangshalle, einen Lichthof mit umlaufenden Galerien, errei-
chen. Seit 1957 wird das Haus vom Sender Freies Berlin (SFB),
heute Rundfunk Berlin-Brandenburg (RBB), genutzt. Das einst
größte und modernste Haus seiner Art in Europa gehört nach
wie vor zu den architektonisch besten Zweckbauten des
20. Jahrhunderts in Berlin.

Als Gegenstück zum ehrwürdigen Funkturm im Westen baute die DDR mitten in ihre Hauptstadt eine „sozialistische Hö-
hendominante", getreu der Parole „Nicht einholen, sondern
überholen!" Und tatsächlich, das mit 365 Metern noch immer
höchste Bauwerk Deutschlands ist unübersehbar und eine
technische Superleistung.

Der *Fernsehturm*, 1969 fertiggestellt und als „Werk der Werk-
tätigen" gefeiert, war zehn Jahre zuvor durch Hermann Henselmann, den Architekten der Karl-Marx-Allee (früher Stalinallee),
angeregt worden. Er hatte einen „Turm der Signale" entworfen, der aus einem geschwungenen Betonschaft, einer gläsernen Kugel und einer Stahlnadel bestand.

„Space design" nannte die raumfahrtbegeisterte Welt so
etwas in der westlichen Hemisphäre. Was als Symbol für den
satellitengleichen Aufstieg des Kommunismus gedacht war,
verdankt seine Entstehung dem Umstand, dass die DDR
endlich eine landesweite Sendeanlage brauchte.

1956 hatte das Staatsfernsehen seinen offiziellen Betrieb als
Deutscher Fernsehfunk in Adlershof aufgenommen, einem
Gelände, das eng mit den Anfängen der deutschen Flugge-
schichte verbunden ist: dem ersten Motorflughafen Deutschlands. In den zu Studiogebäuden umgebauten Hangars wur-

Linke Seite: Foyer im Haus des
Rundfunks in der Masurenallee,
Hans Poelzig, 1929–31, mit
zwei Skulpturen;
Georg Kolbe, *Große Nacht* (1926),
Volkmar Haase, *Hommage à
Kolbe zur „Nacht"* (1988).
Unten: Rundfunkzentrum Nalepa-
straße in Oberschöneweide,
Franz Ehrlich, 1952–56, bis 1990
Sitz des Rundfunks der DDR.

Left page: Foyer in the House of
Radio Broadcasting on Masuren-
allee, Hans Poelzig, 1929–31
with two sculptures;
Georg Kolbe, *Great Night* (1926),
Volkmar Haase, *Hommage à
Kolbe on "Night"* (1988).
Below: Radio Broadcasting Center
Nalepastraße, Oberschöneweide,
Franz Ehrlich, 1952–56, up to
1990: the home of Radio GDR.

galleries. Since 1957, the house has been used by TV and
radio channel Sender Freies Berlin (SFB), or Radio Berlin-
Brandenburg (RBB) today. Once the largest and most modern
building of its kind in Europe, it is still one of the architecturally
most accomplished functional buildings of the 20th century in
Berlin.

As counterpoint to the dignified Radio Tower in the West, the
GDR, in the middle of its capital, built a "socialist vertical
dominant," true to the slogan, "don't just catch up, surpass!"
And indeed, at 365 meters still Germany's highest structure,
it is simply not to be overlooked and constitutes a technological mega-achievement.

The *Television Tower*, completed in 1969 and feted as "work
of the workers," goes back to an inspiration ten years earlier
by Hermann Henselmann, the architect of Karl-Marx-Allee
(former Stalinallee). He had designed a "tower of signals,"
composed of a tapering concrete shaft, a glass sphere and a
steel needle.

"Space design" – this is what the world, enthused by space
travel, called it in the Western Hemisphere. Designed as a
symbol connoting the satellite-like rise of communism, it owes
its existence to the fact that the German Democratic Republic
finally required a countrywide broadcasting facility.

In 1956, GDR television officially started operating as
German Television Broadcasting in Adlershof, a site closely
linked to Germany's early history of aviation: it was the first
German airport for motorized aircraft. Legendary works of
early celluloid history were filmed here later in hangars

den später legendäre Werke der filmischen Frühgeschichte gedreht – „Das indische Grabmal" (1921) etwa oder „Das Testament des Dr. Mabuse" (1933). Heute dreht sich in der verglasten Kuppel des Fernsehturms über dem Alexanderplatz ein Panoramacafé zweimal pro Stunde um die eigene Achse; zwei Personenaufzüge befördern jeweils bis zu fünfzehn Personen mit einer Geschwindigkeit von sechs Metern pro Sekunde hinauf und hinunter. Bei Sturm schwankt die Spitze bis zu sechzig Zentimetern, dabei beträgt die Tiefe des Fundaments nicht mehr als fünf Meter. Der Turmsockel ist von Pavillons eingerahmt, deren plastisch gestaltete Dächer Blatt- und Wurzelwerk eines organischen Schafts symbolisieren sollen. Heute befindet sich hier das Medienzentrum Berlin-Alexanderplatz.

Kongress- und Messeanlagen

Bis zur Neubebauung des Potsdamer Platzes war das *Internationale Congress Centrum* am Messedamm von Ralf Schüler und Ursulina Schüler-Witte, kurz ICC genannt, das umfangreichste Berliner Bauvorhaben der Nachkriegszeit (1974–1979). Von Stadtautobahnen umgeben, liegt der architektonisch kühn anmutende Gesamtkomplex wie eine große aluminiumbekleidete Maschine am Eingang zur Stadt. Auf einer Gesamtlänge von 320 Metern umfängt er achtzig Säle und Räume; der größte fasst bis zu fünftausend Personen. Mit 800.000 Quadratmetern umbautem Raum ist das ICC das größte Kongresszentrum Deutschlands. Wie kein anderer Bau in Berlin steht der tadellos funktionierende Koloss für die Technikgläubigkeit der Entstehungszeit und das Leitbild der motorisierten Stadt. Über ein „Autofoyer" wird der Verkehr auf

converted to studios – such as "The Indian Tomb" (1921) or "The Testament of Dr. Mabuse" (1933). Today, a panorama-café inside the glazed dome of the TV Tower turns round on its axis twice per hour; two elevators transport up to fifteen persons, respectively, up and down at a speed of six meters per second. During storms, the spire can sway up to sixty centimeters, although the tower's foundation is only five meters deep. The base of the tower is framed by pavilions whose sculptured roofs symbolize the leaves and roots of an organic shaft. The Media Center Berlin-Alexanderplatz has its home here today.

Congressional and Trade Facilities

Up to the rebuilding of Potsdamer Platz, the *International Congress Center* at Messedamm, ICC for short, by Ralf Schüler and Ursulina Schüler-Witte, was Berlin's largest postwar building project (1974–1979). Surrounded by city freeways, this architecturally daring complex sits like a large aluminum-clad machine at the gateway to the city. At a total length of 320 meters, it comprises eighty halls and rooms; the largest of these can accommodate up to five thousand people. Containing a building space of 800,000 square meters, the ICC is the largest congress center in Germany. Like no other building in Berlin, this flawlessly functioning colossus represents faith in technology, customary for its period of construction, and the mission statement of the motorized city. Traffic is funneled towards the interior via an "auto-foyer" eight lanes wide; an electronic guidance system directs visitors to the various halls. Besides international congresses and conferences, this

acht Spuren ins Innere geleitet, mittels eines elektronischen Leitsystems finden die Besucher zu den einzelnen Sälen. Neben internationalen Kongressen und Tagungen finden hier renommierte Bälle statt. Die bizarr-futuristischen Interieurs des ICC dienen auch als Filmkulisse, wie jüngst für Dani Levys Komödie „Alles auf Zucker". Da das ICC trotz seiner Funktionalität Defizite verursacht, wurde immer wieder über seinen Abriss nachgedacht. Doch nun – die Würfel sind gefallen – bleibt es der Stadt endgültig erhalten.

Die *Kongresshalle* im Tiergarten war der US-amerikanische Beitrag zur Internationalen Bauausstellung 1957 und ein Geschenk an West-Berlin. Von Anfang an erfreute sich das „Symbol der Freiheit", trotz seiner radikalen Modernität, außergewöhnlicher Popularität. In Sichtweite zur ausgebrannten Reichstagsruine erhob sich die Halle auf einem extra aufgeschütteten Hügel wie ein optimistisches Zeichen des Aufbruchs.

Der technisch und künstlerisch revolutionäre Bau nach Entwürfen des US-Architekten Hugh Stubbins, einem Assistenten von Walter Gropius, entstand in Rekordzeit. Von 1957 an fanden hier internationale Konferenzen und Messen statt, bis 1980 die weit ausschwingende Dachkonstruktion einstürzte. Nach deren Wiederaufbau zog 1989 das Haus der Kulturen der Welt ein.

Sozialistischer Realismus: Detail aus dem 125 m langen, 7 m hohen Fries („Bauchbinde") am Haus des Lehrers am Alexanderplatz mit Alltagsszenen aus dem „glücklichen Leben in der DDR", Mosaik nach einem Tafelbild von Walter Womacka, 1962.

Socialist Realism: Detail of the frieze (nicknamed "Abdominal Belt") on the House of the Teacher at Alexanderplatz, 125 m long, 7 m high; showing everyday scenes from the "happy life in the GDR," mosaic after a panel by Walter Womacka, 1962.

venue also features famous ballroom events. The bizarre-futuristic interiors dof the *International Congress Center* also serve as movie sets, such as for Dani Levy's recent comedy "Go for Zucker!" Since, in spite of its functionality, the ICC has accrued sizable deficit, its demolition has been repeatedly considered. But now – the die is cast – the city will finally get to keep it.

The *Congress Hall* in Tiergarten was the American contribution to the International Building Exhibition in 1957 and a gift to West Berlin. From the beginning, this "symbol of freedom" was extraordinarily popular, in spite of its radical modernity. Visible from the gutted ruin of the Reichstag building, the hall rose up from a newly created hill like an optimistic sign of departure.

Its technologically and artistically revolutionary construction, based on designs by the American architect Hugh Stubbins, an assistant of Walter Gropius, was completed in record time. From 1957 on, it was the site of international conferences and trade fairs, until the widely projecting roof collapsed in 1980. After its reconstruction, the House of World Cultures moved there in 1989.

Flughäfen von Weltbedeutung

Das einstmals größte zusammenhängende Gebäude der Welt zählt auch heute noch zu den weltweit bedeutendsten Verkehrsbauten: der *Flughafen Tempelhof*, der heute keiner mehr ist. 1923 auf einem ehemaligen Exerzierplatz in Betrieb genommen, wurde er 1935 bis 1942 nach Plänen von Ernst Sagebiel im Monumentalstil des Nationalsozialismus ausgebaut. Die „Mutter aller Flughäfen" (Norman Foster) ist ein avantgardistischer Wurf, der allen Anforderungen eines modernen Großflughafens gewachsen war. Auf der Mittelachse durch die Passagierhalle in zwei Hälften geteilt, sah der Komplex getrennte Ebenen für Ankunft, Abflug und Frachtverkehr vor, dazu kamen Hotels, ein Kongresszentrum und Büros. Kurze Wege waren ebenso wichtig wie die Anbindung an den öffentlichen Nahverkehr. Dank seiner kühnen Überdachung – eine 380 Meter lange, 40 Meter weit auskragende Stahlkonstruktion, die zur Zeit des Baus einmalig auf der Welt war – konnten die Passagiere das Flugzeug betreten, ohne sich Wind und Wetter auszusetzen. Ende April 1945 von den Sowjets erobert, im Juli an die US-Amerikaner übergeben, verwandelte sich Hitlers megalomanes Projekt über Nacht in ein Symbol der Freiheit und Selbstbehauptung. Während der sowjetischen

Schwungvolle Innenansichten eines in Funktionalität und Transparenz visionären Gebaudekomplexes der DDR-Architektur: Berliner Congress Centrum (bcc) am Alexanderplatz, Hermann Henselmann, Bernhard Geyer, Jörg Streitparth, 1961–64.

Dynamic interior views of a building complex of GDR architecture, visionary in its functionality and transparency: Berlin Congress Center (bcc) at Alexanderplatz, Hermann Henselmann, Bernhard Geyer, Jörg Streitparth, 1961–64.

Airports of World Renown

Once the largest contiguous building in the world, it still counts among the world's most significant transit structures today: *Tempelhof Airport*, which is no longer an airport. Having started operations in 1923 on a former drill ground, it was expanded in the monumental style of National Socialism in 1935–1942, based on designs by Ernst Sagebiel. The "mother of all airports" (Norman Foster) is an avant-garde feat able to cope with all the demands facing a modern mega-airport. Divided into two halves along its central axis by its passenger concourse, the complex was to contain separate levels for arrival, departure and freight traffic, as well as hotels, a congress center and offices. Short walkways were just as important as the connection to local transit. Due to its daring roof design – a cantilever steel construction 380 meters long and 40 meters wide that was unique in the world at the time of its construction – passengers could enter their planes without being exposed to winds and weather. Conquered by the Soviets in late April 1945, and handed over to the Americans in July, Hitler's megalomaniacal project turned into a symbol of liberty and endurance from one day to the next. During the Soviet Berlin-Blockade of 1948/49, the airport became world

Links oben: Flughafen Tegel,
Tower und Abfertigungsgebäude
mit seinen vierzehn Flugsteigen,
Meinhard von Gerkan, Volkwin
Marg und Klaus Nickels, 1969–74.
Links unten: Das einst weltgrößte
Gebäude des 2008 stillgelegten
Flughafens Tempelhof,
Ernst Sagebiel, 1935–42.

Rechts: Im Monumentalstil des
deutschen Nationalsozialismus –
Seitengang zur ehemaligen
Abfertigungshalle des
Flughafens Tempelhof.

Left above: Tegel Airport, tower
and terminal building with its
fourteen gates, Meinhard von
Gerkan, Volkwin Marg and Klaus
Nickels, 1969–74.
Left below: Tempelhof Airport
building, closed in 2008, once
the largest building in the world,
Ernst Sagebiel, 1935–42.

Right: In the monumentalist style
of German National Socialism –
corridor leading to the former
terminal hall of Tempelhof Airport.

Berlin-Blockade 1948/49 kam der Flughafen zu Weltruhm. Die Stadt wurde von den USA komplett aus der Luft versorgt. In Rekordzeiten starteten hier täglich mehr als tausend Flugzeuge.

Auch der *Flughafen Tegel* (1969–74) hat Maßstäbe gesetzt. Hier herrschen ganz besonders kurze Wege vor. Der „Drive-In-Airport" nach einem Entwurf von Gerkan, Marg und Nickels, dem heute erfolgreichsten Architekturbüro Deutschlands, war beispielgebend für Flughäfen in aller Welt. Seit 2006 befindet sich in Schönefeld ein neuer Zentralflughafen im Bau, der mit seiner Inbetriebnahme nach Tempelhof auch Tegel überflüssig machen soll.

Bahnhöfe im großen und im kleinen Stil

Berlin gehört zu den jüngsten Großstädten, sein Bahnsystem zu den ältesten in Europa. Das macht aus seinen Verkehrsarealen eine Institution mit Patina. Mit fünfhundert Fernzügen täglich fand der Eisenbahnverkehr im Berlin der Vorkriegszeit ein zentrales Drehkreuz zwischen Ost und West. Diese Funktion hat die Stadt mit der Teilung eingebüßt. Jetzt holt sie mit Riesenschritten auf. So ist auf dem Gelände des ehemaligen, bereits 1871 errichteten Lehrter Bahnhofs mit einer Fläche von 90.000 Quadratmetern der größte Kreuzungsbahnhof Europas entstanden: der 2006 eröffnete *Hauptbahnhof*. Er ist Mittel-

Momentaufnahmen des 2006 eröffneten neuen zentralen Hauptbahnhofs nach Plänen von Gerkan, Marg und Partner.

Photographic impressions of the new Central Railway Station, opened in 2006, designed by Gerkan, Marg and Partner.

famous. The city was entirely supplied by air by the Americans. More than one thousand airplanes a day took off from here in record time.

Tegel Airport (1969–74), too, set new benchmarks. Very short walkways are the norm here. The "drive-in airport," designed by Gerkan, Marg and Partner, the most successful architecture firm in Germany today, set an example for airports everywhere in the world. Since 2006, a new central airport has been under construction in Berlin Schönefeld; its opening is to make first Tempelhof Airport, then Tegel Airport, obsolete.

Train Stations in Big and Small Ways

Berlin is one of the youngest big cities, but its railway system is one of the oldest in Europe. This turns its transit areas into an institution hallowed by time. With five hundred long-distance trains running daily, railway transit found in prewar Berlin its central traffic hub linking the East and the West. The city lost this function after its division. Now it is catching up in giant strides. As such, on the site of former Lehrter Bahnhof built back in 1871, the largest European interchange station was constructed on a surface area comprising 90,000 square meters: Berlin's *Central Railway Station*, opened in 2006. It is

304

punkt des gesamten Zugverkehrs der Hauptstadt. Hier treffen sich, auf mehrere Etagen verteilt, Nord-Süd- und Ost-West-Verbindungen, zwei ICE-Linien, Regional- und S-Bahnen. Die Ausmaße dieses Prestigebaus nach den Plänen von Gerkan, Marg und Partner sind gewaltig: Die gläserne Halle in Ost-West-Richtung schwingt sich auf 321 Metern in den Spreebogen, die sie kreuzende Bahnhofshalle ist 160 Meter lang, eingerahmt von zwei 46 Meter hohen, parallelen, gläsernen Gebäuden, die wie Bügel die Gleise überspannen. Durch den neuen Hauptbahnhof haben die bisherigen Zentralstationen der Stadt, besonders der Bahnhof Zoologischer Garten, ihre Bedeutung für den Fernverkehr verloren. Schon ab 1884 hielten am Zoo Fernzüge neben der Vorortbahn. Von 1952 an war er der einzige Fernbahnhof in West-Berlin – mit nur zwei Bahnsteigen, eines der zahlreichen Phänomene, die den unnatürlichen Zustand der Stadt während ihrer Teilung vor Augen führen.

Vom einstmals größten und verkehrsreichsten Fernbahnhof Berlins, dem *Anhalter Bahnhof* (Franz Schwechten, 1876–1880) mit seiner riesigen Halle aus Glas und Gusseisen, steht heute allein der Portikus als kriegsbeschädigte Ruine. Dem Vorbild englischer Industriebauten nachempfunden, war dieser Bahnhof mit seinen prachtvollen Repräsentationsräumen das Tor zum Süden. Rundum reihten sich große Hotels aneinander. Direkt gegenüber befand sich das noble Excelsior, in dem Vicki Baums Weltbestseller „Menschen im Hotel" spielte.

Nach Originalplänen 1989 wiederaufgebaut: Eingangsgebäude zur U-Bahnstation Krumme Lanke in Zehlendorf, Alfred Grenander, 1929.

Rebuilt in 1989, based on the original designs: lobby building of subway station Krumme Lanke in district Zehlendorf, Alfred Grenander, 1929.

the center of the capital's entire railway transport system. This is where all lines meet on multiple levels: the north-south and east-west connections, two ICE lines, regional and city railway-trains. The dimensions of this prestigious building designed by Gerkan, Marg and Partner are tremendous: The glass hall extending in an east-westerly direction follows the curve of the Spree for 321 meters; the main concourse intersects with it and has a length of 160 meters; it is framed by two 46 meters tall, parallel glass buildings which stretch across the tracks like brackets. Because of the new Central Railway Station, the former central rail stations of the city, especially the station of Zoologischer Garten, have lost their significance for long-distance transit. Long-distance trains first began stopping at Zoo Station in 1884, next to suburban trains. In 1952, it was made the only long-distance train station in West Berlin – with only two platforms.

Nothing is left of the once largest and busiest long-distance train station in Berlin, the *Anhalter Bahnhof* (Franz Schwechten, 1876–1880), with its gigantic hall made of glass and cast iron, except the portico that has survived as a war-damaged ruin. Modeled after English industrial buildings, this train station with its magnificent representational halls was the gateway to the south. It was surrounded by grand hotels. Directly opposite from it stood the elegant Excelsior, which provided the setting for Vicki Baum's global bestseller *Grand Hotel*.

Auch ohne den Nahverkehr hätte es das moderne Berlin nicht gegeben. Das Netz der Stadtschnellbahn, S-Bahn genannt, entstand bis 1882, die Untergrundbahn erschloss von 1902 an den städtischen Raum in alle Richtungen. In diesem einst innovativsten Verkehrsnetz der Welt repräsentiert sich auch die Baugeschichte in Berlin. Da die Stadt während der Teilung in Agonie versank, fielen die alten U- und S-Bahnhöfe nicht wie in anderen westlichen Großstädten der Abrisswut zum Opfer. Nach dem Fall der Mauer sorgte eine sorgfältige Restaurierung dafür, dass sich diese Bahnhofe heute als Zeugen einer historischen Gebrauchsarchitektur bewundern lassen können: allen voran die Bahnstationen von Alfred Grenander, die auf der Strecke von Mitte bis zur Krummen Lanke (1929) eine Zeitreise durch die Stilgeschichte von der Jahrhundertwende bis zur sachlichen Formensprache der 1920er Jahre bieten. Mit dem U-Bahnhof Wittenbergplatz (1913) schuf der Architekt ein Theater in schwelgerischem Dekor, eine repräsentative Bühne für alle; der Alexanderplatz versinnbildlichte mit seinen langen Raumlinien die Geschwindigkeit der Metropole. Die meisten Baumeister des Bahnsystems sind zwar vergessen, doch die Zeugnisse ihrer Kunst stehen Solitären gleich im längst veränderten Stadtraum, so die historistischen oder Jugendstil-Empfangsgebäude der Vorortbahnen in Nikolassee, Grunewald und Frohnau oder die sachlich-funktionalen Anlagen des Neuen Bauens an der Bornholmer Straße.

U-Bahnstation Klosterstraße nahe dem Alexanderplatz, mit Motiven des Jugendstils und Assoziationen von Babylons Prozessionsstraße, Alfred Grenander, 1911–13.

Subway station Klosterstraße near Alexanderplatz, with Art Nouveau motifs and suggestions of Babylon's Processional Boulevard, Alfred Grenander, 1911–13.

Without local mass transit, modern Berlin would not have come into being either. The network of the city's rapid railway system (S-Bahn), was completed in 1882; the underground railway opened up the urban terrain in all directions starting in 1902. This once most innovative transit network in the world also reflects Berlin's architectural history. Since the city succumbed to a state of agony during its division, the old U and S stations did not fall victim to the rage of demolition that took place in other cities of the West. After the fall of the Wall, a meticulous restoration made sure they can be admired today as remnants of historical utilitarian architecture: First and foremost are the train stations designed by Alfred Grenander that, on the line running from Mitte to Krumme Lanke (1929), offer passengers a time-traveling tour through the history of styles from the turn of the century up to 1920s Objectivist iconography. With Wittenbergplatz (1913), the architect created a theater of voluptuous décor, a representational stage for everyone; Alexanderplatz Station emblematized the city's speed with its long, geometrical lines. Most of these masterbuilders may be forgotten by now, but testimonies to their art remain standing like stand-alone buildings in a cityscape long since transformed, such as the Historicist or Art Nouveau entrance halls of the suburban train stations in Nikolassee, Grunewald and Frohnau, or the objectivist-functional complexes built in the style of New Building on Bornholmer Straße.

Wohnen, Arbeiten, Sport

Residence, Work, Sports

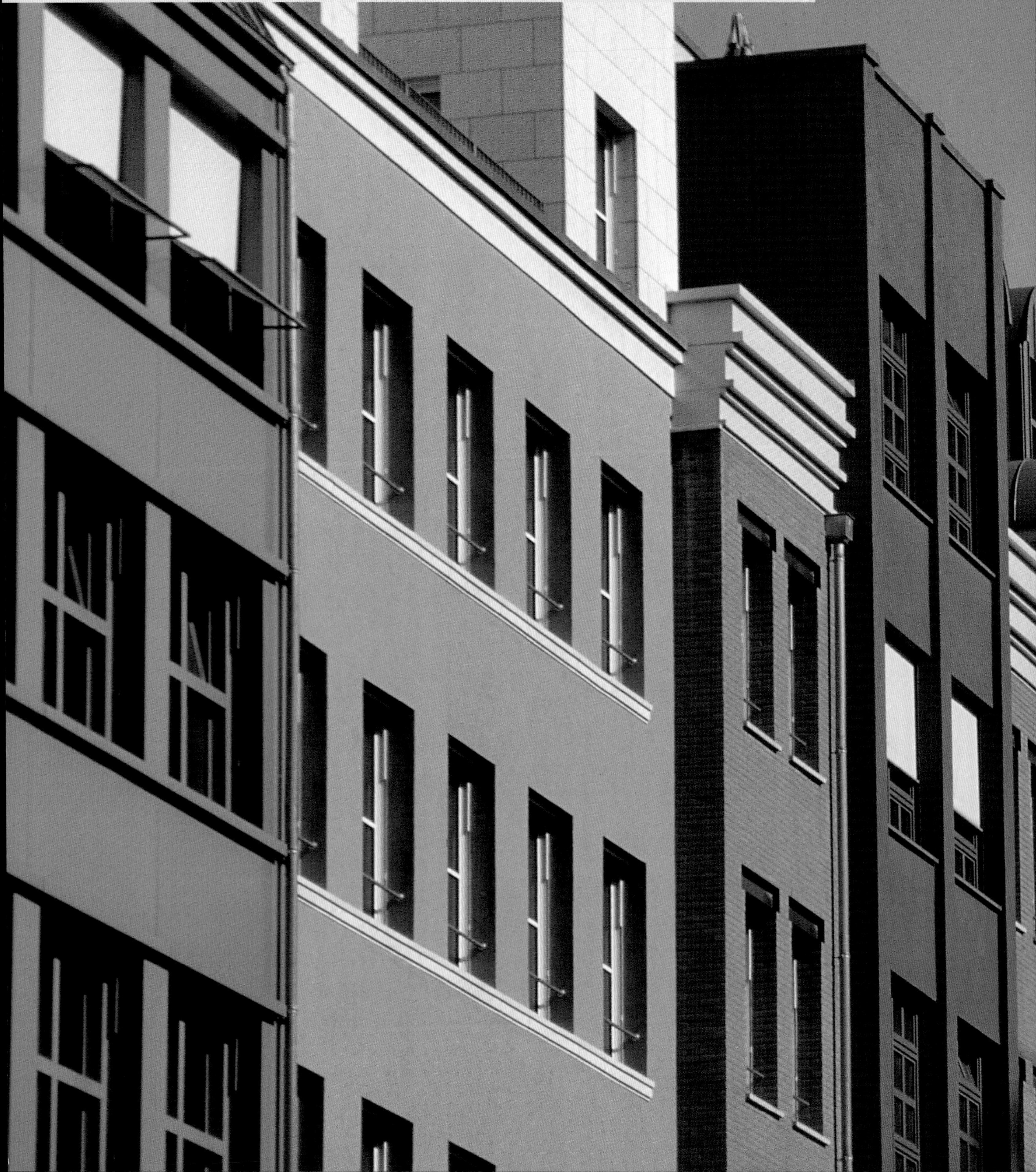

Berlins Wohnhäuser erzählen eine ganz eigene Geschichte der Stadt: Sie beginnt bei den Resten des „Alten Berlin" und führt über die Friedrichstadt des 17. und 18. Jahrhunderts mit ihren singulären Adels- und Bürgerpalais – dem Ribbeck-Haus als einzig erhaltenem Privatbau aus der Spätrenaissance und „der schönsten Ecke Berlins", dem Rokoko-Kleinod des Ephraimpalais – bis zum Klassizismus Schinkelscher Prägung und der alle Quartiere erfassenden Gründerzeit. Diese Epoche wurde vom Bau der Mietskasernen und der geografischen Verlagerung der gesellschaftlichen Mitte in die westlichen Regionen der Stadt bestimmt.

Villen, Wohnhäuser und Siedlungen

Das neue Bürgertum machte sich aus dem Zentrum auf und ließ sich zunächst am Rand des Tiergartens, am Kurfürstendamm und schließlich im Grunewald und am Wannsee nieder,

Ephraimpalais/Ephraim Palace, Friedrich Wilhelm Diterichs, 1761–64, gebaut für Veitel Heine Ephraim, Hofjuwelier Friedrichs II. Unten: Rokoko-Treppenhaus (built for Veitel Heine Ephraim, court jeweler of Frederick II. Below: Rococo stairway).

Rechts oben/Right above: Ribbeckhaus, Hans Georg von Ribbeck, Katharina von Brösicke, 1624, ältestes Wohnhaus in Berlin und einziges erhaltenes Renaissancegebäude (Berlin's oldest residential and sole surviving Renaissance building).

Rechts unten/Right below: Wannsee-Villa, Wilhelm Martens, 1891/92.

Vorherige Seite/Previous page: „Quartier Schützenstraße", Aldo Rossi, 1995–97; dahinter/behind it: GSW-Hochhaus/High-rise, Matthias Sauerbruch, Louisa Hutton, 1989–99, 22 Etagen, Stahl- und Glaskonstruktion mit Segeldach (22 stories, steel and glass construction with sail roof).

Berlin's residential buildings have their own city history to tell: It begins with what is left of "Old Berlin" and moves through Friedrichstadt in the 17th and 18th centuries with its unique aristocratic and bourgeois mansions – the Ribbeck House as the only surviving private building of the late Renaissance and "the most beautiful corner of Berlin," the Rococo jewel that is Ephraim Palace – to Schinkel-style Neoclassicism and the Wilhelminian *Gründerzeit* era that encompassed all city districts. This epoch was determined by the construction of tenement buildings and the geographical relocation of the middle classes to the western regions of the city.

Villas, Apartment Houses and Settlements

The new bourgeoisie left the city center and initially resettled at the edge of Tiergarten, on Kurfürstendamm and finally in Grunewald and at Lake Wannsee, where entirely new *villa*

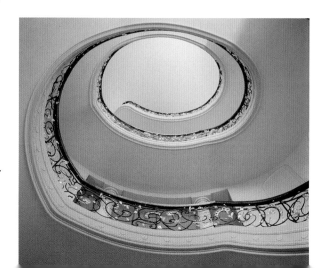

Kreuzberger Mischung.
Linke Seite: Häuserfassaden rund um den Chamisso-Platz.
Oben: Wohnhaus in Riehmers Hofgarten, ein Bauensemble aus der Gründerzeit, nach Plänen von Wilhelm Riehmer und Otto Mrosk, 1880–99, gebaut für Kaufleute, Handwerker und Offiziere.

Unten: Neubauten im Rahmen der Internationalen Bauausstellung (IBA) als Beispiel für eine „behutsame Stadterneuerung" in einem Problembezirk; links das Torhaus am Fraenkelufer, 1982–84, rechts das Wohnhaus an der Admiralstraße nach Plänen von Hinrich Baller, 1987.

Kreuzberg Mix.
Left page: Façades of buildings around Chamisso Square.
Above: Residential building in Riehmers Hofgarten, Wilhelminian architectural complex, designs by Wilhelm Riehmer, Otto Mrosk, built in 1880–99 for merchants, craftsmen and military officers.

Below: New buildings created for the International Building Exhibition (IBA) as an example of "careful urban renewal" in a problem district; on the left: gate building on Fraenkelufer, 1982–84, on the right: house on Admiralstraße designed by Hinrich Baller, built in 1987.

wo ganz neue *Villenkolonien* entstanden. In den inneren Wohn-
bezirken herrschte der Wilhelminismus mit ornamental ge-
schmückten *Fassaden*, die in den Formen von Gotik, Renaissance, Barock oder einer Mischung aus allen Stilen dekoriert
sind. In den besseren Quartieren sind sie durch Erker und
Balkone belebt. Da man in Berlin hauptsächlich zur Miete
wohnte, kam es in den Häusern zu dem für die Stadt charakteristischen Nebeneinander sozial unterschiedlicher Schich-
ten. So lebte im Vorderhaus die gehobenere Klientel, hinten
Dienstboten, Handwerker und Lohnarbeiter.

Besonders für *Kreuzberg* wurde die Durchmischung von
Wohnen und Arbeiten typisch. Die Quergebäude waren oftmals
als komplette Fabriketagen angelegt. In Zuschnitt und Kom-
fort unterschieden sich die Wohnungen je nach Bezirk. Während in Charlottenburg und Wilmersdorf großbürgerliche Häuser mit geräumigen Innenhöfen an der Tagesordnung und
Wohnungen mit zehn und mehr Zimmern keine Seltenheit waren, wurde in den Arbeiterquartieren der Raum rationalisiert.
Auch hier war ein Vorderhaus mit Seitenflügeln und Quergebäuden die Norm, wobei deren Anzahl nach dem Bebauungs-
plan von Stadtplaner James Hobrecht ungeregelt blieb, so dass

Linke Seite: Die Großsiedlung
Siemensstadt, errichtet für die
Arbeiter und Angestellten der
Firma Siemens, Gesamtplanung
Hans Scharoun, gebaut 1929–31;
Fotos um 1935.
Unten: Hufeisensiedlung Britz im
Bezirk Neukölln, Bruno Taut und
Martin Wagner, 1925–33.

Left page: Mega-settlement
Siemensstadt, built for workmen
and employees of Siemens
Company, comprehensive
planning by Hans Scharoun,
built in 1929–31; photos c. 1935.
Below: Horseshoe settlement
Britz, district of Neukölln, Bruno
Taut, Martin Wagner, 1925–33.

colonies came into being. The inner-city residential districts
were dominated by Wilhelminianism with its ornamental
façades decorated with Gothic, Renaissance and Baroque
details or a mixture of all styles. In the more well-to-do quarters,
they are animated by oriels and balconies. Since Berlin residents chiefly rented their living quarters, buildings usually
exhibited the city's characteristic mixture of socially diverse
classes living in close proximity. Socially privileged residents
lived in street-front buildings, while servants, craftspeople
and wage workers had their quarters in the back.

This mixture of living and working was especially typical of
Kreuzberg. Transverse buildings often housed entire floors of
factory facilities. As to layout and comfort, the apartments
differed from district to district. While grand-bourgeois buildings
with spacious interior courtyards were commonplace and
apartments with ten or more rooms no rarity in Charlottenburg
and Wilmersdorf, space was rationed in working-class districts.
Here, too, a street-front building with wings and transverse
buildings was the norm, though their numbers remained
unregulated, true to the building plan devised by city planner
James Hobrecht, so that up to six houses with transverse build-

bis zu sechs eng hintereinander gestaffelte Häuser mit Quergebäuden möglich waren. Nur die Maße der Innenhöfe waren vorgeschrieben: Bis 1887 mussten sie wenigstens 5,34 mal 5,34 Meter groß sein, damit die Feuerwehr dort wenden konnte. In den überbelegten, nur unzureichend mit Sanitäranlagen ausgestatteten Mietshäusern herrschten oft miserable Lebensbedingungen. Heute gehören die komplett sanierten Altbauwohnungen in der einst größten Mietskasernenstadt zu den beliebtesten Wohnformen. Vom Krieg und Zerstörungen der Nachkriegszeit weitgehend verschonte, ungewöhnlich geschlossen erhaltene Ensembles dieser so genannten *Kiezarchitektur* finden sich vor allem in Prenzlauer Berg, Friedrichshain und Kreuzberg.

Nach dem Ende der Monarchie blühten revolutionäre Ideen auf – als radikale Antwort auf die wilhelminische Mietskaserne. Es entstanden *Wohnanlagen* neuen Typs; das Motto hieß: „Licht, Luft und Sonne". Mit ihren über die Stadt bis an die Peripherie verteilten Bauten machten Walter Gropius, Hans Scharoun, Bruno Taut und viele andere Berlin zum architektonischen Brennpunkt der Moderne in Deutschland. Ihr Kennzeichen sind der Verzicht auf repräsentative Details, die Verwendung von industriell gefertigten Baustoffen, weißer Verputz, asymmetrische Gruppierung kubischer Elemente sowie Funk-

Modernes Wohnen, entworfen für die Interbau, Internationale Bauausstellung, 1957.
Oben und unten:
Das Corbusier-Haus nach Plänen von Le Corbusier, 1956–58.
Linke Seite: Das Hansaviertel am Rand des Tiergartens, 1955–60, nach Entwürfen von Walter Gropius, Max Taut, Oscar Niemeyer, Alvar Aalto und vielen anderen.

Modern Living, designed for Interbau, International Building Exhibition, 1957.
Above and below:
Corbusier House, designed by Le Corbusier, 1956–58.
Left page: Hansa Quarter on the edge of Tiergarten, 1955–60, designed by Walter Gropius, Max Taut, Oscar Niemeyer, Alvar Aalto, and many others.

ings stacked one behind the next were quite conceivable. Only the dimensions of the interior courtyards were regulated: Up to 1887, they had to be at least 5.34 by 5.34 meters large so that the fire engines could turn around. Living conditions in these overpopulated tenements inadequately equipped with sanitary facilities were often miserable. Completely renovated, these old-style buildings are among the most popular types of living quarters today in this city once furnished with the greatest number of tenements in the world. Spared by the war and by postwar demolitions, such unusually dense and intact complexes of neighborhood or *Kiez architecture* can above all be found in Prenzlauer Berg, Friedrichshain and Kreuzberg.

After the end of the monarchy, revolutionary ideas flourished – as a radical answer to Wilhelminian tenement buildings. A new type of *residential facility* came into being; its motto: "Light, air and sun." As their buildings covered the city from center to periphery, Walter Gropius, Hans Scharoun, Bruno Taut, and many others made Berlin the architectural focal point of Modernism in Germany. Their hallmarks are the abandonment of representative detail, the use of industrially produced building materials, white plasterwork, an asymmetrical arrangement of cubical elements, as well as functionality, objectivity and an

tionalität, Sachlichkeit und Lichtfülle. Schon die erste Groß-siedlung des sozialen Wohnungsbaus nach dem Ersten Welt-krieg war ein Wurf, sie gehört zu den bekanntesten ihrer Art überhaupt: die *Hufeisensiedlung Britz*. Die 1072 Wohneinhei-ten und Einfamilienhäuser waren für Mieter mit geringem Ein-kommen vorgesehen. Um die Baukosten niedrig zu halten, wurden Aushub und Transport mechanisiert. Die Serienferti-gung erforderte einfache und kostengünstige Formen: Mittels Normierung, dank Flachdächern, der Standardisierung der Fenstergrößen und durch den Einsatz von Farbe, die Taut als „billigstes Gestaltungsmittel" pries, wurde bravourös das wirt-schaftliche Bauen einer Großsiedlung erprobt. 2008 ernann-te sie die UNESCO zum Weltkulturerbe, gemeinsam mit wei-teren großen Wohnanlagen in der Hauptstadt der Weimarer Republik: der *Ringsiedlung Siemensstadt*, der *Weißen Stadt* in Reinickendorf, der *Gartenstadt Falkenberg* in Treptow-Köpenick, der Siedlung *Schillerpark* im Wedding und der *Wohn-stadt Carl Legien* am Prenzlauer Berg.

1945 war Berlin „das größte zusammenhängende Ruinen-gebiet Europas" – rund vierzig Prozent des Wohnraums waren vernichtet, die Innenstadt lag zu zwei Dritteln in Trümmern. So bekam die Stadt ein vollkommen neues Gesicht. Stalinallee, Hansaviertel, die Gebäude der IBA spiegeln heute die politi-

"Moabiter Werder", Wohnanlage für Bundesbedienstete (residential complex for federal employees), Georg Bumiller, 1997–99, Länge/length 320 m, 718 Wohneinheiten, Ziegelfassade (718 residential units, brick façade).

Linke Seite/Left page:
DDR-Architektur/GDR architecture. Plattenbau/ precast concrete slab construction, 1984–89. (oben/above).
Hochhaus Weberwiese mit Fries/ High-rise Weberwiese with frieze, Hermann Henselmann, 1951/52 (unten/below).

abundance of light. Even the first mega-settlement of subsi-dized housing created after World War I was a success; it was the most famous one of its kind: the *Horseshoe Settlement in Britz*. The 1,072 apartment units and single-family homes were reserved for low-income renters. To keep building costs in check, digging and transport were mechanized. Its production in series required simple and inexpensive forms: Thus, the commercially viable construction of a mega-settlement was daringly given its trial run by means of standardization via flat roofs, standard win-dow sizes and the deployment of paint touted, by Taut, as the "cheapest means of design." In 2008, UNESCO declared it a world heritage site, along with other large residential estates of the capital of the Weimar Republic: *Ring Settlement Siemensstadt*, *White City* in Reinickendorf, *Garden City Falken-berg* in Treptow-Köpenick, *Schillerpark* settlement in Wedding, and *Residential City Carl Legien* in Prenzlauer Berg.

In 1945, Berlin was "the largest contiguous field of ruins in Europe" – some 40 percent of residential space had been destroyed; up to two-thirds of the inner city lay in ruins. As such, the city was given an entirely new face. Today, Stalinallee, the Hansa Quarter and the IBA buildings reflect the political development of the divided metropolis. The architectural ideal for reconstructing the West was Weimar Republic Modernism;

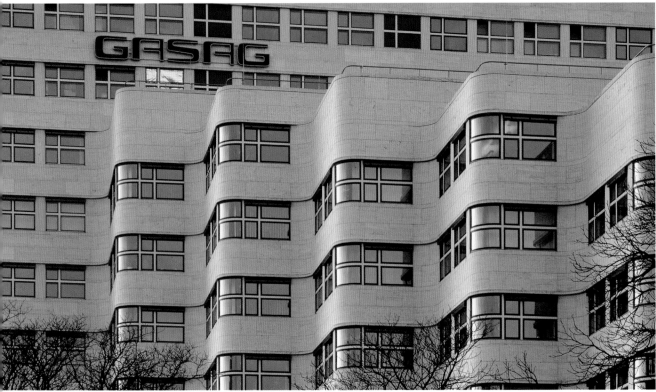

Eines der schönsten Häuser
Berlins, das denkmalgeschützte
Shell-Haus, ein Bürobau am
Landwehrkanal, nach Plänen von
Emil Fahrenkamp, 1930–32.
Die Fassade ist mit römischem
Travertin verkleidet.

One of Berlin's most beautiful
buildings, landmark-protected
Shell House, an office building
on Landwehrkanal, designs by
Emil Fahrenkamp, built in
1930–32. Its façade is clad with
Roman travertine.

Wie ein Gürteltier zieht sich das Ludwig-Erhard-Haus, Sitz der Berliner Industrie- und Handelskammer, mit seinen 15 elliptischen Bögen durch die angrenzende Bebauung. Architekt: Nicholas Grimshaw, 1994–97.

Like an armadillo, the Ludwig Erhard House, seat of Berlin's Chamber of Industry and Commerce, glides among adjacent buildings with its 15 elliptical arches. Architect: Nicholas Grimshaw, 1994–97.

Haus der Deutschen Wirtschaft, der zentrale, mit einem Glasdach überspannte Innenhof (oben und unten), Schweger und Partner, 1997–99.

House of German Business, its central interior courtyard is covered by a glass roof (above and below), Schweger and Partner, 1997–99.

sche Entwicklung der geteilten Metropole wider. Zum architektonischen Leitbild des Wiederaufbaus im Westen wurde die Moderne der Weimarer Republik, deren Protagonisten nun als Verfechter des International Style aus dem Exil in den USA nach Deutschland zurückkehrten. Im Osten huldigte man unter der sowjetischen Besatzungsmacht einem monumentalen Neoklassizismus. Beide Systeme standen nicht nur politisch in direkter Konkurrenz zueinander. Als Antwort auf den propagandistischen Erfolg, den die DDR mit dem Bau der *Stalinallee* 1952 verbuchte, wurde ein Jahr später in West-Berlin die Internationale Bauausstellung (Interbau) ausgerufen, mit ihrem Herzstück, dem neuen *Hansaviertel* am Rand des Tiergartens. Walter Gropius, Max Taut, Oscar Niemeyer, Alvar Aalto – insgesamt mehr als fünfzig hochrangige Planer aus dreizehn Ländern interpretierten ihre Vorstellungen modernen Bauens. So entstanden 1160 Wohnungen in diesem Modellviertel im Grünen inmitten der Stadt. Einen ganz anderen Akzent setzte etwa zwanzig Jahre später die von 1979 bis 1987 stattfindende *Internationale Bauausstellung (IBA)*. Sie war das Ergebnis einer Wende in der Westberliner Stadtplanung, die sich nun von Trabantenstädten und Kahlschlagsanierung verabschiedete. Stattdessen sollte die Stadt, vor allem Kreuzberg, das wegen seiner Randlage an der Grenze zu Ost-Berlin für den Totalabriss vorgesehen gewesen war, wieder belebt werden. Der Planung wurde erstmals seit dem Einzug der Moderne wieder die historische Proportion der Stadt zugrunde gelegt.

Büros, Banken und Wissenschaft

Einen ganz anderen Bauboom erlebte das geeinte Berlin, vor allem in Mitte und in den östlichen Bezirken. Mit der Neubestimmung der Stadt hielt eine vollkommen neue Geschäftswelt Einzug. Banken schufen sich repräsentative Dependancen, internationale Konzerne nutzen die Nobilität historischer Gebäude. Ein architektonisches Schaulaufen hat eingesetzt wie in den 1920er Jahren, als Berlin nicht nur der größte Wirtschaftsstandort Deutschlands, sondern der drittgrößte Europas war. Von den Werks- und Fabrikanlagen wurde die Stadt auch in ihren räumlichen Dimensionen geprägt. Ganz

its protagonists now returned to Germany from their United States exile as advocates of the International Style. Under Soviet occupation, the East paid homage to a monumental type of Neoclassicism. Both systems were competing with each other not only on the level of politics. To counter the building of *Stalinallee*, a 1952 GDR propaganda coup, West Berlin held the International Building Exhibition (Interbau) with its centerpiece, the new *Hansa Quarter* at the edge of Tiergarten. Walter Gropius, Max Taut, Oscar Niemeyer, Alvar Aalto – altogether more than fifty leading architects from thirteen countries interpreted their ideas on modern building. As such, 1,160 apartments were created in this model quarter surrounded by green fields in the middle of the city. Entirely new priorities were set some twenty years later during the *International Building Exhibition (IBA)* which ran from 1979 to 1987. The IBA was the result of a turnaround in West Berlin urban planning, which now said good-bye to satellite settlements and slash-and-burn renovation. Instead, the city was to be revitalized – especially Kreuzberg that, due to its location on the border to East Berlin, had been slated for total demolition. For the first time since the entrance of Modernism into the city, urban planning was based once again on Berlin's historical proportion.

Offices, Banks and Science

Unified Berlin was subject to a very different kind of building boom, especially in Mitte and the eastern districts. As the city was given a new direction, an entirely novel kind of business environment moved in. Banks created representational branches; international concerns made use of the classy cachet of historical buildings. An architectural tournament was

neue Stadtlandschaften wie Siemensstadt, Moabit oder das Gebiet Oberspree entstanden. Von Anfang an legte man Wert darauf, die Firmengebäude und Produktionsstätten funktionsgerecht und dennoch architektonisch ansprechend zu gestalten. Viele dieser heute denkmalgeschützten Zweckbauten werden inzwischen „umgenutzt" und mit neuem Leben erfüllt. Denn Berlin als Industriestandort ist endgültig verloren. Dafür wachsen andere Bedeutungen nach, als Stadt der Dienstleistung, der Bildung und Wissenschaft.

Die schönste Fassade der 1920er-Jahre in der Stadt besitzt Emil Fahrenkamps *Shell-Haus* am Landwehrkanal. Errichtet wurde dieser damals revolutionäre Stahlskeletthochbau in Berlin von 1930 bis 1932 als Niederlassung der Rhenania-Ossag Mineralwerke AG, des heutigen Ölkonzerns Shell. Bis heute überragt der elegante Bürobau nicht nur aufgrund sei-

Oben: Deutsches Institut für Normung, Horst Ziel, 1990–92.
Unten: Büro- und Geschäftshaus Trias an der Holzmarktstraße, drei 13-geschossige Türme, Lucia Beringer, Günther Wawrik, 1994–96.

Above: German Institute for Standardization (DIN), Horst Ziel, 1990–92.
Below: Office and business building Trias on Holzmarktstraße, three 13-story towers, Lucia Beringer, Günther Wawrik, 1994–96.

launched in the 1920s when Berlin was not only the largest business location in Germany, but also the third-largest in Europe. Plant and factory facilities also left their mark on the city's spatial dimensions. Entirely new cityscapes were created, such as Siemensstadt, Moabit or the area of Oberspree. From the start, care was taken to design factory buildings and production sites in ways both functionally capable and architecturally appealing. Protected by landmark status today, many of these utilitarian buildings have in the meantime been "reassigned" as to their usage and filled with new life, because Berlin as a hub of industry has vanished for good. However, other determinations have emerged to make up for this loss, thus turning Berlin into a city of the service industry, culture and science.

The city's most beautiful façade of the 1920s fronts Emil Fahrenkamp's Shell House by the Landwehrkanal. Constructed

ner Höhe alle anderen Gebäude der Gegend. Wie in einer fließenden Bewegung rundet sich das Gebäude an seinen Ecken
auch die stahlgefassten Fensterbänder sind in einem Viertel-
kreis rund um die Ecken herumgezogen. Die Fassade ist mit
römischem Travertin verkleidet. Um diese Platten nach den Zerstörungen des Zweiten Weltkriegs originalgetreu zu ersetzen,
erwirkte man bei der Generalsanierung 1999, dass der bereits
geschlossene Steinbruch in der Nähe Roms wieder geöffnet
wurde.

Eines der großen Bauprojekte der 1990er-Jahre im Westen
Berlins war das neue Domizil der Industrie- und Handelskammer und der Berliner Börse von Nicholas Grimshaw. Wie ein in
sich bewegtes »Gürteltier« aus Stahl und Beton beherrscht das

Oben/Above: Universal Music,
ehemals Eierkühlhaus/former
cold storage building
(Oskar Pusch, 1928/29),
Osthafen, Umbau/remodeled
2000–02, Reinhard Müller.
Unten/Below: Bürohäuser/office
buildings „Treptowers", Gerhard
Spangenberg, Schweger und
Partner, 1995–98.

Links: GSW-Hochhaus/High-rise,
Sauerbruch, Hutton, 1989–99.

in 1930–1932 and then considered revolutionary in Berlin, this
steel frame high rise originally housed the Rhenania-Ossag
Mineral Works Corporation, today's Shell Oil Company. Up to
the present day, this elegant office building towers above all
others in the area, and not merely because of its height.
Creating the effect of one fluid movement, the building's walls
round off at the corners; even the steel-enclosed window
ribbons flow around the corners by curving in quarter circles.
The façade is faced with Roman travertine. To replace these
slabs with replicas of the originals after the damages wrought
by World War II, a special dispensation was obtained during
comprehensive renovation in 1999, so that the already closed
quarry near Rome could be reopened.

Ludwig-Erhard-Haus den gesamten Straßenzug. Fünfzehn stählerne Bögen, die sich entsprechend der wechselnden Breite des Grundstücks zur Mitte hin verschieben, um am Ende mehr als sechzig Meter zu überspannen, bilden das Gerüst für eine komplett stützenfreie Halle.

Eine Stadt für Wissenschaft, Wirtschaft und Medien wird in *Adlershof* aus dem Boden gezaubert. Auf einer Fläche von 120 Fußballfeldern entsteht einer der größten Technologieparks Europas. Bisher wurden für wissenschaftlich-technische Schlüsselbranchen vier Innovationszentren gebaut. Blickfang im gesamten Areal ist das Gebäudeensemble von Sauerbruch & Hutton, das aus einem eingeschossigen und einem dreigeschossigen jeweils amöbenförmigen Glasbau besteht. Hinter den geschwungenen Fensterfronten sind die bunt gefassten Betonteile sichtbar, deren Farbpalette ebenso wie die der bei Sonnenlicht heruntergelassenen Jalousien ein breites Lichtspektrum visualisieren.

Als Inbegriff zukunftsweisender Architektur galt von Anfang an der *Einsteinturm*. Der Bau auf dem Telegrafenberg in Potsdam wurde 1920 bis 1924 im Auftrag der Einstein-Stiftung errichtet. Hier sollte spektralanalytische Forschung betrieben und der Nachweis geführt werden, dass Einsteins Relativitätstheorie in der Praxis zutraf. So entstand ein Zweckbau, das Gehäuse für ein Sonnenobservatorium mit einem eigens entwickelten Spezialteleskop, das bis in die drehbare zwanzig Meter hohe Turmkuppel reichte. Erich Mendelsohn entwarf das Gebäude im expressionistisch-organischen Stil. Sein erstes großes Werk ist eine gleichsam skulpturale Architektur, stromlinienförmig, geschwungen und dabei nahezu ohne

Innenhof des Eugen-Gutmann-Hauses am Pariser Platz, Sitz der Dresdner Bank, Meinhard von Gerkan, 1996/97.
Rechts: Futuristisch gestaltete Raumskulptur im Atrium der DZ-Bank am Brandenburger Tor, Frank O. Gehry, 1996–2001.

Interior courtyard of Gutmann House on Pariser Platz, seat of Dresdner Bank, Meinhard von Gerkan, 1996/97.
Right: Futuristically designed spatial installation in the DZ Bank atrium at Brandenburg Gate, Frank O. Gehry, 1996–2001.

One of the great building projects of the 1990s in the western part of Berlin was the new domicile for the Chamber of Industry and Commerce and the Berlin Stock Exchange designed by Nicholas Grimshaw. The *Ludwig Erhard House* dominates the entire street like an "armadillo" made of steel and concrete and animated by interior movement. Fifteen steel arches that, due to the varying width of the lot, are realigned towards the center to span more than sixty meters at the end, constitute the frame of a completely column-free hall.

In *Adlershof*, a city for science, business and the media is being conjured up out of the soil. On an area covering 120 soccer fields, one of the largest technology parks in Europe is currently under construction. Up to now, four centers of innovation have been built for scientific and technological key industries. The site's most eye-catching structure is the building complex by Sauerbruch & Hutton consisting of two amoeba-like glass buildings, respectively one story and three-stories tall. Behind curved window fronts, colored concrete segments are visible; the colors of these segments as well as those of the blinds shut against the sunlight evoke a broad spectrum of visible light.

The *Einstein Tower* has always been considered the embodiment of progressive architecture. Commissioned by the Einstein Foundation, this structure on Telegrafenberg in Potsdam was constructed in 1920–1924. This is where research in spectral analysis was to be conducted and where proof was to be obtained that Einstein's theory of relativity could be adapted to practical purposes. As such, a utilitarian building was built, a casing for a solar observatory with a special telescope that extended up into the swiveling tower dome, twenty meters

rechte Winkel. Die Inneneinrichtung des Gebäudes ist weitgehend erhalten, darunter auch das mit Originalmöbeln ausgestattete Arbeitszimmer des Nobelpreisträgers. Einstein selbst hat allerdings selten auf dem Telegrafenberg gearbeitet. Heute ist der Turm Teil des Astrophysikalischen Instituts Potsdam.

Antikisierender und minimalistischer Sportstättenbau

Die berühmteste Sportanlage der Stadt, das Olympiagelände, strahlt in ihrer Gesamtheit noch heute den monumentalen Charakter der Architektur des Nationalsozialismus aus: mit dem Reichssportfeld, das eine Freilichtbühne (die heutige Waldbühne), ein Aufmarschgelände, das Maifeld mit der Langemarckhalle, das Sportforum sowie das Schwimm-, Hockey- und Reiterstadion umfasste. Es wurde für die XI. Olympischen Sommerspiele 1936 angelegt und war für die Machthaber eine willkommene Gelegenheit, aller Welt das Bild eines friedlichen Deutschland vorzugaukeln.

Mittelpunkt des Geländes ist das elliptische Stadion für hunderttausend Menschen (heute 74 244). Werner March entwarf es, wobei er die Arena um zwölf Meter absenkte, was dem Gebäude seine monumentale Wucht nahm. Die antikisierende Gestaltung sowie die Steinverkleidung der Stahlbetonkonstruktion gehen auf Albert Speer zurück. 2002 bis 2004 wurde das Stadion von Gerkan, Marg und Partner zu einer modernen und fußballgerechten Multifunktionsarena umgebaut und bekam ein offenes Dach.

Neben Fußball haben Schwimmen und Radfahren Tradition in Berlin. Weil es um die hygienischen Verhältnisse in der Mietskasernenstadt der vorigen Jahrhundertwende nicht zum Besten stand, sah man die Einrichtung von öffentlichen Bade- und Schwimmanstalten als kommunale Aufgabe an. „Badetempel für alle", hieß es damals. Vier davon sind erhalten und in Betrieb. Der schönste liegt im Arbeiterbezirk Neukölln. In freier Nachbildung antiker Vorbilder wurden die beiden mit feinem Marmor, Travertin und Mosaiken verkleideten Schwimmhallen als dreischiffige Basiliken gestaltet. Das architektonische Juwel von 1914 wurde dem damals hohen, sozialen Anspruch gemäß durch eine mit dem Bad verbundene Volksbibliothek (heute Heimatmuseum) ergänzt.

Zentrum für Photonik und Optische Technologien im Technologiepark Adlershof (Center for Photonics and Optical Technologies in Adlershof Technology Park), Matthias Sauerbruch und Louisa Hutton, 1996–98.

Rechte Seite/Right page: Sonnenobservatorium/solar observatory „Einsteinturm", Telegrafenberg in Potsdam, Erich Mendelsohn, 1920–24.

high. Erich Mendelsohn designed the building in the Expressionist style. His first great work is, as it were, a sculptural kind of architecture, streamlined, curved, with barely a right angle. The building's interior has largely survived intact, including the Nobel Prize winner's study with its original furniture. Einstein himself, though, rarely worked on Telegraph Hill. Today, the Einstein Tower belongs to the Astrophysical Institute in Potsdam.

Faux-Antique and Minimalist Sports Facilities

As a whole, the city's most famous sports facility, the Olympic grounds, still today reflect the monumental character of National Socialist architecture: with the Sports Field of the Reich that included an open-air stage (today's Waldbühne), drill grounds, the May Field with Langemarck Hall, the Sports Forum, as well as a swimming pool, hockey stadium and riding ring. It was built for the XIth Olympic Summer Games in 1936 and constituted a prime opportunity for those in power to make the international public believe in a peaceful Germany.

Centerpiece of the grounds was the elliptical stadium for one hundred thousand (today: 74,244) spectators. Werner March designed it by lowering the arena by twelve meters so as to reduce the building's monumental bulk. The faux-antique designs as well as the stone facing covering the iron-steel construction go back to Albert Speer. In 2002–2004, Gerkan, Marg and Partner converted the stadium into a modern multi-function arena with an open roof and capable of accommodating soccer.

In addition to soccer, swimming and cycling are also traditional sports in Berlin. Since sanitary conditions in this city of tenements at the previous turn of the century were not up to par, the installation of public bathing and swimming facilities was considered a community obligation. "Bathing temples for everyone," such was the motto in those days. Four of these have been preserved. The most beautiful of them is located in the working-class district of Neukölln. Its swimming halls, faced with fine marble, travertine and mosaics, were designed as three-aisled basilicas in a liberal imitation of classical models. The architectural jewel of 1914 was complemented with a public library (a museum for local history, today) to accommodate the demanding social standards of those times.

Ausgang
Exit

24

25-41

WC
25-4

Das Berliner Olympiastadion, nach Plänen von Werner March 1934–36 gebaut anlässlich der Olympischen Sommerspiele 1936. Vorhergehende Seite: Das Stadion nach grundlegendem Umbau und Modernisierung sowie Teilüberdachung, Gerkan, Marg und Partner, 2000–04. Links und unten: Unverkennbar der Stil der nationalsozialistischen Auftraggeber – oberer Umgang nach Osten und die Skulpturengruppe *Staffelläufer* von Karl Albiker (1878–1962), Muschelkalk, Höhe 7 m (unten). Rechte Seite: Blick auf das Olympische Tor (Osttor) und das teilüberdachte Stadion nach der Modernisierung (unten).

Olympic Stadium Berlin, designed by Werner March, built in 1934–36 on the occasion of the 1936 Olympic Summer Games. Previous page: The stadium after comprehensive remodeling and modernization, with new partial roof, Gerkan, Marg und Partner, 2000–04. Left and below: The National Socialist style of these structures is unmistakable: upper ring to the east and twin sculptures *Relay Runners* by Karl Albiker (1878–1962), shell limestone, height: 7 m (below). Right page: View of the Olympic Gate (Eastern Gate) and the stadium with partial roof after modernization (below).

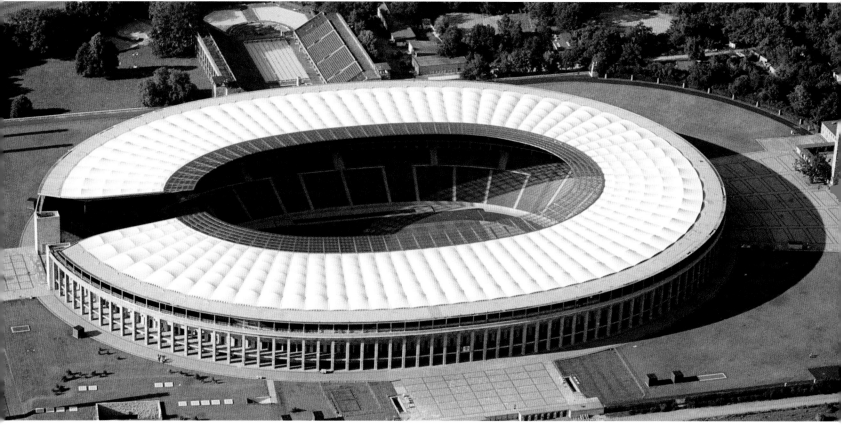

Für avancierte Architektur steht das Schwimm- und Radsportzentrum an der Landsberger Allee, das Dominique Perrault anlässlich der (gescheiterten) Olympia-Bewerbung Berlins entwarf. Nur neunzig Zentimeter ragen die Dächer der beiden Hallen über die Rasenfläche im Europa-Sportpark, darunter verbirgt sich eine der größten Veranstaltungsarenen Europas für bis zu zwölftausend Zuschauer: das Velodrom. Daneben erstreckt sich unter einem rechteckigen, ebenso mit silbernem Metallgewebe bespannten Dach die Schwimm- und Sprunghalle, ein Zentrum für den Hochleistungs-, Schul- und Vereinssport. Siebzehn Meter tief sind die beiden Gebäude ins Erdreich gegraben und von weitem so gut wie unsichtbar – ein minimalistisch selbstbewusstes Gegenmodell zu den weltweit üblichen megalomanen Spiel- und Wettkampfstätten.

Oben: Stadtbad Neukölln, nach Plänen von Reinhold Kiehl, 1914. Unten/Rechte Seite: Europa-Sportpark, Dominique Perrault, 1994–98: Velodrom (unten), Sport- und Sprungbecken, Luftaufnahme von Velodrom und Schwimmhalle.

Above: Neukölln Public Baths, designs by Reinhold Kiehl, 1914. Below/Right page: Europa Sports Park, Dominique Perrault, 1994–98: Velodrome (below), sports and diving pool, aerial photo of Velodrome and swimming hall.

Representing advanced architecture, the Swimming and Cycling Center on Landsberger Allee was designed by Dominique Perrault on the occasion of Berlin's (failed) bid to host the Olympic Games. The roofs of the halls protrudes barely ninety centimeter above the lawn of the Eurosportpark, hidden beneath is one of the largest event arenas in Europe capable of accommodating up to twelve thousand spectators: the Velodrome. Located next to it, under a rectangular roof similarly covered with a silver metal fabric, is the Hall for Swimming and Jumping (1995–1999) – a center for performance, school and club sports. The two buildings burrow seventeen meters deep into the ground and are as good as invisible from a distance – a minimalist, self-confident counter-model to the internationally customary, megalomaniacal facilities for games and competitions.

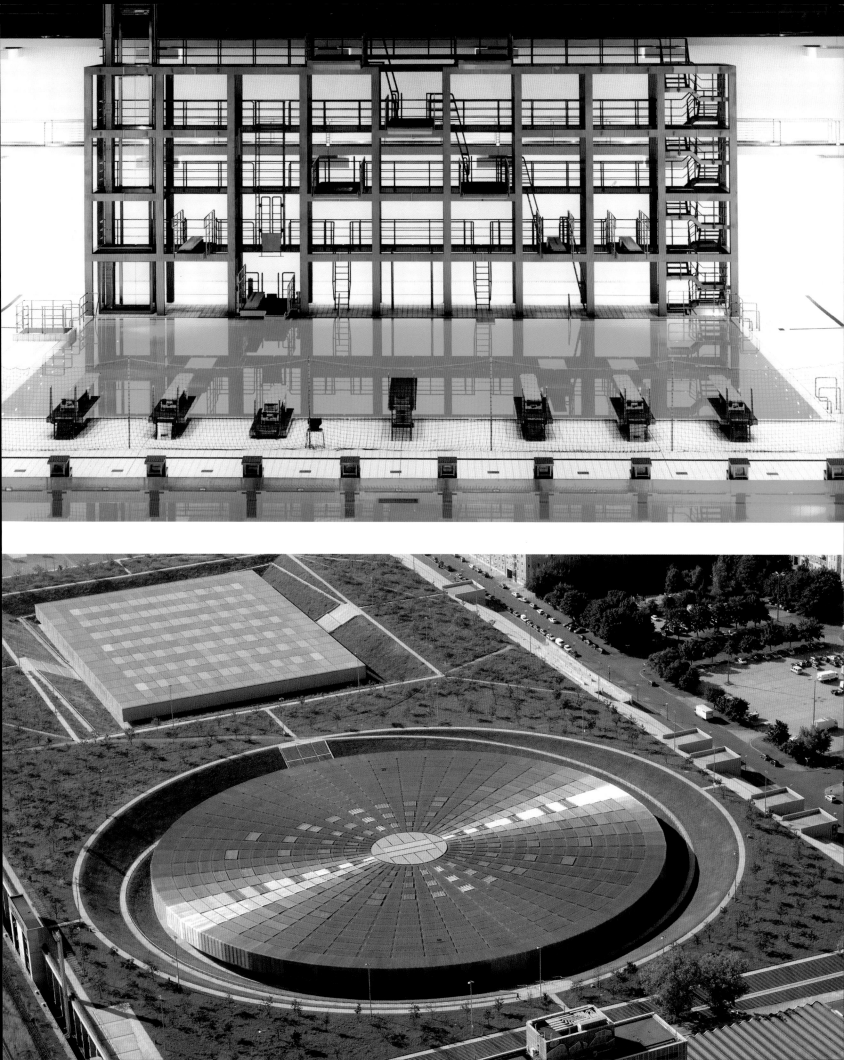

Glaubenshäuser, Friedhöfe, Denkmäler
Devotional Buildings, Cemeteries, Monuments

Trotz seiner vielen Kirchen ist Berlin keine Stadt der religiösen Inbrunst. Aus Sicht der Katholiken gilt sie gar als Diaspora, was man auch am sparsamen Einsatz der Glocken bemerkt. Nicht zufällig ist die bekannteste Glocke die Freiheitsglocke im Rathaus Schöneberg, die jeden Mittag drei Minuten läuten darf, ohne Gläubige zur Andacht zu rufen. Dennoch, Architekturgeschichte in Berlin ist immer auch Kirchengeschichte gewesen.

Kirchen, Synagogen und Moscheen

Die *Friedrichwerdersche Kirche* ist das erste Gebäude Schinkels, das rundum aus roh belassenen Ziegelsteinen besteht. Bei diesem Hauptwerk der deutschen Neugotik mit seinen kubischen Doppeltürmen (1824 bis 1830) ließ sich der Meister des Klassizismus einmal nicht von der Antike anregen. Er griff auf das englische Vorbild der College Chapels zurück. In der Technik des Rohziegelbaus knüpfte er an die heimische mittelalterliche Bautradition an und belebte die Verwendung dieses im steinlosen Preußen billigen, aber wetterfesten Baumaterials wieder, das mit seiner eigentümlich kargen Schönheit im Berliner Kirchenbau des 19. Jahrhunderts Schule machte. Bei der Ausgestaltung bediente sich Schinkel gleichfalls alter Techniken: Auf den Putz der Gewölbe ließ er Backsteinmauer-

Oben links: Nikolaikirche, mit einer bis 1230 zurückreichenden Baugeschichte.
Rechts: Johann Georg Rosenberg (1739–1808), *Klosterstraße mit Turm der Parochialkirche*, Radierung, um 1785, 44 x 69 cm.
Rechte Seite: Marienkirche mit gotischem Chor, 1270–80.
Vorhergehende Seite: Friedrichwerdersche Kirche, Karl Friedrich Schinkel, 1824–30.

Above left: Nikolai Church, its architectural history goes back to 1230.
Right: Johann Georg Rosenberg (1739–1808), *Klosterstraße with Tower of Parochial Church*, etching, c. 1785, 44 x 69 cm.
Right page: St Mary's Church with Gothic choir, 1270–80.
Previous page: Friedrichwerder Church, Karl Friedrich Schinkel, 1824–30.

In spite of all its churches, Berlin is no city of religious fervor. Catholics even rate it as Diaspora, as evidenced by the rare chiming of church bells. It is no coincidence that Liberty Bell in Schöneberg City Hall is the city's most famous bell, allowed to chime everyday at noon for three minutes without calling any of the faithful to prayer. And yet, Berlin architectural history has always also been church history.

Churches, Synagogues and Mosques

Friedrichwerder Church was the first of Schinkel's buildings that consists entirely of unplastered bricks. For this major work of German Neo-Gothic architecture with its cubic twin towers (1824–1830), the master of Neoclassicism for once did not take his inspiration from classical antiquity. He resorted to the English model of college chapels. By choosing the technology of raw brick construction, he continued a domestic medieval building tradition and thereby revived the use of this building material, which, in stoneless Prussia, was inexpensive, if weather-resistant; due to its peculiar beauty, it set a precedent in Berlin church construction of the 19th century. For the interior design, Schinkel likewise made use of old technologies: He had brick masonry patterns painted onto the stucco of the vault and

werk und auf Pfeiler und Wände Sandsteinquader aufmalen. Nach schweren Kriegsschäden ist die Kirche in den 1980er Jahren rekonstruiert und als Museum für Skulpturen eingerichtet worden. Unter den lichthellen Sterngewölben präsentiert sich die Berliner Bildhauerschule mit Werken von Schadow, Rauch, Wolff und Kalide.

Auch die *Nikolaikirche*, das älteste steinerne Zeugnis der Stadt, wird heute als Museum (für Berlin-Geschichte) genutzt. Mit dem Bau der Feldsteinbasilika wurde vermutlich um 1230 begonnen, als Berlin die Stadtrechte erhielt. Im 14./15. Jahrhundert erneuerte man die Kirche und errichtete die heutige dreischiffige Anlage mit Kreuzrippen- und Sterngewölben, den neogotischen Turmaufsatz erhielt sie 1876/77. Kurz vor Ende des Zweiten Weltkriegs wurde das Gotteshaus 1945 von Bomben schwer getroffen, das Innere brannte aus. Erst als anlässlich der 750-Jahrfeier Berlins das gleichfalls zerstörte Nikolaiviertel quasi als Altstadt-Simulation wieder aufgebaut wurde, rekonstruierte man auch die Kirche.

Ebenfalls als Ausstellungshalle dient die 1944 ausgebrannte, barocke *Parochialkirche*, die von Johann Arnold Nering entworfen und von Martin Grünberg vollendet wurde (1695 bis 1705) wurde. Sie zeigt eine für Berlin einmalige Form: Dem kreuzförmigen Zentralbau mit vier Apsiden im Innern ist ein turmbekrönter Vorbau vorgelagert. Die einzige noch als Gotteshaus genutzte mittelalterliche Kirche von Alt-Berlin, die *Marienkirche*, besitzt einen einschiffigen gotischen Chor von 1270/80. Die reichgeschmückte Alabasterkanzel von 1702/03,

Friedrichwerdersche Kirche, Karl Friedrich Schinkel, 1824–30. Rechts: Seit 1987 ist die Kirche Dependance der Alten Nationalgalerie und Schinkel-Museum mit Werken klassizistischer Bildhauer der Berliner Schule; hier das Doppelstandbild der preußischen Kronprinzessin und späteren Königin Luise und ihrer jüngeren Schwester Friederike (*Prinzessinnengruppe*) von Johann Gottfried Schadow (1764–1850), Originalmodell, Gips, 1795.

Friedrichwerder Church, Karl Friedrich Schinkel, 1824–30. Right: Since 1987, the church has been a branch of the Old National Gallery and Schinkel Museum, showing works of Neoclassicist sculptors of the Berlin School; here: the twin statues of the Prussian Crown Princess and future Queen Louise and her younger sister Friederike (*Princess group*) by Johann Gottfried Schadow (1764–1850), original model, plaster, 1795.

sandstone ashlars onto pillars and walls. Heavily damaged by the war, the church was reconstructed in the 1980s and converted into a museum of sculpture. Under the bright stellar vaults, the Berlin school of sculpture presents itself with works by Schadow, Rauch, Wolff, and Kalide.

Nikolai Church, the oldest witness to the city's history that is made of stone, is also used as a museum (for the history of Berlin city) today. Construction of the pillared rock basilica was most likely launched in 1230, when Berlin was granted the city charter. In the 14th and 15th centuries, the church was remodeled and its present triple-naved structure with cross ribs and stellar vaults was built; its Neo-Gothic spires were added in 1876/77. Shortly before the end of world war II, the church was badly damaged by bombs in 1945; the interior was gutted by fire. Only when the Nikolai Quarter, likewise destroyed, was rebuilt as a type of old-town simulacrum on the occasion of Berlin's 750th anniversary, the church was reconstructed.

Baroque *Parochial Church*, designed by Johann Arnold Nering and completed by Martin Grünberg (1695–1705), was gutted by fire in 1944 and currently also serves as an exhibit space. Its design is unique in Berlin: Its cross-shaped central structure with four semicircular interior apses is fronted by a porch-style structure crowned with a tower. The only medieval building of Old Berlin still used as a church, the *St Mary's Church*, has a single-naved Gothic choir dating from 1270/80. Its richly decorated alabaster pulpit of 1702/03, created by

ein Werk Andreas Schlüters, hebt sich mit ihrem üppig ausgestalteten Baldachin von den strengen gotischen Bündelpfeilern und den schlichten Wänden ab. Einzigartig ist das Totentanz-Fresko (um 1490), eines der ältesten seiner Art in Deutschland.

Der wichtigste Sakralbau der späten Gründerzeit in Deutschland, der *Berliner Dom*, gehört nicht zu den allseits geliebten Wahrzeichen der Stadt. An seiner Stelle stand nämlich einst ein barocker Bau, den Friedrich II. durch Johann Boumann d. Ä. 1750 errichten ließ, welcher nach Plänen von Karl Friedrich Schinkel 1816 bis 1821 klassizistisch umgestaltet wurde. Diese Anlage genügte dem Repräsentationswillen des Kaiserreichs nicht mehr. Wilhelm II. ließ den Dom kurzerhand abreißen und zwischen 1893 und 1905 durch Julius Carl Raschdorff neu bauen. Das Ganze war imperial geplant, denn der Berliner

Andreas Schlüter, starkly stands out with its opulently decorated baldachin against the austere, Gothic bundle pillars and unadorned walls. The "Dance of Death" fresco (c. 1490) is unique and one of the oldest of its kind in Germany.

The most important sacred building of Germany's late Wilhelminian *Gründerzeit* period, the *Berlin Cathedral*, is not one of those city emblems loved by everyone. On its site once stood a Baroque building commissioned by Frederick II and built by Johann Boumann the Elder in 1750, then remodeled in 1816–1821 in the Neoclassicist style based on designs by Karl Friedrich Schinkel. This structure was no longer enough to satisfy the imperial hunger for representation. William II had the cathedral torn down without further ado and replaced by a new one, built in 1893–1905 by Julius Carl Raschdorff. The entire venture was an imperial project, because Berlin Cathe-

Berliner Dom/Berlin Cathedral,
Julius Carl Raschdorff, 1893–1905.

Altarraum mit kleiner Kuppel, nach dem Willen des Kaisers am Prunk der Hochrenaissance und des Barock angelehnt.

Chancel with altar and small dome, modeled on High Renaissance and Baroque splendor in obedience to the emperor's wishes.

Dom sollte die Hauptkirche der Protestanten werden und seinem katholischen Gegenstück in Köln den Rang ablaufen. Daher wurde der Petersdom in Rom zum Vorbild gewählt. Die gewaltige Hof- und Grabkirche der Hohenzollern ist an Formen der italienischen Hochrenaissance und des Barock angelehnt. Der überkuppelte Zentralbau, die Fest- und Predigtkirche mit über zweitausend Sitzplätzen, besteht aus schlesischem Sandstein; wie ein Triumphbogen öffnet sich das Hauptportal zum Lustgarten. Der Hauptaltar von 1850, der bereits in der Vorgängerkirche stand, stammt von Friedrich August Stüler. Die Orgel mit 7269 Pfeifen, 113 Registern und vier Manualen wurde von Wilhelm Sauer 1904 in Frankfurt/Oder gebaut und war damals die größte des Landes. 1944 wurde der Dom bei einem Bombenangriff schwer getroffen, ab 1974 wiederhergestellt und 1993, nachdem auch die Innenrenovierung abgeschlossen war, feierlich wiedereröffnet.

Bischofssitz und größtes katholisches Gotteshaus ist die *St.-Hedwigs-Kathedrale*, die Friedrich II. nach der Eroberung Schlesiens für seine neuen katholischen Untertanen erbauen ließ – ein Zeichen der Toleranz im protestantischen Preußen.

Oben: St.-Hedwigs-Kathedrale, G. W. von Knobelsdorff, 1747–73, Außen- und Innenansicht mit Kuppel und Orgel.
Rechte Seite: Teilansicht des Deckenmosaiks der alten und Innenraum der neuen Kaiser-Wilhelm-Gedächtniskirche, Karl Schwechten, 1891–95, Egon Eiermann, 1957–61.

Above: St Hedwig's Cathedral, G. W. von Knobelsdorff, 1747–73, exterior and interior views with dome and organ.
Right page: Partial view of the ceiling mosaics of the old and interior space of the new Kaiser Wilhelm Memorial Church, Karl Schwechten, 1891–95, Egon Eiermann, 1957–61.

dral was to be the main church for Protestants and outrank its Catholic counterpart in Cologne. That is why St Peter's Basilica in Rome was selected as its model. The massive courtly and memorial church of the Hohenzollern dynasty is inspired by Italian High Renaissance and Baroque designs. Its domed central building, the Church for Feasts and Sermons with over two thousand seats, is made from Silesian sandstone; the main portal opens upon the Pleasure Garden like a triumphal arch. Previously located in its predecessor building, the main altar from 1850 was made by Friedrich August Stüler. Its organ with 7,269 pipes, 113 registers and four keyboard consoles was built in 1904 by Wilhelm Sauer in Frankfurt/Oder; it was the largest in the country at the time. In 1944, the cathedral was heavily damaged in bombing raids; its reconstruction was begun in 1974 and in 1993, after its interior renovation had finally been completed, it was solemnly reopened.

A bishop's seat and the city's largest Catholic house of God, *St Hedwig's Cathedral* was commissioned to be built for his new Catholic subjects by Frederick II after his conquest of Silesia – a sign of tolerance in Protestant Prussia. Its dome was mod-

Rechts/Right:
Emile Pierre Joseph de Cauwer
(1827–1873), *Synagoge in der
Oranienburger Straße*,
Öl auf Leinwand/oil on canvas,
1865 (Reproduktion).

Oben links und unten: Hofeingang
und Betraum der Synagoge in der
Rykestraße, Johann Hoeniger,
1903/04, schönstes und
größtes jüdisches Gotteshaus
in Deutschland.

Above left and below: Courtyard
entrance and prayer room of the
Synagogue on Rykestraße,
Johann Hoeniger, 1903/04,
most beautiful and largest Jewish
house of worship in Germany.

Vorbild für den Kuppelbau war das römische Pantheon. Im Zweiten Weltkrieg wurde die Kirche bis auf die Umfassungsmauern zerstört, bis 1963 aber wiederaufgebaut, mit neuer Kuppel aus Stahlbeton und modernisiertem Innenraum.

Der wichtigste Sakralbau für die größte jüdische Gemeinde in Deutschland war die *Neue Synagoge* in der Oranienburger Straße, ein im maurischen Stil gehaltener Bau, der 1859 von Eduard Knoblauch entworfen und bis 1866 von Friedrich August Stüler vollendet wurde. Zur Einweihung fanden sich auch der preußische Ministerpräsident Otto von Bismarck sowie das Kronprinzenpaar in dem dreitausend Plätze umfassenden Hauptgebetsraum ein. Die in der Pogromnacht vom 9. November 1938 dank des Eingreifens eines mutigen Polizeibeamten nur geringfügig beschädigte Synagoge wurde 1943 durch Bomben zu großen Teilen zerstört. 1988 begann der Wiederaufbau von Vorhalle und Repräsentantensaal, nicht jedoch des Hauptgebetsraums. Als Centrum Judaicum ist die Synagoge heute Museum, Gemeindehaus und Gedenkstätte. Die Gegend um die Neue Synagoge ist heute wieder zu einem Zentrum jüdischen Lebens in Berlin geworden.

Das einzige jüdische Gotteshaus, das von den siebzehn Berliner Synagogen der Vorkriegszeit erhalten geblieben ist, liegt am Prenzlauer Berg in der *Rykestraße* und wurde 2007 aufs Schönste neu hergerichtet. Die 1903/04 nach Plänen von

Kuppel der Neuen Synagoge in der Oranienburger Straße, Eduard Knoblauch, Friedrich August Stüler, 1859–1866. Nach schweren Kriegsschäden wurden Wiederaufbau und Erneuerung erst 1993 abgeschlossen.

Dome of the New Synagogue on Oranienburger Straße, Eduard Knoblauch, Friedrich August Stüler, 1859–1866. Heavily damaged in the war, its reconstruction and renovation were not completed until 1993.

eled on the Roman Pantheon. The church was gutted during World War II but rebuilt by 1963 with a new dome made of reinforced concrete and a modernized interior.

The most important sacred building for the largest Jewish congregation in Germany was the *New Synagogue* on Oranienburger Straße, a building suggestive of Moorish architecture designed by Eduard Knoblauch in 1859 and completed in 1866 by Friedrich August Stüler. Its inauguration in the main prayer room, capable of seating 3,000 people, was attended by Prussian Prime Minister Otto von Bismarck as well as the Crown Prince and his spouse. Only slightly damaged during the night of pogrom of November 9, 1938, owing to the intervention of a courageous police officer, the synagogue was largely destroyed during bombing raids in 1943. In 1988, reconstruction of its lobby and hall of representatives was launched, but not of the main prayer room. As Centrum Judaicum, the Synagogue today is a museum, community house, and a site for prayer and memorial. The area around the New Synagogue has once again become a center of Jewish life in Berlin.

The only Jewish house of God left of the seventeen pre-war synagogues in Berlin is located in Prenzlauer Berg on *Rykestraße* and was most beautifully restored in 2007. Built in 1903/04 based on designs by Johann Hoeniger, this synagogue with space for more than one thousand worshippers is not

Johann Hoeniger erbaute Synagoge mit Platz für weit mehr als tausend Gläubige ist heute nicht nur die größte in Deutschland. Sie hat als eine der wenigen den Terror der Nationalsozialisten und den Bombenkrieg nahezu unbeschadet überlebt. Die Lage ihres enormen Baukörpers in einem Hinterhof hat die Synagoge vor antisemitischen Angriffen geschützt. Die eindrucksvolle Schaufront einer in romanisierenden Formen gehaltenen Backsteinbasilika stellt sich bewusst in die Tradition des Abendlandes. Im Innern tragen Pfeiler die Emporen, über dem Kreuzrippengewölbe der Exedra am Ende des Mittelschiffs spannt sich ein blauer, bestirnter Nachthimmel, als hätte ihn Schinkel gemalt – ein offensives Bekenntnis zur Assimilation.

Neben dem Christen- und Judentum kennt die deutsche Metropole freilich auch andere Glaubensrichtungen und deren Sakralbauten. Die älteste Moschee, die 1928 an der Brienner Straße eröffnete *Ahmadiyya-Moschee* im Stil indischer Grabmäler mit Minaretten, Kuppeln und Zinnen, war das erste Bauwerk seiner Art in Deutschland. Entsprechend der islamischgläubigen Bevölkerungszahl gibt es heute rund achtzig Moscheen in Berlin, darunter türkische, arabische, kurdische und bosnische.

Zur Ahmadiyya-Moschee, der ältesten bestehenden Moschee in Deutschland, gehören zwei 32 m hohe Minarette, K. A. Hermann, 1924–28.
Rechts: Innenraum der Sehitlik-Moschee auf dem islamischen Friedhof Columbiadamm, mit zwei knapp 40 m hohen Minaretten die größte in Deutschland, 1983 und 1999–2004 erweitert.

Ahmadiyya Mosque, the oldest surviving mosque in Germany, includes two 32-meter-tall minarets, K. A. Hermann, 1924–28.
Right: Interior of Sehitlik Mosque in the Muslim cemetery in the district of Neukölln; with its two almost 40-meter-tall minarets, it is the largest in Germany, built in 1983, expanded in 1999–2004.

only the largest one in Germany. It is one of the few to have survived Nazi terror and wartime bombing with minimal damage. Its backyard location protected the enormous building from anti-Semitic attacks. Its impressive decorative façade consists of a brick basilica with a Romanizing design that deliberately sides with Occidental tradition. Pillars support the galleries in the interior; above the cross-rib vault of the exedra at the end of the central nave extends a blue, star-spangled night sky, as if Schinkel had painted it – a bold statement of commitment to assimilation.

Apart from Christian and Jewish faiths, this German metropolis is, of course, also familiar with other varieties of belief and their sacred buildings. The oldest mosque, opening in 1928 on Brienner Straße, was *Ahmadiyya Mosque*, designed in the style of Indian tombs with minarets, domes and battlements; it was the first building of its kind in Germany. Commensurate with the percentage of its Muslim population, there are about eighty mosques in Berlin today, including Turkish, Arabic, Kurdish, and Bosnian mosques.

Letzte Ruhestätten

Anders als in Paris, London oder New York begräbt Berlin seine Toten nicht auf zentralen Großfriedhöfen. Sie finden ihre letzte Ruhe auf über zweihundert größeren und kleineren Fried- und Kirchhöfen im gesamten Berliner Stadtgebiet. Diese Verteilung ergibt sich aus der historischen Entwicklung Berlins, das aus mehreren Siedlungskernen zu einer großen Stadt verschmolzen ist. Die ältesten Gräber liegen in unmittelbarer

Friedhof am Mehringdamm, seit Anfang des 18. Jh., damals vor den Toren der Stadt, mit vielen Gräbern prominenter Künstler (unten).

Cemetery on Mehringdamm, dating back to the early 1700s, formerly outside the city gates; it contains many tombs of prominent artists (below).

Final Resting Places

Unlike in Paris, London or New York, Berlin's dead are not buried in large central cemeteries. They find their final rest in over two hundred larger and smaller cemeteries and church-yards all across the Berlin city area. This distribution is the result of Berlin's historical development, as the city was forged through the merging of several settlements into one large city. The oldest graves are situated in the immediate vicinity of their

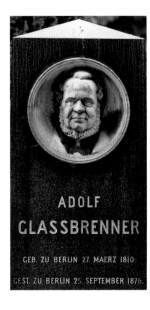

Karl Friedrich Schinkels Grabmal für den Militärreformer Gerhard von Scharnhorst (1755–1813) auf dem Invalidenfriedhof, der vornehmsten Adresse für die letzte Ruhe der preußischen Militärs.
Rechts: Umrissstich von Ferdinand Berger nach einer Schinkelschen Zeichnung, 1826.

Karl Friedrich Schinkel's tomb for military reformer Gerhard von Scharnhorst (1755–1813) in Invalids' Cemetery, the most upscale final resting place for members of the Prussian military.
Right: Outline engraving by Ferdinand Berger after a Schinkel drawing, 1826.

JOH:
FRIEDR: AUG:
BORSIG
GEB: D: 23. JUNI
1804
GEST: D: 6. JULI
1854.

HEINRICH
MANN

1871   1950

Nelly Mann
geb. Kröger
1898 – 1944
Der tapferen
Lebensgefährtin
Heinrich Manns im Exil
gestorben und beigesetzt
Santa Monica, Kalifornie
zum Gedenken

CARL FRIEDRICH SCHIN
GEBOREN
AM XIII MARZ MDCCLX
GESTORBEN
AM IX OCTOBER MDCCC

Letzte Ruhestätte vieler großer
Kulturschaffenden, Gelehrten
und auch Industriellen der Stadt,
der Dorotheenstädtische Friedhof,
angelegt im Jahr 1763.

Final resting place of many of the
city's great creators of culture,
scholars and (also) industrialists,
Dorotheenstadt Cemetery,
created in 1763.

Nähe der jeweiligen Kirchen, so auf dem 1705 angelegten, heute noch vorhandenen Kirchhof der Parochialkirche in der Klosterstraße. Später bestatteten die Gemeinden ihre Toten außerhalb der Stadtmauern, seit 1735 *vor dem Halleschen Tor* oder auf dem *Dorotheenstädtischen Friedhof* im heutigen Bezirk Mitte. Auf dem kleinen romantischen Gottesacker liegen die meisten Prominenten der Stadt begraben, viele Professoren, die hier in Universitätsnähe gelebt hatten, erfolgreiche Industrielle, Dichter, Theaterleute. Das berühmte Quartett des preußischen Klassizismus hat hier nicht nur künstlerisch gewirkt: Schinkel, Schadow, Rauch und Stüler sind hier auch bestattet.

Für seine Militärs hat Preußen als letzte Ruhestätte den *Invalidenfriedhof* bestimmt. Er wurde 1748 nach dem ersten

Charaktervolle Grabsteine auf dem Dorotheenstädtischen Friedhof neben künstlerisch wertvollen wie eines der letzten Werke Schinkels, das Monument für den Erzieher Friedrich Ancillon.

Fanciful tombstones in Dorotheenstadt Cemetery sit next to art-historically valuable ones, such as one of Schinkel's last works, the monument for royal tutor Friedrich Ancillon.

churches, such as the churchyard of Parochialkirche on Klosterstraße, which was created in 1705 and still exists today. Later, the congregations buried their dead outside the city walls, since 1735 *beyond Hallesches Tor* or in the *Dorotheenstädtischer Friedhof* in today's Mitte district. Most of the city's celebrities lie buried in this small, romantic graveyard, many professors who lived here in close proximity to the university, successful industrialists, poets, and theater people. The famous quartet of Prussian Neoclassicism was not only creatively active here: Schinkel, Schadow, Rauch, and Stüler are also buried here.

Prussia designated the *Invalidenfriedhof* as the final resting place for its military. It was established in 1748 after the first

Schlesischen Krieg für die Offiziere und Veteranen aus dem benachbarten Invalidenhaus angelegt. Heute ist er ein Zeugnis der Verwüstungen, welche die Mauer in der Stadt hinterlassen hat. Denn der „Heldenfriedhof" lag direkt im Grenzgebiet. Um ein freies Schussfeld zu haben, wurden große Teile der Grabanlagen eingeebnet. Ein Rest der Mauer ist als Mahnmal erhalten geblieben.

Auf dem mit 115 000 Gräbern größten jüdischen Friedhof Westeuropas in *Weißensee* lässt sich die Geschichte der preußischen Juden im 19. Jahrhundert ablesen. Es war eine Epoche der Emanzipation und des sozialen Aufstiegs. Den einfachen Steinen und Gedenktafeln, wie sie der Tradition jüdischer Grab-

Eingangsensemble mit Holocaust-Gedenkstätte des Jüdischen Friedhofs Weißensee.
Unten: Grabanlage des Berliner Zigarettenfabrikanten Josef Garbáty-Rosenthal (1851–1939).

Entrance building with Holocaust Memorial at Weißensee Jewish Cemetery.
Below: Burial site of Berlin cigarette factory owner Josef Garbáty-Rosenthal (1851–1939).

Silesian War for the officers and war veterans of the adjacent Invalidenhaus hospital. Today it testifies to the city's devastation left behind by the Wall, because the "Heroes' Cemetery" was situated in the middle of border territory. To obtain an unobstructed view and a clear line of fire, much of its gravesites were leveled. A piece of the Wall has been preserved as a memorial.

The history of Prussian Jews in the 19th century is told by the largest Jewish cemetery in Western Europe; it contains 115,000 graves. It was an epoch of emancipation and social advancement. Plain stones and simple memorial plaques consistent with the principles of traditional Jewish grave design are found

Orte des Gedenkens der Toten in allen Facetten auf dem Jüdischen Friedhof in Weißensee: einfache Tafeln wie für die Eltern Kurt Tucholskys, stilsichere Entwürfe wie von Walter Gropius für den Arzneimittel-Großhändler Albert Mendel, von wildem Efeu überwucherte Grabsteine der Namenlosen oder repräsentative Familiengrabstätten.

All kinds of memorials for the dead can be found in Weißensee Jewish Cemetery: simple tablets, such as for Kurt Tucholsky's parents; stylistic coups, such as Walter Gropius' design for pharmaceutical wholesale merchant Albert Mendel; ivy-covered tombstones for the many nameless ones; or representational family tombs.

gestaltung entsprechen, stehen hier hoch repräsentative Anlagen gegenüber. Wie christliche Friedhöfe um die Jahrhundertwende, entfalten auch hier manche Wandarchitekturen und Mausoleen eine außergewöhnliche Pracht. Die Kaufhauskönige Hermann Tietz (1837–1907) und Adolf Jandorf (1870–1932) sind hier bestattet, der Zeitungsmogul Rudolf Mosse (1843–1920), der Verleger Samuel S. Fischer (1859–1934) und der Maler Lesser Ury (1861–1931). Viele sehr alte Grabsteine sind erhalten, so auch jener für Louis Grünbaum, der hier als erster Toter 1880 beigesetzt wurde. Daneben die Urnenstätten von in Konzentrationslagern ermordeten Juden, die Gräber von dreitausend Menschen, die in der Zeit des Nationalsozialismus Selbstmord begingen, sowie das Grab des Widerstandskämpfers Herbert Baum (1912–1942).

Obwohl sich der Arzt und Epidemiologe Rudolf Virchow schon 1875 aus Gründen der Stadthygiene für die Feuerbestattung ausgesprochen hatte, wurde sie in Berlin erst 1911 erlaubt

Krematorium Baumschulenweg, Axel Schultes und Charlotte Frank, 1996–1999.
Rechte Seite: Nachempfunden Ägyptischer Architektur ist die Kondolenzhalle mit 29 frei angeordneten Betonsäulen und einem Brunnen, über dem ein Ei als Symbol des Lebens schwebt.

Baumschulenweg Crematorium, Axel Schultes and Charlotte Frank, 1996–1999.
Right page: Reminiscent of Egyptian architecture: the Hall of Condolence with 29 arbitrarily placed concrete columns and a fountain above which floats an egg symbolizing life.

next to highly representational tomb groups. Comparable to the style of Christian cemeteries around the turn of the century, the wall architectures and mausoleums here, too, exhibit an extraordinary magnificence. Department store kings Hermann Tietz (1837–1907) and Adolf Jandorf (1870–1932) are buried here, as are newspaper mogul Rudolf Mosse (1843–1920), publisher Samuel S. Fischer (1859–1934) and painter Lesser Ury (1861–1931). Many very old gravestones have survived, such as that of Louis Grünbaum, the first person to be entombed here in 1880. The cemetery also contains the burial urns of Jews murdered in the concentration camps, the graves of three thousand people who committed suicide during the era of National Socialism, as well as the grave of resistance fighter Herbert Baum (1912–1942).

Even though, for reasons of city hygiene, physician and epidemiologist Rudolf Virchow had spoken out in favor of cremation as early as 1875, it was first permitted only in 1911,

Oben und rechts: Siegessäule mit „Viktoria", Heinrich Strack, 1864–73.
Unten: Karl Friedrich Schinkels Nationaldenkmal auf dem Kreuzberg in Erinnerung an die Siege in den Befreiungskriegen, 1818–21.
Rechte Seite: Schinkels Neue Wache, 1816–18, heute zentrale deutsche Gedenkstätte, mit der *Pietà* von Käthe Kollwitz, 1937, eine persönliche Klage über den im Ersten Weltkrieg gefallenen Sohn, im Original 38 cm groß.

Above and right: Victory Column with "Victoria," Heinrich Strack, 1864–73.
Below: Karl Friedrich Schinkel's National Monument on Kreuzberg Hill commemorating victories won in the Liberation Wars, 1818–21.
Right page: Schinkel's New Guard House, 1816–18, now a pivotal German memorial site, with Käthe Kollwitz's *Pietà*, 1937, a personal lament for her son fallen in World War I, original height: 38 cm.

und damit auch die ersten Krematorien gebaut. Das jüngste, das Krematorium am Baumschulenweg in Treptow, entstand zwischen 1996 und 1999 nach einem Entwurf der Berliner Architekten Axel Schultes und Charlotte Frank. Kubische Formen, Sichtbeton und durch Lamellen gegliederte Glasflächen kennzeichnen das Äußere. Mit geradezu magischer Ausdruckskraft spricht das Innere, die Kondolenzhalle. Über den 29 unregelmäßig im Raum verteilten Säulen aus marmorglattem Sichtbeton, welche die Dachkonstruktion tragen, liegen kreisrunde Öffnungen. Das durch sie einfallende Licht lässt die Säulen als riesige Fackeln erscheinen. In der Hallenmitte: ein spiegelglattes Wasserbecken.

In Erinnerung an Sieger, Retter, Opfer und Helden

Berlin kennt viele Zeugen seiner wechselvollen Geschichte. Wie die Stadt aber ihre Vergangenheit selbst sieht, belegen ihre Denkmäler – von den Monumenten auf dem Kreuzberg und Unter den Linden, die das gloriose Ende der Befreiungskriege wachrufen, zur *Siegessäule*, die für ein neues Zeitalter, die Gründerzeit, steht; vom niedergeschlagenen Widerstand gegen die Hitler-Diktatur am 20. Juli 1944, woran der *Bendlerblock* gemahnt, über die an das Kriegsende erinnernden *Sowjetischen Ehrenmale*, bis zur wichtigsten, seit der Gründung der Bundesrepublik Deutschland entstandenen Gedenkstätte.

Denkmal für die ermordeten Juden Europas, Peter Eisenman, 2003–05, 19 000 Quadratmeter Fläche, an zentralem Ort nahe dem Brandenburger Tor.

Memorial to the Murdered Jews of Europe, Peter Eisenman, 2003–05; 19,000 square meter of surface area, in a central location close to Brandenburg Gate.

and so the first crematoria were built. The youngest, the crematorium on Baumschulenweg in Treptow, was built in 1996–1998 based on a design by Berlin architects Axel Schultes and Charlotte Frank. Cubic forms, exposed concrete and glass surfaces articulated by louvers characterize its exterior. Its interior, the Hall of Condolences, speaks with an almost magical expressivity. Supporting the roof, 29 columns made of marble-smooth, exposed concrete are scattered about the space in irregular intervals; above them are circular openings. The light falling through these make the columns appear like gigantic torches. In the center of the hall: a water basin smooth as glass.

In Memory of Victors, Saviors, Victims, and Heroes

Berlin has many witnesses to its history full of vicissitudes, but how the city itself sees its past is documented by its memorials – from the monuments on Kreuzberg Hill and Unter den Linden Boulevard that recall the glorious end of the Liberation wars; to the *Victory Column* that represents a new age, the Wilhelminian Gründerzeit; to the *Bendler Block*, commemorating failed resistance against Hitler's dictatorship on July 20, 1944; to the *Soviet Cenotaphs* that recall the end of the war; to the most important memorial to emerge since the founding of the Federal Republic of Germany.

Das *Denkmal für die ermordeten Juden Europas* ist ein Labyrinth ohne Zentrum, bestehend aus einem zu ebener Erde angelegten Feld von unterschiedlich hohen Stelen: 2711 Betonpfeiler, die zwischen 0,5 und 4,7 Meter emporragen, verteilen sich auf dem unregelmäßig abgesenkten, zwei Hektar großen Gelände. Das Denkmal wurde nach langen Diskussionen, die schon in den 1980er Jahren begannen, 2003 bis 2005 nach einem Entwurf von Peter Eisenman gebaut.

Es befindet sich in bester Berliner Lage – unmittelbar zwischen Brandenburger Tor und Potsdamer Platz. Geschichtsträchtiger dürfte kaum ein Flecken deutschen Bodens sein: Die Stelen stehen dort, wo sich Goebbels im Bunker versteckte, unweit der Stelle, an der Hitlers Leiche verbrannt wurde. Nach dem Krieg zerschnitten hier Mauer und Todesstreifen die Stadt und das Gelände. Die Botschaft, die mit der Wahl dieses Platzes verbunden war, hat dem New Yorker Architekten Eisenman imponiert: „Keine andere Nation der Welt hätte so einen wichtigen Ort mitten in der Hauptstadt zur Verfügung gestellt."

In einer unterirdischen Halle am Südostrand des Denkmalgeländes ergänzt der Ort der Information das Holocaust-Mahnmal. Dort wird an die jüdischen Opfer erinnert durch Namen und exemplarische Familiengeschichten. Erst unter der Erde wird also das historische Ausmaß dessen, woran an der Oberfläche gedacht werden soll, erkennbar: der Holocaust, die Ermordung von Millionen Menschen in deutschen Vernichtungslagern.

Auf der gewellten Fläche stehen 2711 Stelen (Betonquader) mit identischem Grundriss und unterschiedlicher Höhe, zwischen ebenerdig und 4,7 m Höhe.

On the undulating plain, there are 2,711 stelae (concrete slabs) with identical ground plans and varying heights, from ground level to 4.7 m tall.

The *Memorial to the Jews Murdered in Europe*. It is a labyrinth without a center, consisting of a ground-level field covered with stelae of varying heights: 2,711 concrete pillars that rise above ground between 0.5 and 4.7 meters are distributed across an unevenly sloping terrain of about two hectares. Following long discussions starting as far back as the 1980s, the monument was finally built in 2003–2005 based on a design by Peter Eisenman.

It is located on prime Berlin territory – just between Brandenburg gate and Potsdamer Platz. Hardly another site in Germany is so impregnated with history as this one: The stelae are standing where Goebbels hid in the bunker, not far from the place where Hitler's corpse was burnt. After the war, the Wall and the death strip cut the city and terrain in two here. The message linked to the selection of this area impressed New York architect Eisenman: "No other nation in the world would have provided such a significant site in the middle of the capital."

A "Place of Information" situated in an underground hall at the southeastern border of the memorial site complements the Holocaust Memorial. Jewish victims are remembered by name and via exemplary family histories. Only underground does the historical extent of what is memorialized above become recognizable: the Holocaust, the murder of millions of people in German extermination camps.

Links: Marx-Engels-Denkmal,
Ludwig Engelhardt, 1987, Bronze.
Rechts: Ernst-Thälmann-Denkmal,
Lew Kerbel, 1981–86, Bronze auf
Sockel aus ukrainischem Granit,
Höhe 14 m, Breite 15 m.
Unten: Sowjetisches Ehrenmal
im Bezirk Tiergarten für die im
Zweiten Weltkrieg gefallenen
Soldaten der Roten Armee, Lew
Kerbel, 1945; mit der Bronzefigur
eines sowjetischen Soldaten.

Left: Marx Engels Memorial,
Ludwig Engelhardt, 1987, bronze.
Right: Ernst Thälmann Memorial,
Lew Kerbel, 1981–86, bronze on a
base made of Ukrainian granite,
height: 14 m, width: 15 m.
Below: Soviet War Memorial in
the district of Tiergarten for the
Red Army soldiers fallen during
World War II, Lew Kerbel, 1945;
with bronze statue of a Soviet
soldier.

Rechts: Gedenkstätte Berliner Mauer in Erinnerung an die Teilung der Stadt und ihrer Opfer, Bernauer Straße, Kohlhoff und Kohlhoff, 1998, zwei Stahlwände, Höhe 7 m.
Unten: Bendlerblock, Gedenkstätte Deutscher Widerstand für die Widerstandsgruppe des Hitler-Attentats vom 20. Juli 1944; Skulptur von Richard Scheibe, *Junger Mann mit gebundenen Händen*, 1953, Bronze.

Right: Berlin Wall Memorial in memory of the city's division and its victims, Bernauer Straße, Kohlhoff and Kohlhoff, 1998, two steel walls, height: 7 m.
Below: Bendlerblock, Memorial to the German Resistance for the group of resistance fighters planning the attack on Hitler on July 20, 1944; sculpture by Richard Scheibe, *Young Man with Hands Tied*, 1953, bronze.

364

Von der Renaissance bis zum Klassizismus – die Schlösser und Herrenhäuser, die sich die Hohenzollern und andere Adelsdynastien in Berlin und rund um die Residenzstadt errichten ließen, bieten ein vielgesichtiges Bild höfischer Kunst und Architektur. Sie dienten als Jagdschlösser, Sommerresidenzen und als repräsentative Wohnsitze weitverzweigter Familien. Die besten Architekten ihrer Zeit wurden für deren Bau engagiert. Ihre Entwürfe und gestalterischen Einfälle haben Maßstäbe gesetzt, sie nahmen Einfluss auf die Entwicklung des Berliner Umlandes ebenso wie auf die Physiognomie der Stadt. Die Schlösser waren Vorbilder, sie wurden munter kopiert. Von den Adelspalais des 17. Jahrhunderts in der Friedrichstadt bis zu den Gründerzeitvillen des Großbürgertums im Grunewald – man bediente sich ungeniert des Formenschatzes der splendiden Architektur. Heute sind die meisten Schlösser, umgeben von ausgedehnten Parkanlagen, viel besuchte Ausflugsziele, Museen, Orte herausragender Kunstsammlungen oder historische Kulisse für festliche Anlässe.

Vorhergehende Seite und unten: Schloss Charlottenburg, im Auftrag Königin Sophie Charlottes 1695–99 nach Plänen von Johann Arnold Nering als barocke Sommerresidenz gebaut; erweitert und verändert u. a. durch Eosander von Göthe, Andreas Schlüter und auch Carl Gotthard Langhans.

Previous page and below: Charlottenburg Palace, built in 1695–99 at the behest of Queen Sophie Charlotte, designed by Johann Arnold Nering as a Baroque summer residence; expanded and modified by Eosander von Göthe, Andreas Schlüter and also Carl Gotthard Langhans, et al.

From the Renaissance to Neoclassicism – the palaces and mansions the Hohenzollerns and other aristocratic dynasties had built for themselves in Berlin and around the royal residence city offer a multifaceted picture of courtly art and architecture. They served as hunting palaces, summer residences and representational mansions for families with many branches. The best architects of their period were commissioned for their construction. Their designs and creative ideas set benchmarks; they influenced the development of Berlin's environs as much as the physiognomy of the city itself. The palaces were models; they were blithely copied. From the aristocratic palaces of the 17th century in Friedrichstadt to the Wilhelminian *Gründerzeit* villas of the haute bourgeoisie in Grunewald – the wealth of forms informing this splendid architecture was shamelessly recycled. Today, most of these palaces surrounded by extensive landscaped grounds are often visited places of excursion, museums, sites housing outstanding art collections, and historical backdrops for festive occasions.

Friedrich Wilhelm Weidemann
(1668–1750), *Königin Sophie
Charlotte* (Queen Sophie
Charlotte) um/c. 1701,
Öl auf Leinwand/oil on canvas,
65,8 x 64,1 cm, Schloss
Friedrichshof, Kronberg.

In der Stadt: Charlottenburg und Jagdschloss Grunewald

Berlins größtes und prachtvollstes Schloss trägt den Namen der Stammmutter aller preußischen Könige. Sophie Charlotte, eine ungewöhnliche Fürstin, hoch gebildet und mit Gottfried Wilhelm Leibniz befreundet, ließ es sich nach einem Entwurf von Johann Arnold Nering 1695 bis 1699 als kleine Sommerresidenz vor den Toren Berlins errichten. Als sich ihr Gemahl 1701 zum ersten König in Preußen krönte, wurde das *Charlottenburger Schloss* mit seinen zweieinhalb Geschossen zu einer dreiflügeligen Anlage erweitert. Auf die Mittelachse setzte der an Versailles geschulte Baumeister Johann Friedrich Eosander von Göthe einen 48 Meter hohen Turm, an der Westseite errichtete er die 143 Meter lange Orangerie. Im Ehrenhof erhebt sich heute eines bedeutendsten barocken Reiterdenkmäler überhaupt, das Monument des Großen Kurfürsten (1696–1700) von Andreas Schlüter, das bis 1943 auf der Langen Brücke (heute Rathausbrücke) stand. Den dritten Bauabschnitt gab Friedrich II. in Auftrag. 1740 bis 1746 ließ er seinen ersten Baumeister den östlichen, später nach diesem benannten Knobelsdorff-Flügel errichten. Carl Gotthard Langhans, der Architekt des Brandenburger Tores, entwarf unter Friedrich Wilhelm II. das Schlosstheater (1787–1791) in Verlängerung der Orangerie und das ursprünglich auf einer Insel gelegene Belvedere. Das im Zweiten Weltkrieg schwer beschädigte Schloss wurde in den 1950er Jahren wieder aufgebaut. Auch die Interieurs wurden weitgehend wiederhergestellt, so die einstigen Wohnräume Friedrichs II. mit der bedeutenden Gemäldesammlung der französischen Schule vom Anfang des 18. Jahrhunderts,

Aus der Gemäldesammlung von Friedrich II./paintings from the collection of Frederick II: Antoine Pesne (1683–1757), *Kronprinz Friedrich mit seiner Schwester Wilhelmine* (Crown Prince Frederick with his sister Wilhelmine), 1714, Öl auf Leinwand/ oil on canvas, 174 x 163 cm (links/left).

Jean Baptiste Simeon Chardin (1699–1779), *Die Briefsieglerin* (Lady sealing a letter), 1733, Öl auf Leinwand/oil on canvavs, 146 x 147 cm (rechts/right).

In the City: Charlottenburg and Grunewald Hunting Palace

Berlin's largest and most magnificent palace is named after the matriarch of all Prussian Kings. Sophie Charlotte, an unusual princess, highly educated and a friend of Gottfried Wilhelm Leibniz', had it built for herself in 1695–1699 as a small summer residence outside the gates of Berlin and based on a design by Johann Arnold Nering. When her spouse crowned himself the first King in Prussia in 1701, *Charlottenburg Palace* with its two and a half stories was expanded into a three-wing structure. Trained at Versailles, its master builder Johann Friedrich Eosander von Göthe set up a 48-meter-high tower on its central axis; on the western side, he installed the 143-meter-long Orangery. The court of honor today contains one of the most important of Baroque equestrian statues of all times, the monument to the Great Elector (1696–1700) by Andreas Schlüter, which had been sitting on Lange Brücke (Long Bridge, today's Rathausbrücke) until 1943. The third building stage was initiated by Frederick II. In 1740–1746, he had his first master builder construct the eastern wing that was later named Knobelsdorff Wing in his honor. Under Frederick William II, Carl Gotthard Langhans, the architect of Brandenburg Gate, designed the Schlosstheater (Palace Theater, 1787–1791) as an expansion of the Orangery and Belvedere Palace, which had originally been set up on an island. Heavily damaged in World War II, the palace was reconstructed in the 1950s. Most of the interior was likewise, such as the former residential quarters of Frederick II with its important collection of paintings by the French School of the early 18th century, among them

Sammlungsstücke aus dem Museum für Vor- und Frühgeschichte, heute im Westflügel von Schloss Charlottenburg: Rechts und unten: Spitze und Fuß des „Berliner Goldhutes", vermutlich Kopfbedeckung eines Priesters aus der Bronzezeit, um 1000–800 v. Chr., Goldblech, Höhe 74,5 cm, Gewicht, 490 g.

Pieces from the collection of the Museum of Prehistory and Early History, now in the west wing of Charlottenburg Palace: Right and below: Tip and foot of the "Berlin Golden Hat," presumably the headdress of a Bronze Age priest, c. 1000–800 B. C., gold leaf, height: 74.5 cm, weight: 490 g.

Oben: Ohrgehänge aus Troja, um 2300 v. Chr., ausgegraben unter Heinrich Schliemann, Replik, Silber, vergoldet. Unten: Goldschätze aus Brandenburg, 12. bis 9. Jh. v. Chr. Viele Goldgegenstände werden nur als Abgüsse gezeigt, da die Originale, wie auch der berühmte „Schatz des Priamos", zur so genannten „Beutekunst" gehören.

Above: Trojan drop earrings, c. 2300 B. C., excavated under the direction of Heinrich Schliemann, replica, silver, gold-plated. Below: Hoards of gold from Brandenburg, 12th–9th centuries B.C. Many of the gold objects on exhibit are mere replicas since the originals, including the famous "Priam's treasure," belong to the category of "looted art."

Antoine Watteau (1684–1721),
Die Einschiffung nach Kythera
(Embarkation for Cythera),
um/c. 1717, Öl auf Leinwand/
oil on canvas, 129 x 194 cm.

darunter Antoine Watteaus „Ladenschild des Kunsthändlers Gersaint" (1720). Spitzenleistungen des europäischen Rokoko im Schloss sind die beeindruckenden Raumfluchten Eosanders, die Enfiladen, und vor allem die von Knobelsdorff 1740 bis 1747 gestalteten Festsäle. Im Park an der Spree, der ab 1697 von dem Le-Nôtre-Schüler Siméon Godeau im französischen Stil angelegt und später von Peter Joseph Lenné weitgehend in einen englischen Landschaftsgarten umgewandelt wurde, stellte man nach dem Krieg das sogenannte Broderieparterre des Barockgartens wieder her. Der Westflügel des Schlosses beherbergt heute das Museum für Vor- und Frühgeschichte.

In den westlichen Wäldern und Seen, wo der Berliner Hof vierhundert Jahre lang dem Jagdvergnügen nachging, ließ sich Kurfürst Joachim II. vermutlich von Caspar Theyss, einem der Baumeister der Hohenzollernresidenz, 1542 einen bewehrten Ausflugspunkt errichten, das *Jagdschloss Grunewald*. Über dem Portal kann man bis heute die Inschrift „Zum grünen Walde" lesen, ein Name, der bald auf die Gegend selbst überging. Der zweigeschossige Bau wurde im 17. Jahrhundert aufgestockt und war bis 1709 ein von einem Graben umspültes Wasserschloss. Der große Saal mit bemalter Holzdecke ist der einzige erhaltene profane Innenraum aus der Renaissancezeit in Berlin. Repräsentative barocke Erweiterungen und kleinere Hofgebäude kamen Anfang des 18. Jahrhunderts hinzu. Um 1830 führte der benachbarte Glienicker Schlossherr Prinz Carl von Preußen die Parforcejagd wieder ein: „Par force de chiens" (durch Hundekraft) wurde das Wild gehetzt und von den nacheilenden Jägern abgefangen. Zahlreiche Gemälde im Schloss veranschaulichen diese Art von höfischer Unterhaltung ebenso wie monströse Tierdarstellungen, die der barocken Vorliebe fürs Spektakuläre entsprachen. In dem seit 1932 als Museum dienenden Gebäude sind in wohnlicher Atmosphäre neben Möbeln, Porzellanen und Zinnzeug über zweihundert

Jagdschloss Grunewald, Berlins ältester erhaltener Schlossbau, vermutlich nach Plänen von Caspar Theyss, 1542/43. Rechts: Hans Fincke nach einer Zeichnung von Gustav Adolf Boenisch (1802–1887), *Das königliche Jagdschloss Grunewald bei Berlin*, 1838, Stahlstich, 23,8 x 30,3 cm.

Grunewald Hunting Palace, Berlin's oldest surviving palace, presumably designed by Caspar Theyss, built in 1542/43. Right: Hans Fincke after a drawing by Gustav Adolf Boenisch (1802–1887), *Royal Grunewald Hunting Palace near Berlin*, 1838, steel engraving, 23.8 x 30.3 cm.

Antoine Watteau's "Store Sign for the Art Dealer Gersaint" (1720). Outstanding achievements of European Rococo in the palace are the imposing flights of rooms by Eosander, the Enfilades, and above all Knobelsdorff's ballrooms, created in 1740–1747. In the park along the Spree, created in the French style by Le Nôtre student Siméon Godeau starting in 1697 and later transformed for the most part into an English landscape garden by Peter Joseph Lenné, the so-called Parterre de Broderie of the Baroque garden was reconstructed after the war. Today, the western wing of the palace houses the Museum for Prehistory and Early History.

Among the western woods and lakes, where the Berlin Court engaged in the pastime of hunting for four hundred years, Elector Joachim II had himself built, most likely by Caspar Theyss, a master builder of the Hohenzollern residence, a reinforced place of excursion in 1542: *Grunewald Hunting Palace*. To this day, the inscription above its portal reads "To the Green Forest," a name that soon transferred to the area itself. The two-story structure was raised in the 17th century and up to 1709, it was a water palace surrounded by a moat. The large hall with its painted wood ceiling is the sole surviving secular interior room dating back to the Renaissance period in Berlin. Representational Baroque expansions and smaller court buildings were added in the early 18th century. Around 1830, the landlord of nearby Glienicke Palace, Prince Carl of Prussia, reintroduced par force hunting: The game was run down "par force de chiens" (by the power of dogs) and intercepted by the pursuing hunters. Numerous paintings in the palace illustrate this type of courtly entertainment; they also depict monstrous animals consistent with the Baroque predilection for the spectacular. Serving as a museum since 1932, the building displays—in a residential setting—furniture, porcelain and pewter wares, but also two hundred paintings by German

Lucas Cranach d. Ä./the Elder (1472–1553), *Judith mit dem Haupt des Holofernes* (Judith with the head of Holofernes), 1530, Öl auf Lindenholz/oil on linden wood, 75 x 56 cm, Jagdschloss Grunewald.

Gemälde deutscher und niederländischer Meister ausgestellt, u. a. von Peter Paul Rubens, Jan Gossaert, Jan Steen, Anton Graff, Franz Krüger und Antoine Pesne. Die Attraktion aber ist die mit dreißig Bildern größte Cranach-Sammlung Berlins, darunter bekannte Werke von Lucas Cranach d. Ä.: „Joachim II. als Kurprinz" (um 1517/18), „Auferstehung Christi" (um 1537/38) sowie Darstellungen der Lucretia und einer Quellnymphe (um 1515). Von seinem Sohn Lucas Cranach d. J. stammt neben anderen Werken ebenfalls ein Porträt des Erbauers, des etwa fünfzigjährigen Joachim II. (um 1555).

Johann Gabriel Friedrich Poppel (1807–1882) nach/after Ludwig Rohbock, *Humboldt im Park von Schloss Tegel* (Humboldt in the park of Tegel Palace), um/c. 1850, kolorierter Stahlstich/hand-colored steel engraving.

and Dutch masters, such as by Peter Paul Rubens, Jan Gossaert, Jan Steen, Anton Graff, Franz Krüger, and Antoine Pesne. The main attraction, however, is – at thirty paintings – Berlin's largest Cranach collection, among them familiar works by Lucas Cranach the Elder: "Joachim II as Electoral Prince" (c. 1517/18), "Christ's Resurrection" (c. 1537/38), as well as representations of Lucretia and a nymph of the spring (c. 1515). Works by his son Lucas Cranach the Younger likewise include a portrait of the building master: Joachim II at about fifty years of age (c. 1555).

Am Rand gelegen: Tegel, Spandau, Friedrichsfelde, Köpenick

Wie sein geografisches Pendant im Süden gehen die Anfänge des *Humboldt-Schlosses* (*Schloss Tegel*) im Norden auf einen Waidmannssitz zurück. In der Waldeinsamkeit nahe dem großen See, der heute nach dem Ort Tegel heißt, ließ ihn sich ein Hofsekretär Joachims II. im Stil der Renaissance errichten. Nach mehrmaligen Eigentümerwechseln 1766 in den Besitz der Familie von Humboldt übergegangen, verlebten hier die Brüder Wilhelm und Alexander ihre Kindheit. Nach dem Tod der Mutter kehrte 1797 der Ältere, der Gründer der später nach ihm benannten Universität, hierher zurück. Karl Friedrich Schinkel gestaltete das Anwesen 1820 bis 1824 zu einem Ruhesitz für ihn um: In

Sitting on the Edge: Tegel, Spandau, Friedrichsfelde, Köpenick

Like its geographical counterpart in the south, the origins of *Humboldt Palace* (*Tegel Palace*) in the north go back to a hunter's residence. A court secretary of Joachim II's had it built in the style of the Renaissance in the sylvan solitude close to the great lake that today is called Tegel after the town. After landing in the hands of the Humboldt family in 1766 following several changes of ownership, the brothers Wilhelm and Alexander spent their childhood years there. When their mother died, the elder brother and founder of the university named after him, returned to it in 1797. Karl Friedrich Schinkel remodeled the estate in 1820–1824 to serve as Wilhelm's retirement

Schloss Tegel, ursprünglich 1558 als Renaissance-Herrenhaus gebaut, ab 1766 Landsitz der Familie Humboldt; Umbau durch Karl Friedrich Schinkel 1820–24. Rechts: Das erste preußische Antikenmuseum, der 1824 fertiggestellte Antikensaal im Schloss Tegel, von Schinkel an das bestehende Gebäude angefügt, Foto, um 1935.

Tegel Palace, originally built as a Renaissance manor in 1558, since 1766 the country seat of the Humboldt Family; remodeled by Karl Friedrich Schinkel in 1820–24. Right: The first Prussian Museum of Antiquities, the Hall of Antiquities in Tegel Palace, completed in 1824, attached to the existing building by Schinkel, photo, c. 1935.

Die Statt vnd. Vestung Spandaw.

Spre · Fluß

Anspielung auf die italienische Villenarchitektur und die griechische Antike schuf er einen makellos weißen, streng gegliederten Bau. Den südlichen Renaissanceturm des Altbaus kopierte der Architekt für die übrigen Ecken, sodass ein symmetrisches Ganzes entstand. Im Inneren erwuchsen helle, großzügige Räume, Bibliothek und Blauer Salon, Vestibül und Antikensaal. Der ursprünglich vom Lehrer Gottlob Johann Christian Knuth angelegte Park wurde von Humboldt selbst später weiterentwickelt. Eine Lindenallee führt an der Humboldteiche vorbei zur Grabstätte der Familie, die Wilhelm von Humboldt nach dem Tod seiner Frau Caroline 1829 ebenfalls von Schinkel errichten ließ. Auch er sowie sein Bruder Alexander sind hier begraben.

Das älteste und zugleich wehrhafteste Profanbauwerk Berlins liegt im Westen der Stadt. Der Juliusturm von 1200 krönt als höchste Erhebung eine der am besten erhaltenen Festungen in Europa. Die *Zitadelle Spandau* entstand auf dem Gelände einer slawischen Siedlung. Bereits im 16. Jahrhundert war sie zu einem machtvollen Militärstützpunkt geworden, der die Stadt am Fernhandelsweg vom Rheinland nach Polen sicherte. Francesco Chiaramella da Gandino, der erste italienische Baumeister in brandenburgischen Diensten, entwarf die ganz von Wasser umflossene Anlage nach norditalienischen Vorbildern mit vier pfeilförmigen Bastionen, die dem einfachsten hierarchischen Prinzip folgend „König", „Königin", „Kronprinz" und „Brandenburg" hießen. Die Festung galt als uneinnehmbar. Im Dreißigjährigen Krieg zogen sich die Schweden hierher zurück, während des Siebenjährigen Krieges suchten Elisabeth Christine und ihr Hofstaat vor den Österreichern hinter den Mauern Zuflucht. Ein einziges Mal, 1813, fand während der napoleonischen Besatzung eine kriegerische

seat: Taking his cues from Italian villa architecture and Greek Antiquity, he created a flawlessly white, austerely articulated structure. The architect replicated the southern Renaissance tower of the old building for its remaining corners so as to create a symmetrical whole. The interior was outfitted with bright, spacious rooms, a library and the Blue Salon, a vestibule and the Hall of Antiques. The park, originally designed by teacher Gottlob Johann Christian Knuth, was developed further by Humboldt himself. A linden tree avenue leads past the Humboldt Oak Tree to the family tomb, also constructed by Schinkel at Wilhelm von Humboldt's behest after the death of the latter's wife, Caroline, in 1829. He and his brother Alexander are also buried here.

The oldest and simultaneously most fortified secular building in Berlin is located in the western part of the city. Dating back to 1200, Julius Tower crowns as its highest elevation one of the best-preserved fortresses in Europe. *Spandau Citadel* was built on the site of a Slavic settlement. As early as the 16th century it had developed into a mighty military fortress able to secure the city located on the trade route going from the Rhineland to Poland. Francesco Chiaramella da Gandino, the first Italian master builder in the service of the Brandenburgians, designed the facility wholly surrounded by water based on northern Italian models with four arrow-headed bastions that, consistent with the simplest hierarchical principle, were named, "King," "Queen," "Crown Prince," and "Brandenburg." The fortress was considered invincible. The Swedes retreated to it during the Thirty Years' War; during the Seven Years' War, Queen Elisabeth Christine and her royal household sought shelter from the Austrians inside its walls. Only once, in 1813

Auseinandersetzung statt. Die Zitadelle war aber auch ein Gefängnis, und sie bewährte sich als Staatstresor. Der Julius-turm barg den kurfürstlichen Silberschatz, und von 1874 bis 1919 die französischen Reparationsgelder. Heute beherbergt der Bau das Stadtgeschichtliche Museum Spandau.

Auch das Stadtmuseum Berlin zeigt einen Teil seiner Be-stände an einem historischen Schauplatz, im *Schloss Fried-richsfelde* im Osten der Stadt. 1695 von Johann Arnold Nering im Auftrag des holländischen Hasardeurs Benjamin von Raulé als Lusthaus errichtet, wechselte das Schloss mehrfach Ausse-hen und Besitzer, bis es die Herzogin Katharina von Holstein-Beck, die für ihre schillernden Gartensoireen berühmt war, um 1800 im frühklassizistischen Stil umbauen ließ. Der säulen-verzierte Festsaal im Obergeschoss erinnert an diese Zeit, während die reich geschnitzte Holztreppe im Mittelbau noch aus der Zeit des ersten Umbaus um 1719 stammt. Lenné gestal-tete 1822 den nach holländischer Art angelegten Garten in einen Landschaftspark um. Die symmetrischen Parterres aus den Anfangsjahren wurden erst in den 1980er Jahren rekonstru-iert. Seit 1955 ist der Ostberliner Tierpark in das Gelände einge-zogen. Das Schloss, das den Zweiten Weltkrieg überstand, ohne äußerlich großen Schaden zu nehmen, wurde in den 1970er Jahren von Grund auf restauriert und im Zustand von 1800 wiederhergestellt. Die nahezu verlorene Innenaus-stattung ersetzte man durch Dekor und Mobiliar aus zerstörten märkischen Schlössern und Herrenhäusern.

Auch *Schloss Köpenick*, das dem Kurprinzen Friedrich, dem späteren ersten Preußenkönig, als Sommerresidenz für

Schloss Friedrichsfelde, Johann Arnold Nering, 1665, Erweiterung/ expansion 1719, Parkgestaltung/ landscaping by Joseph Peter Lenné, 1822.

during the Napoleonic occupation, did a martial conflict occur there. The citadel was also an effective prison, and it proved its mettle as a state vault. Julius Tower preserved the Electoral silver hoard; and from 1874 to 1919, it safeguarded the French reparation monies. Today, the building houses the Museum of Municipal History, Spandau.

The Berlin City Museum, too, exhibits a portion of its holdings in a historical setting, in *Friedrichsfelde Palace* in the eastern part of the city. Built in 1695 by Johann Arnold Nering as a pleasure seat commissioned by the Dutch soldier of fortune Benjamin von Raulé, the palace changed looks and hands several times before it was remodeled around 1800 in the early Neoclassicist style by Duchess Katharina von Holstein-Beck, famous for her colorful garden soirees. The column-studded banquet hall on the upper floor commemorates this period, while the richly carved wooden staircase in the center build-ing dates back to the era of its first remodeling around 1719. In 1822, Lenné redesigned the garden, first conceived in the Dutch style, into a landscape garden. The symmetrical parterres from the early years were not reconstructed until the 1980s. In 1955, the former East Berlin Zoo moved into the grounds. Sur-viving World War II without incurring major damage, the palace was thoroughly restored to its 1800 condition in the 1970s. Lost for the most part, its interior décor was replaced with acces-sories and furnishings from Brandenburgian castles and manor houses that had been destroyed.

Having once served Electoral Prince Frederick, Prussia's first king-to-be, as summer residence for his Baroque pleasure

Oben: Das Rokokozimmer mit
Wandbespannungen aus Schloss
Ostrau, eingerichtet um 1750.
Rechts: Blick in das Jagdzimmer
von Schloss Friedrichsfelde, das
seinen Namen den Jagd- und
Tierszenen an den Wänden
verdankt.

Above: The Rococo Room with
wall coverings from Ostrau
Palace, furnished c. 1750.
Right: View of the Hunting Room
in Friedrichsfelde Palace, which
owes its name to the scenes of
hunting and animals depicted
on its walls.

Unbekannter Künstler/unknown
artist, *Schloss Friedrichsfelde*,
Gouache, um/c. 1780.

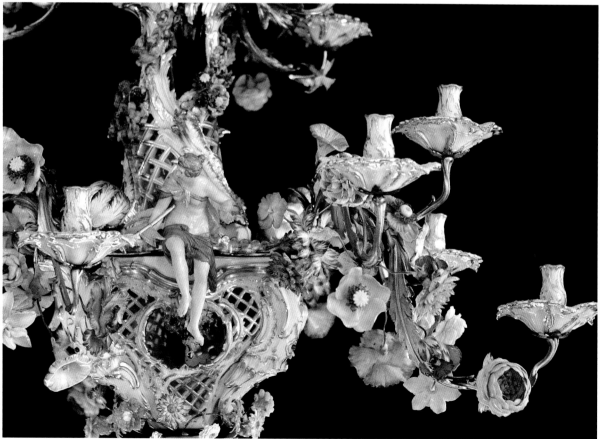

Schloss Köpenick, nach Plänen
von Wilhelm Zacharias, 1558,
Erweiterung für den Kurprinzen
Friedrich durch Rutger van
Langervelt, 1677. Die Schloss-
kirche (linke Seite) baute Johann
Arnold Nering, 1685.
Oben: Barocke Stuckarbeiten des
italienischen Künstlers Giovanni
Carove im „großen Saal" des
Schlosses; links: Kronleuchter
aus Berlins Königlicher Porzellan-
Manufaktur (KPM).

Köpenick Palace, designed by
Wilhelm Zacharias, built in 1558,
expansion for Electoral Prince
Frederick by Rutger van
Langervelt, 1677. The Palace
Church (left page) was built by
Johann Arnold Nering, 1685.
Above: Baroque stucco work by
Italian artist Giovanni Carove in
the "Great Hall" of the palace;
left: Chandelier made by Berlin's
Royal Porcelain Manufactory
(KPM).

barocke Lustbarkeiten diente, ist heute Museum. Im Inneren des Schlosses, wo ein dreiläufiges Treppenhaus und prächtige Vestibüle sowie in fünfzehn Räumen originale Deckengemälde von Jacques Vaillant und kunstvolle Stuckarbeiten des italienischen Meisters Giovanni Carove erhalten sind, zeigt das Kunstgewerbemuseum reiche Schätze der Raumkunst aus den Zeiten der Renaissance, des Barock und des Rokoko mit Möbeln, Tapisserien, Fayencen und Porzellan. Einer der Höhepunkte der Sammlung: das berühmte Silberbuffet von 1695 aus dem Berliner Schloss.

Am Wasser gebaut: Pfaueninsel, Glienicke, Babelsberg

Einst war die *Pfaueninsel* inmitten der Havel, weit vor den Toren Berlins und Potsdams, ein Liebesnest. Kronprinz Friedrich Wilhelm II. verbrachte hier seine ersten heimlichen Rendezvous mit der Hoftrompeterstochter Wilhelmine Encke, bevor er knapp dreißig Jahre später – das Mädchen war längst zu seiner Mätresse und vertrauten Freundin geworden – auf der verschwiegenen Insel ein Schloss bauen ließ. Wilhelmine, alias Gräfin Lichtenau, wirkte ab 1794 wesentlich an der Planung des Sommersitzes mit, der wie eine kunstvolle Ruine anmutet. Vor allem die vollständig erhaltene Innenausstattung, die ein einzigartiges Zeugnis aus der Zeit des frühen Klassizismus ist, geht auf sie zurück. In den intimen Räumen verweisen zahlreiche Rom-Zitate auf die Italiensehnsucht der „Bauherrin", ebenso wie antikisierende Wandtäfelungen, zart und diskrete Wand- und Deckenmalereien. Stendhal soll sich auf der Pfaueninsel in südliches Ambiente – „wie auf den Borromäischen Inseln" im Lago Maggiore – versetzt gesehen haben. Und Theo-

Ein Ort der Lust und der Liebe: die Pfaueninsel; das Schlösschen wurde ohne Architekt, nur unter Leitung eines Hofzimmermeisters gebaut, jedoch unter planerischer Aufsicht der Geliebten, Mätresse und vertrauten Freundin Wilhelms II., Wilhelmine Encke, später Gräfin Lichtenau.
Rechts: Carl Blechen (1798–1840), *Das Palmenhaus auf der Pfaueninsel*, 1832, Öl auf Leinwand, 183 x 201 cm, Alte Nationalgalerie.

A place of love and leisure: Peacock Island; the small palace was built without an architect, only under the guidance of a master carpenter of the court, though Wilhelmine Encke, the future Countess Lichtenau, William II's beloved, mistress and confidante, supervised its construction and design.
Right: Carl Blechen (1798–1840), *The House of Palms on Peacock Island*, 1832, oil on canvas, 183 x 201 cm, Old National Gallery.

activities, *Köpenick Palace* today is a museum. Inside the palace, which contains a well-preserved triple-ramp staircase and a gorgeous vestibule, as well as fifteen rooms decorated with original ceiling paintings by Jacques Vaillant and artful stucco works by Italian master Giovanni Carove, the Museum of Decorative Arts exhibits vast holdings of interior design treasures dating from the Renaissance, Baroque and Rococo periods including furniture, tapestries, faiences and porcelain. A collection highlight: the famous 1695 silver buffet from Berlin Palace.

Built on the Water's Edge: Pfaueninsel, Glienicke, Babelsberg

Once upon a time, *Peacock Island*, situated in the middle of the Havel, far outside the gates of Berlin and Potsdam, was a love nest. Crown Prince Frederick William II used it for his first secret trysts with the Court Trumpeter's daughter, Wilhelmine Encke, before some thirty years later – the girl had long since become his mistress and confidante – he had a castle built on this secretive island. In 1794, Wilhelmine, alias Countess Lichtenau, started to contribute substantially to the planning of the summer residence that has the air of an artful ruin. Most to her credit is the comprehensively preserved interior décor that provides a unique testimony to the era of early Neoclassicism. Numerous Rome citations decorating its intimate rooms point to this "lady-builder's" nostalgia for Italy, as do the classically themed wall panels and the delicate and discrete paintings on walls and ceilings. Stendhal, on Peacock Island, was to have felt himself transported to a southern ambience – "like the Borromean Islands" in Lago Maggiore. And Theodor

dor Fontane nannte das Eiland eine „rätselvolle Oase in der Mark". Friedrich Wilhelm III. ließ nach Plänen Schinkels auf der Insel andere Bauten (1824 bis 1832) hinzufügen. Für seine einstigen Bewohner war die Pfaueninsel ein Rückzugsort jenseits des höfischen Zeremoniells. Heute ist sie ein luftiges Denkmal aus der romantischen Epoche in Preußens Geschichte.

Schräg gegenüber, auf einer Anhöhe, die sich sanft zur Havel hin neigt, erhebt sich das *Schloss Klein-Glienicke*. Den südlich anmutenden Landsitz schuf Schinkel ab 1825 für Prinz Carl von Preußen, der damals von einer Grand Tour nach Rom, Florenz und Neapel zurückgekehrt war. Das zweigeschossige, winkelförmige Hauptgebäude und die bis 1829 angefügten Kavalier- und Hofdamenflügel umschließen einen italienischen Gartenhof mit Brunnen, während die Frontseite des Schlosses mit Balkon, breiter Freitreppe und Gartenterrasse von einer großen, durch goldene Löwen flankierten Fontäne betont wird, die Schinkel nach dem Vorbild der Villa Medici in Rom entwarf. Nördlich des Komplexes liegt der Remisenhof, in dem heute ein nobles Restaurant untergebracht ist; am Havelufer thront das Casino im Stil einer italienischen Villa mit Pergolen. Den 116 Hektar großen, ganzjährig geöffneten Park gliederte Lenné nach englischem Prinzip in drei Partien, in Blumengärten sowie Pleasureground rund um das Schloss und eine großräumige „Landschaft", die wie in einem grandiosen Theater die nordeuropäische Natur in eine „alpine" Szenerie und schließlich in mediterrane Gefilde übergehen lässt. Persius entwarf die passenden Gebäude dazu, das Matrosen-, Gärtner- und

Perspektivische Ansichten von Karl Friedrich Schinkel: „Häuschen am See in Glinicke", das Casino, 1824/25 (oben) und „Ansicht des ganzen Schlosses" von Klein-Glienicke (1825–28), Kupferstich und Lithographie aus der „Sammlung architektonischer Entwürfe", 1819–40.
Rechts: Löwenfontäne und Schloss, wie sie sich heute von der Straße nach Potsdam aus gesehen präsentieren.
Unten: Blick von der Havel auf das Casino von Klein-Glienicke.

Perspective views by Karl Friedrich Schinkel: "Little House on the Lake in Glinicke," the Casino, 1824/25 (above) and "View of the Entire Palace" of Klein-Glienicke (1825–28), copper engraving and lithograph from the "Collection of Architectural Designs," 1819–40.
Right: Lion Fountain and palace, as seen today from the road to Potsdam.
Below: View of the Casino of Klein-Glienicke from the Havel.

Fontane called the island a "mysterious oasis in Brandenburgian lands." Frederick William III had other buildings (1824–1832) added to the island that were all based on Schinkel's designs. For its erstwhile inhabitants, Peacock Island was a refuge beyond courtly ceremony. And today, it is an airy memorial to the romantic epoch in Prussia's history.

Diagonally across from it, on a hill gently sloping towards the Havel, there arises *Klein-Glienicke Palace*. Starting in 1825, Schinkel created this country seat with a southern feel for Prince Carl of Prussia, who had just returned from his Grand Tour to Rome, Florence and Naples. The two-story, angled main building and the Cavalier and Court Ladies' Wings, both attached by 1829, enclose an Italian garden courtyard with a fountain, while the front of the palace with balcony, external stairs and garden terrace is accentuated by a large fountain flanked by golden lions and designed by Schinkel, who modeled it on the Villa Medici in Rome. To the north of the complex lies the courtyard of the carriage building that today houses an elegant restaurant; on the banks of the Havel sits the ochre-colored casino in the style of an Italian villa with pergolas. The park, 116 hectares large and open year-round, was divided by Lenné into three sections based on the English design principle: into flowerbeds, pleasure grounds around the palace and a spacious "landscape" that, as in a grandiose theater, shows northern European nature changing into an "Alpine" scenery and finally into Mediterranean regions. Persius designed suitable buildings for them: the Sailors', Gardeners', and Machine

Maschinenhaus. Am südlichen Rand der Schlossanlage schuf Schinkel zwei Aussichtspunkte, einen anmutigen Teepavillon und einen dem Lysikrates-Denkmal in Athen nachempfundenen Rundtempel, dessen Dach auf korinthischen Säulen ruht: Hochromantisch nannte er sie Kleine und Große Neugierde .

Direkt vis-à-vis von Glienicke steigt der Babelsberg auf. Am Hang zur Havel hin ließ sich Prinz Wilhelm, später König und erster deutsche Kaiser, nach 1833 einen Sommersitz anlegen. Das *Schloss Babelsberg* entwarf ebenfalls Schinkel, und zwar nach der Art englischer Landsitze. Den Tudor-Stil imitierend schuf er eine malerische Anlage aus turmähnlichem Polygon als Hauptbau mit Erker, Zinnen und türmchenhaften Strebepfeilern sowie einer Bogenhalle. Große, dicht aneinander gereihte Spitzbogenfenster geben reizvolle Ausblicke auf die Landschaft frei. Zwischen dem Baumeister und Prinzessin Augusta, der Gemahlin des Prinzen, kam es immer wieder zu Differenzen. Die Bauherrin wünschte überreichen Dekor, Schinkel plante maßvolle gotische Formen. Auch sein Nachfolger Ludwig Persius hatte sich – gleichfalls widerstrebend – den fürstlichen Wünschen zu beugen. Erst Johann Heinrich Strack traf den Geschmack der Auftraggeberin. Er erweiterte von 1844 bis 1849 das Schloss durch einen Anbau, der durch einen Turm abgeschlossen wird und dessen gleichfalls achteckiger Tanzsaal über zwei Etagen reicht. Die Fassaden zieren Türmchen, Erker und weitere dekorative Spielereien, die dem Ganzen den Charakter einer mittelalterlichen Burg verleihen. Auch das Innere zeigt sich gotisch mit Sterngewölben und in altdeutscher Ausmalung. Den Park entwarf Lenné als englischen Garten, den Hermann von Pückler-Muskau dann ab 1843 mit Panoramawegen und theatralischen Sichtachsen veränderte.

G. Hess nach Friedrich August Borchel, *Schloss Babelsberg bei Potsdam*, Ansicht von Norden mit der Terrasse, kolorierter Stahlstich, um 1850.
Rechte Seite: Schinkel, Persius, schließlich Johann Heinrich Strack planten und arbeiteten an Schloss Babelsberg, Lenné und Pückler-Muskau nahmen sich im Wechsel des Gartens an, bis als Ergebnis herausgekommen war, was Prinz Wilhelm, später deutscher Kaiser, und Gattin Augusta sich gewünscht hatten.

G. Hess after Friedrich August Borchel, *Babelsberg Palace near Potsdam*, view from the north with terrace, hand-colored steel engraving, c. 1850.
Right page: Schinkel, Persius, finally Johann Heinrich Strack designed and worked on Babelsberg Palace; Lenné and Pückler-Muskau took turns creating the garden until they achieved the design desired by Prince William, the future German emperor, and his consort, Augusta.

Houses. On the southern border of the palace grounds, Schinkel created two vista points, a graceful Tea Pavilion and a round temple designed after the Monument of Lysicrates in Athens, with its roof resting on Corinthian columns: in the manner of High Romanticism he called them Small and Large Curiosity.

Just opposite Glienicke, Babelsberg Hill rises upward. On the slope down towards the Havel, Prince William, the future king and first German emperor, had a summer seat installed after 1833. *Babelsberg Palace* was likewise designed by Schinkel – and in the style of an English countryseat. Imitating Tudor style models, he created a picturesque structure with a polygon shaped like a tower as principal building that was furnished with oriel windows, battlements and turret-like counterforts, as well as an arcade. Large ogival windows strung closely together grant charming views of the landscape. The master builder and Princess Augusta, the prince's spouse, frequently engaged in differences of opinion. The princess builder wanted a lavish décor; Schinkel designed restrained Gothic forms. His successor, Ludwig Persius, as well had to submit just as reluctantly to her princely desires. Only Johann Heinrich Strack met his client's wishes on the level of taste. In 1844–1849, he enlarged the palace with an annex capped by a tower whose equally octagonal ballroom took up two stories. The facades were adorned with small towers, oriel windows and other decorative baubles that gave the entire building the appearance of a medieval castle. The interior looks gothic as well with its stellar vaults and Old German interior paint job. Lenné designed the park as an English garden which, starting in 1843, Hermann von Pückler-Muskau modified by installing panorama pathways and theatrical lines of sight.

Drüben in Potsdam

Over there in Potsdam

A. das vortreffliche Lust Schloß.
B die auf beiden Seiten befindlichen Pavillons.
C. Gebüsch, die Lerchenheide genañt.
E. das Glaß haüß. F. die Orangerie. G. Aleen. H. Mauer, so den Weinberg umgiebt.

Prospect des königlichen Lust-Schlosses

zu Berlin, zu finden bei I.

Soucy, bei Potsdam

D. der durch die Kunst sehr magnifique angeordnete Weinberg, bestehet aus 6 Absätzen oder
Gangen, zu welchen man in der mitten vermittelst der Stiegen (a) und an beiden Enden auf denen von
Erde gemachten Erhohungen, bequem auf und absteiget. Diese Absätze sind mit Mauren eingefasset
... welche ... ... viel rundten Behältnüssen stehen, so oben mit einer Fallthüre, und auf
den Seiten mit gläsernen Thüren versehen, wie bei d zusehen.

Die von Kanälen und zahlreichen Seen umgebene Stadt an der Havel, nur durch eine Brücke (heute die Glienicker Brücke) von Berlin getrennt, war die zweite Residenz der preußischen Könige und deutschen Kaiser. Obwohl die Bomben des Zweiten Weltkriegs den historischen Stadtkern schwer beschädigten und die Abrisswut der DDR-Stadtplaner das, was davon noch erhalten war, ein zweites Mal zerstörte, gewinnt Potsdam heute neben dem traditionellen Holländischen Viertel und der Russischen Kolonie in ganzen Straßenzügen sein barockes Gesicht zurück. Prachtvolle Villenviertel am Rande der Parks und Seen zeugen vom einstigen Glanz der Residenz. Vor allem aber ist Potsdams einzigartiges Ensemble aus Schlössern und Parks geblieben, das die bedeutendsten Landschaftsarchitekten, Baumeister, Maler und Bildhauer Preußens von der Mitte des 18. Jahrhunderts an geschaffen haben. Die gesamte Kunst- und Naturlandschaft Potsdams ist 1990 von der UNESCO zum Weltkulturerbe erklärt worden – die Parkanlagen von Sanssouci, der Neue Garten, Babelsberg, Glienicke und die Pfaueninsel.

Vorhergehende Seite/Previous page: Johann David Schleuen d. Ä./the Elder (1711–1771), *Prospect des Königlichen Lustschlosses Sans-Souci bei Potsdam*/View of the Royal Pleasure Palace of Sanssouci near Potsdam, 1748, kolorierter Kupferstich/hand-colored copper engraving, 38,5 x 59,6 cm.

Rechts/Right: Carl Blechen (1798–1840), *Schloss Sanssouci*, um/c. 1830–32, Öl auf Pappe/ oil on cardboard, 41 x 33 cm, Alte Nationalgalerie.

Unten/Below: Schloss Sanssouci (Palace), Georg Wenzeslaus von Knobelsdorff, 1745–47.

Surrounded by canals and lakes, the city on the Havel, only a bridge (today the Glienicke Bridge) away from Berlin, was the second residential seat of the Prussian kings and the German emperor. Even though World War II bombs badly damaged the historical center of the city and demolition madness by GDR urban planners destroyed all over again what was still standing, Potsdam today is regaining not only its traditional Dutch Quarter and Russian Colony, but also its Baroque aspect along the lengths of entire city streets. Magnificent villa districts at the edge of parks and lakes testify to the former splendor of this royal residential seat. Above all, what has survived is Potsdam's unique ensemble of palaces and large parks, created by Prussia's most important landscape architects, master builders, painters, and sculptors starting in the mid-18th century. In 1990, UNESCO declared the entire artistic and natural landscape of Potsdam a World Heritage Site. It includes the parks of Sanssouci, the New Garden, Babelsberg, Glienicke, and Peacock Island.

PLAN von Sans-Souci und Charlottenhof

Maaßstab von der Ruth. Bre.

1836.

Das Paradies von Sanssouci

Herzstück dieses preußischen „Arkadiens" ist die Sommerresidenz Friedrichs des Großen, ein königlicher Bungalow, den
der Bauherr wie eine zum privaten Gebrauch bestimmte Villa
nannte: „Sans souci" – „ohne Sorge". Zuerst entstand nach
seinen Entwürfen ein Weinberg mit sechs konkav gekrümm-
ten Terrassen. Dann ließ der König, gleichfalls nach seinen Ideen,
1745 von Georg Wenzeslaus von Knobelsdorff, dem auch die
Anlage des 290 Hektar großen Parks zu verdanken ist, in nur
zweijähriger Bauzeit das Schloss im Stil des französischen
Rokoko errichten. Die südliche Fassade ist als Fest Rubensscher
Körperlichkeit gestaltet. Bacchanten, angefertigt vom Hofbild-
hauer Friedrich Christian Glume, sind paarweise zwischen den
bodentiefen Fenstern gruppiert und tragen als Karyatiden das
Gebälk. Ernster wirkt hingegen die Nordseite, wo eine halb-
kreisförmige Kolonnade den Ehrenhof umschließt. Den ellip-

Peter Joseph Lenné (1789–1866),
*Plan von Sans-Souci und
Charlottenhof*
(Ground plan of Sanssouci and
Charlottenhof Palaces),
Lithographie/lithograph, 1836.

Sanssouci Paradise

The centerpiece of this Prussian "Arcadia" is Frederick the
Great's summer residence, a royal bungalow, which its builder
called by a name suitable for a villa meant for private purposes,
"sans souci" – "without a care." At first, a vineyard with six
concavely curving terraces was created based on his own
designs. Then, in 1745, and likewise designed by himself, the
king had Georg Wenzeslaus von Knobelsdorff, who also created
the 290-hectare park, build the palace in the style of French
Rococo; its construction took only two years. Its southern
façade is designed as a feast of Rubensian physicality. Between
the long windows that extend down to the ground, pairs of
Bacchantes made by court sculptor Friedrich Christian Glume
support the frame in the form of caryatids. Its northern side,
where a semicircular colonnade encircles the court of honor,
bears a more serious aspect. The elliptical marble hall inside

Oben/Above: Antoine Pesne
(1683–1757), *Bildnis Friedrichs
des Großen als Kronprinz*
(Portrait of Frederick the Great,
as Crown Prince), 1739/40,
Öl auf Leinwand/oil on canvas,
80,5 x 65 cm, Gemäldegalerie.

Adolph von Menzel (1815–1905),
*König Friedrichs II. Tafelrunde in
Sanssouci* (King Frederick II's
round table at Sanssouci), von
links/from left Marishal, (?),
Voltaire, von Stille, Friedrich,
d'Argens, Keith, Algarotti,
Rothenburg, de Lamettrie, 1850,
Öl auf Leinwand/oil on canvas,
204 x 175 cm, Nationalgalerie,
Kriegsverlust/lost in the war.

tischen Marmorsaal im Inneren krönt gleich dem Pantheon en miniature eine zum Himmel sich öffnende Kuppel. Hier hielt Friedrich der Große seine berühmt gewordenen Tafelrunden ab. Im Konzertzimmer, einem der schönsten Räume des deutschen Rokoko, feiert das Lieblingsmotiv der Epoche, die Rocaille, an Wänden und Decke wahre Triumphe. Östlich und westlich wird Schloss Sanssouci von zwei ähnlichen Gebäuden flankiert, den *Neuen Kammern* und der 1755 bis 1764 von Johann Gottfried Büring geschaffenen *Bildergalerie*, das erste nur für die Ausstellung von Gemälden bestimmte Gebäude in der Museumsgeschichte. 39 Jahre lebte Friedrich der Große in Sanssouci. Hier wünschte er auch begraben zu sein, in einer Gruft auf der obersten Weinbergterrasse, neben seinen Lieblingshunden. Sein Wunsch ging, wenn auch erst im Jahr 1991, in Erfüllung.

Noch zu seinen Lebzeiten, aber auch unter seinen Nachfolgern wurde der Park erweitert. Dabei entwickelte sich eine etwa zwei Kilometer lange Allee, die im Osten durch ein

is crowned like a miniature Pantheon with a cupola opening up to the skies. This is where Frederick the Great held his famous dinner receptions. In the concert room – one of the most beautiful rooms of German Rococo – the favorite motif of the epoch, the Rocaille, celebrates veritable victories on walls and ceilings. To the east and the west, Sanssouci Palace is flanked by two similar buildings, the *New Chambers* and the *Picture Gallery*, created in 1755–1764 by Johann Gottfried Büring, the first structure in the history of museums to have been built exclusively for the exhibition of paintings. Frederick the Great lived in Sanssouci for 39 years. It was his wish to be buried there as well, in a tomb on the uppermost vineyard terrace, next to his favorite dogs. His wish was granted – even though it took until 1991 for it to happen.

The park was developed further even during his lifetime, but also under his successors. During this process, an avenue some two kilometers long was created, which was accentuated

394

Die Neue Orangerie im Park von Sanssouci, nach Plänen von Ludwig Persius und Friedrich August Stüler, 1851–64. Im imposanten Raffaelsaal sind knapp fünfzig Kopien aus dem 19. Jh. nach Werken des italienischen Meisters Raffael zu bewundern.

The New Orangery in Sanssouci Park, designed by Ludwig Persius and Friedrich August Stüler, built in 1851–64. Its imposing Raphael Hall contains some fifty 19th century copies of works by the Italian master Raphael.

Das Chinesische Teehaus im Park
von Sanssouci, entworfen von
Johann Gottfried Büring,
1754–57. Im 18. Jh. wichtigstes
Beispiel europäischer
Chinoiserie, heute ist hier
Meißener und ostasiatisches
Porzellan ausgestellt.

The Chinese Tea House in
Sanssouci Park, designed by
Johann Gottfried Büring,
1754–57. Most important
instance of European Chinoiserie
in the 18th century, used today to
exhibit Meißen and East Asian
porcelains.

Adolph von Menzel (1815–1905),
*Flötenkonzert Friedrich des
Großen in Sanssouci*
(Flute concert of Frederick the
Great in Sanssouci), auf dem
Sofa/on the sofa Wilhelmine von
Bayreuth, Friedrichs Lieblings-
schwester/Frederick's favorite
sister, 1850/52, Öl auf Leinwand/
oil on canvas, 142 x 205 cm,
Alte Nationalgalerie.

Obelisk-Portal, im Westen durch das Neue Palais markiert ist. Dazwischen reihen sich Bauten, Ziergärten, Marmorrondelle, Haine und Wäldchen wie Perlen auf einer Kette aneinander: das *Chinesische Teehaus*, ein vergoldeter Rokoko-Pavillon, den Johann Gottfried Büring zwischen 1755 und 1764 nach Skizzen Friedrichs II. auf kleeblattförmigem Grundriss errichtete. Oder der dreihundert Meter lange Bau der *Orangerie*. Diese Hommage an die Renaissancepaläste von Tivoli und Florenz ließ Friedrich Wilhelm IV. 1840 unter dem Eindruck seiner Italienreise von Ludwig Persius entwerfen. Glanzpunkt ist der Raffaelsaal, der eine Sammlung von über fünfzig aus dem 19. Jahrhundert stammenden Kopien von Gemälden des italienischen Renaissancemeisters beherbergt, darunter Nachbildungen berühmter Werke wie der „Sixtinischen Madonna".

Im *Neuen Palais*, dem gewaltigsten Schlossbau im Park Sanssouci, hielten die königliche Familie und ihre fürstlichen Gäste auf höchst repräsentative Weise Hof, anders als im intimen Weinbergschloss. In nur siebenjähriger Bauzeit entstand der

Innenansichten von Schloss Sanssouci, Konzertzimmer mit Wandbildern des französischen Meisters Antoine Pesne; hier feierte Friedrich der Große seine musikalischen Auftritte, koloriertes Foto, 1898.

Interior views of Sanssouci Palace, Concert Room with wall paintings by French master Antoine Pesne; this is where Frederick the Great gave his musical performances, hand-colored photo, 1898.

in the east by an Obelisk Portal, in the west by the New Palace. Along the way, buildings, flower gardens, marble circles, groves, and small woods are strung up like pearls on a necklace: the *Chinese Tea House*, a gilded Rococo pavilion built by Johann Gottfried Büring in 1755–1764 on a clover-shaped ground plan, based on sketches by Frederick II. Or the building of the *Orangery*, three hundred meters long. This homage paid to the Renaissance palaces of Tivoli and Florence was designed in 1840 by Ludwig Persius at the behest of Frederick William IV, still captivated by his impressions of Italy during his Grand Tour. Its highlight is Raphael Hall, which contains a collection of more than fifty 19th century copies of paintings by the Italian Renaissance master, among them replicas of famous works such as the "Sixtinian Madonna."

In the *New Palace*, the most massive palatial building in Sanssouci Park, the royal family and their noble guests held court in a most representational manner, a style quite different from the intimate vineyard palace. Designed at the behest of

Das so genannte Voltairezimmer auf Schloss Sanssouci mit Wanddekorationen von Johann Christian Hoppenhaupt d.J.; hier wohnte der französische Philosoph als Gast Friedrichs, koloriertes Foto, 1898.

The so-called Voltaire Room in Sanssouci Palace with wall decorations by Johann Christian Hoppenhaupt the Younger; the French philosopher stayed here as Frederick's guest, hand-colored photo, 1898.

Rechts/Right: Peter Haas (1754–1813), *Friedrich der Große und Voltaire unter den Kolonnaden von Sanssouci* (Frederick the Great and Voltaire under the colonnades in Sanssouci), kolorierter Kupferstich/colored copper engraving).

dreiflügelige, 240 Meter lange Bau – viermal so lang und dreimal so hoch wie Sanssouci – den Friedrich II. ab 1763 von Büring, dann von Carl von Gontard entwerfen ließ. Er wird von einer zentralen Kuppel bekrönt, auf der drei Grazien unter Preußens Königskrone tanzen. In vielen Räumen stehen noch die originalen Möbel und Porzellane, auch Wandmalereien mit fantastischen Trompe-l`oeil-Effekten haben sich erhalten. Das Theater im südlichen Hauptflügel gehört zu den wenigen bis heute bespielten Schlosstheatern des 18. Jahrhunderts in Deutschland.

Was unter dem heimischen Himmel fehlte, um „glücklich zu sein wie in Italien", ließ sich Kronprinz Friedrich Wilhelm (IV.) nach eigenen Ideenskizzen in den Park von Sanssouci stellen: die *Römischen Bäder* sowie einen Sommersitz nach dem Vorbild antiker Villen, *Schloss Charlottenhof*. Die Anlage geht auf einen 1756 von Baumeister Büring errichteten eingeschossi-

Neues Palais/New Palace, Johann Gottfried Büring, Heinrich Ludwig Manger, Carl von Gontard, 1763–69, Länge/length 240 m, Kuppelhöhe/dome height 55 m.

Links/Left: Otto Günther-Naumburg (1856–1941), *Neues Palais bei Potsdam, Sommerresidenz des deutschen Kaisers* (New Palace near Potsdam, summer residence of the German emperor), Kaiser Wilhelm II. mit Familie/Emperor William II with his family, Farbdruck nach Aquarell/color print after a watercolor, 1889.

Frederick II, first by Büring (as of 1763), then by Carl von Gontard, the three-wing, 240-meter-long building was constructed in only seven years – it was four times as long and three times as high as Sanssouci. It is crowned by a central dome on top of which the Three Graces are dancing under a Prussian Royal Crown. Many of the rooms still contain the original furniture and porcelains; murals with fantastic trompe-l'œil effects have also survived. The theater in the southern main wing is one the few 18th century palace theaters in Germany still in use today.

What was lacking under domestic skies for him to be "as happy as in Italy," Crown Prince Frederick William (IV) had set up in Sanssouci Park based on his own ideas and sketches: the *Roman Baths* as well as a summer seat modeled on antique villas, *Charlottenhof Palace*. Its layout originates in a single-story farming estate built by master builder Büring in 1756,

Vorhergehende Seite:
Julius Umbach (1815–1877) nach
Zeichnung von Ludwig Rohbock,
Der Charlottenhof bei Potsdam,
kolorierter Stahlstich, um 1850,
11 x 16 cm.
Links: Marmorpalais im Neuen
Garten, Entwurf Carl von Gontard,
Carl Gotthard Langhans, 1787–92,
vollendet mit zwei Seitenflügeln
von Michael Philipp Boumann,
ab 1797, koloriertes Foto 1898.

Previous page:
Julius Umbach (1815–1877) after
a drawing by Ludwig Rohbock,
Charlottenhof Palace near
Potsdam, hand-colored steel
engraving, c. 1850, 11 x 16 cm.
Left: Marble Palace in the New
Garden, design: Carl von Gontard,
Carl Gotthard Langhans, 1787–92,
completed with two wings by:
Michael Philipp Boumann, from
1797, hand-colored photo, 1898.

Gotische Bibliothek am Heiligen
See, Carl Gotthard Langhans,
1792–94, diente als königliche
Bibliothek deutscher Literatur
und französischer Klassiker.

Gothic Library on Holy Lake,
Carl Gotthard Langhans,
1792–94, served as royal
library for German literature
and French classics.

406

gen Gutshof zurück, den Schinkel von 1826 bis 1829 mit einem offenen dorischen Portikus, Pergola und Terrasse in ein klassizistisches Kleinod verwandelte. Ihm zur Seite stand Peter Joseph Lenné. Der zauberte aus dem bis dahin landwirtschaftlich genutzten Terrain einen englischen Landschaftsgarten.

Neuer Garten und Pfingstberg

Der Wegbereiter des Klassizismus in Preußen, Friedrich Wilhelm II., leitete nach dem Tod seines Onkels und Vorgängers, Friedrich II., den künstlerischen Epochenwechsel ein. Mit der Anlage eines neuen Gartens nordöstlich von Sanssouci ließ er sich zur selben Zeit ein neues Schloss errichten, das *Marmorpalais*. Seinen Namen erhielt das aus rotem Backstein nach Plänen von Carl von Gontard 1787 bis 1792 errichtete zweigeschossige Gebäude nach den Schmuck- und Gliede-

Schloss Cecilienhof, nach Plänen von Paul Schultze-Naumburg, 1913–17, der letzte Schlossbau der Hohenzollern; Auftraggeber war Kaiser Wilhelm II.

Cecilienhof Palace, designed by Paul Schultze-Naumburg, built in 1913–17, the last palace built by the Hohenzollerns; commissioned by Emperor William II.

which Schinkel, in 1826–1829, transformed into a Neoclassicist gem by adding an open Doric portico, a pergola and a terrace. He was helped by Peter Joseph Lenné, who conjured up an English landscape garden out of the terrain that had hitherto been used for agricultural purposes.

New Garden and Pfingstberg Hill

Neoclassicism's trailblazer in Prussia, Frederick William II, initiated an art-historical change after the death of his uncle and predecessor, Frederick II. While creating a new garden northeast of Sanssouci Palace, he also had himself built a new palace, *Marble Palace*. Built in 1787–1792 and designed by Carl von Gontard, the two-story building made of red brick owes its name to the decorative and structural elements made of gray and white Silesian marble that adorn its exterior façade. On

Die Heilandskirche in Sacrow, am Ufer der Havel, mit freistehendem Campanile, Ludwig Persius im Auftrag und nach Zeichnungen von Friedrich Wilhelm IV., des „Romantikers auf dem Thron", 1841–44; Geländegestaltung durch P. J. Lenné mit Sichtachsen zu den Parkanlagen in Potsdam.

Church of the Holy Redeemer in Sacrow, on the banks of the Havel, with free-standing campanile, built by Ludwig Persius on commission and after drawings by Frederick William IV, the "Romanticist on the Throne," 1841–44; landscape design by P. J. Lenné with lines of sight towards the parks of Potsdam.

Belvedere auf dem Pfingstberg,
Doppelturmanlage, inspiriert von
Vorbildern der italienischen
Renaissance, nach Plänen von
Friedrich Wilhelm IV., ausgeführt
durch Ludwig Persius, Friedrich
August Stüler und Ludwig
Ferdinand Hesse, 1847–52 und
1860–62.
Links: N. Buchholz, *Ansicht des
Belvedere auf dem Pfingstberg*,
um 1910, Radierung, 15 x 22 cm.

Belvedere on Pfingstberg Hill,
twin tower construction,
inspired by models of the Italian
Renaissance, designed by
Frederick William IV, realized by
Ludwig Persius, Friedrich August
Stüler and Ludwig Ferdinand
Hesse, 1847–52 and 1860–62.
Left: N. Buchholz, *View of the
Belvedere on Pfingstberg*,
c. 1910, etching, 15 x 22 cm.

rungselementen aus grauem und weißem schlesischen Marmor an der Außenfassade. Auf dem flachen Dach des kubischen Baukörpers, der ab 1797 durch zwei Seitenflügel ergänzt wurde, thront ein Belvedere in Miniatur, dem der gesamte Neue Garten zu Füßen liegt. Johann August Eyserbeck, Sohn des Architekten der Dessau-Wörlitzer Anlagen, hat daraus eine frühklassizistisch-empfindsame Landschaft mit Sichtachsen, Hügeln und in das Gelände komponierten, bizarren architektonischen Staffagen gemacht. Ab 1816 entwickelte Lenné den Park im englischen Stil weiter, mit Sichtachsen zur Pfaueninsel, Glienicke, Babelsberg und Sacrow. Auch gegenüber schuf er für die *Heilandskirche*, die wie ein mediterranes Sehnsuchtsbild am Ufer der Havel steht, den passenden Landschaftsrahmen. Die dreischiffige Basilika mit separatem Campanile war von Friedrich Wilhelm IV., dem „Romantiker auf dem Thron", bei Persius in Auftrag gegeben worden.

Das letzte Schloss der Hohenzollern im Neuen Garten entstand unter dem letzten deutschen Kaiser, Wilhelm II., von 1913 bis 1917: *Schloss Cecilienhof* nach dem Vorbild eines englischen Landsitzes. Weltweit bekannt wurde es als Verhandlungsort der alliierten Siegermächte im Sommer 1945. Truman, Attlee als Nachfolger von Churchill und Stalin unterzeichneten

Karl Friedrich Schinkel (1781–1841), *Pomonatempel auf dem Pfingstberg* (Pomona Temple on Pfingstberg Hill), 1800, Aquarell über Feder auf Papier/watercolor over ink on paper, 13,1 x 18,4 cm.

the flat roof of the cube-shaped body of the building, to which were added (starting in 1797) two lateral wings, there sits a miniature Belvedere with the entire New Garden spread out at its feet. Johann August Eyserbeck, son of the architect who designed the Dessau-Wörlitz Gardens, turned these grounds into an early Neoclassicist/Culture-of-Sensibility landscape with lines of sight, hills and bizarre, architectural staffages that are composed directly into the landscape. Starting in 1816, Lenné further developed the park following English stylistic models and creating lines of sight towards Peacock Island, Babelsberg and Sacrow. Across from it, as well, he created a suitable framing landscape for the *Church of the Savior* sitting like a Mediterranean picture of longing on the banks of the Havel. Built by Persius, its triple-nave basilica with separate campanile was commissioned by Frederick William IV, the "Romanticist on the Throne."

The final palace built by the Hohenzollerns in the New Garden was created in 1913–1917 under the last German emperor, William II: *Cecilienhof Palace*, modeled on an English country manor. It acquired international fame as the site of negotiations by the victorious Allied Forces in the summer of 1945. Truman, Churchill's successor Attlee, and Stalin were the signatories

hier am 2. August das „Potsdamer Abkommen", das die Zukunft Nachkriegsdeutschlands und von ganz Europa festlegte.

Der schönen Aussicht wegen ließ Friedrich Wilhelm IV. auf dem benachbarten Pfingstberg nach eigenen Plänen das *Belvedere* errichten. Ausgeführt wurde der von der italienischen Renaissance beeinflusste Bau ab 1847 von Persius, Stüler und Ludwig Ferdinand Hesse. Von der begehbaren Plattform der mächtigen Doppelturmanlage aus hat man heute einen phantastischen Rundumblick über die gesamte Potsdamer Kulturlandschaft. Unterhalb des Belvedere liegt ein kleiner Picknickpavillon, benannt nach der römischen Göttin der Feldfrüchte, der *Pomonatempel*. Er ist das erste Werk des damals gerade 19 Jahre alten Karl Friedrich Schinkel – und es ist schon alles da: Antike, Anmut und Strenge, Präzision und Witz.

Die geschichtsträchtige Stadt

Potsdam verkörpert preußisches Lebensgefühl par excellence. Neben der Kapitale Berlin behauptete sie sich stets als die kleinere Residenzstadt mit eigenem Charakter, das von Beamten, dem Militär und Manufakturen geprägt war. Beherrscht wird Potsdams Stadtsilhouette bis heute von der Kuppel der *Nikolaikirche*, die Schinkel ab 1830 als einen Zentralbau entwarf, der sich vor allem an der Londoner St. Paul's Cathedral orientierte. Zunächst nur mit einem flachen Satteldach ver-

Neben der mächtigen Nikolaikirche (Karl Friedrich Schinkel, 1830–37, damals noch mit flachem Dach) und dem Alten Rathaus (Johann Boumann, 1753–55) sowie dem Marmorobelisken (1753) liegt heute eine große Brache: Vom Stadtschloss ist auf dem Alten Markt nur noch das Fortunaportal zu sehen. Das soll sich bald ändern.

Next to mighty Nikolai Church (Karl Friedrich Schinkel, 1830–37, still with a flat roof in those days) and the Old City Hall (Johann Boumann, 1753–55), as well as the Marble Obelisk (1753), there currently lies a great wasteland: Nothing is left of City Palace on the Old Market but the Fortuna Portal. This is supposed to change soon.

to the "Potsdam Agreement" of August 2, 1945, which determined the future of postwar Germany and of all of Europe.

Based on his own designs, Frederick William IV had the *Belvedere* built on neighboring Pfingstberg Hill because of its beautiful views. Starting in 1847, the building influenced by Italian Renaissance designs was constructed by Persius, Stüler and Ludwig Ferdinand Hesse. The accessible platform of the massive twin-tower facility grants fantastic panoramic views of the entire Potsdam cultural landscape. Beneath the Belvedere, there sits a small picnic pavilion named after the Roman goddess of field crops, *Pomona Tempel*. It was the first work by Karl Friedrich Schinkel, only 19 years old at the time – and everything is already present: antiquity, grace and austerity, precision and wit.

The Historic City

Potsdam embodies the Prussian way of life as such. Next to the capital of Berlin, it always asserted itself as the smaller royal residence city with its own character, defined by civil servants, the military and manufactories. To the present day, Potsdam's skyline is dominated by the dome of *Nikolai Church*, designed (starting in 1830) as a central-plan structure modeled primarily on London's St Paul's Cathedral by Schinkel. Initially covered with nothing but a flat saddle roof, the church was not

411

Links: Schinkel hat den Bau seiner Idee einer Kuppel nicht mehr erlebt; realisiert durch Friedrich August Stüler, 1843–50, Höhe bis zum Kuppelscheitel 52 m.
Oben: Der vergoldete Atlas auf dem Alten Rathaus, nachgebildet der Turmfigur auf dem Rathaus von Amsterdam.

Left: Schinkel did not live to see the realization of his idea of a dome; built by Friedrich August Stüler, 1843–50, dome height rim to apex: 52 m.
Above: Gilded Atlas on the Old City Hall, modeled on the statue topping the tower of Amsterdam's city hall.

Das Dampfmaschinenhaus mitten in der Stadt, Pumpstation für die Fontänenanlage im Park von Sanssouci, Ludwig Persius, 1841–43, auf Wunsch von Friedrich Wilhelm IV. „nach Art der türkischen Moscheen mit einem Minarett als Schornstein" gebaut und ausgestattet mit einer Zweizylinder-Dampfmaschine der Firma Borsig.

The Steam Pump House in the center of the city, pump station for the fountains in Sanssouci Park, Ludwig Persius, 1841–43, built at the request of Frederick William IV "in the manner of Turkish mosques with a minaret for a chimney" and furnished with a two-cylinder steam engine made by Borsig Company.

Rechts: Seit 1981 Filmmuseum; erst Orangerie, 1685, seit 1714 Marstall für die königlichen Pferde; Umbau durch Georg Wenzeslaus von Knobelsdorff, 1746.
Unten: Älter als jenes in Berlin – Potsdams „kleines" Brandenburger Tor, Carl von Gontard und Georg Christian Unger, 1770.

Right: Since 1981, Film Museum; initially Orangery, 1685, from 1714 on, stables for the royal horses; remodeled by Georg Wenzeslaus von Knobelsdorff, 1746.
Below: Older than its Berlin counterpart – Potsdam's "small" Brandenburg Gate, Carl von Gontard and Georg Christian Unger, 1770.

414

sehen, erhielt die Kirche ab 1843 unter der Leitung Stülers die 78 Meter hohe Tambourkuppel.

Nur wenig erinnert daran, dass zwischen der Nikolaikirche und der ehemals bebauten Wasserkante an der Alten Fahrt bis 1945 der historische Kern Potsdams lag, der repräsentative Mittelpunkt einer Garnisons- und Residenzstadt. Einzig das Alte Rathaus, das Johann Boumann von 1753 bis 1755 errichtete und mit Palladio-Fassade, Kolossalsäulen und Kuppel ausstattete, sowie Knobelsdorffs Wohnhaus von 1750 wurden nach den Kriegsbeschädigungen ab 1960 wiederaufgebaut. Auch der Marmorobelisk von 1753 fand in veränderter Form 1979 wieder seinen Platz. Auf dem Alten Markt hat einst das unter dem Großen Kurfürsten 1664 bis 1670 errichtete, später mehrfach umgestaltete *Stadtschloss* gestanden: Vor allem Knobelsdorff hatte daraus ab 1744 eine prächtige barocke Anlage gemacht. Nachdem es bei einem Bombenangriff 1945 völlig ausgebrannt war, wurde die Ruine des Schlosses 1959/60 trotz großer Proteste abgerissen. Jetzt ersteht es mit Sitz des Land-

Im Auftrag Friedrich Wilhelms I., des „Soldatenkönigs", angelegtes Viertel im holländischen Stil in Erwartung niederländischer Handwerker, Johann Boumann, 1734–42: unverputzter roter Backstein mit weißen Fugen und weiß-grün dekorierten Türen und Fensterläden.

Commissioned by Frederick William I, the "Soldier King," as a quarter in the Dutch style in preparation for the arrival of Dutch craftsmen, Johann Boumann, 1734–42: raw red brick with white joints, doors and windows decorated with white-and-green patterns.

given its 78-meter-high tambour cupola from 1843 under the direction of Stüler.

There is not much left to show that, until 1945, the historical center of Potsdam was located between Nikolai Church and the formerly developed waterfront at Alte Fahrt – once the representational focus of a garrison town and royal residence city. Only Old City Hall, built by Johann Boumann in 1753–1755 and outfitted with a Palladio-style façade, colossal columns and a dome, as well as Knobelsdorff's residence of 1750, were rebuilt after war damages starting in 1960. The marble obelisk of 1753 was likewise returned to its original spot in 1979 – though its form was modified. The Old Market used to be the site of *City Palace*, built under the Great Elector in 1664–1670 and later repeatedly remodeled: Knobelsdorff, especially, began transforming it into a glorious baroque structure in 1744. After being thoroughly gutted by a bombing raid in 1945, the ruined palace was demolished in 1959/60, in spite of widespread protests. Now it is being reconstructed at its original site to

tages neu, als Rekonstruktion am alten Ort. Gegenüber dem Alten Markt liegt das einzige Gebäude des Schlossensembles, das Kriegs- und Nachkriegszeit überlebt hat, der einstige *Marstall*. 1685 als Orangerie nach den Plänen von Johann Arnold Nering erbaut, ließ der Soldatenkönig das Gebäude 1714 in einen Stall für die königlichen Reitpferde umwandeln. Seine heutige Form erhielt es 1746 durch Knobelsdorff. Aus dieser Zeit stammen auch die dramatisch bewegten Reitergruppen von Friedrich Christian Glume über den Portalen. Seit 1981 residiert hier das Filmmuseum Potsdam.

Obwohl es im 19. Jahrhundert durchaus üblich war, fremde Baustile zu kopieren, konnte nur ein Romantiker auf die Idee kommen, 81 PS als Moschee zu verkleiden. Das Haus für die stärkste Dampfmaschine Preußens, die vom noch jungen Unternehmer August Borsig gebaut worden war, ließ Friedrich Wilhelm IV. von 1841 bis 1843 durch Ludwig Persius nach maurischem Vorbild errichten – „mit einem Minarett als Schornstein". Das *Dampfmaschinenhaus*, damals das höchste Bauwerk in der Gegend, verdankt die aufwendige Gestaltung vermutlich seiner exponierten Lage am Havelufer, denn es war von der königlichen Gartenterrasse in Sanssouci aus zu sehen.

Als die Zuwanderer nicht in der erwarteten Zahl kamen, zogen französische und preußische Handelsvertreter, Künstler und Soldaten in das mit rund 150 Typenhäusern europaweit einmalige Bauensemble ein.

When the immigrants did not arrive in the numbers expected, French and Prussian trade representatives, artists and soldiers moved into the complex which, with its some 150 single model "type houses," is unique in Europe.

house the Diet of Brandenburg. Across from the Old Market lies the only building of the palatial complex to have survived the war and postwar eras, the former royal stables or, *Marstall*. Built in 1685 as an orangery based on designs by Johann Arnold Nering, the Soldier King had the building transformed into a stable for his royal horses in 1714. It was given its current form by Knobelsdorff in 1746. The dramatically animated groups of riders above the portals by Frederick Christian Glume date from the same period. Since 1981, the Film Museum Potsdam has had its home there.

Although it was fairly common in the 19th century to copy foreign architectural styles, only romanticists could get the bright idea of dressing up 81 HP as a mosque. Housing Prussia's strongest steam engine built by entrepreneur August Borsig when he was still young, the structure was commissioned by Frederick William IV who had it constructed by Ludwig Persius after Moorish models in 1841–1843 – "with a minaret for a chimney." The highest building in the region at the time, the *Pump House* most likely owes its elaborate design to its exposed position on the shores of the Havel, because it could be seen from the royal garden terrace at Sanssouci.

Carl Hasenpflug (1802–1858),
Die Garnisonskirche in Potsdam
(Garrison Church in Potsdam),
1827, Öl auf Kupfer/oil on copper,
63 x 81 cm, Stiftung Stadtmuseum.

Ein europaweit einzigartiges Bauensemble: das zwischen 1734 und 1742 entstandene *Holländische Viertel*. Der Soldatenkönig ließ es von Johann Boumann d. Ä. errichten in Erwartung holländischer Einwanderer – in deren Heimatstil. Es besteht aus vier Karrees mit etwa 150 Backsteinhäusern, geschmückt mit weißgrünen Portaldekorationen und Fensterläden.

Gleichfalls vom Soldatenkönig wurde die *Garnisonkirche* in Auftrag gegeben. 1732 eingeweiht, gehörte der von Philipp Gerlach entworfene schlichte Barockbau zu den weithin sichtbaren Wahrzeichen der Stadt. Friedrich Wilhelm I. und sein Sohn, Friedrich II., waren hier, in der Hofkirche der Hohenzollern, bestattet. Am 21. März 1934 nahm der Reichspräsident Hindenburg dem Reichskanzler Hitler hier den Eid auf die Verfassung ab – propagandistische Inszenierung, die als „Tag von Potsdam" in die Geschichte einging. Wegen dieser symbolischen Bedeutung ist der Wiederaufbau der im Krieg ausgebrannten, 1968 gesprengten Garnisonkirche umstritten.

An architectural complex unique in Europe: the *Dutch Quarter*, created in 1734–1742. The Soldier King commissioned Johann Boumann the Elder to build it for immigrants expected to arrive from the Netherlands – in the style of their homeland. It consists of four square blocks with some 150 brick houses decorated with white-and-green portals and window shutters.

Garrison Church was likewise commissioned by the Soldier King. Dedicated in 1732, the unpretentious Baroque building designed by Philipp Gerlach was one of the city's emblems visible from afar. Frederick William I and his son, Frederick II, were buried here, in the court church of the Hohenzollerns. On March 21, 1934, Imperial President Hindenburg received Imperial Chancellor Hitler's oath on the constitution – a propagandistic performance that went down in history as the "Day of Potsdam." Because of this symbolic significance, reconstruction of Garrison Church, burnt down during the war and blown up in 1968, is contested.

Oben: Unbekannter Künstler, *Potsdamer Stadtschloss, von der Nikolaikirche aus gesehen*, 1769, Reproduktion eines Kupferstichs. Unten: Das Stadtschloss mit Lustgarten, errichtet unter dem Großen Kurfürsten, 1664–70, Umgestaltung durch Georg Wenzeslaus von Knobelsdorff, 1744–52; koloriertes Foto, 1898.

Above: Unknown artist, *Potsdam City Palace, seen from the direction of Nikolai Church*, 1769, reproduction of a copper engraving. Below: City Palace with Pleasure Garden, built under the Great Elector, 1664–70, remodeled by Georg Wenzeslaus von Knobelsdorff, 1744–52, hand-colored photo, 1898.

418

Xaver Sandmann (1805–1856),
*Das königliche Schloss in
Potsdam* (Royal Palace in
Potsdam), um/c. 1840,
gouachierte Lithographie/
gouached lithograph, 31,5 x 44 cm.

Matthias Koeppel (geb. 1937),
Sanssouci, 1993, Diptychon/
diptych, Öl auf Leinwand/oil on
canvas, 200 x 300 cm.

Werkregister / Index of Works

Im Folgenden sind alle künstlerischen Werke verzeichnet, die in diesem Buch gezeigt oder im Text erwähnt werden. Die Titel in deutscher Sprache sind kursiv, die Titel in englischer Sprache sind in gerader Schrift.

Below are indexed all works of art displayed in the book or mentioned in the text. Titles in German are italicized; titles in English are printed in regular font style.

5-7-9 Serie Brunneninstallation, Walter de Maria 187

5-7-9 Serie fountain installation, Walter de Maria 187

The Abduction of Europe, Paul Gauguin 210

Abreise König Wilhelms I. zur Armee am 31. Juli 1870, Adolph von Menzel 62f.

Akhenaten and his spouse Nefertiti in front of Aten's sun disk, relief panel 147

Der Alchimist, Pieter Bruegel d. Ä. 204

The Alchemist, Pieter Bruegel the Elder 204

Alexander von Humboldt und Aimé Bonpland im Tal von Tapia am Fuß des Vulkans Chimborazo, Friedrich Georg Weitsch 176

Alexander von Humboldt and Aimé Bonpland in the Valley of Tapia at the Foot of Chimborazo Volcano, Friedrich Georg Weitsch 176

Alexander von Humboldt, Georg Friedrich Weitsch 175

Allegorische Figur, den Kunstunterricht symbolisierend, Moritz Schulz 151

Allegorical figure symbolizing art instruction, Moritz Schulz 151

Das alte Berliner Rathaus, Carl Graeb 226

Amor als Sieger, Caravaggio (eigentl. Michelangelo Merisi) 191

Amor Victorious, Caravaggio (orig. Michelangelo Merisi) 191

Amphora des „Berliner Malers" 148

Amphora by the "Berlin Painter" 148

Angriff der Kavallerie auf das vor dem Schloss versammelte Volk am 18. März, F. Mesmer 181

Ansicht aus dem Zuschauerraum auf die Scene der beim Einweihungsprolog aufgestellten Decoration, Louis Normand 278

Ansicht der Schlossbrücke, Eduard Gaertner 80

Ansicht der Städte Berlin und Cölln von Norden gesehen, P. von der Aa 8

Ansicht des Belvedere auf dem Pfingstberg, N. Buchholz 408

Apple Heads on Swiss Cheese, Paul McCarthy 266

Arbeiter an der Deichsel des Transport wagens, Adolph von Menzel 209

The Archer, Henry Moore 214

Archiv der Deutschen Abgeordneten, Christian Boltanski 98, 102

Archive of the German Delegates, Christian Boltanski 98, 102

Area of Treptow with view of Stralau, August von Rentzell 228

The Artist and his Family in His House on Lake Wannsee, Max Liebermann 263

The Artist's Garden in Wannsee, Max Liebermann 261

Artistin – Marcella, Ernst Ludwig Kirchner 254

Assyrischer König Asarhaddon führt Besiegte am Nasenring, babylonische Granitstele 138

Assyrian King Esarhaddon leads the vanquished by nose rings, Babylonian granite stela 138

At the Employment Agency; Menial Staff Rental Office, Fritz Paulsen 169

Athena im Kampf mit Alkyoneus, Pergamonaltar 132

Athena Fighting Alcyoneus, Pergamon Altar 132

Athenischer Staatsmann und Heerführer Perikles, Porträtbüste 147

Athenian statesman and military leader Pericles, portrait bust 147

Auf der Digue, Ostende, Franz Skarbina 235

Auferstehung Christi, Lucas Cranach d. Ä. 372

Babelsberg Palace near Potsdam, G. Hess after Friedrich August Borchel 386

Badehaus an der Havel, Max Slevogt 29

*Das Balkonzimmer/*Balcony Room, Adolph von Menzel 156

Bathers Throwing Reeds, Ernst Ludwig Kirchner 253

Bathhouse on the Havel, Max Slevogt 29

Bei der Stellenvermittlung – Gesinde-Vermietungsbureau, Fritz Paulsen 169

Berlin Beach Life, Heinrich Zille 30

Berlin Cathedral, Carl Hasenpflug 225

Berlin Colour Sphere, Olafur Eliasson 268

Berlin Market Scene, Franziska Kobes 168

Berlin Street Scene, Lesser Ury 231

Berlin, Brigitte Matschinsky-Denninghoff, Martin Matschinsky-Denninghoff 72, 74f.

Berlin, Unter den Linden, Lovis Corinth 62

Berliner Marktszene, Franziska Kobes 168

Berliner Strandleben, Heinrich Zille 30

Berliner Straßenszene, Lesser Ury 231

Der betende Knabe, Bronze-Skulptur 149

Big Nudes, Helmut Newton 242

Bildnis Franz Marc, August Macke 220

Bildnis Friedrichs des Großen als Kronprinz, Antoine Pesne 393

Birth of Christ, Martin Schongauer 190

Black Red Gold, Gerhard Richter 96

Blick auf die Kurfürstenbrücke vom Mühlendamm aus, Johann Heinrich Hintze 228

Blick in Griechenlands Blüte, Karl Friedrich Schinkel, Kopie von Wilhelm Ahlborn 11

Blick vom Dach der Friedrich-Werderschen Kirche auf das Friedrichsforum, Eduard Gärtner 160f.

Die Blumenterrasse im Wannseegarten nach Nordwesten, Max Liebermann 261

Body of Christ with Angels, Giovanni Pisano 127

Der Bogenschütze, Henry Moore 214

Die Borsig'sche Werkstatt am Oranien-burger Tor in Berlin, Karl Eduard Biermann 20f.

Borsig Factory at Oranienburg Gate in Berlin, Karl Eduard Biermann 20f.

Brandenburg Gate and Paris Square, H. A. Forst after F. A. Schmidt 46

Brandenburger Tor und Pariser Platz, H. A. Forst nach F. A. Schmidt 46

Die Briefsieglerin, Jean Baptiste Simeon Chardin 366

Die Brüder Schadow mit Thorvaldsen, Wilhelm von Schadow 158

Capricorne, Max Ernst 223

Carol Singers, Emil Koller 227

Cavalry Attack on the People Assembled in Front of the Palace on March 18, F. Mesmer 181

Charles V, Portrait with Baton, Peter Paul Rubens 165

Der Charlottenhof bei Potsdam, Julius Umbach 402f.

Charlottenhof Palace near Potsdam, Julius Umbach 402f.

Christ Appearing to Mary Magdalena, Tilman Riemenschneider 126f.

Christ's Resurrection, Lucas Cranach the Elder 372

Christian Daniel Rauch, Carl Adolph Henning 16

The City and Fortress of Spandau, Matthäus Merian 374

Clock of Flowing Time, Bernhard Gitton 73

Congress of Berlin, Anton von Werner 24f.

Construction and Installation of Tared Forms, Santiago Sierra 269

Coronation of William I as King of Prussia on October 18, 1861, in the Palace Church at Königsberg, Adolph von Menzel 18

Courtyard of the Royal Porcelain Manufactory Berlin, 4 Leipziger Straße, Eduard Gaertner 17

Crouching Girl, Ernst Ludwig Kirchner 233

Crown Prince Frederick with his sister Wilhelmine, Antoine Pesne 366

The Dance, Antoine Watteau 203

The Dangolsheim Madonna, Niclaus Gerhaert von Leyden 128f.

Death of Medusa, Adelchi-Riccardo Mantovani 234

Death of the Virgin Mary, Bartolome Bermejo (Bartolomé de Cardenás) 190

Der Denker, Auguste Rodin 159

Departure of King William I for the Army on July 31, 1870, Adolph von Menzel 62f.

Der Bevölkerung, Hans Haacke 98

Desk with Power Unit, Joseph Beuys 97

Die Domkirche in Berlin, Carl Hasenpflug 225

Don't gawk so romantically, Karl-Ernst Herrmann 276

Die drei Grazien, Rebecca Horn 106

Dürers Mutter, Albrecht Dürer 207

Dürer's Mother, Albrecht Dürer 207

Dutch Proverbs, Pieter Bruegel the Elder 194

Echnaton und seine Gemahlin Nofretete vor der Sonnenscheibe Atons, Relief-platte 147

Eight-Seater Racing Canoes, Christiane Möbius 103

Ein moderner Maler, Georg Baselitz 232

Einsamer Baum, Caspar David Friedrich 155

Die Einschiffung nach Kythera, Antoine Watteau 368f

Eisenwalzwerk, Adolph von Menzel 157

Embarkation for Cythera, Antoine Watteau 368f.

Die Entführung der Europa, Paul Gauguin 210

Entry of Napoleon into Berlin on October 27, 1806, Charles Meynier 47

Equestrian Statue of Frederick the Great, Christian Daniel Rauch 65

Die Erbsenesser, Georges de La Tour 196

*Ernst-Thälmann-Denkmal/*Memorial, Lew Kerbel 360

Die Eröffnung des Deutschen Reichstages im Weißen Saal des Berliner Schlosses durch Wilhelm II. am 25. Juni 1888, Anton von Werner 26f.

Die Erscheinung Christi vor Maria Magdalena, Tilman Riemenschneider 126f.

Façade der Hauptfronte des neuen Museums, Carl Friedrich Thiele 143

Façade of the Main Front of the new Museum, Carl Friedrich Thiele 143

Fall of Man, Lucas Cranach the Elder 192

Female Artist – Marcella, Ernst Ludwig Kirchner 254

Female Figure with Pomegranate 139

Fighting Amazon, August Kiss 144

Figur in großer Höhe II, Rolf Szymanski 250

Figure study of St. Anthony of the Isenheim Altar, Mathis Gothart Grünewald 209

Figure Up High II, Rolf Szymanski 250

Figurenstudie zu dem Heiligen Antonius des Isenheimer Altars, Mathis Gothart Grünewald 209

Flachsscheuer in Laren, Max Liebermann 157

Flax Spinning in Laren, Max Liebermann 157

Flötenkonzert Friedrich des Großen in Sanssouci, Adolph von Menzel 156, 396f.

Flower Terrace in Wannsee Garden Facing Northwest, Max Liebermann 261
Flute Concert by Frederick the Great in Sanssouci, Adolph von Menzel 156, 396f.
Frau am Fenster, Caspar David Friedrich 152
Frauenstatue mit Granatapfel 139
Frederick the Great and Voltaire under the colonnades in Sanssouci, Peter Haas 399
Frederick the Great Honors a Fallen Officer, unknown artist 166
Frederick William II of Prussia, Anton Graff 9
Friedrich der Große ehrt einen gefallenen Offizier, unbekannter Künstler 166
Friedrich der Große und Voltaire unter den Kolonnaden von Sanssouci, Peter Haas 399
Friedrich Wilhelm II. von Preußen, Anton Graff 9
Friedrichs Melancholie, Georg Baselitz 97, 102

Die Garnisonskirche in Potsdam, Carl Hasenpflug 416
Garrison Church in Potsdam, Carl Hasenpflug 416
Der Garten des Künstlers in Wannsee, Max Liebermann 261
Das Gastmahl des Plato, Anselm Feuerbach 156
Die Geburt Christi, Martin Schongauer 190
Gegend von Treptow mit Aussicht auf Stralau, August von Rentzell 228
Der gelbe Pullover, Pablo Picasso 247
Genealogical Tree of a Saxon Family, Daniel Bretschneider the Younger 167
Gesellschaft in Altberliner Destille, Heinrich Zille 31
Get-Together in Old Berlin Pub, Heinrich Zille 31
Das Glas Wein, Jan Vermeer van Delft 200
The Glass of Wine, Jan Vermeer van Delft 200
Glimpse of Greece's Golden Age, Karl Friedrich Schinkel, 1825, copy by Wilhelm Ahlborn 11
Glotzt nicht so romantisch, Karl-Ernst Herrmann 276
Die Granitschale im Berliner Lustgarten, Johann Erdmann Hummel 224
Granite Bowl in Pleasure Garden, Johann Erdmann Hummel 224
The Great Elector an His Wife Louise Henriette of Orange, Matthias Czwiczek 9
Great Night, Georg Kolbe 294
Greifswalder Hafen, Caspar David Friedrich 153
Greifswald Harbour, Caspar David Friedrich 153
Große Kniende, Wilhelm Lehmbruck 221
Der Große Kurfürst und seine Gemahlin Luise Henriette von Oranien, Matthias Czwiczek 9
Große Nacht, Georg Kolbe 294
Ground plan of Sanssouci and Charlottenhof Palaces, Peter Joseph Lenné 92

Group of Turkish Riders, Daniel Nikolaus Chodowiecki 208
Grundgesetz 49, Dani Karavan 105
Grunewaldsee oder Schlachtensee, Walter Leistikow 249
A Gun For Hire, Helmut Newton 242

Häuschen am See in Glienicke, Karl Friedrich Schinkel 384
Head of the Güstrow Memorial, Ernst Barlach 244
Heads and Tail, Alexander Calder 214
Die heilige Anna mit ihren drei Ehemännern, Tilman Riemenschneider 125
Die Heilige Anna Selbdritt, Jacob Cornelisz van Amsterdam 192
Die Heilige Elisabeth von Thüringen, Jacob Cornelisz van Amsterdam 192
Der Hexensabbat, Hans Baldung Grien 204
Hinterhaus und Hof, Adolph von Menzel 19
Hof der königlichen Porzellanmanufaktur Berlin, Leipziger Straße 4, Eduard Gaertner 17
Hommage à Kolbe zur „Nacht", Volkmar Haase 294
Hommage à Kolbe on "Night", Volkmar Haase 294
Hospital Market, Eduard Gaertner 57
The House of Palms on Peacock Island, Carl Blechen 383
Die Huldigung der preußischen Stände vor Friedrich Wilhelm IV. in Berlin am 15. Oktober, 1840, Franz Krüger 182
Humboldt im Park von Schloss Tegel, Johann Gabriel Friedrich Poppel nach Ludwig Rohbock 372
Humboldt in the park of Tegel Palace, Johann Gabriel Friedrich Poppel after Ludwig Rohbock 372
Humboldt und Bonpland am Orinoco, Eduard Ender 177
Humboldt and Bonpland at Orinoco, Eduard Ender 177

The Imperial Family in Sanssouci Park, William Pape 169
The International, Otto Griebel 171
Die Internationale, Otto Griebel 171
Iron Rolling Mill, Adolph von Menzel 157
The Island of Death, Arnold Böcklins 156

Jacob Wrestling with the Angel, Harmensz van Rijn Rembrandt 198
Jakob Fugger II. (der Reiche), Albrecht Dürer 191
Jakob Fugger II (the Rich), Albrecht Dürer 191
Jakobs Kampf mit dem Engel, Harmensz van Rijn Rembrandt 198
Joachim II. als Kurprinz, Lucas Cranach d.Ä. 372
Joachim II as Electoral Prince, Lucas Cranach the Elder 372
Judith mit dem Haupt des Holofernes, Lucas Cranach d. Ä. 371

Judith with the head of Holofernes, Lucas Cranach the Elder 371
Junge Dame mit Perlenhalsband, Jan Vermeer van Delft 201
Junger Mann mit gebundenen Händen, Richard Scheibe 361
Junges Mädchen mit Puppe, Paul Cézanne 248

Die kaiserliche Familie im Park zu Sanssouci, William Pape 169
Kämpfende Amazone, August Kiss 144
Kardinal Julian, Andreas Hofer 265
Karl August von Hardenberg, Porträtbüste/portrait bust, Christian Daniel Rauch 168
Karl Friedrich Schinkel, Carl Friedrich Schmid 10
Karl V., Portrait mit dem Kommandostab, Peter Paul Rubens 165
Kauerndes Mädchen, Ernst Ludwig Kirchner 233
Kentaur und Nymphe, Arnold Boecklin 210
King Frederick II's round table at Sanssouci, Adolph von Menzel 393
King's Bridge, Eduard Gaertner 82
Klosterstraße mit Turm der Parochialkirche, Johann Georg Rosenberg 336
Klosterstraße with Tower of Parochial Church, Johann Georg Rosenberg 336
Komposition Z VIII, László Moholy-Nagy 222
Der Kongress zu Berlin, Anton von Werner 24f.
König Friedrichs II. Tafelrunde in Sanssouci, Adolph von Menzel 393
Königin Luise als Hebe vor dem Brandenburger Tor, Karl Wilhelm Wach nach P.E. Stroehling 227
Königin Sophie Charlotte, Friedrich Wilhelm Weidemann 365
Das königliche Jagdschloss Grunewald bei Berlin, Hans Fincke nach Gustav Adolf Boenisch 370
Das königliche Schloss in Potsdam, Xaver Sandmann 418f.
Das Königliche Schloss, W. Loeillot 180
Die Königsbrücke, Eduard Gaertner 82
Konstruktion und Installation von teerbeschichteten Formen, Santiago Sierra 269
Kopf des Güstrower Ehrenmals, Ernst Barlach 244
Köpfe und Schwanz, Alexander Calder 214
Kore „Ornithe" 139
Krach in der Destille, Heinrich Zille 211
Krieg (Holzschnittzyklus), Käthe Kollwitz 244
Kriegsgefangen, Anton von Werner 230
Kronprinz Friedrich mit seiner Schwester Wilhelmine, Antoine Pesne 366
Krönung Wilhelms I. zum König von Preußen am 18. Oktober 1861 in der Schlosskirche zu Königsberg, Adolph von Menzel 18
Der Künstler und seine Familie in seinem Haus am Wannsee, Max Liebermann 263
Kurrendesänger, Emil Koller 227

Ladenschild des Kunsthändlers Gersaint, Antoine Watteau 370
Lady sealing a letter, Jean Baptiste Simeon Chardin 366
Lake Grunewald or Lake Schlachtensee, Walter Leistikow 249
Lange Brücke und Schloss, Maximilian Roch 82
Large Kneeling Woman, Wilhelm Lehmbruck 221
Leap over the Spree, Stephan Braunfels 105
Leib Christi mit Engeln, Giovanni Pisano 127
Leipziger Platz, Otto Antoine 170
Liebknecht-Luxemburg-Gedenkdemonstration im Januar 1948 auf dem Friedhof von Friedrichsfelde, Alfred Stiller 34
Liebknecht-Luxemburg Memorial Demonstration Held in January 1948 on the Friedrichsfelde Cemetery, Alfred Stiller 34
Life Enigma, Anselm Reyle 269
Lion Fighter, Albert Wolff 144
Little House on the Lake in Glinicke, Karl Friedrich Schinkel 384
Lonesome Tree, Caspar David Friedrich 155
Long Bridge and Palace, Maximilian Roch 82
Löwenkämpfer, Albert Wolff 144
Lucretia und eine Quellnymphe, Lucas Cranach d. Ä. 372
Lucretia and a nymph of the spring, Lucas Cranach the Elder 372

Die Macht der Frau Minne, Meister Caspar von Regensberg 205
The Making of Große Geister, Thomas Schütte 265
Der Maler und sein Modell, Pablo Picasso 249
Mann und Frau in Betrachtung des Mondes, Caspar David Friedrich 154
Man and Woman Contemplating the Moon, Caspar David Friedrich 154
Mann auf der Leiter, Neo Rauch 105
Man on the ladder, Neo Rauch 105
Der Mann mit dem Goldhelm, Harmensz van Rijn Rembrandt 186
Man with a Golden Helmet, Harmensz van Rijn Rembrandt 186
Maria, Joseph Anton Feuchtmayer 128
Marientod, Bartolome Bermejo (Bartolomé de Cardenás) 190
Die Marsham-Kinder, Thomas Gainsborough 202
The Marsham Children, Thomas Gainsborough 202
Das Martyrium der Hl. Agathe, Giovanni Battista Tiepolo 202
The Martyrdom of St Agatha, Giovanni Battista Tiepolo 202
Marx-Engels-Denkmal/Memorial, Ludwig Engelhardt 360
Masken der Sterbenden Krieger, Andreas Schlüter 172
Masks of the Dying Warriors, Andreas Schlüter 172

Max Liebermann in seinem Atelier, Ernst Ludwig Kirchner 255

Max Liebermann in his Studio, Ernst Ludwig Kirchner 255

Michael Jackson Gold, Paul McCarthy 266

Military Parade on Opera Square, Franz Krüger 60

Mill on the Couleuvre near Pontoise, Paul Cézanne 155

Mit Schilf werfende Badende, Ernst Ludwig Kirchner 253

A Modern Painter, Georg Baselitz 232

Mönch am Meer, Caspar David Friedrich 155

Mondaufgang am Meer, Caspar David Friedrich 156

Monk by the Sea, Caspar David Friedrich 155

Moonrise by the Sea, Caspar David Friedrich 156

Der Morgen, Georg Kolbe 252

Morgenspaziergang, Georges Seurat 248

Morning, Georg Kolbe 252

Morning Stroll, Georges Seurat 248

Moses zerschmettert die Gesetzestafeln, Harmensz van Rijn Rembrandt 199

Moses Smashing the Tables of Law, Harmensz van Rijn Rembrandt 199

The Mother, Pieter de Hooch 197

Mühle an der Couleuvre bei Pontoise, Paul Cézanne 155

Die Mutter, Pieter de Hooch 197

Die Muttergottes aus Dangolsheim, Niclaus Gerhaert von Leyden 128f.

Napoleons Einzug in Berlin am 27. Oktober 1806, Charles Meynier 47

Nationaldenkmal für die Befreiungskriege 1818–21, Karl Friedrich Schinkel 356

National Monument for the Liberation Wars, 1818–21, Karl Friedrich Schinkel 356

Nefertiti 120ff., 146f.

Neptun und Amphitrite, Jan Gossaert, genannt/known as Jan Mabuse 193

Die neue Bauschule, von der Schloss-brücke aus gesehen – Die Werderschen Mühlen, Friedrich Wilhelm Klose 12f.

Der Neue Markt mit der Marienkirche, Johann Heinrich Hintze 56f.

Neues Palais bei Potsdam, Sommer-residenz des deutschen Kaisers, Otto Günther-Naumburg 400

The New Academy of Architecture, as Seen from Palace Bridge – The Werder Mills, Friedrich Wilhelm Klose 12f.

New Market with St Mary's Church, Johann Heinrich Hintze 56f.

New Palace near Potsdam, summer residence of the German emperor, Otto Günther-Naumburg 400

Die niederländischen Sprichwörter, Pieter Bruegel d. Ä., 194

Nofretete 2, 120ff., 146f.

Nollendorfplatz bei Nacht, Lesser Ury 219

Nollendorfplatz at Night, Lesser Ury 219

Die Öffnung der Berliner Mauer, Matthias Koeppel 36

Ohne Titel, Katja Strunz 271

Ohne Titel, Monika Sosnowska 269

Old City Hall in Berlin, Carl Graeb 226

On the Boardwalk, Ostend, Franz Skarbina 235

The Opening of the Berlin Wall, Matthias Koeppel 36

The Opening of the German Reichstag in the White Hall of the Berlin Palace by William II on June 25, 1888, Anton von Werner 26f.

Outside the Gates of Berlin, Leopold Zielke 229

The Painter and His Model, Pablo Picasso 249

The Palace Garden of Prince Albert, Adolph von Menzel 19

Palaisgarten des Prinzen Albrecht, Adolph von Menzel 19

Das Palmenhaus auf der Pfaueninsel, Carl Blechen 383

Panoramic View of Berlin, as Seen from the Armory, Carl Pescheck 14f.

Panoramische Ansicht von Berlin, vom Zeughaus aus gesehen, Carl Pescheck 14f.

Parade auf dem Opernplatz, Franz Krüger 60

Parade on Opera Square, Franz Krüger 60

The Pea Eaters, Georges de La Tour 196

Perspectival depiction of the concert hall, by Carl F. Thiele 278

Perspectival View of the Gallery of the Main Stairs, Hans Fincke 143

Perspectivische Ansicht von der Galerie der Haupt-Treppe, Hans Fincke 143

Perspectivische Darstellung des Concertsaales, von Carl F. Thiele 278

Peter Joseph Lenné, Carl Joseph Begas 16

Pietà, Käthe Kollwitz 356f.

Plan von Sans-Souci und Charlottenhof, Peter Joseph Lenné 392

Plato's Symposium, Anselm Feuerbach 156

Pomonatempel auf dem Pfingstberg, Karl Friedrich Schinkel 409

Pomona Temple on Pfingstberg Hill, Karl Friedrich Schinkel 409

Portrait Franz Marc, August Macke 220

Portrait Madame Cézanne, Paul Cézanne 248

Portrait of Frederick the Great, as Crown, Antoine Pesne 393

Potsdam City Palace, seen from the direction of Nikolai Church, unknown artist 417

Potsdamer Stadtschloss, von der Nikolaikirche aus gesehen, unbekannter Künstler 417

Potsdamer Platz, Ernst Ludwig Kirchner 218

The Power of Lady Love, Meister Caspar von Regensberg 205

Prayer for Peace, Speelman Mahlangu 118

Praying Boy, bronze statue 149

Princess Group, Johann Gottfried Schadow 339

Prinzessinnengruppe, Johann Gottfried Schadow 339

Prisoner of War, Anton von Werner 230

The Prodigal Son, Max Slevogt 28

Profilbildnis einer jungen Frau, Antonio del Pollaiuolo oder Domenico Veneziano 187

Profile Portrait of a Young Woman, Antonio del Pollaiuolo oder Domenico Veneziano 187

Prospect des Königlichen Lustschlosses Sans-Souci bei Potsdam, Johann David Schleuen d. Ä. 388f.

The Prussian Estates Render Obeisance to Frederick William IV in Berlin on October 15, 1840, Franz Krüger 182

Quadriga, Johann Gottfried Schadow 43

Queen Louise as Hebe in front of Brandenburg Gate, Karl Wilhelm Wach, after P.E. Stroehling 227

Queen Sophie Charlotte, Friedrich Wilhelm Weidemann 365

Rear of House and Backyard, Adolph von Menzel 19

Red 2000, 875 / 99, Rupprecht Geiger 96

Red, Yellow, White, Blue 1-4, Imi Knoebel 105

Das Reichstagsgebäude, Albrecht Kurz 92

Reichstag Building, Albrecht Kurz 92

Reichstag Building. Western façade, Eduard Obermayer 92f.

Reichstags-Gebäude zu Berlin. Westfront, Eduard Obermayer 92f.

Reigning Queens – Queen Beatrix of The Netherlands, Andy Warhol 118

Reiterstandbild Friedrich des Großen, Christian Daniel Rauch 65

Relay Runners, Karl Albiker 330

Relief mit Darstellung des Wettergottes aus Tell Halaf 138

Relief representing the weather god of Tell Halaf 138

Rennachter, Christiane Möbius 103

Das Riesengebirge, Caspar David Friedrich 156

Riesengebirge Mountains, Caspar David Friedrich 156

Rot 2000, 875 /99, Rupprecht Geiger 96

Rot, Gelb, Weiß, Blau 1-4, Imi Knoebel 105

Royal Grunewald Hunting Palace near Berlin, Hans Fincke after Gustav Adolf Boenisch 370

Royal Palace in Potsdam, Xaver Sandmann 418f.

The Royal Palace, W. Loeillot 180

Ruckus at the Pub, Heinrich Zille 211

Saint Anne and Her Three Husbands, Tilman Riemenschneider 125

Saint Anne with Virgin and Child, Jacob Cornelisz van Amsterdam 192

Saint Elisabeth of Thuringia, Jacob Cornelisz van Amsterdam 192

Sanssouci Palace, Carl Blechen 391

Sanssouci, Matthias Koeppel 420f.

The Schadow Brothers with Thorvaldsen, Wilhelm von Schadow 158

Schiller-Denkmal (Monument), Reinhold Begas 48f.

Schloss Babelsberg bei Potsdam, G. Hess nach Friedrich August Borchel 386

Schloss Sanssouci, Carl Blechen 391

Schlüter Courtyard of City Palace, Eduard Gaertner 178f.

Der Schlüterhof des Stadtschlosses, Eduard Gaertner 178f.

Schwarz Rot Gold, Gerhard Richter 96

Seated Harlequin, Pablo Picasso 249

Selbstbildnis – Akt, Paula Modersohn-Becker 220

Selbstbildnis mit Palette an der Staffelei, Profil rechts, Max Liebermann 262

Selbstbildnis mit Pelzmütze, Harmensz van Rijn Rembrandt 206

Selbstbildnis, Käthe Kollwitz 245

Selbstbildnis, Tizian, eigentl. Tiziano Vecelli(o) 195

Self-Portrait – Nude, Paula Modersohn-Becker 220

Self-Portrait in Fur Hat, Harmensz van Rijn Rembrandt 206

Self-Portrait with Palette at the Easel, profile right, Max Liebermann 262

Self-Portrait, Käthe Kollwitz 245

Self-Portrait, Tizian, orig. Tiziano Vecelli(o) 195

Siegessäule, Heinrich Strack 78, 356

Silhouette etching of Palace Bridge, Ferdinand Berger 80

Die Singakademie am Festungsgraben, Ludwig Eduard Lütke 274

Der Sitzende Harlekin, Pablo Picasso 249

Der Spittelmarkt, Eduard Gaertner 57

Spree-Sprung, Stephan Braunfels 105

Staffelläufer, Karl Albiker 330

Stammbaum einer sächsischen Familie, Daniel Bretschneider d. J. 167

Standing Child, Erich Heckel 255

Die Statt und Vestung Spandaw, Matthäus Merian 374

Stehendes Kind, Erich Heckel 255

Still Life with Dead Hare, Pieter Bol 197

Stilleben mit totem Hasen, Pieter Bol 197

Store Sign for the Art Dealer Gersaint, Antoine Watteau 370

Die Straße, Max Beckmann 231

The Street, Max Beckmann 231

Der Sündenfall, Lucas Cranach d. Ä. 192

Synagoge in der Oranienburger Straße, Emile Pierre Joseph de Cauwer 344

Der Tanz, Antoine Watteau 203

The Thinker, Auguste Rodin 159

The Three Graces, Rebecca Horn 106

Tisch mit Aggregat, Joseph Beuys 97
To the Population, Hans Haacke 98
Der Tod der Medusa, Adelchi-Riccardo
   Mantovani 234
Torso der Großen Stehenden, Wilhelm
   Lehmbruck 221
Torso of Large Standing Woman, Wilhelm
   Lehmbruck 221
Die Toteninsel, Arnold Böcklins 156
Trust, Norbert Schwontkowski 270
Türkische Reitergruppe, Daniel Nikolaus
   Chodowiecki 208

Uhr der fließenden Zeit, Bernhard Gitton 73
Umrissstich der Schlossbrücke, Ferdinand
   Berger 80
Die Universität, W. Loeillot 172
The University, W. Loeillot 172
Unschlitt/Tallow, Joseph Beuys 267
Untitled, Katja Strunz 271
Untitled, Monika Sosnowska 269
Untitled Restaurant, Jorge Pardos 105
Us and Them, Helmut Newton 242

Venus and the Organist, Tizian, orig.
   Tiziano Vecelli(o) 196
Venus mit dem Orgelspieler, Tizian,
   eigentl. Tiziano Vecelli(o) 196

Venus und Amoretten in einer Landschaft,
   Battista Dossi 193
Venus with Cupids in Landscape, Battista
   Dossi 193
Der verlorene Sohn, Max Slevogt 28
Victory Column, Heinrich Strack 78, 356
View from the auditorium of the scene
   showing the decor set up for the
   inaugural prologue, Louis Normand 278
View from the North of the Cities of Berlin
   and Cölln, P. von der Aa 8
View of Frederick's Forum from the Roof of
   Friedrich-Werder Church, Eduard
   Gärtner 160f.
View of Palace Bridge, Eduard Gaertner
   80
View of the Belvedere on Pfingstberg, N.
   Buchholz 408
View of the Bridge of the Elector from
   Mühlendamm, Johann Heinrich Hintze
   228
View of the Royal Pleasure Palace of
   Sanssouci near Potsdam, Johann David
   Schleuen the Elder 388f.
Volcans d'air de Turbaco, Marchais &
   Bouquet nach einer Skizze von/after a
   sketch by Louis de Riens 176
Vor den Toren Berlins, Leopold Zielke 229

*Wannseegarten mit Villa – Die Birkenallee
   im Wannseegarten nach Westen*, Max
   Liebermann 260
Wannsee Garden with Villa – Birch-Lined
   Avenue in Wannsee Garden Facing West,
   Max Liebermann 260
War (woodcuts cycle), Käthe Kollwitz 244
Der Watzmann, Caspar David Friedrich 155
Watzmann Mountain, Caspar David
   Friedrich 155
The Wave, Gustave Courbet 158
Weavers' Revolt, Käthe Kollwitz 244
Weberaufstand, Käthe Kollwitz 244
Weimar's Golden Days - Weimar Court of
   the Muses, Theobald Reinhold Freiherr
   von Ör 175
*Weimars goldene Tage - Der Weimarer
   Musenhof*, Theobald Reinhold Freiherr
   von Ör 175
Weißbieridyll, Hans Baluschek 234
Die Welle, Gustave Courbet 158
Weltkugelbrunnen, Joachim Schmettau 58
Wheat Beer Idyll, Hans Baluschek 234
Who's Afraid of Red, Yellow and Blue IV,
   Barnett Newman 217
Wilhelm v. Humboldt, J. L. Raab nach/after
   Franz Krüger 175
Wilhelm von Bode, Max Liebermann 125

Winter, Balthasar Permoser 183
Witches' Sabbath, Hans Baldung Grien 204
Woman at the Window, Caspar David
   Friedrich 152
Workers at the Drawbar of the Trolley,
   Adolph von Menzel 209
World Globe Fountain, Joachim Schmettau
   58

The Yellow Sweater, Pablo Picasso 247
Young Girl with Doll, Paul Cézanne 248
Young Lady with Pearl Necklace, Jan
   Vermeer van Delft 201
Young Man with Hands Tied, Richard
   Scheibe 361

Zeus Fighting Porphyrion, Leader of the
   Giants, and Two Adolescent Giants,
   Pergamon Altar 132f.
*Zeus kämpft gegen den Gigantenführer
   Porphyrion und zwei jugendliche
   Giganten*, Pergamonaltar 132f.

Namen- und Ortsregister/ Index of Names and Places

Aalto, Alvar 315, 320
Abbado, Claudio 283
Academy of Architecture see Bauakademie
Academy of Singing see Sing-Akademie
Ackermann, Franz 268
Admiralspalast/Admiral's Palace 274, 276f.
Ägyptisches Museum/Egyptian Museum 145
Ahlborn, Wilhelm 11
Ahmadiyya-Moschee/Mosque 346
Ahrend, Werner 293
Akademie der Künste/Acadamy of Arts 45f.
Akhenaten see Echnaton
Albiker, Karl 330
Albrecht, Thomas 187, 246
Aleppo-Zimmer/Aleppo Chamber 141
Alexanderplatz 34, 54f., 75, 293, 297ff., 305
Alliierten Museum/Allied Museum 225
Alsenviertel/Alsen Quarter 90
Alt, Peter 113
Alte Nationalgalerie 10f., 122f., 125, 150ff., 216, 338, 382, 390
Altenbourg, Gerhard 101
Altes Museum 15, 58, 122, 142ff., 187
Altes Palais/Old Palace 163
Anhalter Bahnhof 23, 287f., 304
Antoine, Otto 170
Armory see Zeughaus
Arnim, Achim von 45
Art Library see Kunstbibliothek
Asarhaddon 138
Attlee, Clement 410
August Ferdinand von Preußen/of Prussia 90
Augusta, Prinzessin/Princess 386
Aust, Heinz 284
Austria, Embassy see Österreich, Botschaft
Auswärtiges Amt/Foreign Office 104f.

Babelsberg, Schloss/Palace 386f., 390, 409
Babylon 135ff.
Babylon, Kino/movie theater 284, 287
Bachmann, Jürgen 111
Baden-Württemberg, Vertretung/Mission 112
Baker, Josephine 73
Baller, Hinrich 311
Baluschek, Hans 234
Band des Bundes/Federal band 89ff., 92, 100f.
Bangert, Dietrich 112
Barenboim, Daniel 283
Barlach, Ernst 244
Barnhelm, Minna von 57
Baselitz, Georg 97, 102f., 232
Bastian, Céline 270
Bastian, Heiner 270
Bauakademie/Academy of Architecture 12ff.
Bauhaus-Archiv/Archive 224, 340f.

Baum, Herbert 354
Baum, Vicki 304
Baumgarten, Paul Otto 28, 96f., 260
Bebelplatz 173
Beckmann Max 32, 216f., 231
Begas, Carl Joseph 16
Begas, Reinhold 48, 51, 156, 279
Behnisch, Günter 46
Behrens, Peter 23, 28, 54f., 96f.
Bellevue, Schloss/Palace 90f.
Belling, Rudolf 216f.
Bendlerblock 109, 358, 361
Benn, Gottfried 32
Berger, Alfred 113, 116
Berger, Ferdinand 80, 349
Berggruen Collection see Sammlung Berggruen
Berggruen, Heinz 246, 249
Berggruen, Nicolas 249, 267
Berghaus, Ruth 279
Beringer, Lucia 321
Berlin Cathedral see Berliner Dom
Berlin Gallery see Berlinische Galerie
Berlin Goddess see Berliner Göttin
Berlin International Film Festival see Berliner Filmfestspiele
Berliner Dom/Berlin Cathedral 58f., 64, 143f., 225, 340f.
Berliner Ensemble 272ff., 276
Berliner Filmfestspiele/Berlin International Film Festival 58f., 286, 288
Berliner Göttin 139
Berlinische Galerie/Berlin Gallery 122, 230ff.
Bermejo, Bartolome 190
Bernhard, Karl 23
Beuys, Joseph 97, 267
Biermann, Karl Eduard 22
Bismarck, Otto von 24, 276, 345
Blechen, Carl 16, 382f., 390f.
Bleyl, Fritz 253
Blücher, Gebhard Leberecht von 48
Böcklin, Arnold 156
Bode, Wilhelm von 125, 129, 187, 256
Bode-Museum 22, 122ff., 187
Boecklin, Arnold 210
Boenisch, Gustav Adolf 370
Bofinger, Helge 109, 116
Bol, Pieter 197
Boltanski, Christian 98, 100f.
Bonpland, Aimé 176f.
Borchel, Friedrich August 386
Bornemann, Fritz 285
Boros, Christian 268f.
Borsig, Johann Friedrich August 350, 415
Borsigwerk/Borsig faktory 20ff.
Boumann d. Ä./the Elder, Johann 162f., 340, 410, 414, 416
Boumann, Michael Philipp Daniel 90, 405
Brahm, Otto 275
Brandenburger Tor, Brandenburg Gate, Potsdam 413
Brandenburger Tor/Brandenburg Gate 10, 14, 33, 43, 45ff., 60, 62, 227, 358f.
Brandt, Marianne 240

Brandt, Willy 111
Braque, Georges 249
Braunfels, Stefan 96f., 102f.
Brecht, Bertolt 32, 73, 276f., 279, 351
Breitscheidplatz 58
Bretschneider d. J./the Younger, Daniel 167
Breuer, Marcel 240f.
Britz, Thomas 113
Brodersen, Albert 260
Bröhan, Karl H. 250
Bröhan-Museum 224, 246, 249f.
Brösicke, Katharina von 308
Bruchhäuser, Joachim 112
Brücke-Museum 224, 253ff.
Bruegel d. Ä./the Elder, Pieter 188, 194, 204
Brüggemann, Hans 129
Bruskin, Grisha 102f.
Bruyn, Günter de 48
Buchholz, N. 408
Bülow, Hans von 280, 283
Bumiller, Georg 317
Bundeskanzleramt/Chancellor's Office 85ff., 101
Bundespräsidialamt/Federal President's Office 91
Bundespressekonferenz/Federal Press Conference 100, 108
Büring, Johann Gottfried 393, 395, 398, 401, 406
Busch, Ernst 276

Calatrava, Santiago 96f.
Calder, Alexander 214
Callas, Maria 274
Canova, Antonio 156
Caravaggio 191
Carove, Giovanni 381f.
Caruso, Enrico 274
Catherine the Great see Katharina die Große 213
Cayart, Jean Louis 50
Cecilienhof, Schloss/Palace 406, 409
cemeteries see Friedhöfe
Central Railway Station see Hauptbahnhof
Centrum Judaicum 345
Cézanne, Paul 155, 248
Chamber Music Hall see Kammermusiksaal
Chancellor's Office see Bundeskanzleramt
Chardin, Jean Baptiste Simeon 366
Charité 10, 177
Charles V see Karl V.
Charlottenburger Schloss/Palace 10, 202, 362ff.
Charlottenhof, Schloss/Palace 392, 401ff., 405
Chiaramella da Gandino, Francesco 374
Chillidas, Eduardo 90
China, Botschaft/Embassy 115
Chipperfield, David 145, 270
Chodowiecki, Daniel 11, 193, 208
Christl, Michael 112
Christo und/and Jeanne-Claude 96f.
Churchill, Winston 410
City Palace see Stadtschloss

City Palace, Potsdam see Stadtschloss Potsdam
Clever, Edith 274
Cobb, Henry N. 69
Coin Cabinet see Münzkabinett
Collection Scharf-Gerstenberg see Sammlung Scharf-Gerstenberg
Cölln 8
Commerzbank 46
Concert Hall see Konzerthaus
Congress Hall see Kongresshalle
Contemporary Fine Arts 270
Corbusier-Haus/Corbusier House 315
Corinth, Lovis 29, 62
Cornelisz van Amsterdam, Jacob 192
Courbet, Gustave 155, 158
Cranach d. Ä./the Elder, Lucas 188, 192, 371f.
Cranach d. J./the Younger, Lucas 372
Cresilas see Kresilas 147
Crown Prince Bridge see Kronprinzenbrücke
Culture Forum see Kulturforum
Czar Alexander I see Zar Alexander I.
Czwiczek, Matthias 9

Dahlem Museum Center see Museumszentrum Dahlem
DaimlerChrysler-Areal/Area 53
Dali, Salvador 216f., 250
Dampfmaschinenhaus/Steam Pump House 412, 415
de Bodt, Jean 168f.
de Cardenás, Bartolomé 190
de Cauwer, Emile Pierre Joseph 344
de Feo, Vittorio 116
de Hooch, Pieter 197
de La Tour, Georges 196
de Lamettrie, Julien Offray 393
de León, Teodoro González 113, 119
de Maria, Walter 187f.
de Portzamparc, Christian 46
de Riens, Louis 176
debis-Haus 53
Degas, Edgar 155
Degen, Kurt 285
del Pollaiuolo, Antonio 189
Denkmal für die ermordeten Juden Europas/Memorial to the Murdered Jews of Europe 358f.
Deutsche Oper 285
Deutscher Dom/German Cathedral 48ff.
Deutsches Historisches Museum/German Historical Museum 34, 163ff.
Deutsches Theater 275f.
Diener & Diener 90
Diepenbrock, Alexander 276
Dieter, Fritz 293
Dietrich, Stefan 116
Diterichs, Friedrich Wilhelm 308
Dix, Otto 32, 216f., 234
Döblin, Alfred 32, 54, 57, 286
Domäne Dahlem/Dahlem Domain 225
Dossi, Battista 193
Dresdner Bank 44, 46

Dubuffet, Jean 250
Dudler, Max 174
Dürer, Albrecht 188, 191, 207
Düttmann, Werner 253, 293
DZ-Bank 46, 324

East Side Gallery 36
Echnaton/Akhenaten 147
Egyptian Museum see Ägyptisches
    Museum
Eiermann, Egon 342
Einstein, Albert 177, 324, 326f.
Einsteinturm/Einstein Tower 324
Eisenman, Peter 358f.
El Greco 192
Eliasson, Olafur 268
Elisabeth Christine 374
Emin, Tracey 268
Emperor William Memorial Church see
    Kaiser-Wilhelm-Gedächtniskirche
Encke, Wilhelmine (Gräfin/Countess
    Lichtenau) 382
Ender, Eduard 177
Engelhardt, Ludwig 360
Enslen, Johann Carl 15
Eosander von Göthe, Johann Friedrich 9,
    364, 366, 370
Ephraim, Veitel Heine 308
Ephraimpalais/Ephraim Palace 230, 308
Ermisch, Richard 292f.
Ernst, Max 223, 250
Ernst-Thälmann-Denkmal/Memorial 360
Ethnologisches Museum/Ethnological
    Museum 256ff.
Eumenides II. 136
Europa-Center 58f., 72f
Eyserbeck, Johann August 409

Fahrenkamp, Emil 318, 321
fairgrounds see Messegelände
Federal President's Office see
    Bundespräsidialamt
Federal Press Conference see
    Bundespressekonferenz
Feininger, Lyonel 216f.
Fellner, Ferdinand 285
Felsenstein, Walter 285
Fernsehturm/Television Tower 36, 64, 108,
    293, 295, 297
Feuchtmayer, Joseph Anton 128
Feuerbach, Anselm 156
Feuerbach, Ludwig 173
Fichte, Johann Gottlieb 173
Filmmuseum/Film Museum, Potsdam 413,
    415
Fincke, Hans 143, 370
Fischer von Erlach, Johann Bernhard 163
Fischer, Samuel S. 354
Flavin, Dan 264
Flickenschildt, Elisabeth 279
Flughafen Tegel/Tegel Airport 300f., 303
Flughafen Tempelhof/Tempelhof Airport
    33, 299ff., 303
Fontana, Lucio 217
Fontane, Theodor 57, 384

Foreign Office see Auswärtiges Amt
Förg, Günther 268
Forst, H. A. 46
Fortunaportal/Fortuna Portal 410
Forum Fridericianum 11, 162, 172f.
Foster, Norman 94ff., 101, 299
Frank, Charlotte 88f., 354, 358
Franke, Günter 293
Frankreich, Botschaft/embassy 46
Französischer Dom/French Cathedral 48ff.
Frederick I see Friedrich I.
Frederick II (the Great) see Friedrich II.
    (der Große)
Frederick III see Friedrich III.
Frederick William I („Soldier King") see
    Friedrich Wilhelm I. („Soldatenkönig")
Frederick William II see Friedrich Wilhelm II.
Frederick William III see Friedrich
    Wilhelms III.
Frederick William IV see Friedrich
    Wilhelms IV.
Freed, James Ingo 69
Freiheitsglocke/Liberty Bell 111
French Cathedral see Französischer Dom 48
Fricke, Jörg 231
Friederike (Prinzessin/Princess) 338
Friedhöfe/cemeteries 348ff.
Friedrich Christian Flick Collection 267
Friedrich I./Frederick I 9, 11
Friedrich II. (der Große)/Frederick II
    (the Great) 10f., 16, 50, 64f., 149, 156,
    163, 166, 172, 174, 184, 187, 213, 283,
    308, 340, 342, 366, 392f., 396ff., 406,
    416
Friedrich III./Frederick III 128
Friedrich Wilhelm I. („Soldatenkönig")/
    Frederick William I („Soldier King") 10,
    45, 65, 414, 416
Friedrich Wilhelm II./ Frederick William II
    9, 11, 47, 366, 382, 406
Friedrich Wilhelm III./Frederick William III
    58f., 172, 174, 192, 384
Friedrich Wilhelm IV./Frederick William IV
    11, 16, 90, 122, 154, 183f., 398, 401,
    407ff., 412
Friedrich, Caspar David 16, 102f., 152ff.
Friedrich, Götz 285
Friedrichsfelde (Schloss/Palace) 90, 122,
    230, 376ff.
Friedrichstraße 36, 66ff.
Friedrichwerdersche Kirche/
    Friedrichwerder Church 162, 336, 338
Froh, Martin 44, 46
Fugger II., Jakob 191
Funkturm/Radio Tower 292f.
Furtwängler, Wilhelm 280, 283

Gaertner, Eduard 16f., 57, 80, 82, 162, 177
Gainsborough, Thomas 192, 202
Galeries Lafayette 68
Gallé, Émile 194
Ganz, Bruno 274
Garbáty-Rosenthal, Josef 352
Garnisonkirche/Garrison Church 416
Gauguin, Paul 210

Gehry, Frank O. 46, 324
Geiger, Rupprecht 96
Gemäldegalerie/Picture Gallery 123, 128,
    187ff.
Gendarmenmarkt 9, 43
George, Heinrich 54
George-Marshall-Haus 293
Georg-Kolbe-Museum 224, 252
Gerhaert von Leyden, Niclaus 128f.
Gerkan, Meinhard von 44, 46, 287f., 293,
    301, 303f., 324, 326, 330
Gerlach, Philipp 237
German Cathedral see Deutscher Dom
German Historical Museum see
    Deutsches Historisches Museum
Geyer, Bernhard 299
Giacometti, Alberto 249
Giehse, Therese 276
Gilly, David 14
Gilly, Friedrich 14
Gitton, Bernhard 73
Glienicker Brücke/Glienicke Bridge 85,
    390
Glume Friedrich, Christian 392, 415
Godeau, Siméon 370
Goebbels, Joseph 109, 359
Goethe, Johann Wolfgang 175, 276
Gontard, Carl von 50, 401, 405f., 413
Göring, Hermann 108
Gossaert, Jan 193, 372
Goya, Francisco de 250
Graeb, Carl 226
Graf von der Mark, Alexander 156
Graf zu Lynar, Rochus 374
Graff, Anton 9, 372
Great Britain/Embassy see
    Großbritannien/Botschaft
Grenander, Alfred 304f.
Griebel, Otto 171
Grien, Hans Baldung 204
Grimm, Jacob 173
Grimm, Wilhelm 173
Grimmek, Bruno 293
Grimshaw, Nicholas 319, 323
Gropius, Walter 172, 240, 298, 315, 320,
    353
Großbritannien, Botschaft/Great Britain,
    Embassy 114
Großer Kurfürst/Great Elector 9, 65, 187,
    192, 366, 414, 417
Grosz, George 32, 216f.
Gruber, Martin 90, 92
Grünbaum, Louis 354
Grünberg, Martin 50, 168f., 338
Gründgens, Gustaf 32, 279
Grunewald Hunting Palace see
    Jagdschloss Grunewald
Grünewald, Mathis Gothart 209
Grützke, Johannes 217
Günther-Naumburg, Otto 401
Gursky, Andreas 267
Gutbrod, Rolf 194

Haacke, Hans 98f.
Haas, Peter 399

Haase, Volkmar 295
Hagemeister, Karl 251
Hals, Frans 192
Hamburger Bahnhof 264ff.
Hansaviertel 34, 314f., 320
Hanson, Duane 267
Hardenberg, Karl August von 168
Hartmann, Egon 78
Hasenpflug, Carl 225, 416
Hauptbahnhof/Central Railway Station
    290f., 293, 302ff.
Hauptmann, Gerhart 275
Haus am Waldsee 225
Haus der Kulturen der Welt/House of
    World Cultures 297f.
Haus des Rundfunks/House of Radio
    Broadcasting 293ff.
Haus Liebermann 44, 46
Heartfield, John 32
Heckel, Erich 253, 255
Hegel, Georg Wilhelm Friedrich 173
Heilandskirche/Church of the Holy
    Redeemer 407, 409
Heiliger Georg/St George 212
Heinle, Erwin 113
Heinrichskreuz/Henry's Cross 212
Helmer, Hermann 285
Henning, Carl Adolph 16
Henry's Cross see Heinrichskreuz
Henselmann, Hermann 78, 293, 295, 299,
    317
Herder, Johann Gottfried 175
Hermann, K.A. 346
Hermannplatz 77
Herrmann, Karl-Ernst 276
Hess, G. 386
Hesse, Ludwig Ferdinand 408, 410
Hessen, Vertretung/Mission 112
Hilmer, Heinz 53, 187, 246
Hindemith, Paul 32
Hindenburg, Paul von 416
Hintze, Johann Heinrich 57, 228
Hirst, Damien 268
Hitler, Adolf 32, 88, 109, 186, 359, 361, 416
Hitzig, Friedrich 90
Hobrecht, James 17, 313
Höch, Hannah 32, 216f., 234
Hoeniger, Johann 344ff.
Hofer, Andreas 265
Höfer, Candida 267
Hoffmann, E.T.A 14
Hoffmann, Erika 268
Hoffmann, Josef 251
Hoffmann, Ludwig 28, 135, 226
Holländisches Viertel/Dutch Quarter 390,
    414ff.
Hollein, Hans 116
Holzer, Jenny 102f.
Hopp, Hanns 78
Hoppe, Marianne 279
Horn, Rebecca 106
Horseshoe settlement see
    Hufeisensiedlung
Hospital Market see Spittelmarkt 57
Hoss, Nina 275

Hotel Adlon 47
House of World Cultures see
    Haus der Kulturen der Welt
Hufeisensiedlung/Horseshoe settlement
    313, 317
Hufeland, Christoph Wilhelm 173
Humann, Carl 137
Humboldt, Alexander von 174ff., 180, 276,
    372, 374
Humboldt, Caroline 374
Humboldt, Wilhelm von 173ff., 177, 180,
    372, 374
Humboldt-Schloss (Schloss Tegel)/
    Humboldt Palace (Tegel Palace) 372f.
Humboldt-Universität/Humboldt
    University 11, 64f., 67, 163, 172ff., 180
Hummel, Johann Erdmann 224
Hutton, Louisa 308, 320, 324, 326

IBA 36
Ibsen, Henrik 275
Iffland, August Wilhelm 14
Ihne, Ernst von 128
Indien, Botschaft/India, Embassy 115
Innenministerium/Ministry of Interior 104f.
Interbau 315, 320
Internationale Bauausstellung (IBA)/
    International Architecture Exhibition
    231, 311, 317, 320
Internationales Congress Centrum (ICC) 297f.
Ischtar-Tor/Ishtar Gate 135, 138
Isozaki, Arata 53
Italien, Botschaft/Italy, Embassy 113, 116
Itten, Johannes 240

Jagdschloss Grunewald/Grunewald
    Hunting Palace 224, 370f.
Jahn, Helmut 38, 53, 70, 73
Jakob-Kaiser-Haus 100f., 105
Jandorf, Adolf 354
Japan, Botschaft/Embassy 113
Jessner, Leopold 279
Jewish Museum see Jüdisches Museum
Joachim II., Kurfürst/Elector 225, 370, 372
Johne, Sven 270
Jucker, C. J. 241
Jüdisches Museum/Jewish Museum 122,
    234, 236ff.
Juliusturm/Julius Tower 8, 374ff.
Jürgensen, Peter 111
Justi, Ludwig 123

Kaiser, Josef 284, 287
Kaiser-Wilhelm-Gedächtniskirche/
    Emperor William Memorial Church 22,
    58, 77, 342
Kalide, Theodor 338
Kammermusiksaal/Chamber Music Hall
    186, Hall 280f.
Kandinsky, Wassily 217, 240
Karajan, Herbert 283
Karavan, Dani 105
Karl V./Charles V 165
Karl-Marx-Allee (siehe auch/also see
    Stalinallee) 34f., 78, 287, 295, 320

Karstadt (Kaufhaus/department store) 77
Katharina die Große/Catherine the Great
    213
Käthe-Kollwitz-Museum 244f.
Kaufhaus des Westens (KaDeWe) 75
Kaufmann, Oskar 275
Kennedy, John F. 111
Kerbel, Lew 360
Kiaulehn, Walther 67
Kiefer, Anselm 101, 267
Kiehl, Reinhold 332
Kino International/movie theater 284, 287
Kippenberger, Martin 267
Kirchner, Ernst Ludwig 217f., 233, 253ff.
Kiss, August 144
Klee, Paul 216f., 240, 249
Kleihues, Josef Paul 44, 46, 264, 267
Klein, Yves 217
Kleine-Kraneburg, Helmut 90, 92
Klein-Glienicke, Schloss/Palace 384, 390,
    409
Kleist, Heinrich von 14, 274
Klemperer, Otto 285
Klose, Friedrich Wilhelm 12, 14
Klotz, Rainer-Michael 47
Knobelsdorff, Georg Wenzeslaus 10, 162f.,
    173, 282f., 342, 366, 370, 390, 392,
    413ff., 417
Knoblauch, Eduard 345
Knoebel, Imi 105
Knuth, Gottlob Johann Christian 374
Kobes, Franziska 168
Koch, Robert 177
Koeppel, Matthias 36f., 420
Kohlhoff und Kohlhoff 361
Koidl, Roman Maria 270
Kokoschka, Oskar 216f.
Kolbe, Georg 252, 295
Koller, Emil 227
Kollhoff, Hans 43, 53, 55, 57
Kollwitz, Käthe 29, 172, 244f., 356
Kollwitz-Platz 43
Komische Oper 285
Kongresshalle/Congress Hall 297f.
Königin Anna/Queen Anna 212
Königin Elisabeth/Queen Elisabeth 184
Königin Luise/Queen Louise 227, 338f.
Königlich Preußische Porzellanmanufaktur/
    Royal Prussian Porcelain Manufactory
    (KPM) 17, 213, 381
Konrad-Adenauer-Haus 109, 116
Konzerthaus/Concert Hall 48, 279
Koolhaas, Rem 119
Köpenick, Schloss/Palace 202, 380ff.
Kore „Ornithe" 139
Kracauer, Siegfried 51
Krauß, Werner 279
Kresilas/Cresilas 147
Kronprinzenbrücke/Crown Prince Bridge 96f.
Krüger, Franz 60, 16, 183, 372
Krumme Lanke 305
Kulturforum 34
Kulturforum/Culture Forum 34, 122, 186ff.,
    202, 280
Kunstbibliothek/Art Library 187, 202

Kunstgewerbemuseum/Museum of
    Decorative Arts 186, 194, 202, 212f.
Kunst-Werke 267
Kupfer, Harry 285
Kupferstichkabinett/Museum of Prints and
    Drawings 186f., 192f., 204ff.
Kurfürst Friedrich III. (= König Friedrich I./
    King Frederick I) 9
Kurfürstendamm 28, 58f., 70, 73
Kurz, Albrecht 92

Lampe, Jutta 32, 274, 285f.
Langhans, Carl Gotthard 14, 45, 47, 90,
    364, 366, 405
Le Corbusier 315
Lehmbruck, Wilhelm 221
Leibniz, Gottfried Wilhelm 10, 366
Leinberger, Hans 129
Leipziger Platz 45, 53, 10, 170
Leistikow, Walter 29, 249, 251, 260
Lenné 15f., 370, 384, 386, 392, 406f., 409
Léon, Hilde 115
Lessing, Gotthold Ephraim 57
Leucht, Kurt W. 78
Levy, Dani 298
Levy, Lucien 23
Lewandowsky, Via 234, 270
Liberty Bell see Freiheitsglocke
Libeskind, Daniel 234, 237f.
Lichtwark, Alfred 263
Liebermann House see Haus Liebermann
Liebermann, Max 29, 45, 125, 156f., 255,
    260ff.
Liebermann-Villa/Villa Liebermann 122
Liebknecht, Karl 88
Lincke, Paul 289
Löbe, Paul 96f.
Loeillot, W. 172, 180
Lortzing, Albert 283
Louis, Morris 217
Lüders, Marie-Elisabeth 96f.
Ludwig-Erhard-Haus/Ludwig Erhard House
    319, 323
Luise Henriette von Oranien/Louise
    Henriette of Oranien 9
Lustgarten/Pleasure Garden 58f., 67, 144,
    180, 224
Lütke Ludwig, Eduard 274
Luxemburg, Rosa 275

Mabuse, Jan 193
Macke, August 220
Magritte, René 250
Mahlangu, Speelman 118f.
Manet, Edouard 155
Manger, Heinrich Ludwig 401
Mann, Heinrich 350
Mann, Thomas 260
Mantovani, Adelchi-Riccardo 234
Manzel, Dagmar 275
Marble Palace see Marmorpalais
Marc, Franz 220
March, Werner 288, 326, 330
Marg, Volkwin 44, 46, 293, 301, 303f., 326,
    330

Marie-Elisabeth-Lüders-Haus 89, 94f.,
    101ff., 105
Marienkirche/St Mary's Church 8, 56f.,
    336ff., 340
Märkisches Museum/Museum of the Mark
    Brandenburg 46, 82, 162, 224ff.,
Markttor von Milet/Market Gate of Miletus
    136f., 140
Marlene-Dietrich-Platz 53, 287
Marmorpalais/Marble Palace 404ff.
Martens, Wilhelm 308
Marx, Erich 267
Marx-Engels-Denkmal/Memorial 57, 360
Masur, Kurt 285
Matschinsky-Denninghoff, Brigitte 72, 75
Matschinsky-Denninghoff, Martin 72, 75
Matthes, Ulrich 275
Maxim-Gorki-Theater/Maxim Gorky
    Theater 279
McCarthy, Paul 266
Mehringplatz 45
Meister Caspar von Regensberg 205
Memhardt, Johann Gregor 9
Memling, Hans 188
Memorial to the Murdered Jews of Europe
    see Denkmal für die ermordeten Juden
    Europas
Mendel, Albert 353
Mendelsohn, Erich 275f., 324, 326
Mendelssohn Bartholdy, Felix 276
Mendelssohn, Moses 57
Menzel, Adolph von 62, 16ff., 156, 193,
    209, 393, 396f.
Menzel, Ludwig 283
Merisi, Michelangelo 191
Messegelände/fairgrounds 292f.
Messel, Alfred 28, 75f., 135
Messter, Oskar 286
Mexiko, Botschaft/Embassy 113, 119
Mexikoplatz 43
Meyerbeer, Giacomo 45
Meynier, Charles 47
Mies van der Rohe, Ludwig 214, 216, 240
Ministry of Interior see Innenministerium
Miró, Joan 217
Möbius, Christiane 103
Modersohn-Becker, Paula 220
Moholy-Nagy, László 222, 240f.
Molkenmarkt/Molken Market 57
Moltkebrücke/Moltke Bridge 85
Mommsen, Theodor 177
Moneo, Jos Rafael 53
Monet, Claude 155
Moore, Charles 44, 46
Moore, Henry 214, 297
Mosse, Rudolf 354
Mozart, Wolfgang Amadeus 285
Mpahlwa, Luyanda 119
Mrosk, Otto 311
Mschatta-Fassade/-façade 135, 141
Mueller, Otto 253
Mühe, Ulrich 275
Mühsam, Erich 73
Müller, Heiner 275
Müller, Reinhard 323

Müller, Thomas 105
Müller, William 275f.
Multscher, Hans 129
Munch, Edvard 216f., 227
Münzkabinett/Coin Cabinet 123, 129
Murnau Friedrich, Wilhelm 286
Museum Europäischer Kulturen/Museum
    of European Cultures 257f.
Museum für Asiatische Kunst/Museum of
    Asian Art 257f.
Museum für Byzantinische Kunst/Museum
    for Byzantine Art 123, 129
Museum für Gegenwart/Museum of the
    Present 265
Museum für Islamische Kunst/Museum of
    Islamic Art 141
Museum für Vor- und Frühgeschichte/
    Museum of Prehistory and Early History
    367, 370
Museum of Asian Art see Museum für
    Asiatische Kunst
Museum of Decorative Arts see
    Kunstgewerbemuseum
Museum of European Cultures see
    Museum Europäischer Kulturen
Museum of Musical Instruments see
    Musikinstrumenten-Museum
Museum of Natural History see
    Naturkundemuseum
Museum of Prints and Drawings see
    Kupferstichkabinett
Museum of the Present see
    Museum für Gegenwart
Museumsinsel/Museum Island 34, 122ff., 172
Museumszentrum Dahlem/Dahlem
    Museum Center 256ff.
Musikinstrumenten-Museum/Museum of
    Musical Instruments 186
Muthesius, Hermann 28

Nalbach, Gernot 108
Nalbach, Johanne 108
Napoleon Bonaparte 47f., 90
Naturkundemuseum/Museum of Natural
    History 122
Nauman, Bruce 267f.
Nebukadnezar II. 136, 138
Nefertiti see Nofretete
Nelson, Rudolf 73
Neptunbrunnen/Neptune Fountain 110f.
Nering, Johann Arnold 9, 168f., 338, 364,
    366, 381, 415
Netherlands, Embassy see Niederlande,
    Botschaft
Neue Nationalgalerie 186, 214ff.
Neue Synagoge Oranienburger
    Straße/New Synagogue Oranienburger
    Straße 344f.
Neue Wache/New Guard House 14f., 65,
    67, 172, 356f.
Neuer Garten/New Garden 390, 404f., 409
Neues Kranzler-Eck/New Kranzler Corner
    70
Neues Museum 122f., 141,145f.
Neues Palais/New Palace 401

Neuhaus, Friedrich 264
New Garden see Neuer Garten
New Guard House see Neue Wache
New Palace see Neues Palais
New Synagogue on Oranienburger Straße
    see Neue Synagoge Oranienburger
    Straße
Newman, Barnett 217
Newton, Helmut 242f.
Newton, June 242
Nickels, Klaus 301, 303
Niederlande, Botschaft/Netherlands,
    Embassy 119
Nielsen, Asta 286
Niemeyer, Oscar 315, 320
Nikisch, Arthur 280 283
Nikolaikirche/St Nicholas Church 8, 230,
    336, 338
Nikolaikirche, Potsdam/St Nicholas
    Church, Potsdam 410f., 414, 417
Nishizawa, Ryue 240
Nofretete/Nefertiti 120ff., 145ff.
Nolde, Emil 253
Nordische Botschaften/Nordic Embassies
    113, 116f.
Normand, Louis 279
Nouvel, Jean 69

Oberbaumbrücke/Oberbaum Bridge 82
Obermayer, Eduard 92
Old Palace see Altes Palais
Olympiastadion/Olympic Stadium 288,
    326ff.
Opernplatz/Opera Square 60f.
Ör, Theobald Reinhold Freiherr von 175
Österreich, Botschaft/Austria, Embassy
    116
Ottmer, Carl Theodor 276

Palace Bridge see Schlossbrücke
Palais am Pariser Platz 44
Palais Podewils/Podewils Palace 226
Panhans, Stefan 270
Pape, William 169
Pardos, Jorge 105
Pariser Platz 10, 43ff.
Parkkinen, Tiina 113, 116
Parochialkirche/Parochial Church 336,
    338, 351
Patzschke, Jürgen 47
Patzschke, Rüdiger 47
Paul, Bruno 256
Paulick, Richard 67, 78, 283
Paul-Löbe-Haus 96f., 100ff., 105
Paulsen, Fritz 169
Pechstein, Max 253
Pei, Ieoh Ming 69, 163f., 172
Peichl, Gustav 96f.
Pergamonaltar 132f., 135f.
Pergamonmuseum 122f., 130ff., 144ff.
Perikles/Pericles 147
Permoser, Balthasar 183
Perrault, Dominique 332
Persius, Ludwig 15, 384, 386, 394, 398,
    407ff., 412, 415

Pescheck, Carl 15
Pesne, Antoine 11, 366, 372, 393, 398
Petzinka, Karl-Heinz 109, 116
Peymann, Claus 279
Peyton, Elizabeth 268
Pfaueninsel/Peacock Island 382ff., 390,
    409
Philharmonie/Philharmonic Hall 186, 280f.
Piano, Renzo 53, 286, 288
Picasso, Pablo 216f., 242f., 249f.
Picture Gallery see Gemäldegalerie
Pink, Thomas 109, 116
Piranesi, Giovanni Battista 250
Pisano, Giovanni 127
Pleasure Garden see Lustgarten
Podewils Palace see Palais Podewils
Poelzig, Hans 284, 287, 292f., 295
Pomonatempel/Pomona Temple 409f.
Poppel, Johann Gabriel Friedrich 372
Porten, Henny 286
Potsdamer Platz 40f., 50ff., 186, 287, 359
Poussin, Nicolas 192
Priam's treasure see Schatz des Priamos
Prinz Heinrich/Prince Henry 163
Prinzessinnengruppe/Princess group 338f.
Prozessionsstraße von Babylon/
    Processional Boulevard of Babylon
    135ff., 305
Puccini, Giacomo 274
Pückler-Muskau, Hermann von 386
Pusch, Oskar 323

Quadriga 14, 43, 47f., 227
Quartier 206 69
Queen Anna see Königin Anna
Queen Elisabeth see Königin Elisabeth
Queen Louise see Königin Luise

Radio Tower see Funkturm
Raffael 394, 398
Raschdorff, Julius Carl 340
Rattle, Simon 283
Rauch, Christian Daniel 15f., 65, 156, 168,
    338, 351
Rauch, Neo 101, 105
Rauschenberg, Robert 267
Red City Hall see Rotes Rathaus
Redon, Odilon 250
Reichstag 33, 36, 88ff., 92ff.
Reimann, Ivan 105
Reinhardt, Max 32, 275f.
Rembrandt 188, 198f., 206
Renoir, Auguste 155
Rentzell, August von 228
Reuter, Ernst 111
Reyle, Anselm 268f.
Reynolds, Joshua 192
Rheinland-Pfalz/Rhineland-Palatinate,
    Vertretung/Mission 113
Ribbeck, Hans Georg von 308
Ribbeck-Haus/Ribbeck House 308
Richter, Gerhard 101, 268
Rieckhallen/Rieck Halls 267
Riehmer, Wilhelm 311
Riemenschneider, Tilman 125ff.

Rist, Pipilotti 267
Roch, Maximilian 82
Rodin, Auguste 156, 159
Roentgen, Abraham 194
Rogers, Richard 53
Rohbock, Ludwig 372, 405
Rosenberg, Johann Georg 336
Rossi, Aldo 308
Roters, Eberhard 230
Rotes Rathaus/Red City Hall 57, 110f., 113
Royal Prussian Porcelain Manufactory
    (KPM) see Königlich Preußische
    Porzellanmanufaktur
Rubens, Peter Paul 192, 372
Ruble, John 44, 46
Rüdesheimer Platz 43
Rudolf I. 212
Ruff, Thomas 267
Ruisdael, Jacob van 192

Saarland, Vertretung/Mission 113
Sagebiel, Ernst 33, 108, 299, 301
Sammlung Berggruen/Berggruen
    Collection 224, 246ff.
Sammlung Haubrock 268
Sammlung Scharf-Gerstenberg/Collection
    Scharf-Gerstenberg 224, 250f.
Samuels, Alun 119
Sandmann, Xaver 418
Sanssouci 149, 169, 388ff., 412, 415, 420
Sattler, Christoph 53, 187, 246
Sauerbruch, Matthias 308, 320, 324, 326
Savignyplatz 43
Schadow, Johann Gottfried 14, 45, 48, 156,
    158, 338, 351
Schadow, Ridolfo 158
Schäfer, Philipp 77
Scharnhorst, Gerhard von 349
Scharoun, Hans 34, 186, 280, 313, 315
Schatz des Priamos/Priam's treasure 367
Schaubühne 274, 276f.
Schauspielhaus 15, 48, 50, 278f.
Scheffler, Karl 36
Scheibe, Richard 361
Scheidemann, Philipp 92
Schiller, Friedrich 90, 175
Schiller-Denkmal/Monument 48, 50
Schinkel, Karl Friedrich 10f., 14ff., 48, 50,
    58, 65, 67, 80, 122, 143f., 146, 172, 187,
    193, 216, 264f., 276, 279, 308, 336, 338,
    340, 349ff., 356, 372ff., 384, 386, 406,
    409ff.
Schlegel, August Wilhelm 14
Schlegel, Friedrich 14
Schleiermacher, Friedrich 173
Schlemmer, Oskar 240
Schleuen d. Ä./the Elder, Johann David 390
Schliemann, Heinrich 367
Schlossbrücke/Palace Bridge 60f., 67, 80,
    82
Schlüter, Andreas 9, 164, 168f., 364, 366
Schlüterhof/Schlüter Courtyard 168f., 177
Schmeling, Max 289
Schmettau, Joachim 58
Schmid, Carl Friedrich 10

Schmidt, F. A. 46
Schmidt-Rottluff, Karl 253
Schneider, Gregor 268
Schöneberger Rathaus/Schöneberg City
    Hall 111
Schongauer, Martin 190
Schoszberger, Hans 58f.
Schüler, Ralf 297
Schüler-Witte, Ursulina 297
Schultes, Axel 88f., 354, 358
Schultze-Naumburg, Paul 406
Schulz, Moritz 151
Schulze, Friedrich 107
Schütte, Hans 111
Schütte, Thomas 265
Schwebes, Paul 58f.
Schwechten, Franz 23, 304
Schwechten, Karl 342
Schweger, Peter W. 320, 323
Schweitzer, Heinrich 276
Schweiz, Botschaft/Swiss Embassy 90
Schwontkowski, Norbert 270
Seeling, Heinrich 274, 276
Sehring, Bernhard 28, 274, 2283
Sejima, Kazuyo 240
Serrano, Francisco 113f., 116, 119
Seurat, Georges 248f.
Shell-Haus/Shell House 318, 321, 323
Sherman, Cindy 267
Siegessäule/Victory Column 29, 78, 356, 358
Siemensstadt 312f.
Sierra, Santiago 268f.
Silens Oreimachos 148
Simon, James 145
Sing-Akademie/Academy of Singing 14,
    274, 276
Skarbina, Franz 235
Skladanowsky, Max 285
Skulpturensammlung/Sculptures
    Collection 123
Slevogt, Max 28f., 260
Sony Center 38, 53
Sophie Charlotte 10, 78, 364ff.
Sosnowska, Monika 268f.
Souradny, Karl 78
South Africa, Embassy see Südafrika,
    Botschaft
Spandau Citadel see Zitadelle Spandau
Spangenberg, Gerhard 323
Speer, Albert 32f., 78, 88, 326
Spittelmarkt/Hospital Market 57
Spontini, Gaspare 283
St George see Heiliger Georg
St Mary's Church see Marienkirche 57
St Nicholas Church see Nikolaikirche
St. Matthäuskirche/St Matthew's Church
    186, 214
St.-Hedwigs-Kathedrale/St Hedwig's
    Cathedral 11, 162, 342
Staatsbibliothek/State Library 186
Staatsoper/State Opera 67, 162, 282f.
Stadtschloss/City Palace 9, 36, 39, 177ff.,
    202
Stadtschloss/City Palace, Potsdam 410,
    414, 417ff.

Stahn, Otto 83, 85
Stalin, Josef 410
Stalinalle 34f., 78, 320
State Library see Staatsbibliothek
State Opera see Staatsoper
Steam Pump House see
    Dampfmaschinenhaus
Steen, Jan 372
Stein, Peter 274
Stella, Franco 39, 180
Stendhal 8, 382
Sternberg, Josef von 285
Stiller, Alfred 34
Strack, Johann Heinrich 15, 47, 151, 154,
    356, 386
Straße des 17. Juni 78
Straumer, Heinrich 292f.
Strausberger Platz 79
Strauss, Richard 283
Streitparth, Jörg 299
Stridbeck d. J./the Younger, Johann 60
Stroehling, P.E. 227
Strunz, Katja 270f.
Struth, Thomas 267
Stubbins, Hugh 297f.
Stüler, Friedrich August 15, 141, 151, 154,
    186, 214, 246, 249ff., 264f., 342, 345,
    351, 394, 408, 410f., 414
Südafrika, Botschaft/South Africa,
    Embassy 118f.
Swiss, Embassy see Schweiz, Botschaft
Szymanski, Rolf 250

Tauentzienstraße 70, 73, 77
Taut, Bruno 313, 315
Taut, Max 315, 320
Tegel Airport see Flughafen Tegel
Television Tower see Fernsehturm
Tempelhof Airport see Flughafen Tempelhof
Tempodrom 287f.
Thaer, Albrecht Daniel 173
Thalheimer, Michael 275
Theater des Westens/Theater of the West
    274, 283
Theyss, Caspar 225, 370
Thiele, Carl Friedrich 143, 279
Thielemann, Christian 285
Thorvaldsen, Bertel 158
Tieck, Christian Friedrich 184
Tiepolo, Giovanni Battista 202
Tietz, Hermann 354
Tillmanns, Wolfgang 268
Timmermann, Helga 43
Titz, Eduard 275
Tizian (eigentl./orig. Tiziano Vecelli(o))
    165, 193, 195f.
Treptowers 323
Trias 321
Truman, Harry S. 409
Tschechow, Anton 274
Tschudi, Hugo von 155
Tucholsky, Kurt 32, 353

Uecker, Günther 102f.
Umbach, Julius 405

Unger, Georg Christian 413
Ungers, Oswald Mathias 141
Unter den Linden 9, 11, 6off., 67
Urania-Weltzeituhr/World Time Clock 54
Ury, Lesser 219, 231, 354
USA, Botschaft/embassy 44, 46

Vaillant, Jacques 382
van de Velde, Henry 251
van Gogh, Vincent 249
van Langervelt, Rutger 381
Velázquez, Diego 192
Velodrom/Velodrome 332f.
Verdi, Giuseppe 274, 285
Vermeer van Delft, Jan 200f.
Victory Column see Siegessäule
Viktoria-Luise-Platz 43
Villa Liebermann see Liebermann-Villa
Villazòn, Rolando 285
Virchow, Rudolf 354
Volksbühne 275
Voltaire 393, 399
von der Aa, P. 8

Wach, Karl Wilhelm 227
Waesemann, Hermann Friedrich 111
Wagenfeld, Wilhelm 241
Wagner, Martin 292, 313
Wagner, Richard 279
Waldbühne 288f.
Wallot, Paul 92, 100
Walter-Benjamin-Platz 43
Warhol, Andy 119, 268
Watteau, Antoine 192, 203, 368ff.
Wawrik, Günther 321
Weber, Carl Maria von 279
Weberwiese 316f.
Weidemann Friedrich, Wilhelm 365
Weidendammer Brücke/Weidendamm
    Bridge 85
Weigel, Helene 276, 279, 351
Weill, Kurt 32, 73
Weitsch, Georg Friedrich 174, 176
Weltkugelbrunnen/World Globe Fountain
    58
Werner, Anton von 24ff., 29, 227, 230
Wernik, Siegfried 115
Wertheim (Kaufhaus/department store) 76
Wessel, Ivo 268, 270
Whiteread, Rachel 267
Wieland, Christoph Martin 175
Wiene, Robert 285f.
Wilford, Michael 114
Wilhelm I./William I 62f., 163
Wilhelm II. (Kaiser)/William II (Emperor) 11,
    26, 96f., 128, 340f., 401, 406, 409
Wilhelmine von Bayreuth 396
William I see Wilhelm I.
William II (Emperor) see Wilhelm II.
    (Kaiser)
Willy-Brandt-Haus 109, 116
Winking, Bernhard 44, 46
Wischer, Robert 113
Wittenbergplatz 305
Wohlhage, Konrad 115

Wolff, Albert 144
Wolff, Emil 338
Womacka, Walter 54, 298
World Globe Fountain see
    Weltkugelbrunnen
Wuhlheide 289

Yudell, Buzz 44, 46

Zacharias, Wilhelm 381
Zadek, Peter 279
Zar Alexander I./Czar Alexander I 54
Zelter, Carl Friedrich 14, 276
Zeughaus/Armory 9, 6of., 64f., 144, 162ff.,
    168f., 172
Ziel, Horst 321
Zielke, Leopold 228f.
Zille, Heinrich 29ff., 211, 234,
Zitadelle Spandau/Spandau Citadel
    8, 374ff.
Zobeltitz, Fedor von 75, 77
Zweig, Arnold 351

Abbildungsnachweis / Illustration Credits

Der Verlag bedankt sich bei den Künstlern, Museen, Sammlern, Archiven und Fotografen für die erteilte Abdruckerlaubnis ihrer Werke und Abbildungen sowie für die freundliche Unterstützung bei der Produktion dieses Buches. Der Verlag hat sich bemüht, alle Inhaber von Abbildungsrechten ausfindig zu machen. Personen oder Institutionen, die möglicherweise nicht erreicht wurden und Rechte an den verwendeten Abbildungen beanspruchen, werden gebeten, sich nachträglich mit dem Verlag in Verbindung zu setzen.

The publisher would like to thank the artists, museums, collectors, archives and photographers for the right to reproduce their works and images, and for their friendly cooperation in the production of this book. The publisher made every effort at the time of publication to contact all copyright holders of the images in this book. Private or institutional image copyright holders who may not have been contacted are hereby requested to contact the publisher.

Alle Abbildungen von picture alliance, Frankfurt/Main, mit Ausnahme der folgenden:
All images by picture alliance, Frankfurt/Main, exept for:

23 above Deutsches Technikmuseum Berlin; 34, 171 © picture alliance/Stiftung Deutsches Historisches Museum; 37, 421/22 picture alliance/© Matthias Koeppel/VG Bild-Kunst, Bonn 2013; 39 all © Förderverein Berliner Schloss e.V./eldaco, Berlin; 54 left © Deutsche Kinemathek; 55 below © Berliner Senatsverwaltung für Stadtentwicklung, Abt. II; 96 above picture alliance/© Gerhard Richter, 2013; 96 below picture alliance/© Rupprecht Geiger/VG Bild-Kunst, Bonn 2013; 97 above, 232 picture alliance/© Georg Baselitz; 97 below, 267 picture alliance/© Joseph Beuys/VG Bild-Kunst, Bonn 2013; 98 picture alliance/© Christian Boltanski / VG Bild-Kunst, Bonn 2013; 103 above picture alliance/ © Christiane Möbus/ VG Bild-Kunst 2013; 99 picture alliance/© Hans Haacke/VG Bild-Kunst, Bonn 2013; 106 below picture alliance/© Rebecca Horn/VG Bild-Kunst, Bonn 2013; 114 above picture alliance/ © Tony Cragg/ VG Bild-Kunst 2013; 117 all © Nordische Botschaften/Florian Bolk; 118 above Courtesy of Netherlands Embassy Berlin/Christian Richters; 126 © bpk/Skulpturensammlung, Museum für Byzantinische Kunst, Staatliche Museen zu Berlin/Rudolf Nagel; 127, 128 © bpk/Skulp-turensammlung, Museum für Byzantinische Kunst, Staatliche Museen zu Berlin/Jörg P. Anders; 132 below, 139 left © bpk/Antikensammlung, Staatliche Museen zu Berlin/Jürgen Liepe; 135, 138 right © bpk/Vorderasiatisches Museum, Staatliche Museen zu Berlin/Olaf M. Teßmer; 141 © bpk/Museum für Islamische Kunst/Georg Niedermeiser; 145 © bpk/Altes Museum, Staatliche Museen zu Berlin/Martin Specht; 148 © bpk/Antikensammlung, Staatliche Museen zu Berlin/Johannes Laurentius; 162, 163 © Deutsches Historisches Museum; 174 © Humboldt-Universität zu Berlin/Jacob und Wilhelm Grimm-Zentrum/Max Dudler; 206 © bpk/Kupferstichkabinett, Staatliche Museen zu Berlin/Jörg P. Anders; 214 © picture alliance/© Alexander Calder/VG Bild-Kunst, Bonn 2013; 216 above right picture alliance/ © Rudolf Belling/ VG Bild-Kunst 2013; 222 picture alliance/© László Moholy-Nagy/VG Bild-Kunst, Bonn 2013; 223 © Max Ernst/ VG Bild-Kunst, Bonn 2013, photo: bpk/Nationalgalerie, Staatliche Museen zu Berlin/Reinhard Friedrich; 231 © Max Beckmann/VG Bild-Kunst, Bonn 2013; 236, 238/39 all © Jüdisches Museum/Jens Ziehe, Berlin; 241 above © Wilhelm Wagenfeld/VG Bild-Kunst, Bonn 2013; photo: Bauhaus-Archiv Berlin/Gunter Lepkowski; 241 below © Bauhaus Archiv Berlin/Fotostudio Bartsch; 242 above, 243 all © Helmut Newton Foundation/Stefan Müller; 245, 357 above picture alliance/© Käthe Kollwitz/VG Bild-Kunst, Bonn 2013; 247, 217 below right picture alliance/© Pablo Picasso, Succession Picasso/VG Bild-Kunst, Bonn 2013; 250 picture alliance/© Rolf Szymanski/VG Bild-Kunst, Bonn 2013; 252, 294 below © Georg Kolbe/VG Bild-Kunst, Bonn 2013; 255 left picture alliance/© Nachlass Erich Heckel, Hemmenhofen; 257 left, 258 left © bpk/Ethnologisches Museum, Staatliche Museen zu Berlin/Martin Franken; 259 right © bpk/Museum für Asiatische Kunst, Staatliche Museen zu Berlin/Jürgen Liepe; 265 below left picture alliance/© Thomas Schütte/VG Bild-Kunst, Bonn 2013; 265 below right picture alliance/© Andreas Hofer/Hauser & Wirth Zürich London; 266 all picture alliance/© Paul McCarthy/Hauser & Wirth Zürich London; 268 right Olafur Eliasson/Courtesy of Collection Christian Boros/Foto Noshe; 269 above © Anselm Reyle, and Courtesy of Collection Christian Boros/Foto Noshe; 269 below left Santiago Sierra/Courtesy of Collection Christian Boros/Foto Noshe; 269 below right Monika Sosnowska/Courtesy of Collection Christian Boros/Foto Noshe; 270 Norbert Schwontkowski/Courtesy of Contemporary Fine Arts, Berlin/Jochen Littkemann; 271 Katja Strunz/Courtesy of Contemporary Fine Arts, Berlin/Jochen Littkemann; 282 above right © Manfred Schürmann; 298 picture alliance/ © Walter Womacka/VG Bild-Kunst 2013; 333 above picture alliance/ © Dominique Perrault/ VG Bild-Kunst 2013; 352 all, 353 above all, 359 © Hannah Schweizer; 394, 395 © Dirk Laubner; 409 © Stiftung Stadtmuseum Berlin/Michael Setzpfandt

© h.f.ullmann publishing GmbH

Original title: *Berlin. Kunst und Architektur*
ISBN 978-3-8331-5246-7

Concept: Dr. Harro Schweizer, from an idea by Jeannine Fiedler
Project management: Kristina Scherer, Swetlana Dadaschewa
Image selection, final image and text editing, index and overall production: Dr. Harro Schweizer, Berlin
Translation from German: Cathy Lara, Sebastopol, CA
Graphic design, layout and cover design: Dorén + Köster, Berlin
Lithography: LVD GmbH, Berlin

© for this edition: h.f.ullmann publishing GmbH
Special edition

Overall responsibility for production: h.f.ullmann publishing GmbH, Potsdam, Germany

Printed in China, 2013

ISBN 978-3-8480-0314-3
ISBN 978-3-8480-0406-5

10 9 8 7 6 5 4 3 2 1
X IX VIII VII VI V IV III II I

www.ullmann-publishing.com
newsletter@ullmann-publishing.com